Print to Fit

*The New York Times,
Zionism and Israel*
1896–2016

Antisemitism in America

Series Editor
Eunice Pollack (University of North Texas, Denton, Texas)

Other Titles in this Series:
From Antisemitism to Anti-Zionism: The Past & Present of a Lethal Ideology
Edited by Eunice G. Pollack

Hating the Jews: The Rise of Antisemitism in the 21st Century
Gregg Rickman

Antisemitism on the Campus: Past and Present
Edited by Eunice G. Pollack

For more information on this series, please visit:
academicstudiespress.com/antisemitism-in-america

ACADEMIC
STUDIES
PRESS

Print to Fit
The New York Times, Zionism and Israel
1896–2016

JEROLD S. AUERBACH

Boston
2019

Library of Congress Cataloging-in-Publication Data

Names: Auerbach, Jerold S.

Title: Print to Fit: The New York times, Zionism and Israel, 1896-2016 / Jerold S. Auerbach.

Description: Brighton, MA: Academic Studies Press, 2019. | Series: Antisemitism in America | Includes bibliographical references and index.

Identifiers: LCCN 2018055398 (print) | LCCN 2019000992 (ebook) | ISBN 9781618118998 (ebook) | ISBN 9781618118974 (hardcover: alk. paper) | ISBN 9781618118981 (pbk.: alk. paper)

Subjects: LCSH: Arab-Israeli conflict—Press coverage--United States. | New York times. | Journalism—Objectivity—United States.

Classification: LCC DS119.7 (ebook) | LCC DS119.7 .A8435 2019 (print) | DDC 070.4/49569405—dc23

LC record available at https://lccn.loc.gov/2018055398

Book design by Kryon Publishing Services Pvt. Ltd.
http://www.kryonpublishing.com
Cover design by Ivan Grave

Published by Academic Studies Press
28 Montfern Avenue
Brighton, MA 02135, USA
press@academicstudiespress.com
www.academicstudiespress.com

Jacob and Minnie Auerbach
Dora and William Soloff
Morry and Sophie Auerbach
Z"L

Table of Contents

Introduction

The New York Times has long occupied the pinnacle of American daily news journalism. In August 1896, two months after Adolph S. Ochs, thirty-eight-year-old publisher of the *Chattanooga Times,* purchased the flagging newspaper he added the masthead motto: "All the News That's Fit to Print." Enduring as a firm, yet ambiguous, pledge of comprehensive news coverage, it left the meaning of "fit" to be determined by reporters, editors and, not least, by the publisher himself.

Ochs was a proud American Jew. The son-in-law of Rabbi Isaac Mayer Wise, leader of the nascent Reform movement in the late nineteenth century, he passionately embraced its definition of Judaism as a religion, not a national identity. That enabled American Jews whose families had arrived a generation earlier (primarily from Germany) to pledge their undivided loyalty to the United States. Their patriotic affirmation became more urgent once two million Eastern European Jews, among the immigrants memorably identified by Emma Lazarus as "huddled masses yearning to be free," began to arrive on American shores. The foreign languages, customs, and politics of the newcomers prompted vigorous assertions of American patriotism from prominent Reform Jews.

Several months before Ochs purchased the *Times,* Viennese journalist Theodor Herzl had published a slim "pamphlet" (as he called it) entitled *The Jewish State.* Herzl urged restoration of Jewish national sovereignty in Palestine, "our ever-memorable historic home." Zionism posed a potentially menacing challenge to the ardent Reform affirmation of the patriotic loyalty of American Jews to the United States. With the ominous cloud of dual loyalty hovering nearby, the very idea of Jewish nationalism, to say nothing of the eventual reality of the State of Israel, would torment members of the Ochs-Sulzberger publishing dynasty.

Until World War I Zionism remained a remote European movement, only occasionally noticed by the *Times* and invariably disparaged. It did not have a reporter in Palestine until 1928 when Joseph W. Levy, whose boyhood had been spent in Jerusalem, was hired as a foreign correspondent. Fascinated with archeological explorations and discoveries, his reporting was transformed by the festering conflict between Arabs and Zionists that erupted violently one year later. Murderous riots leading to the slaughter of Jews in their ancient capital cities of Hebron and Jerusalem prompted Levy to become a partisan advocate. He participated in secret meetings with the Grand Mufti, Hebrew University Chancellor Judah L. Magnes (who advocated a bi-national Palestinian state), and former British civil servant H. St. John Philby, an Arabist who vigorously opposed the idea of a Jewish national home in Palestine. The *Times* journalist guided statements by Magnes and Philby into his newspaper, launching an anti-Zionist critique that would long remain a *Times* editorial refrain.

The convergence of religious Reform and anti-Zionism had far more serious journalistic consequences once Adolph Hitler ascended to power. Adolph Ochs, by then in declining health, was torn between ancestral attachment to Germany and steadfast American patriotism. *Times* editors, who had dismissed the Nazi menace as a gross exaggeration in 1930, were slow to respond three years later when Hitler became Chancellor. Its foreign correspondent was charmed by Hitler's "childlike" eyes and "sincere" manner, while its European reporter found the commandant of Dachau equally appealing.

Following Ochs's death in 1935 his son-in-law Arthur Hays Sulzberger succeeded him as publisher, launching the family dynasty that has remained intact ever since. Sulzberger echoed Ochs's concern lest Zionism raise doubts about the loyalty of American Jews. His unease over "showcasing" Jews in the *Times* prompted instructions that they were to be identified as "people of the Jewish faith," not members of "the Jewish people." Reporters named Abraham were granted by-lines with their initials only. The idea of a Jewish editorial page editor was anathema to the publisher. The convergence of Sulzberger's Reform Judaism and fervent anti-Zionism had especially serious consequences for his newspaper between 1939 and 1945 when the Holocaust, in the title of Laurel Leff's meticulous scrutiny of its evasion of the Nazi slaughter of six million Jews, was *Buried by The Times*.

During the war years Sulzberger's newspaper became a sounding board for the vehemently anti-Zionist American Council for Judaism, extensively reporting and frequently echoing its discomfort over the prospect of Jewish statehood. Three months after Israel proclaimed its independence in May 1948 the *Times* reporter in Jerusalem still was identified as its "Palestine" correspondent. The Council, avidly supported by Sulzberger, was more prominently covered in the *Times* than Israel. Not until Independence Day in 1953 did the editorial page recognize the Jewish state as "an outpost of democracy in the Middle East."

Times support was short-lived. Discomfort mounted with repeatedly cited, but grossly exaggerated, numbers of Palestinian refugees, often by foreign correspondent Cyrus Sulzberger (the publisher's nephew). By the mid-fifties respected *Times* columnists Arthur Krock and James Reston had joined the growing chorus of disapproval of Israel's determination to respond forcefully to Arab aggression. The publisher expressed concern over the prospect of posting a "Jewish specialist" in Jerusalem and unwillingness to put a Jew in "the show-case," lest the *Times* be diminished in Gentile eyes.

Between the capture and trial of Nazi war criminal Adolf Eichmann in 1960 and the Six-Day War seven years later, *Times* disquiet with Israel intensified. Given Sulzberger's brimming concern lest the Jewish state be perceived as representing the Jewish people, Eichmann's trial by Israel for crimes committed in Europe was deeply disturbing. Anticipating Hannah Arendt's noxious label, correspondent Homer Bigart was struck by Eichmann's self-image as "a petty bureaucrat," not worth fussing over.

Far more consequential was Israel's stunning 1967 victory over the hostile Arab armies massed at its borders. If the very idea of a Jewish state had long agitated the *Times,* a triumphant Israel deepened its unease. *Times* editors focused on the necessity of Israeli redress for "the legitimate grievances of the Arab world," especially the plight of Palestinian refugees from the 1948 war. They expected Israel to display "magnanimity" toward the Arab "victims" who had been prepared to annihilate it. Six years later, on Yom Kippur, Egyptian and Syrian military forces attacked Israel. Condemning their aggression, the *Times* demanded Israeli restraint.

The 1977 election of Menachem Begin, the Irgun leader despised by the *Times* during Israel's struggle for independence, posed the challenge to provide fair coverage of Israel's first right-wing (and religiously identified) prime minister. His support for settlements in what had been Jordan's West Bank elicited incessant criticism of Israeli "occupation" that shows no sign of abating four decades later. Claiming to align itself with "friends of Israel," the *Times* identified the Jewish state as the major impediment to Middle East peace.

With Palestinian terrorist attacks increasing, editors and columnists found multiple opportunities to berate Israel for responding with force. Viewing Israel as a malevolent occupying power, they disregarded its historic claims and international legal rights to land between the Jordanian border and pre-1967 armistice lines, rarely identified as biblical Judea and Samaria. A bevy of Op-Ed contributors blamed Israel for Palestinian violence; assertions of moral equivalence between Palestinian terrorists and Israeli settlers became a repetitive trope of *Times* coverage.

In 1979 the *Times* selected David Shipler as its first Jerusalem Bureau Chief, focusing responsibility, and accountability, for Israel coverage. There would be more than occasional tension between his nuanced reports and the relentless criticism of Washington columnists and editors in New York. It was most vividly on display in 1981 when Israel launched a preemptive bombing attack that destroyed the Iraqi nuclear reactor. While Shipler grasped the danger that Israel confronted, an editorial furiously denounced its "inexcusable ... aggression." *Times* (Jewish) columnists, especially Anthony Lewis, formed a chorus of disapproval of Israel's moral failings.

The selection of Thomas Friedman as Shipler's successor represented a decision by editor A.M. Rosenthal to discard "the old unwritten rule" at the *Times* not to permit a Jew to report from Jerusalem. (Evidently neither Rosenthal nor Friedman knew of Joseph Levy.) Friedman, who had embraced Israel as a teenage kibbutz volunteer, became active as a Brandeis student in Breira, a left-wing Jewish advocacy group that favored a two-state solution along pre-1967 lines. His *Times* posting in Beirut during the Lebanon war featured sharp condemnation of Israel. After his relocation to Jerusalem he refocused on Palestinian suffering under Israeli occupation. Along the way, he came to rely on a trio of Israelis whose criticism of their country guided his refrain (echoed in the reporting of his successors) about the Jewish David that had become the menacing Israeli Goliath.

Political liberalism entwined with American patriotism continued to frame *Times* coverage of Israel, providing a strong buffer against insinuations of dual loyalty. Right-wing prime ministers Menachem Begin, Yitzhak Shamir, Ariel Sharon, Benjamin Netanyahu and Jewish settlers provoked the persistent ire of editors and columnists alike. Israeli "occupation" (of its biblical homeland) became a repetitive trope of condemnation, rivaled only by evident discomfort with (Jewish) religious Orthodoxy. The obduracy of Palestinian leaders who rejected Israeli offers of "land for peace" in 2000 and 2008, and waged war against Israel after its unilateral withdrawal from Gaza, did not weigh nearly as heavily in editorials or columns as the perceived intransigence of the Jewish state.

Israel has repeatedly been blamed for causing the death of innocent civilians, among whom Palestinians in Gaza and the West Bank embedded their fighters and launched their attacks. While columnists chastised Israel for excessive military force, editorials, invariably blaming "both sides" for the carnage, called on the Jewish state to be "measured" in its responses to Palestinian rockets and terrorism. The funerals of Palestinian terrorists (and the mourning tents of their families) were reported far more expansively and sympathetically than the deaths of their Israeli victims.

Since the turn of the twenty-first century *Times* columnists have launched a fusillade of criticism of Israel. Thomas Friedman, writing from Washington, delighted in role-playing as the Saudi king and American presidents to proffer his own fantasy peace plan to Israel's detriment. Roger Cohen, like Anthony Lewis before him, wrapped himself in his Jewish identity to badger Israel for the absence of peace. Demonstrating little evident familiarity with the Israeli-Palestinian conflict, Nicholas Kristof blamed Israel for Palestinian terrorism and suffering. The fallback position of *Times* editors, even at a time of rising Palestinian violence, invariably was moral equivalence. Israelis and Palestinians alike were blamed for the carnage inflicted on Israeli civilians riding buses, food shopping, eating pizza, or celebrating Passover.

Israeli op-ed contributors, prominent left-wing writers Amos Oz and David Grossman and *Haaretz* journalist Ari Shavit among them, were incessant critics of their country. Far more newsworthy than the deaths of Israelis from Palestinian terrorist attacks were the deaths of civilians in Gaza and the West Bank from Israeli retaliation. News coverage from Palestinian territory was invariably provided by *Times* reporters who were guided by, and dependent on, local Palestinian sources for contacts, translation and interpretation.

Between 2009 and 2016 *Times* editorial policy was framed within the acrimonious tension between a liberal American president and a right-wing Israeli prime minister. Barack Obama's determination to improve relations with the Muslim world, while speaking (his) "truth" to Israel, guided editorial judgment. Benjamin Netanyahu, in turn, was routinely criticized for his stubborn defense of Israeli security. The *Times* critique of Israel intensified once Jerusalem Bureau Chief Jodi Rudoren and reporter Isabel Kershner were joined by Diaa Hadid, a Muslim advocate of the Palestinian cause who was hired in response to the Public Editor's suggestion that an Arabic-speaking journalist would enhance *Times* coverage. Their entwined reporting was driven by the narrative of Palestinian victimization and Israeli culpability.

In August 2016 the Ochs-Sulzberger family publishing dynasty reached its 120th anniversary. To be sure, the biblical life span that God assigned to Moses (Genesis 6:3) was intended for people, not newspapers. But it provides an appropriate chronological framework for analyzing *Times* coverage of Zionism before 1948 and the State of Israel ever since. The *Times* remained faithful to the principles of Reform Judaism and American patriotism embraced by Adolph Ochs and his Sulzberger descendants: Judaism is a religion without national content; assimilation assures the patriotic loyalty of American Jews; Zionism, compounded by the birth of the State of Israel, remains a lurking problem. An extensive network of editors, columnists, reporters (occasionally with their spouses) and contributors implemented coverage of Zionism and Israel. All the news "fit to print" became news that fit *New York Times* discomfort with the idea, and since 1948 the reality, of a thriving democratic Jewish state in the historic homeland of the Jewish people.

CHAPTER 1

Patriotic Loyalty:
1896–1927

A Tennessee youngster named Adolph S. Ochs, born in 1858 to immigrant parents from Bavaria, exemplified the Horatio Alger ascent from rags to riches that American opportunity afforded to hard-working young men, even if they were Jewish. His highly educated father (whose family name was Ochsenhorn), master of six languages including Hebrew, became an itinerant peddler in the South. He served as lay rabbi for scattered Jewish communities along his route before settling in Knoxville after the Civil War. Young Adolph launched his career in journalism as an eleven-year-old delivery boy for the Knoxville *Chronicle*. His evident determination to succeed elevated him to printer's "devil," sorting type, sweeping floors and running errands. In a whirl-wind ascent up the publishing ladder he relocated briefly to Louisville, where he became a reporter for the *Courier-Journal*, before moving to Chattanooga to become business solicitor for the *Dispatch*. At the age of nineteen he borrowed $250 to purchase the *Chattanooga Times*.

Wishing his mother a happy birthday that year, Adolph expressed the ambitious hope that she would see one of her sons become president, the other a senator, and their sister "a large-salaried rabbi's wife." In an ironic twist six years later he married Iphigenia Wise, daughter of Rabbi Isaac Mayer Wise, the prominent leader of Reform Judaism and founder of Hebrew Union College, its rabbinical institute in Cincinnati. Rabbi Wise, a German immigrant, was determined to reconcile the religion of Judaism with American patriotism. Ancient Israel, he passionately believed and proudly proclaimed, provided the model for American democracy. Loyalty to Judaism, in Rabbi Wise's formulation, required loyalty to the American homeland. Reform Judaism appealed to American Jews, predominantly of German origin, who were determined to blend their religion into an affirmation of American national identity.[1]

The tight braiding of Jewish and American values was threatened by the arrival in the 1880s of the first wave of Jewish immigrants from Russia, fleeing pogroms and compulsory service in the Czar's army. The presence of hundreds of thousands of Russian Jews who were impoverished, Yiddish-speaking, evidently foreign and conspicuously Jewish concerned assimilated German Jews who had preceded them by a generation to the American promised land. No one tried harder, or more ingeniously, than Oscar S. Straus to affirm the loyalty of Jews to the United States. A Bavarian immigrant (like Adolph Ochs's father), he (like Ochs) was raised in the American South and drawn to Reform Judaism as the proclamation of Jewish identity and American loyalty.

Straus seized on the Constitutional centennial in 1887 to affirm the bond between ancient Israel and modern America. The history of Israel, he wrote in a celebratory essay, had served as "a glorious example and inspiring incentive to the American people" in their own "mighty struggle for the blessings of civil and religious liberty." "In the spirit and essence of our Constitution," Straus asserted (with little but his own patriotic yearning to support it), "the influence of the Hebrew commonwealth was paramount." The appropriation of biblical imagery for patriotic purposes became an identifying trope of Reform Judaism. Rabbi Kaufmann Kohler, who would succeed Rabbi Wise as its intellectual leader, heard "the mighty resonance of Sinai's thunder" in "the jubilant tocsin peals of American liberty." For Reform Jews America was the new Zion.[2]

The golden years of Reform in the closing decades of the nineteenth century afforded unprecedented opportunity for mobility, success, and stature in American society. German American Jews who rose from peddling to prosperity, Straus conspicuous among them, often did so in the world of finance. Adolph S. Ochs, equally ambitious and determined, followed a different path to financial success, national prominence and Jewish distinction. But it took time. After more than fifteen years in Chattanooga, with his newspaper languishing and burdened by debt, Ochs traveled to New York in search of financial loans. He toyed with the idea of purchasing a local newspaper with better prospects. Considering the fading New York *Mercury*, he learned from its financial reporter that *The New York Times*, founded nearly half a century earlier, was in desperate straits, virtually bankrupt with a shrinking readership. Ochs described his yearning to make it "a successful and very profitable business enterprise, and at the same time make it a model American newspaper ... for fairness, cleanliness, independence and enterprise."

In August 1896 Ochs became its owner. He was astonished by his own audacity: "Just twenty years ago I was working as an apprentice in Louisville," he marveled, "and now to be the responsible head of one of the greatest newspapers in the world – and a Jew!" In his publisher's declaration of principle, Ochs promised "to give the news impartially, without fear or favor." His pledge "to write intelligent discussion from all shades of opinion" was embedded, two months later, in the new motto for his newspaper. First appearing on the editorial page, "All the News That's Fit to Print" was soon relocated to the top left corner of Page 1, where it has remained ever since.[3] Unstated was Ochs's fervent determination that the *Times* would never appear to be a "Jewish" newspaper.

Six months before Ochs purchased the *Times* a Jewish lawyer turned journalist named Theodor Herzl published a pamphlet entitled *Der Judenstaat* (*The Jewish State: An Attempt at a Modern Solution of the Jewish Problem*). Herzl asserted that Jews are "a people – one people," who "have honestly endeavored everywhere to merge ourselves in the social life of surrounding communities and to preserve the faith of our fathers." But, he lamented, "We are not permitted to do so. … In countries where we have lived for centuries we are still cried down as strangers." He envisioned a Jewish state that would become "an outpost of civilization against barbarism."[4] *Der Judenstaat* propelled Zionism to international awareness, where it has remained ever since.

The first mention of Herzl in *The New York Times* came in August 1897, one year after Ochs purchased the newspaper. It identified him as "originator of the Zionist scheme," which had been "so coldly received by those to whose attention it has been called in this country." Relying on an interview conducted by a British reporter, the *Times* noted that Herzl's plan is "entirely practical – whatever may be the case as to its practicability." Echoing a familiar derogatory trope about Jews, it emphasized that Herzl had spoken "not of the fulfillment of prophecy, but of the raising of money with which to buy concessions from the Sultan."[5]

In anticipation of the approaching Zionist conference in Basel, the *Times* paid closer attention to "The Jewish State Idea." The "religious world," it noted, "has recently been interested by the report of a plan for the re-establishment of Palestine as a Jewish State at the hands of certain German leaders." This "altogether novel idea" had been presented "to feel the pulse of the public"; among Jews it was greeted with both "criticism and endorsement" and even "enthusiastic support in some quarters." But "is it feasible," the *Times* asked, "even if it is advisable?" Both in Europe and the United States, it noted, "there are many Jews who oppose the founding of this State on the ground that it could only be a small, weak State, existing by sufferance." It was also "urged," although the *Times* did not identify those doing the urging, "that Israel's mission is no longer political, but purely and simply religious, and that the establishment of the State would do incalculable harm, and could do no good."[6]

Inspired by Herzl, delegates to the First Zionist Congress adopted the Basel Program, proclaiming: "Zionism seeks to secure for the Jewish people a publicly recognized, legally secured home in Palestine." Herzl took it as a positive sign that Jews no longer would be "tortured by the idea of assimilation." But his envisioned Jewish state was itself the dream of an assimilated Jew. Amid lugubrious details of land development, manufacturing priorities, and plans for Jewish migration "in accordance with scientific principles," *Der Judenstaat* envisioned "an aristocratic republic" where "a federation of tongues" (as in Switzerland) would prevail. "Who amongst us," Herzl famously asked, "has a sufficient acquaintance with Hebrew to ask for a railway ticket in that language?" He was no less dismissive of the religion of Judaism. "We shall keep our priests within the confines of their temples," Herzl wrote, where they could not "interfere in the administration of the State." Above all, however, "We shall live at last as free men on our own soil."

Once the delegates in Basel endorsed the idea of Jewish statehood "with great enthusiasm," the *Times* became even more wary. It identified Herzl as "the so-called 'New Moses'" and "originator of the scheme to purchase Palestine and resettle the Hebrews there." Less than a week after the Basel Conference adjourned it reprinted a sharply critical article from *American Israelite*, the newspaper of Reform Judaism published in Cincinnati. Referring to Herzl and his followers as "romantic Zealots," it excoriated them for lacking even "the least intention to benefit Judaism." The establishment of a Jewish state in Palestine, it declared, was "an impossibility. . . . None can leap over two thousand years of history and commence anew where all things were left then." The author of that scathing critique was Rabbi Isaac Mayer Wise, Adolph Ochs's father-in-law.[7]

Two months later Louis Zangwill, brother of the prominent British Zionist, lacerated Herzl (reprinted in the *Times* from *Cosmopolis)* for his "ignorance of the people he would lead and the country he would lead them to." Reform Rabbi Samuel Schulman, who labeled Zionism "the fruit of the poisonous seed of religious indifference," subsequently warned (in *Menorah*, also reprinted) that it would "add fuel to the flame of Jew-baiting in Europe." An independent Jewish commonwealth in Palestine would be "disastrous to the Jews of Occidental countries."[8]

Sparse *Times* coverage of Zionism in the early years of the new century was largely derivative from critical Reform sources. It reprinted an article warning of "The Evil of Zionism" from *The American Israelite* and cited an editorial in

The London Jewish Chronicle warning that "the ostentatious proclamation of a Jew nationality that cannot be content with anything but a Jewish state is merely playing into the hands of the enemies of their race." Zionism, it lamented, had done "more harm to Israel than Christian anti-Semitism." Indeed, Zionism and anti-Semitism were "twin enemies of the Jews, and the former is potentially the more dangerous."[9]

Within a two-week span the *Times* twice provided extensive coverage of anti-Zionist sermons by Reform rabbi Joseph Silverman of Temple Emanu-El in Manhattan, Adolph Ochs's synagogue. Zionism, the rabbi asserted, "is not feasible. It is based on the false premise that the Jews are a nation. ... Israel is not a nation, but a religious community." It expressed "a feigned, fictitious, or imaginary love of Zion. . . It would become a dumping ground upon which every nation of the earth would spew out all its undesirable Jews." The "greatest blessing" for Jews was "the dispersion of Israel throughout the world." The "fiction of Jewish nationality" must yield to assimilation, with Jews preserving their "distinctive character" – and, to be sure, patriotic loyalty – through their religion alone.[10]

Given scant *Times* coverage of Zionism, except to highlight critiques from Reform sources, it was hardly surprising that Herzl's death of heart failure in July 1904 elicited slight notice. A brief four-paragraph obituary mentioned that his early work in law and journalism "was in no way related to the Jews." But moved by the Dreyfus affair, he wrote *Der Judenstaat* and planned and presided over the First Zionist Congress. He had recently negotiated with the Egyptian government for a charter to permit Jewish settlement in the Sinai region of Al'Arish, "but the scheme failed."[11]

Times coverage of Zionism remained sparse during the decade following Herzl's death. The London *Times* served as its primary source for European developments; in the United States it most frequently relied on articles published in *The American Israelite* and *The American Hebrew*, a New York weekly newspaper. Zionist activities were overshadowed by a steady trickle of letters, reports and articles expressing the discomfort with Jewish nationalism that Ochs shared with other prominent Reform Jews. A letter signed by British Jewish luminaries, including Lord Rothschild, Sir Edwin Samuel Montagu and Claude Montefiore, among others, labeled Zionism a "scheme" that was "quite outside the range of practicability" and likely to establish a "Ghetto State."[12]

In a lengthy *Times* article subtitled "An Argument Against the Ambition for Separate National Existence," Count Leo Tolstoy dismissed Zionism as "an awakening of the thirst for imperialism and an evil desire to govern" that was "neither progressive nor national." The "real Jewish spirit," he asserted, "is against a separate territory of their own. It does not want the old toy of empire." For Tolstoy, "the grandest moment in the history of Judaism" had occurred nearly nineteen centuries earlier, during the Roman siege of Jerusalem, when Rabbi Yohanan ben Zakkai had himself smuggled out of the besieged city in a coffin to request from emperor Vespasian the remote village of Yavneh. There peaceful Jews, not zealots for national independence, might be permitted to study Torah. "It is not the land, but the Book," Tolstoy wrote, that became the "fatherland" of the Jewish people. Zionism was nothing but "toy congresses" and "childish colonial banks," exemplifying "the great sin" of nationalism that "borders on blasphemy."[13]

A litany of anti-Zionist criticism from American Reform Jews punctu- ated the pages of the *Times* during the first decade of the twentieth century. Foremost among them was Jacob Schiff, the German-born immigrant who achieved wealth and prominence as a banker with Kuhn, Loeb & Co. before becoming a generous philanthropist and pillar of the (anti-Zionist) American Jewish Committee. When Schiff spoke, the *Times* eagerly reported his words of Jewish wisdom. In a speech at the Jewish Chautauqua in Atlantic City in 1907 he firmly asserted that "the promised land of the Jew was in America." Schiff dreamed of "an American Israel" where "Jews in faith" were "warmly attached to their country, of which they have become part and parcel." Reiterating the theme propounded by Oscar Straus twenty years earlier for the Constitutional Centennial, he spoke glowingly of "descendants of Jewish Pilgrim Fathers, true Americans of the Jewish faith."[14]

The following month the *Times* headlined a letter from Schiff to Rabbi Solomon Schechter, the distinguished scholar and president of the Jewish Theological Seminary. Originally published in *The American Hebrew*, it expressed regret that the leader of Conservative Judaism had become "an adherent of Zionism." Schiff rejected the proposition that "a Jew can be a true American and a good Zionist at the same time." He warned that Zionists, believing in the "ultimate restoration of Jewish political life and the reestablish- ment of a Jewish nation," place "a prior lien" on their citizenship. A Jew, Schiff asserted, must not "feel that he has only found an 'asylum' in this country; he must not feel that he is in exile."[15]

Apprehension over divided loyalty continued to torment Reform leaders and arouse *Times* concern. It provided two columns of coverage for a speech deliv- ered by Reform Rabbi Emil G. Hirsch at a meeting of the Central Conference of American Rabbis (1909) condemning "Zionists and nationalistic Jews who see in the Jewish race and the restoration of Palestine the chief concern of Judaism." In "blending Americanism with Judaism," declared President Kaufman Kohler of the Hebrew Union College (1911), "we have, like Joseph of yore, stored up the treasures of life" for native and immigrant Jews alike. "There is no room for ghetto Judaism in America," he warned, at a time when tens of thousands of recent Jewish immigrants packed the Lower East Side of Manhattan.[16]

The *Times* paid close attention to the words of wealthy and prominent anti-Zionist American Jews. It reported the keynote speech of Oscar S. Straus, recently Theodore Roosevelt's Secretary of Commerce and Labor (and the first Jewish Cabinet member), at the concluding dinner of the Reform Union of American Hebrew Congregations. Conceding that Zionism might appeal to Jewish "victims of oppression" in other countries, Straus asserted that "the Republicanism of the United States is the nearest approach to the ideals of the prophets that has ever been incorporated in the form of a state." Jews, he insisted, "are not any less patriotic Americans because they are Jews, nor any less loyal Jews because they are primarily patriotic Americans."[17]

Similarly, Jacob Schiff's wealth, prominence, devotion to Reform principles – and hostility to Zionism – kept him in the *Times* limelight. Warning at a gathering of the Menorah Society of "the siren-song of the Jewish Nationalist," he insisted that Zionism "threatened the very existence of the Jewish race." Schiff asserted: "As an American, though a good Jew I seek to be, I cannot become a Jewish Nationalist." Only religion assured Jewish survival. The *Times* subsequently reported his appeal to an audience of Reform rabbis for "Americanism above Zionism." He passionately urged: "Be Americans above all else. Tell your children to hold fast and high the banner of Judaism. But don't forget that, first of all, your children are Americans."[18]

Events affecting Jews far from American shores occasionally rippled through the *Times*. The eruption of a horrific pogrom in Kishinev, led by priests on the day after Easter in 1903, resulted in the murder of nearly fifty Jews who, the *Times* reported, were "slaughtered like sheep" in "scenes of horror...beyond description." In the aftermath of another pogrom in Kishinev two years later, prominent American Jews (including Schiff, Straus, Cyrus Adler and Louis Marshall) organized the American Jewish Committee "to aid in securing the civil and religious rights of the Jews in all countries where such rights are denied or endangered." The Committee became the anti-Zionist "ethnic lobby" for the wealthy Reform Jews with whom Adolph Ochs identified.[19]

The Zionist trajectory of Louis D. Brandeis made him newsworthy for the *Times*. An unexpected encounter with European Zionist leader Nahum

Sokolow proved transformative. Stirred by Sokolow's appeal for participation in the effort to "recreate Zion" in Palestine, Brandeis confessed: "You have brought me back to my people." Several weeks later he met Aaron Aaronsohn, the Palestinian Zionist on a fundraising mission for his agricultural field station near Haifa. Brandeis was fascinated by "the possibilities of scientific agriculture" and by Aaronsohn. Not long afterward, he urged American Jews to identify with the "noble traditions" that inspired the Zionist pioneers. In his memorable articulation of their linkage, he declared in 1914: "To be good Americans, we must be better Jews, and to be better Jews, we must become Zionists." Zionism, he declared, was "the Pilgrim inspiration and impulse all over again." Zionist ideals, he asserted, "are essentially American."[20]

With his seductive *non sequitur*, Zionism as Americanism, Brandeis emerged at the forefront of the American Zionist movement. His assurance to European Zionist leader Nahum Sokolow that American Jews would support "well matured and carefully devised plans" for "opening up Palestine to the masses" received attention in the *Times*. As chairman of the Provisional Committee for General Zionist Affairs, Brandeis proclaimed the wartime necessity for American Jews to assume "responsibility for preserving Jewish customs and ideals," reiterating his credo that being a Zionist made one a good Jew and, therefore, a good American.[21]

The *Times* announced the program of the Federation of American Zionists annual conference in 1915 (immediately followed, in order of importance, by a story headlined "Trout Fisher Nets a Pig"). Two days later it informed readers that Brandeis had concluded his speech with the rousing plea: "Let us Americans ... lead earnestly, courageously, and joyously in the struggle for the liberation of the Jewish people." Liberation, he asserted, required "the consummation of the specific Zionist purpose of securing a publicly recognized, legally secured home in Palestine." Brandeis had come a long way and, so it seemed, had the *Times*. By then it was anticipating "A New Palestine if the Allies Win," with British capitalists expected to play a major role in its modernization once the war ended. Trolley lines would surely follow, along with "moderate-rate hotels" and the development of a seaport so that "all the world will journey thither." Endangered Polish Jews would find a home there "since Jews are at home in Palestine," but only if they did not already live in the United States.[22]

At the urging of respected attorney Louis Marshall the *Times* supported Leo Frank, who had been found guilty in 2013 of the rape and murder of thirteen-year-old Mary Phagan. Her body was discovered in the basement of Frank's Atlanta factory. Frank was targeted by Southern anti-Semites; a prominent Georgia newspaper referred to him as the "filthy, perverted Jew of New York." Persuaded by Marshall that Frank was the victim of a "horrible miscarriage of justice," Ochs rallied the *Times* to Frank's defense, demanding a new, and fair, trial. The *Times* vigorously campaigned for the commutation of his death sentence to life imprisonment; two months after Georgia governor John Slayton complied, Frank was seized from prison and lynched. Accused by a Georgia newspaper of "outside interference of the Jews" in defending Frank, especially "offensive propaganda" in the *Times,* Ochs was stung by attacks on his "Jewish" newspaper. "Never again," wrote Susan E. Tifft and Alex S. Jones in their illuminating study of the Ochs-Sulzberger family dynasty, would Ochs offer public support for a cause, "certainly not one involving Jews."[23]

President Wilson's nomination of Brandeis to the Supreme Court in January 1916 caught the *Times* – and, the newspaper suggested, the nation – by surprise. Identifying him as a "noted 'trust-buster,'" and "a man of remarkable ability as a lawyer," its lengthy news story expressed concern about his "judicial temperament." Sub-headlined "First Jew Named for Supreme Court," it suggested that the appointment "might appeal to advocates of religious tolerance because Mr. Brandeis is of Jewish blood and a leader in the Zionist movement." An editorial recognized Brandeis as "a very distinguished member of the bar, a man learned in the law" and "deeply interested" in public affairs. But his "purely political activity" suggested that a more appropriate place for him might be the legislature. The Supreme Court did not need "some advocate of 'social justice.'"[24]

The *Times* was occasionally receptive to Zionist advocacy – within Reform confines. It quoted liberally from a sermon delivered by Rabbi Stephen S. Wise at Carnegie Hall proclaiming that "Zionism is not irreligious, not un-American. ... A Jew can be a Jew and still be a good American." It was far more attentive to warnings from Henry Morgenthau after his resignation as American ambassador to Turkey in 1916: "It is utterly impossible to place several millions of people in Palestine." But it was "a good idea to have a model colony there," primarily for the development of Jewish art and literature.[25]

Jacob Schiff's discomfort with Zionism continued to command *Times* attention. "The men who tell you [that] you are a separate nation and try to make you look at the American problem from a Jewish viewpoint," he warned early in 1916, "are like the men who made the Golden Calf." When, in June, Schiff renounced further activity in "Zionism, nationalism, ... and Jewish politics," he was praised in a *Times* editorial for his philanthropic generosity "for the good of his race" and for inspiring "those of his faith with a love for the principles of good citizenship."[26]

Revolutionary convulsions in Russia the following year prompted concern about the implications for Jews. The *Times* reprinted the prophecy of Rabbi David Philipson of Hebrew Union College, originally published in *The American Israelite*, that "the messianic age is dawning for our brethren in Russia. ... The obtaining of full rights by Jews in Russia ought to mean the beginning of the end of the Zionistic movement," which was "a counsel of despair" from those who doubted "the increasing triumphs of the spirit of freedom." It also reprinted Schiff's letter in *The American Hebrew*, stating his preference for "a large Jewish population, not a Jewish nation" in Palestine. The majority of Jewish nationalists, he warned, were "either atheists or agnostics," with "absolutely no interest in the Jewish religion."[27]

The *Times* gave prominent attention to a critique of Zionism by Dr. Henry Moskowitz, co-founder of the National Association for the Advancement of Colored People, who labeled the movement "romantic and impracticable." In a *Times Magazine* article the Romanian-born Moskowitz, who was active in the Ethical Cultural Society and New York City politics, insisted that fidelity to the Jewish religion better assured Jewish survival than an embrace of nationalism, which led to "spiritual domination – to a lack of humility." Since a Jewish state would generate "spiritual inbreeding," it was preferable that Jews "get in touch with other places, to grow by struggle, and even at times by suffering." American Jews, for whom "Zionism has no positive message," would not tolerate "any other national political loyalty."[28]

The proclamation in November 1917 by British Foreign Secretary Lord Arthur James Balfour that "His Majesty's Government view with favour the establishment in Palestine of a national home for the Jewish people" was briefly noted in the *Times*, its significance not yet grasped – or, perhaps, evaded. Reprinting Balfour's letter to Lord Rothschild, it merely quoted from *The Jewish Chronicle* in London, the world's oldest continuously published Jewish newspaper, praising the "lifting of the cloud of centuries" from the Jew: instead of remaining "a wanderer in every clime there is to be a home for him in his native land."[29]

But as Zionist promise moved closer to reality with the impending fall of Jerusalem to British soldiers, *Times* editors expressed unease. They noted that the "restoration of Jewish nationality" was not a universal Jewish yearning. Furthermore, "multitudes of Orthodox Jews" (not a Jewish community to which the *Times* normally paid attention) were either indifferent or dubious about Zionism. And Jews of "modern ways of thinking" feared that Zionism would provoke a resurgence of anti-Semitism. The editors favored "practical" policies over "yearning and idealism."[30]

The *Times* published a two-column letter from Henry Morgenthau identifying America as "a holy land." American Jews, he asserted, "are Jews in religion and Americans in nationality." It reprinted an essay from *The American Hebrew* by Rabbi Samuel Shulman of Reform Temple Beth El in New York entitled "Jewish Nation Not Wanted in Palestine." Jews, he wrote, constituted "a spiritual entity" with a home "in all lands of the world." The most important provisions of the Balfour Declaration, Shulman suggested, protected the rights of non-Jews in Palestine and preserved the civil and religious rights of Jews elsewhere. Jews living "in Western lands cannot for a moment grant the idea that they are without a home." Belonging to the nation "in whose midst they dwell," they have properly "refused to acknowledge that Israel is a nation." Zionism, for Rabbi Shulman, raised "sinister possibilities" of "hyphenated nationality." Jewish "destiny" was "to remain scattered all over the world."[31]

Several days later the *Times* published an article excoriating Zionism by Whitman College English professor Ralph P. Boas. It was, he protested, more than a proposal for Jewish statehood; "it is a program for Jewish life everywhere," demanding that "a complete Jew" must "believe in Jewish theology" and "faithfully obey the minute prescriptions of the traditional Jewish law, to speak a Jewish language, ... to live in a Jewish land under a Jewish government." But Jews must be left free "not to separate from society": "If Judaism is so far gone that its salvation lies in becoming a little State it had much better die." Worse yet, Boas asserted ominously, "Zionists would, consciously or unconsciously, dragoon us into a citizenship and a nationality which we do not want. ... We will not be dragooned out of America into Palestine." It was "inconceivable" that American Jews would "allow their future to be determined by a group of men who will control the Zionist State," for Zionism is "insidiously dangerous."[32]

Between 1914 and 1917 the unanticipated consequences of war in Europe resulted in the collapse of the Ottoman Empire, the emergence of Great Britain as a major power in the Middle East, and the transformation of Zionist yearnings from fantasy to reality. The Balfour Declaration, with its pledge of "the establishment in Palestine of a national home for the Jewish people," was as galvanizing to Zionists determined to return to the ancient Jewish homeland as it was ominous for diaspora Jews whose apprehension over divided loyalty it activated. Among assimilated Jews in Reform temples, conferences and publications – and in the pages of *The New York Times* – their anxiety was palpable.

The best that could be said in the *Times* for the scattered Jewish communities in Palestine was their resemblance to "New England Townships." Arriving

British soldiers discovered "thriving colonies of Russo-Polish Jews" that were "far superior, as to scientific cultivation and housing, to the Arab farmers." In Rishon-le-Zion, already known for its fine wine, inhabitants lived in stone houses "rescued from the debris of Biblical buildings." Smaller villages had a "Beth-am" (people's house) that resembled "the New England town hall." Their Vaads – village councils – mirrored "the Selectmen of a New England township."[33] Complementing Oscar Straus's celebration of the biblical sources of American constitutional government, the *Times* discovered the source of Zionist inspiration in colonial New England.

Such fanciful comparisons soon yielded to more disturbing concerns, most frequently expressed in defense of Reform Jewish principles. The *Times* published a two-column letter from former New York Attorney General Simon W. Rosendale reiterating that Zionism lacks the "general sympathy or approval" of Reform Jews, who are Jews "by religion only and American by nationality." The implications of Jewish statehood in Palestine were dire: "distasteful, dangerous, and outworn doctrines" that merged Church and State. But Reform Jews "refuse to be hyphenated"; our nationality and religion are "distinct and separate." Referring to "un-American Zionists," Rosendale fretted: "What would be the attitude of 'Zionists' in case of war between our country and their 'national homeland'?"[34]

Concern over President Wilson's apparent sympathy for Zionism prompted a *Times Magazine* critique from Republican Congressman Julius Kahn. Wilson's support, Kahn believed, was attributable to "some of his closest friends" (presumably Brandeis) being "avowed Zionists." But most American Jews were "thoroughgoing Americans" who "owe no allegiance and desire to any other country in the world." The United States is their "Zion." A "so-called Jewish homeland in Palestine" would be nothing but a "hindrance" to Jews, creating "divided allegiance." Kahn, who had emigrated from Germany as a young boy with his parents, was apprehensive lest Zionism make Diaspora Jews seem like "aliens" rather than "respected citizens." Several weeks later an American Jewish Committee statement appeared in the *Times* warning against the "reorganization of the Jews as a national unit to whom, now or in the future, territorial sovereignty in Palestine shall be committed." It was signed, among others, by Adolph Ochs.[35]

The *Times* paid slight attention to events in Palestine, barely noticing the sudden eruption of Arab violence in Jerusalem on Easter Sunday in April 1920. Incited by speeches from Muslim dignitaries urging resistance to the Balfour Declaration, Arab celebrants of the Nabi Musa festival on their way to the al-Aqsa Mosque attacked Jews in the Jewish Quarter of the Old City. When a group of young Zionists arrived to protect Jewish residents, rioting erupted. British soldiers fired weapons to scatter the crowds; five Jews and four Arabs were killed.

The *Times* report (from Cairo) merely cited travelers' accounts of anti-Semitism that had sparked clashes resulting in "mostly light" casualties. In a brief editorial the following day entitled "These Piping Times," one paragraph referred to 188 casualties in the Jerusalem rioting; another reported the death of a "scab student" in Buenos Aires who crossed a picket line to take exams; and the concluding paragraph was devoted to an explosion that wrecked a store in the Italian neighborhood of New York. Taken together, they demonstrated to *Times* editors that "the war is over, but these days of peace are not yet so tame that they cannot furnish some 'moral equivalents' for most of its phenomena." Several days later, the *Times* referred to "considerable effervescence in the Jerusalem district" (ten civilians were killed) but concluded that "the situation is well in hand." *Times* editors remained deeply uneasy over the prospect of Jewish statehood. Although the League of Nations Mandate for Palestine referred to "a national home for the Jewish people," an editorial noted that it had not "set up a Jewish State or nation in Palestine." Rather, its "effect" was "to create a national home or refuge for Jews who, because of oppression or persecution in any other land, may desire to seek shelter there."[36] American Jews, by implication, had no need for such a refuge.

Another wave of Arab violence erupted in 1921 during a May Day march of Zionists from Jaffa to Tel Aviv. In three days of bloody fighting that spread to nearby Jewish agricultural settlements, forty-three Jews (and fourteen Arabs) were killed. The *Times* report from Paris by Edwin L. James (who would become Managing Editor a decade later) endorsed allegations by British officials of a "Bolshevik peril." Jewish immigrants from Russia, James wrote, "appear to have included a number of Bolshevist agents" who aroused "the resentment of the natives, both Christian and Mohammedan" and "succeeded in stirring up serious trouble."[37] Arabs killed Jews and the *Times* blamed Jews.

Zionist economic development received approving notice. Sir Alfred Mond, visiting Palestine with Chaim Weizmann in 1921, reported "a very fine class of young Jews from the Ukraine and Galicia" who are "assisting in the reconstruction of the country with enthusiasm and real patriotism." These Zionists, engaged in "fruit growing and farming," demonstrated that "the race will go back to their original role of cultivation of the soil." And, Mond observed, "They are all anti-Bolshevists." Palestine, according to the prominent American Jewish educator Dr. Samson Benderly, had the potential to become "the Southern California of the old world" if "the business acumen and ingenuity of the Pacific Coast" could be transplanted there. Months later the *Times* quoted German Professor Otto Warburg's identification of Palestine as "the California of the East."[38] The more that Palestine resembled America, the better it suited the *Times*.

The appointment of John Finley in 1921 as associate editor (a position he held until he became editor-in-chief sixteen years later) nudged the *Times* editorial page even further away from Jewish nationalism. After heading the Red Cross Commission in Palestine during the war Finley had become "a pilgrim in Palestine," the title of his postwar journey of discovery and self-discovery. In his Preface he thanked Great Britain "for making it possible for Christendom to walk again in its holy places free of the Turk." Finley envisaged Palestine as the place for fulfillment of "a practicable internationalism" that transcends "national frictions." By reason of "genius and the universality of his experience," Finley wrote, "the Jew" was "fitted above others to help nations reach that internationalism, of practice as well as of spirit, through nationality." But Jews in Palestine must not segregate themselves, once again becoming "a 'peculiar people' and a separate nation." Palestine must become "an international Homeland," not a parochial Jewish nation that "accentuates difference of race or creed."[39]

During the 1920s, under Finley's editorial guidance, criticism of Zionism was a staple of *Times* coverage. Pope Benedict's expression of "deep anxiety over the situation in Palestine, owing to the activity of the Jews in the Holy Land," was highlighted. Two weeks later the *Times* devoted three columns to Henry Morgenthau's article in *World's Week* declaring "Zionism is the most stupendous fallacy in Jewish history ... wrong in principle and impossible of realization." Zionism, Morgenthau asserted, is "a surrender, not a solution," a "betrayal" that will "cost the Jews of America most that they have gained of liberty, equality, and fraternity." It was "enlightened Jews" of the United States who had discovered "the true road to Zion." In a lengthy exploration of Palestine as "a land of problems," correspondent T. Walter Williams noted that "the flooding of Palestine with thousands of penniless Jews" had "antagonized the natives."[40]

Even with British Mandatory governance in Palestine secured the *Times* continued to provide a welcoming forum for hostile critics of Zionist activities. A "prominent American missionary" deplored newly arriving Jewish immigrants from Europe who were "unnecessarily arrogant." A letter from Yale English professor Edward Bliss Reed asserted that Zionist methods and goals were "opposed to the principles of liberty and justice generally held by

Americans." Everyone who was not a Zionist, wrote a New York neurologist, believed that the British Government and Zionist advocates were launching "an experiment of political anachronism" unrecorded in history. It was fine for Jews to build a great university in Jerusalem, colonies such as Rishon-le-Zion, and schools and hospitals in Jaffa. But it was ominous if Jews were "sent into a country and maintained there at the expense of their prosperous co-religionists of other lands" until they become strong enough "to get the native's substance and soil from him."[41]

The *Times* published a sharp response from Professor William H. Worrell, formerly director of the American School of Oriental Research in Jerusalem. Anyone acquainted with Palestine "through study and research," he observed pointedly, would find it "strange" that such a statement "should have sufficient news value to find a place on the crowded page of our greatest newspaper." Jerusalem, Worrell noted, has always been "a city of strife" and Palestine "the political battleground of the nations"; and, during Arab occupancy, "a land of decay, misery, insecurity and obscurity." Zionism, he asserted, "is the latest, if not the last, attempted solution of the Jewish problem. It seems only fair that it be given a trial."[42]

Adolph Ochs remained skeptical. Interviewed at length in *The American Israelite* after his first visit to Jerusalem in 1922, the *Times* publisher identified with "that very large school of Jewish thought in America that think that the greatest heritage of the Jew is his religion ... and that as a distinctive race the Jews need no place in modern civilization." Ochs was "greatly impressed by the earnest and able men and women of the Zionist organization," and "astonished" at their accomplishments. But he believed that "their cause is hopeless" in the face of Arab hostility. He remained "unsympathetic with Zionism ... because the Jewish religion is secondary." He wished "only to be regarded as a Jew by religion."[43]

In the month following his return the *Times* published sharply contrasting editorials about Armenian and Jewish pursuits of a national homeland. "Where is this exiled people to find its homeland," the *Times* movingly implored – about Armenians. Two weeks later it sharply criticized a proposed Congressional resolution supporting the Balfour Declaration, warning that "A religious question is being thrust into American politics." Congress was "catering" to "the Jewish vote," a decision likely to contribute to "the evils of hyphenated citizens." Jews would suffer most from such efforts and were likely to confront "a separation between them and the rest of their fellow-Americans, with whom it is their earnest desire to associate themselves in every patriotic sentiment and national aspiration."[44] The enticing prospect of Jewish assimilation must not be impeded by Zionism.

Without its own correspondent in Palestine the *Times* relied on visiting journalists, tourists, and Reform rabbis to inform readers about the Zionist project. Henrietta Szold's Hadassah, and its offshoot the American Zionist Medical Unit, were praised for efforts that were "purely humanitarian and philanthropic, as distinct from any political aims or activities." The farming "colony" of Hadera, established before the turn of the century by members of Hovevei Zion ("Lovers of Zion"), symbolized the "spirit of progress." Its residents, wrote Bernard A. Rosenblatt, a member of the World Zionist Executive, "are building the new Judea even as the Puritans built a New England three hundred years ago." Embracing a favorite *Times* trope he identified new immigrants as "Jewish Puritans," bringing "prosperity and happiness to the Arabs in Palestine." Zionist community building also reminded him of a "booming Western town," with the growth potential of Los Angeles. But a six-column excerpt from popular journalist Ray Stannard Baker's *America and the World Peace*, entitled "Against Palestine As Jewish State," highlighted "the injustice of the Zionist program."[45]

The *Times* celebrated American identity and loyalty and Reform superiority. Covering the Golden Jubilee convention of the Union of American (Reform) Hebrew Congregations, under the sub-heading "Idea of Exile Discarded," it featured the comments of Rabbi Jonah B. Wise, son of the founder of Reform Judaism (and Effie Wise Ochs's half-brother). America may not be "a Jewish nation," he conceded, but Jews are "identified with American ideals" because their adopted homeland embraces Hebrew scripture, prophecy and justice. The idea of "galuth" (exile) was unacceptable to "American Israel."[46]

For reassurance about Zionism the *Times* relied on the observations of American visitors who shared Adolf Ochs's assimilationist concerns. Former ambassador to Turkey Oscar Straus, who spent a month in Palestine in 1925, reported "a fine spirit of sacrifice and devotion among the settlements where modern scientific methods are fast replacing archaic methods still employed by the Arabs, as 2,000 years ago." But Zionism was no more than a "pious hope," with its realization dependent on British benevolence. German-born American banker Felix Warburg found the most "disheartening" aspect of Palestine to be the absence of synagogues, especially one of "architectural grandeur." He expressed relief that he had not heard "a single word about the nationalistic ambitions of the Jews to make of the Holy Land a Jewish political State." At the dedication of a temple in Glens Falls, Adolph Ochs reiterated: "I know nothing else, no other definition for a Jew except religion."[47]

If the *Times* avoided – or, through Reform proxies, criticized – political Zionism, it nonetheless displayed interest in archeological discoveries, especially those that "substantiate biblical evidence." The excavation of the four-thousand-year-old walls of the ancient Jebusite City of David, breached by King David's army in his conquest of Jerusalem in 1000 BC, had been located with the "Bible as guide." According to the *Times,* the discovery in Jerusalem's Kidron Valley of the adjacent ancient tombs of Absalom (David's son), King Jehoshaphat, and the prophet Zechariah, "appear to confirm certain chapters of Jewish legend."[48]

The *Times* gave prominent coverage to the inauguration of Hebrew University in 1925, on the Mt. Scopus site where Titus had camped when the Roman army besieged Jerusalem eighteen centuries earlier. From the amphitheater facing east, it noted, there was an "unrivaled panorama full of biblical associations": past the Judean desert, across the Jordan Valley and Dead Sea, to the hills of Moab. Lord Balfour, in his dedication speech, proudly proclaimed: "We are now engaged in adapting Western methods and the Western form of the university to an Eastern site," a "new experiment."[49] But any link between Zionism and ancient Jewish sovereignty was avoided.

Rabbi Samuel Schulman of Temple Beth El in Manhattan identified the university as the symbol of the new "secular Palestine," the "most characteristic expression of modern Zionism." For Reform Jews, however, "the highest symbol for Judaism would be a magnificent House of God, erected on the holy mountain." He complained that by its very name the Hebrew University "emphasizes the importance of the race, the nation, the native language and not the religion." In his subsequent Yom Kippur sermon (reported in the *Times*), Rabbi Shulman insisted that Palestine "can never be the solution of the Jewish problem." Israel's "destiny is to remain scattered all over the world … and to cooperate with the best spirits of the world for progress and human freedom, in social justice and in humanitarian sympathies."[50]

In 1925, three years after his previous visit to Palestine, *Times* correspondent T. Walter Williams concluded that the Zionist aim was to establish "colonies" for "the oppressed members of the race in Europe," not to claim Palestine as "the national home for the Jews." He was most impressed by the "macadamized roads" and flourishing Jewish "colonies" between Haifa and Nazareth. In Jerusalem Williams focused on improved sanitation, noting: "people have been taught to cover the garbage cans outside their doors at night."[51]

But Zionism remained problematic for the *Times*. According to Reform Rabbi Jonah B. Wise, America was "the new Jerusalem" for American Jews, "the interpreter of the traditions and spirit of Israel." Dr. Henry S. Pritchett, President of the Carnegie Endowment for International Peace, declared the Zionist project to be "unfortunate and visionary." In a four-column critique he warned that "No greater misfortune can come to a people or to a nation than to cherish the illusion that it is a chosen people." Pritchett concluded: "The segregation of any national group by itself has seldom failed to develop a type of personality and national character that was aggressive, egotistic and without capacity for cooperation with the rest of the world."[52]

Pritchett's assessment was sharply challenged. Chaim Weizmann, president of the World Zionist Organization, rejected his "superficial and biased observations" and failure to recognize the "historic justice and necessity" that propelled "the effort of the Jewish people for national redemption." But Pritchett's report "compels attention," an editorial response deferentially concluded, because it is "the judgment of a non-Jewish observer" whose objectivity "may be presumed." The editors wondered whether there was "a sound economic foundation for large-scale Jewish settlement." With evident concern they asked: "Can a large Jewish population be developed without displacing the native Arabs?"[53]

Several months later the *Times* published another lengthy anti-Zionist critique by Rev. Harry Emerson Fosdick of the Park Avenue Baptist Church. Expressing his wish that "a modified form of Zionism succeed," Rev. Fosdick warned that "the Jew has got to stop his chauvinism." Jews in Palestine were "confident and aggressive," but Arabs were "angry and resentful." Citing Reform Rabbi Judah Magnes as a model of enlightened Zionism, with "educational and cultural revival instead of political ambition as its motive," Rev. Fosdick deplored (Jewish) nationalism as "a false god."[54]

Ever since Adolph S. Ochs purchased the *Times* the parameters of Jewish legitimacy in its pages had been defined by the assimilationist ideology of Reform Judaism that he passionately embraced. The nascent Jewish national revival in Palestine, with its perceived challenge to his proud identity as an American Jew, evoked abiding discomfort. Wary lest the *Times* be seen as a "Jewish" newspaper, Ochs guided its resolute affirmation of the patriotic loyalty of American Jews to the United States.

CHAPTER 2

The Zionist Menace: 1928–1939

Joseph M. Levy is the forgotten pioneer of *New York Times* reporting from Jerusalem. Born in New Jersey in 1901, he was taken there as an infant by his parents and spent his boyhood in the Ottoman ruled city. He attended the American University of Beirut before serving as private and political secretary to Sir Ronald Storrs, governor of Jerusalem during the early years of the British Mandate. Then he spent seven months living with a Bedouin tribe in Trans-Jordan. Fluent in Hebrew and Arabic, he was hired as a foreign correspondent by the *Times* in 1928. That November, Levy was identified as "Palestine Correspondent of *The New York Times*."[1]

Levy's reporting carefully skirted the political reverberations of Zionism. He was fascinated by archeology and history, reporting excavations at ancient Beit El and Megiddo and (in a front-page article) the discovery of pottery and bones from the Canaanite period at a site near Hebron. "An imposing array of evidence," Levy wrote, "linked these artifacts to the Israelite conquest of Canaan and to the land assigned by Moses to his loyal follower Caleb." With these discoveries, he concluded with palpable excitement, the biblical account "becomes more vivid and intelligible than ever."[2]

Levy also reported extensively on Zionist land development and the resulting bountiful harvests of fruit, vegetables, and grain, although not without occasional conflict as unemployed Jewish workers expressed anger over their employers' preference for hiring cheap Arab labor. Following a severe mid-decade financial crisis in Palestine the "dark clouds" of economic depression and high unemployment were finally lifting. With patience, determination, and an infusion of capital for industrial development, Levy concluded optimistically, "the future of the Holy Land is assured."[3]

Zionist cultural institutions also attracted Levy's interest. He noted that the three-year-old Hebrew University, committed to the revival of the Hebrew language, had sparked "a new literature" that displayed "the highest type of poetry, fiction and drama." Jews in Palestine, he concluded, "are living up to their reputation, earned through the ages, as a people eager for learning and culture." He enthusiastically embraced the Zionist narrative, describing a land "bare and barren through lack of care and cultivation," finally "flowing with milk and honey." Even the "new type of Jew," while indistinguishable in dress from Gentiles, "is yet conscious of his peculiar vocation as a member of the chosen people, once again a free citizen in his ancestral homeland."[4]

Levy reported "rapid development and progress" in Palestine under British Mandatory rule. The simultaneous celebration in Jerusalem of Easter, Passover and Nebi Musa affirmed his optimism about inter-communal harmony. Friction, he concluded, "has to a very great extent been set at rest" as the result of shared confidence in "the justice of the rule" of British High Commissioners. Lord Plumer, Levy noted, was not "an instrument of Zionism"; he responsibly governed "a British administration."[5]

At the end of September 1928, during Yom Kippur prayer at the Western Wall, the British Deputy District Commissioner abruptly ordered police to remove a wooden partition separating men and women. His decision sparked conflict, not across gender lines but between Muslims and Jews. The *Times* (not Levy) reported that the disruption was grounded in Muslim concern over "professional wailers" at the Wall. Muslim authorities anticipated that the partition, with benches provided for "old and feeble men [to] rest when not wailing," would be followed by walls and a roof, and "soon after the Jews would claim this as their own land." The Yom Kippur provocation stirred Jewish protest throughout Palestine. Chief Rabbi Abraham Isaac Kook proclaimed a day of fasting and mourning for the "outrages" inflicted on the holiest day in the Jewish calendar.[6]

Levy wrote a column about the disturbance for the editorial page. He focused, for the first time, on "the abyss of race and religion which divides Jew and Moslem"; even under "a most modern [British] administration," the "turbulent history of Palestine" lingered. Levy did not doubt the "sincerity" of British attempts to bring order out of chaos following the departure of Turkish rulers. But Palestine, he concluded, was not yet prepared for self-government. Although British authorities claimed that the Muslim Supreme Council had requested removal of the Western Wall partition for violating the status quo, there was "no excuse," Levy wrote, "for the disrespect displayed by the interruption of the sacred prayer on the holiest day of the year." It was "natural" that Jews throughout the world had "raised their voices in indignant protest," claiming the Western Wall as "their rightful property."[7]

Once the conflict receded Levy resumed his coverage of less volatile developments. During the early months of 1929 he touted economic progress in Palestine, citing an influx of tourists, flourishing hotels, the expansion of paved roads and a bountiful orange harvest. To be sure, the problem of beggars in the Old City of Jerusalem endured, creating "the most heartrending spectacles" in the narrow alley leading to the Western Wall, where "miserable wretches" displayed "all manner of afflictions" and "mumble invocations through toothless gums." Levy also provided a window on developments elsewhere in the Middle East. Displaying remarkable journalistic versatility, he wrote about Ibn Saud's effort to contain the Bedouin tribes in the Arabian peninsula, Iraq-Persian relations, the discovery of Byzantine relics in Trans-Jordan, Maronite-Muslim conflict in Damascus, and political turbulence in Lebanon.[8]

In late August Haj Amin al-Husseini, the British-appointed Grand Mufti of Jerusalem, claimed in a public statement that Jews planned to "usurp" the Western Wall and endanger Muslim Holy sites on the Temple Mount. There were "many incidents," the *Times* reported, when Jewish prayer at the Wall was obstructed, but protests and demands for protection were "ineffectual." Following the Tisha b'Av mourning service commemorating the destruction of the ancient Temples, an Arab mob swarmed through the site, attacking the prayer leader, destroying sacred objects, and burning prayer books. The funeral procession for a Jew was disrupted by Arab rioters, "incited to the highest pitch of frenzy," who attacked the pallbearers and uncovered the body.[9]

Tension was also rising in another ancient holy city. Twenty miles south in Hebron, the traditional site of the burial caves of the patriarchs and matriarchs of the Jewish people, a Jewish teacher was ominously warned by a local Arab: "This time we are going to butcher you all." The solitary British police officer in Hebron concluded, after meeting with local Arab and Jewish notables, that "any trouble ... was out of the question." But incited by the frenzied claim of a local sheikh that the blood of "thousands" of Muslims was being shed in Jerusalem, Hebron Arabs screaming "Itbach al Yahud" ("Kill the Jews") swarmed through the Jewish Quarter. A mob broke into the spacious home of Eliezer Dan Slonim, the Jewish community leader who served on the Hebron municipal council, where more than seventy terrified Jews had taken refuge. Virtually the entire Slonim family (except for one-year-old Shlomo), along with nearly twenty other Jews, were brutally slaughtered. Sixty-seven Jews, including twenty-seven yeshiva students, were murdered in Hebron during the Arab rampage.[10]

The headline over Levy's front-page report, two days later, read: "12 Americans Killed by Arabs in Hebron." The "most serious attack," he reported, had occurred at the Hebron yeshiva, where a dozen American students, "mostly youths," were murdered and fifteen wounded. As the extent of the carnage became known the *Times* noted that thirty Slobodka yeshiva students, including eight Americans, had been killed in the "savage" attack, while eighteen Jews had been murdered in the "Banker's House" owned by Slonim. "The barbarity of the attackers," its report concluded, "knew no bounds." Calling for "A Firm Hand in Palestine," a *Times* editorial assigned "chief responsibility" for "the tragic outburst of racial and religious feuds" to "a breakdown in British administrative efficiency." British authorities had not displayed the "show of force" necessary to "overawe" the "fanaticism" in Palestine.[11]

Levy wrote from Jerusalem: "There is not one corner of the land where Jews are to be found, from Dan to Beersheba, which has been left unmolested." His visit to the Nathan Straus Health Center, where several hundred terrified Hebron refugees had arrived following their evacuation by British soldiers, belatedly alerted him to the extent of the horrific massacre that had destroyed the millennia-old Jewish community. He heard "the heart-breaking cries of hysterical men, women and children bemoaning the losses of their dear ones and friends." He learned details of the "tragic and stirring tales of these Hebron atrocities," including "butchery, robbery and pillage." The horror of "the wholesale slaughter" in Hebron remained with him. "What explanation can be given," Levy wondered, "for the cruel, barbaric slaughter" of innocent rabbinical students, women, and children?[12]

"The horror in Palestine does not come to me as a surprise," wrote Adolph Ochs from his Lake Placid summer home. In a letter to humanitarian reformer Lillian D. Wald, he identified himself as "an anti-Zionist. I almost have an obsession on the subject." He blamed Zionists for attempting "to superimpose an aggressive minority in Arabia with unacceptable political and economic ideas, aims and purposes." Ochs feared that "Zionist activities in Palestine would not only result in massacres there, but would be a menacing danger to Jews throughout the world." Zionism, he claimed, "is doomed and the sooner it is a matter of the past and forgotten the better it will be for the Jews of the world."[13]

Levy eagerly anticipated the arrival of a British commission of inquiry to investigate "all phases of the Palestine problem" and determine "how far Zionism can succeed here and how the Arabs may be pacified," given "the ever-growing Jewish strength in the country." The "fundamental cause" of the riots, he concluded, was "acknowledged to be a revolt by Arabs against Zionism and the alleged Zionist policy of the government." Their goal, he learned from an official of the Palestine Arab executive committee, was "retraction of the Balfour

Declaration and the establishment of a national democratic government. ... Palestine cannot become 'the' Jewish national home."[14] It was a message that lingered with Levy.

The *Times* balanced Levy's coverage of the deadly consequences of Arab terror and murder with criticism of Jewish settlement in Palestine from Arab groups in New York and Jews in Baghdad who joined Muslims (and the *Times*) in denouncing the Jewish national movement. It published a statement from Yale religion professor John Clark Archer declaring "Jews have no right to a State in so predominantly a Moslem community." Zionism, he concluded, was "a mistaken policy and a misreading of Jewish history."[15]

Yom Kippur in Jerusalem, Levy wrote, probably was "the most mournful" in centuries. Even "Hebrews" known to be "avowed atheists" attended synagogue. But British authorities imposed stringent restrictions on Jewish prayer at the Western Wall. Barely a handful of Jews attended evening Kol Nidre services there when, at the insistence of the Grand Mufti, lighting was prohibited. British High Commissioner Sir John Chancellor instructed Chief Rabbi Kook that shofar blowing also was banned, lest Muslims be offended. Kook responded that not since "the darkest epochs of the Middle Ages" had such draconian restrictions been imposed on Jewish worshippers.[16]

Levy provided extensive and balanced coverage of the hearings conducted by the British Shaw Commission, appointed to investigate the causes and consequences of the recent rioting. But in early November there was a discernible shift in the tone and content of his reports. "The critical political situation between the Arabs and the Jews in Palestine," he wrote, "is daily becoming more serious as the Arabs continue to gain strength." Moslems had closed ranks behind the Grand Mufti and Christian Arabs were united with them in calling for abolition of the Balfour Declaration, establishment of "a national democratic government," and suspension of Jewish immigration. "Unfortunately," Levy continued, "the Zionist leaders seem unable to cope with the situation and are floundering about without finding a political solution of the problem." They had "failed to realize" that Palestine, with an Arab population of more than 600,000 (quadruple the number of Jews), "is not a new country." Zionists "have overlooked the fact that cooperation with these natives is most essential and have made no efforts to reach an understanding with them."[17]

The Arab riots propelled Levy into the vortex of political debate over the Balfour Declaration, Zionism and the future of Palestine. He participated in covert discussions with H. St. John Philby, a disgruntled former British civil servant who had denounced the Declaration as "an act of betrayal for whose parallel … we have to go back to the garden of Gethsemane"; Judah L. Magnes, the prominent American Reform rabbi and outspoken proponent of a bi-national state in Palestine who had recently become Chancellor of the new Hebrew University; and the Grand Mufti of Jerusalem Haj Amin al-Husseini, convicted of inciting the 1921 riots.[18]

Philby, from the inner circles of elite British society, had served British interests (and his own) in India, Iraq and the Arabian Peninsula before replacing T.E. Lawrence as chief British representative in Trans-Jordan. He was dismissed by British authorities for providing secret information designed to facilitate the ascendancy of Ibn Saud over the Hashemites in the Arab peninsula. On the return journey to his adopted home in Jidda (where he lived in a sixty-room palace bestowed on him by the Saudi king) he met with the Grand Mufti in Jerusalem to offer advice about securing Arab national interests in Palestine.[19]

After describing his visit with the Grand Mufti and his chief lieutenants at the office of the Muslim Supreme Council, Philby recounted to Lord Passfield: "I had the pleasure of making the acquaintance of the Near East correspondent of *The New York Times*, Mr. Joseph Levy, and of discussing the Palestine situation with him. We found ourselves substantially in agreement as to the practical steps now necessary for the permanent solution of the Palestine problem." Levy was "apparently so impressed with the possibility of my scheme for a settlement" that he asked Philby "to prepare a statement of my considered views for publication in his paper." At Levy's urging, Philby returned from Cairo for a "vigorous discussion of a possible solution" with Magnes, the Mufti, and the *Times* journalist.[20]

Levy was already familiar with Magnes, the maverick American Reform rabbi whose "spiritual" Zionism blended pacifism and universalism. Although Magnes had protested that given the Arab demographic majority in Palestine the Balfour Declaration violated "almost every principle of democracy," he passionately believed that the Hebrew University could facilitate Arab-Jewish reconciliation. So, too, might Brit Shalom, an organization founded by Martin Buber, Gershom Scholem, and other prominent intellectuals whose commitment to a bi-national state Magnes vigorously and publicly supported. Speaking at the Winter term convocation in November 1929, he declared that if a Jewish national home could only be established "upon the bayonets of some empire," it would be preferable for "the eternal people" to demonstrate "patience, planning and waiting to enter the promised land." Jews must do "nothing that cannot be justified before the conscience of the world." His comments provoked an "uproar" and a *Times* headline: "Students Hiss Head of Hebrew College."[21]

By then Levy had become the coordinator of an anti-Zionist cohort comprising Philby, Magnes (with whom Levy shared Philby's proposal), and the Grand Mufti. He relayed word of Philby's meeting with the Mufti to Magnes and met with them to prepare an article presenting their critique of Zionist nationalism. Then he forwarded a "final draft" of Philby's proposal for "a solution of the existing political situation in Palestine" to the Grand Mufti for his approval, noting: "I was asked by Mr. Philby to carry on negotiations in his absence and to report to him to Jidda." Proposing that "Palestine shall henceforth be administered on a democratic constitutional republican basis," the document would vest all legislative and executive authority in a representative assembly and council comprising Arabs and Jews "in proportion to their numbers in the population."[22] In effect, and by design, it would eviscerate the Balfour Declaration, endorsed by the League of Nations, promising "a national home for the Jewish people" in Palestine.

Levy secured *Times* publication of lengthy statements by Magnes and Philby that were prominently featured three days apart. Magnes urged that Palestine become the "World Holyland." Praising Philby (identified by the *Times* only as a "British journalist and traveler") for his proposal, Magnes granted to Jews the right to an "intellectual centre" in Palestine, but they "must renounce all ideas of political domination." Three days later the *Times* ran a five-column article under Levy's by-line entitled "Suggests Solution for Palestine Ills," featuring Philby's proposals (approved by the Grand Mufti and endorsed by Magnes). To be sure, Levy acknowledged, the "Wailing Wall dispute" was the "hidden spark" that that had aroused "the religious fanaticism of the Arab fellaheen," kindling the "nationwide anti-Jewish campaign" that had raged through Palestine since August. But responsibility for the upheaval lay elsewhere.[23]

The implicit message was that the problem in Palestine was Zionism. Levy glowingly introduced "one of the greatest British authorities on Arab affairs today, a man who is the Arabs' greatest friend, Mr. St. John Philby." In Levy's judgment, Philby offered "perhaps the most logical and fair proposal thus far suggested" for resolving the Palestine conundrum. While the Balfour Declaration could not be abrogated, "the unquestionable moral and legal rights of the Arabs" must be recognized. The establishment of a national government, with representation based on population, was essential. The Jewish Agency could continue "to watch over and protect the interests of the Jews," assuring "freedom of immigration subject to the capacity of the country to absorb immigrants." But political power would reside elsewhere.

The "practical effect on Jews," Philby acknowledged, would be their recognition that "the political Zionist dream of ultimate domination of the Holy Land is dead forever." But "in the interest of the peace of the Holy Land that is all to the good." Philby assured *Times* readers that "the best elements of Jewry will still come to Palestine with a legitimate and useful purpose": to study and teach at the university and "settle down to the tilling of the soil." But Jews with "political tendencies and ambitions" fostered by political Zionism will "keep away." His proposal, Philby asserted, would not "jeopardize any legitimate interest of the Jews."[24]

Philby's plan was endorsed by Magnes, introduced by Levy as "an important moderate Jewish leader" who opposed the "extravagant interpretation" of the Balfour Declaration advocated by Zionists. Indeed, Magnes asserted, the Balfour Declaration "emphasized unduly the Jewish relationship to Palestine" rather than Palestine as "an international holy land." Remaining permanently under international control, it should be no more than "a spiritual and intellectual centre for Judaism and the Jewish people." Magnes favored a bi-national government for "an inter-religious and an interracial home" grounded in "understanding and peace" that included "all three religions equally." He firmly rejected "the Joshua method ... of entering the Promised Land" by conquest.[25]

By then Levy had become the *Times* conduit for the anti-Zionist consensus comprising the Grand Mufti, Philby and Magnes. He "played a crucial part in the Magnes-Philby negotiations," concludes historian Naomi W. Cohen; and he assured expansive *Times* coverage – and endorsement – of their views. Levy also encouraged Magnes to summarize his rebuttal to critics in a pamphlet entitled "Like All the Nations" in which Magnes reiterated his willingness to "yield on the question of a Jewish State and a Jewish majority." Rebuked by Jerusalem journalist Gershon Agronsky for undermining the Zionist administration in Palestine, Levy conceded that if he succeeded it would represent the fulfillment of years of effort.[26] Whether that was his retrospective wish, or the disclosure of a long hidden agenda, remains unknown.

Recognizing that Zionists had expressed "the greatest indignation" over Magnes's proposals, Levy afforded him two opportunities within a week to respond to his critics. Expounding on the anti-Zionist ideas presented in his new booklet, which Levy summarized at length, Magnes praised Philby's "moderate expression of opinion." He would be content if "immigration and settlement in the land and Hebrew life and culture can be guaranteed to Jews in Palestine." For that, Magnes would "yield on the question of a Jewish State and a Jewish majority." Palestine, he wrote, "should be neither an Arab national

State nor a Jewish national State." It was the appropriate place for "a bi-national country." Jews could establish a homeland "only by being true democrats and internationalists," using "brotherly, friendly instruments" to achieve the "great ethical mission" of Palestine.[27]

By 1930 the *Times,* guided by Levy's behind-the-scenes maneuvering, served as a platform for anti-Zionist critics. Jewish nationalism, Henry Morgenthau complained, had stirred "serious trouble" between Jews and Arabs who had lived peacefully together in Palestine before the war. "The Zionists have spoiled Palestine for the Jews," he wrote, "by making demands to which the Arabs could not afford to agree." Zionism, he concluded, "is doomed to failure." Thomas Mann, visiting Palestine to gather material for what became the magisterial *Joseph and His Brothers,* contributed a column cautioning Jews to "go carefully" because Arabs, present in Palestine for more than one thousand years, also have "historical associations and rights to the land." Mann pointedly identified with "spiritual," not political, Zionism. On the first anniversary of the Arab riots the *Times* (once again) provided Rabbi Samuel Shulman of Temple Emanu-El with an opportunity to present his Reform critique of Zionism. It was the duty of American Jews, he asserted, to "oppose uncompromisingly and with all their might the philosophy of Jewish nationalism and the Zionistic ideal." Jews had "long ago outgrown the stature of a nation as a political entity." Their belief in Palestine as the location for Jewish salvation undermined "the aspirations of the world for harmony and peace."[28]

In the wake of the 1929 riots the British Simpson Report proclaimed "the duty of the administration under the mandate to insure that the position of the Arabs is not prejudiced by Jewish immigration." It was quickly followed by the Passfield White Paper, rejecting "independent and separative ideals" for a Jewish national home and declaring that suspension of Jewish immigration to Palestine was "fully justified." In a lengthy editorial the *Times* enthusiastically endorsed these anti-Zionist conclusions. "The claims of 'political Zionism' were always inadmissible," it asserted. "The imposition of Jewish ascendancy by high-pressure methods" contradicted principles of justice, (Arab) nationalism, and British pledges (to Arabs, not to Jews). *Times* editors applauded British policy affirming that "there has been too great haste in the building of the Jewish Homeland."[29]

By then, Levy had expanded his coverage to include rising opposition to British Mandatory rule in other Muslim countries. On his return to Palestine in July 1931 he wrote two articles offering unbounded admiration for the Grand Mufti and contempt for Zionist "extremists." The Mufti, "a most intelligent person with an exceptionally charming personality," had initiated a "real Arab Nationalist and anti-Zionist movement." But it had remained dormant until Zionist leaders, lacking "an elementary understanding of the Arab," had rejected "diplomacy and tact" while elevating removal of the partition at the Western Wall into "a vital issue." Levy conceded that the Wall had been "a sacred shrine for centuries" to "pious Jews." But rather than permit the conflict to be resolved by Jewish and Moslem religious leaders, Zionists made it seem that "the fate of 16,000,000 Jews throughout the world depended on the Wailing Wall." The Mufti, Levy wrote, had "set a trap for the Zionists, in which the latter allowed themselves to be caught." Zionists, Levy concluded, had "themselves only to blame for this strong movement against them."[30]

Two weeks later, Levy embellished his indictment, blaming the worsening conflict on the failure of Zionists to establish "friendly relationships and cooperation" with local Arabs. Such "lack of foresight" undermined the Zionist cause. He chastised "the extreme militant wing" of Revisionists, still a fringe Zionist group, for demanding "nothing less than a Jewish majority in Palestine, which should become a Jewish state." The Labor Party, favoring the exclusive employment of Jewish workers, was another "stumbling block." To be sure, Levy conceded, "the group of extremists headed by the Mufti" also was "one of the main obstacles."[31]

By mid-1931 Arab opposition to Zionism dominated Levy's coverage of Palestine. He enjoyed access to Arab leaders and quoted extensively from his interviews with them, while virtually ignoring their Zionist counterparts (except Magnes, who by then had become marginalized on the Zionist periphery). Based in Egypt during the early months of 1932, Levy returned to Palestine to cover the opening of the first Maccabiah games, known as the Jewish Olympics, in Tel Aviv. Still riveted by archeological excavations, he described the discovery of an ancient gate in Mizpah destroyed by Sennacherib in 701 BC. The discovery of ivory objects in another excavation left Levy, who excitedly cited the book of Kings and the prophet Amos, with "no doubt that they belonged to the palace of the Israelite kings."[32]

Ancient history aside, Levy recognized – and admired – Zionist economic progress. "Everywhere from Dan to Beersheba," he reported, "building, planting and manufacturing are proceeding at a swift pace" while recently "bare and barren land" was "blooming" with orange and grapefruit groves. Tel Aviv was "bustling," displaying "all the comforts and conveniences," and "bohemian atmosphere," of a metropolis in Europe or the United States. Haifa, emerging as "one of the most prosperous seaports" on the Mediterranean, had "a brilliant" future.[33] But his collaboration with Philby, Magnes and the Mufti, implicating the *Times* in his covert anti-Zionist agenda, had seriously compromised any claim to objective reporting about political Zionism.

Levy was hardly alone at the *Times*. Its publisher assumed that the "temporary prosperity" in Palestine "doubtless will attract a great many Jews." But, Ochs reiterated in a letter to Levy, "I am not a believer in the Zionist movement." He could not understand "why so many men, whom I regard as intelligent, are encouraging the movement." They did not "see the danger arising from the fact that the Christian and Mohammedan world have their holy and sacred places there, and are fearful and suspicious of the ultimate object of the Jews," believing that "they have aspirations for political domination."[34]

Levy was attentive to newly arrived German Jews, privileged yet persecuted. In the summer of 1933, six thousand fleeing immigrants were "able to establish themselves comfortably" in Palestine, where they felt "so much at home" (except for hundreds, without any livelihood, who were "absolutely helpless"). But for stringent immigration restrictions 50,000 other German Jews might have joined them in Palestine. Levy expressed surprise that "despite their exile," German Jews "still exert themselves painstakingly to protect the name of their fatherland."[35]

Another eruption of Arab violence in October 1933, spurred by protests against any Jewish immigration, elicited a more nuanced view of responsibility than Levy had provided four years earlier. Rioting in Haifa, Nablus, and especially Jaffa, where twenty-two Arabs were killed and more than one hundred injured in clashes with British police, prompted "wholesale arrests of Arab leaders and agitators," extensive military preparation, and the dispatch of two squadrons of Royal Air Force planes from Cairo. The eruption occurred despite a government announcement that only 5,500 Jewish immigrant work certificates would be issued during the following six months, leaving Jews "keenly disappointed and despondent."[36]

Levy cited the determination of Arab leaders "to show the outside world that the Arabs were fighting a national cause." Targeting the British government and its policies, not the Jews, they would prove that they were not "a savage people." Their intentions "are not just to kill and loot but [to demonstrate] that we are actually fighting for our right to exist." Jews, Levy's Arab sources asserted, "are encroaching upon us, and since they are buying up all the land in Palestine they are bound to ... ultimately dominate us and drive us out of our country." In the end, Levy concluded, Arab-Jewish conflict was "a puzzle and a paradox." While Arabs strenuously protested against the sale of land to Jews, even their own leaders sold, or brokered, property to them. Levy learned that a close relative of one of the "chief leaders" had offered to sell a large tract of land to a Jewish orange plantation company. There were "many similar instances of Arab patriots and Nationalists" prepared to do likewise. Yet it was Zionists, "from the very beginning of their work in Palestine," who failed to realize that "cooperation with the Arabs would avert constant anxiety."[37]

With Jews in Germany increasingly endangered by the Nazi rise to power, the *Times* embraced universalism. Early in 1933 it reported a new organization, initiated by Rabbi Pereira Mendes, to encourage "the creation of an altruistic nation seeking blessing for all the world," not merely the return of Jews to Palestine. He advocated "a country where the brotherhood of man is emphasized," with a temple "where all races and religions might worship in peace." *Times* Moscow Bureau Chief Walter Duranty cited Odessa as the exemplar of Jewish opportunity. Jews who had been viewed as "parasites" under the Czar now enjoyed favorable business and employment prospects in "an autonomous Jewish country" where conditions were "far more suitable to Russian Jewry than ... even Palestine itself." Duranty, who had recently won a Pulitzer Prize for his reporting from the Soviet Union, would soon become known as "Stalin's Apologist" (for what the *Times* eventually acknowledged was "some of the worst reporting" to appear in the newspaper).[38]

Discomfort with Zionism aside, the *Times* remained fascinated by archeological explorations in Palestine. "Bible Stories Born Out By Archeology" declared the headline of a four-column report by British journalist P.W. Wilson. His discovery of archeological "corroborations of Biblical history" led him to conclude that Noah's flood, the crossing of the Red Sea during the exodus from Egypt, Joshua's invasion, Samson's exploits and King David's capture of Jerusalem, the "great sequence of events" recounted in the Hebrew Bible, "is not fiction. It happened." During March and April 1935 the *Times* ran nine stories in three weeks reporting the discovery of Hebrew inscriptions on fragments of broken pottery at the site of ancient Lachish. There Jewish fighters were besieged by Babylonian King Nebuchadnezzar in the war that culminated in the destruction of the First Temple in Jerusalem. Dating from the time of the prophet Jeremiah, the inscriptions were described by a Hebrew University Semitic language expert as "the most valuable find ever made" from the First Temple period. As another scholar noted, "these writings are among the oldest texts that we have of the Hebrew language and their connection with the Bible is of utmost significance."[39]

Archeological discoveries might have provided a compelling link between ancient Jewish history in the Land of Israel and Zionist renewal in Palestine.

But there was a conspicuous disconnect in the *Times* between Jewish antiq-
uity and modern Zionist efforts to restore Jewish national sovereignty. Editorial
policy, echoing Adolph Ochs, had long since determined that Judaism was a
religion only, devoid of national content. Under no circumstances would Jewish
nationalism be permitted to confront American Jews with the dreaded prospect
of competing national loyalties.

Although Levy continued to file occasional reports from Jerusalem, by
1934 Cairo had become his primary base. His political analysis remained
sharply critical of Zionist leaders, who had "inflated" the Balfour Declaration
to imply that "Great Britain had promised the Jews a return to Zion and their
ancient glory." The "ambiguity" of the Declaration had transformed Palestine
into "a seething centre of strife and hatred." Zionist leaders bore responsibility
for "arousing false hopes in the hearts of the Jewish masses by exaggerating the
promise contained in the ambiguous declaration." To be sure, Jews "built; they
planted; they established factories and industries; ... they drained thousands of
acres of swamp lands. They bought up land from the Arabs and paid dearly for
every inch of it." This, Levy acknowledged, was accomplished "with the spirit
and enthusiasm of a people rebuilding and restoring its own home. ... Why,
then, worry about the Arabs? And they didn't."[40]

Following the eruption of a far more violent and prolonged Arab revolt
in the spring of 1936, initiated by the Arab High Command (led by the Grand
Mufti) and enduring for three years, Levy returned periodically to Palestine.
His initial reporting described rather harmless disruption led by "militant Arab
youths" who relied on young children to throw stones, impose store closures,
and pour kerosene on purchases from Jewish-owned shops. But after three
weeks of "chaos, panic, arson and terrorism," the seriousness of the situation
was evident. "Never were the possibilities of an Arab-Jewish understanding in
Palestine," Levy concluded, "more remote than at present." Any Arab leader who
pursued accommodation with the Zionists would be labeled a traitor because
the Grand Mufti would not permit it. "Clever, intelligent and ambitious," the
Mufti, whose most devoted followers were "fanatic Moslems," realized that "his
career depends upon his popularity as an Arab hero and defender of Islam."[41]

Levy was convinced that "Mohammedanism," whose "motto" was "religion
by the sword," propelled the violence. "Once the Arab's religious fanaticism is
aroused he becomes wild and almost uncontrollable" unless confronted with
"strong force" and "iron-handed methods." Levy focused on young "hotheads"
who aroused "the Arab masses with the spirit of opposition." He described
these "ambitious young Arab patriots," who spread "sensational propaganda

and arouse Moslem fanaticism," as "militant and most sincere." To be sure, they committed "minor acts of terrorism" against Jews to "nourish the movement," but they also threatened the lives and property of wealthy Arabs who failed to provide financial support for their militancy.[42]

Levy believed that feuding between the powerful rival Husseini and Nashashibi families in Jerusalem had sparked the uprising, with Jews merely serving as "convenient scapegoats." After losing the Jerusalem mayoralty to his political nemesis in the Husseini family, Ragheb Bey Nashashibi had turned "extremist." He dispatched "hot-headed youths" (Levy's favorite descriptive label) to incite Arab masses against British authorities and Jewish residents. These agitators, Levy belatedly acknowledged, were not merely "brigands" and "bandits" but "young terrorists," prepared "to go to any length of agitation, incitement or terrorism" to secure their demands for the termination of Jewish immigration and land purchases. After six weeks of "rioting, murder and acts of brigandage by Arabs in Palestine," Levy concluded, "irresponsible terrorists" bore responsibility for the intensification of violence.[43]

"A reign of terror is prevailing throughout Palestine," Levy wrote two months later. The "bloodiest" and most "barbarous" attacks, he noted, targeted Jews. But Arab leaders and police, no less than "Britons and Jews," were also assaulted by "Arab youths," "rebellious hotheads" who comprised "the most militant of the extremist Nationalists." Although Palestinian Jews had demonstrated "almost super-human self-restraint" by not retaliating, Zionists were hardly blameless for the eruption of violence. The "faith and trust" of their leaders in Great Britain, coupled with "their extreme nationalism and idealism," had "blinded" them to the wishes of the Arab majority. They had made "no real effort" to cooperate with Arabs; indeed, "they ignore them." Levy held Zionist leaders, with their "blunders and mistakes," "equally responsible" for the turmoil in Palestine.[44]

The *Times* editorial response to the violent Arab upheaval in Palestine reached a different conclusion: five months of British "patient adherence to a policy of conciliation" had failed. Noting that nearly eighty Jews had already been "defenselessly murdered by the terrorists," it called on Britain to demonstrate "its determination to maintain its obligations under the Balfour Declaration." Violence, it asserted, must be combatted by "overwhelming military force."[45]

The imminent arrival of a British Royal Commission, chaired by Lord Peel, left Levy pessimistic. The Palestine problem, he concluded, was one that "no commission could ever solve to the satisfaction both of Arabs and Jews." Levy blamed them both for the difficulties it would encounter. Jews, he wrote, "deemed it their right to obtain more assistance from the mandatory than had actually been given," while ignoring the protection afforded by the Balfour Declaration to the rights of non-Jewish communities. To be sure, the Grand Mufti and his followers displayed "intransigence" in demanding the abandonment of a Jewish national home, a halt to Jewish immigration, and the prohibition on land sales to Jews. But even "more moderate Arabs" also opposed "radical and uncompromising [Zionist] demands." They, too, believed that once Jews comprised a majority they would destroy Moslem mosques on the Temple Mount and rebuild Solomon's Temple on its ancient site.[46]

The Peel Commission report, Levy concluded, served "to strengthen the argument that the Palestine question has no solution." Jews were "bitterly disappointed" with its partition proposal, which they perceived as designed to "appease the Arabs" rather than ease the plight of their "suffering brethren" in Europe. The loss of Jerusalem, "decapitating" their prospective state, meant "Zionism without Zion." Testifying before the Commission David Ben-Gurion, chairman of the Palestine Zionist Executive, had declared: "We are coming to our own country by our own right of historic connection with the land." The Bible, he asserted, "is our mandate."[47] The *Times* quoted Ben-Gurion's statement in an unsigned wireless report. Levy ignored it.

A *Times* editorial vigorously endorsed the Peel Commission partition proposal for Palestine. Rejected by "Zionist and Arab extremists," "moderates" (including *Times* editors) favored "a compromise which would maintain, at least for the time being, the minority status of the Jew in Palestine and keep alive the conception of a united Holy Land of three great religions." It was "most important" to set "a maximum of Jewish immigration" to Palestine for the next decade. Unrestricted immigration would be "calamitous" – for Jews. Intensifying conflict in Palestine, it would also "block the entry of Jews into other Arab lands" and "make matters worse for Jewish minorities" in European nations. With restrictions, however, "Zionist and Arab would have a better opportunity to reconcile their views."[48] The *Times* ignored the fate of Jews in Nazi Germany confronting restrictive immigration quotas for Palestine.

Ten days later Judah Magnes vigorously supported the *Times* endorsement of the Peel partition plan, which he praised as "a great State paper." Although "two fierce nationalisms," in conjunction with British "mandatory imperialism," were unable to reconcile, Magnes focused on Jewish failings. Jewish rights, he asserted, "are a thousand times less important than the consent ... of the Arabs who live in the land." Citing the "long and high ethical tradition" of the Jewish people, he asserted that "our duty in Palestine is to make peace." Disregarding its Jewish majority, Magnes proposed that Jerusalem, "the center of religions of the world," be internationalized.

In April 1937, after nearly a decade of reporting from Jerusalem, Levy's byline newly identified him as the *Times* "Near-East correspondent." In a nostalgic farewell to the city of his youth Levy wrote an elegiac description of "Sabbath in Jerusalem." Framed by the "purple hills of Moab" and the "blue mist" of the Dead Sea in the distance, the city blended the "dark, medieval, cobbled lanes" of the Old City, Orthodox Jews and Moslems who strolled along Jaffa Road, and the tranquility of the elegant Jewish neighborhood of Rehavia and its adjacent Arab Christian enclave of Talbieh. Everywhere, he observed, life was serenely "routine."[49]

The Arab Revolt periodically returned Levy to Jerusalem. As had been true since 1929, when he first encountered the Grand Mufti, the centerpiece of his narrative was Arab frustrations and demands. He had little to say about Zionist leaders (who reluctantly accepted the Peel partition proposal), other than to note that "hot-headed" (Revisionist) "extremists" were demanding "all [of] Palestine."[50] From his "many conversations" with young Arab "extremists," Levy transmitted their desire for Arab-Jewish cooperation. Agreement could be reached "easily," they assured him, if only Zionist leaders embraced the views of Magnes, whose "sincerity" they "respected." But (unnamed) "veteran observers," he wrote, "all agree that the Revisionist Zionists have caused more harm to their co-religionists ... than have any Arab terrorists." It would be "far better" for Zionists, his Arab contacts suggested, to relinquish the "nationalistic and political aims of a Jewish state and have many more Jews spread throughout the Arab countries of the Near and Middle East." That outcome "would solve the Jewish problem much more effectively than a Jewish State within Palestine."[51]

In mid-September Levy described Palestine in "a state of anarchy," with terrorism rampant. Arab rebels "were roaming about freely, fully armed," and "boldly murdering innocent persons, both Jews and Arabs," while British authorities were "helpless." He reported a "series of killings," including of British officials, and "daring terrorist activities." Primary blame fell on Jewish Revisionists, some of whom were "apparently making terror its aim." Once they "let loose with acts of retaliation against innocent Arabs," even "moderate enlightened Arabs" held all Jews responsible.[52] Regarding the rising number of Jewish victims of Arab attacks, or the deepening alliance between the Mufti and Nazi officials, Levy had virtually no comment.

The Arab uprising returned Levy to a volatile Jerusalem during the summer of 1938. With Arabs "uncompromising in their demands" and "terrorist gangs" displaying "ever-increasing zeal," he nonetheless apportioned blame equally among "Arab terrorists, hotheaded Jewish Revisionists ... and agents provocateurs" employed by foreign governments to "annoy" Great Britain and "harass" Jews. "Veteran observers" in Palestine, he wrote, "all agree that the Revisionist Zionists have caused more harm to their co-religionists ... than have any Arab terrorists."[53]

Early in 1939 Levy prominently reported a statement by King Ibn Saud, who broke his silence on the Palestine conflict in an interview with H. St. John Philby. The Saudi King then sent a letter to President Roosevelt warning that "the ambition of the Zionists renders Arabs of all countries apprehensive." Levy gave prominence to Arab demands for annulment of the Balfour Declaration and termination of Jewish immigration. Jews, he wrote, were undeterred by the draconian new British immigration restrictions promulgated in the White Paper; they "will now proceed with their usual activities of building, industry and agriculture." But Levy could not resist reiterating his familiar warning that "some hot-headed revisionist youths may commit some acts of violence." He concluded that "the Holy Land cannot hope for peace and tranquility for a long time to come."[54]

In May Levy wrote his final articles from Palestine. They summarized the lessons he had learned a decade earlier when Philby, Magnes, and the Grand Mufti had swept him into their vortex of hostility to Zionism. The primary cause of the conflict, Levy asserted yet again, was "Revisionist provocation." Some young Jews, increasingly dissatisfied with the "passive resistance" urged by Zionist leaders, had come to believe that "violence is the only method" that would be noticed by British authorities and achieve Zionist goals. Levy was told: "We are ready to be killed rather than be ruled by Arabs." He allotted ample space (for the first time) to David Ben-Gurion, who denounced England for its White Paper restriction on Jewish immigration. Jews, the Zionist leader asserted, will not stop coming to their homeland "because some law terms it illegal." Nor would they tolerate "a Hitler regime in a country that was internationally pledged to them as a national home." Filling two columns, Ben-Gurion's statement marked the only comprehensive expression of mainstream Zionism to appear under Levy's by-line in a decade of reporting.[55]

An intelligent, ambitious young journalist, eager to comprehend the past, present and future of Palestine, Levy had become the conduit to the *Times* for the Mufti's Muslim nationalism and Magnes's dream of bi-nationalism, converging in their shared hostility to Zionism. An increasingly explosive conflict between Arabs and Jews had pulled him into its vortex, undermining his objectivity and turning him against Zionist national aspirations. Even after his arrival in Cairo in 1940, complaints about his lack of objectivity prompted Sulzberger to instruct Managing Editor Edwin James to cable Levy: "Reports again received your confusing political with reportorial work."[56]

Levy's political aversion to Zionism complemented the Reform anti-Zionism embraced by the *Times* ever since Adolph Ochs purchased the newspaper. His legacy was his bias, embedded in the pages of the *Times* long after his departure from Jerusalem – even as the rising menace of Nazism heightened the desperate plight of European Jews and the urgency of a Jewish national home.

CHAPTER 3

Denial and Discomfort: 1939–1948

Between 1933, when Adolph Hitler became Chancellor of Germany, and 1945, when the horrors of the Holocaust could no longer be evaded, *The New York Times* confronted its most serious challenge of journalistic responsibility. Adolph Ochs, torn between sentimental attachment to Germany through family ancestry and fervent loyalty to the United States, initially believed that Hitler's rise to power was not cause for alarm. Following elections in 1930 that elevated National Socialists to the second largest party in the Reichstag, a *Times* editorial declared: "The menace of Adolph Hitler has been grossly exaggerated." Three weeks later the *Times* confidently predicted: "Germany has no idea of delivering itself over to a madcap Austrian."[1]

After Hitler became Chancellor in 1933 an editorial complimented him for urging his followers to "refrain from acts of individual terrorism." Interviewing the Nazi leader, foreign news correspondent Anne O'Hare McCormick was charmed by his "curiously childlike and candid eyes" and "indubitably sincere" manner. Visiting Dachau, *Times* European correspondent G.E.R. Gedye provided its first coverage of a concentration camp, where "those who have incurred the displeasure of the present rulers of Germany" were imprisoned. Describing Dachau as a "huge Nazi internment camp," he was nonetheless impressed by the commandant, "a quiet-mannered, blond, blue-eyed young former officer," who facilitated the reporter's "thorough inspection." Gedye was assured that prisoners were "grateful for regular work and food." Indeed, he concluded, many of them "looked as if the community would not suffer from their seclusion."[2]

Adolph Ochs observed developments in Nazi Germany with deepening despair. Anguished by the persecution of Jews, he remained determined that the *Times* must not be identified as a Jewish newspaper. After his death in 1935, his son-in-law Arthur Hays Sulzberger succeeded him as publisher. Sulzberger had grown up in privileged German Jewish circles in Manhattan. His father was president of a prosperous cotton goods company; his mother was the grand-daughter of a founder of the New York Stock Exchange. While a Columbia student he met Iphigene Ochs. After their wedding in 1917 Sulzberger assured his father-in-law: "I am truly grateful that I was born a Jew. I have a Jewish feeling – a Jewish religion."[3] They shared the conviction that Judaism was a religious faith without ethnic or national content.

Eager for the *Times* to remain within his own family, but initially dubious about Sulzberger's qualifications as a journalist, Ochs appointed his son-in-law to an inconsequential position as tabulator for the annual Hundred Neediest Cases Fund. During the post-war decade Sulzberger slowly ascended the *Times* hierarchy to become a vice president. Sharing Ochs's strong aversion to any perception of the *Times* as a "Jewish" newspaper, he insisted that journalistic integrity depended on reporters "who have no common denominator other than their Americanism."[4]

Sulzberger described Jews as "a people of perfect loyalty to the countries of their birth." Like other wealthy and privileged American Jews of German ancestry, he feared that Zionism would "exacerbate doubts about every Jew's ultimate loyalty." He was a non-Zionist, he explained, "because the Jew, in seek-ing a homeland of his own, seems to me to be giving up something of infinitely greater value to the world." As he stated: "If I, as a Jew, can help to impress the world that what Jews want far more than a home of their own is the right to call any place home, then I believe I shall have been faithful to the tradition of justice which is my heritage as an American of Jewish faith."[5]

Sulzberger's loyalty anxiety framed his pervasive uneasiness about "show-casing" Jews in the *Times*. Editors were instructed not to refer to "the Jewish people" but to "people of the Jewish faith." Reporters whose first name was Abraham received by-lines with their initials only. When Washington Bureau Chief Arthur Krock was bypassed for appointment as editorial page editor Sulzberger explained that "he would be criticized if he appointed a Jew as Editor, since the ownership was in the hands of Jews." (Krock was Episcopalian by conversion.) As head of the *Times* Washington Bureau, Krock developed a reputation for not wanting Jewish reporters assigned to him.[6]

Following his first trip to Palestine in 1937 Sulzberger made clear his discomfort with singling out Jews, whether as victims of persecution or advo-cates for their own homeland. "If the Jew was to have this land as his own then in any and in every land save this he was a foreigner," he wrote shortly after his return. "If there was to be any emotional conflict between America as my land and this as my land I must choose America, even if that were to mean that I can no longer be a Jew." Offended by the suggestion that a Jewish state in Palestine could deepen the roots of American Jews, he responded that his ancestors had arrived in America in the seventeenth century "and my roots in America are deep enough."[7]

Hitler identified Jews as a despised race, but Sulzberger insisted that they must not be identified in the *Times* as a distinctive group. "I must act as an American and not as a Jew," he asserted. "The Jews are not a people.... Certainly there is no such common denominator between the poor unfortunate Jew [in Poland] ... or myself." Defending restrictive American immigration quotas (which went unfilled for German Jews), the *Times* declined to identify the refugee issue as a Jewish problem; rather, it was "the problem of mankind."[8]

The *Times* was erratic, at best, in its coverage of the plight of desperate Jewish refugees. Sailing from Germany to Cuba in May 1939, 900 Jews aboard the *S.S. St. Louis* were denied entry in Havana and turned away from the United States by the American government. Although *Times* editorials referred to "the saddest ship afloat," they declined to identify the refugees as Jews: "It is decency and justice that are being persecuted – not a race, a nationality or a faith."[9]

An editorial the following year (entitled "Human Flotsam") anticipated the dire fate of 500 Jewish refugees, desperate to reach Palestine, who had been stranded for four months on a Danube River steamer. But the Jewish passengers were identified only as "helpless and terrified human beings ... human flotsam on the authoritarian sea of death." The 1942 sinking of the *Struma*, with 768 Jews on board who had been denied entry in Turkey while awaiting permits to enter Palestine, was briefly reported on an inside page as the sinking of a "Black Sea ship." Only three weeks later did an editorial identify it as a "Jewish refugee ship."[10]

When the Vichy government in France urged the Roosevelt Administration to facilitate the immigration of "thousands of refugees," especially Jews, the *Times* opposed the rescue proposal and supported American restrictions. It endorsed State Department policy that Jews should not receive favored treatment as immigrants. Editorials and front-page stories urged Congress to permit British children to find refuge in the United States, but the *Times* ignored the plight of Jewish children. British White Paper restrictions on Jewish immigration to Palestine were praised as necessary "to save the homeland itself from overpopulation." Sulzberger stated his position on his newspaper's coverage of Jewish refugees: "Not that many [Jews] do not need a place of refuge, but so do countless others who are not Jews."[11]

Given its evasion of the accelerating lethal danger confronting European Jews during the 1930s, muted *Times* coverage of their subsequent slaughter was hardly surprising. Lest it be accused of being a "Jewish" newspaper, Sulzberger adamantly opposed identification of Jews as the primary victims of Nazi extermination. Editorials referred to "Europe's Dispossessed," "The Uprooted People," and "War of Extermination" – without mentioning Jews. When mentioned they were invariably submerged among other "persecuted minorities."[12]

The *Times* adopted various strategies to evade the annihilation of European Jewry. Jews were identified as "persons" who were confined to ghettos and deported to extermination camps. A headline noted, without mentioning Jews: "Death Rate Soars in Polish Ghettos." The fate of Jews was described as "similar to that of other oppressed peoples under the Nazi yoke." The first published account in the *Times* of the Nazi plan to exterminate Jews, identifying it as "probably the greatest mass slaughter in history," appeared on an inside page at the bottom of a column of unrelated stories. Only rarely were Jews mentioned on the front page or identified as the primary victims. As Laurel Leff concluded in her aptly titled *Buried by The Times*, "the murder of millions of Jews was a relatively unimportant story." Indeed, Sulzberger's newspaper made "a deliberate effort" to suppress news of the Holocaust. It "never acknowledged that the mass murder of Jews, *because they were Jews*, was something its readers needed to know."[13]

In the summer of 1942 the *Times* cited a report by Szmul Zygielbojm, a member of the Polish National Council in London, documenting the "slaughter" of 700,000 Jews: "Children in orphanages, old persons in almshouses, the sick in hospitals and women were slain in the streets." Since early winter, the *Times* noted (on page 5), Germans had been "methodically proceeding with their campaign to exterminate all Jews." The front page that day featured articles about tennis shoes and canned fruit. The *Times* report of a Madison Square Garden protest rally received front-page coverage focused on "Hitler atrocities" but Jews were barely mentioned. Several months later Sulzberger publicly criticized Zionist efforts to create a Jewish army, which "serves no useful purpose," and encouraged Muslim enmity.[14]

The following spring the *Times* described the Warsaw Ghetto uprising in brief inside page stories. The first account, nearly three weeks after Jews had launched their struggle "against annihilation by the Nazis," occupied four paragraphs. One week later, via an American rabbi in London, it relayed a report of "the final massacre" when "all Jews in Warsaw's ghetto have been 'liquidated.'" In its solitary editorial about the revolt, the *Times* referred to 500,000 "persons" who had been confined to the ghetto and 400,000 "persons" who were deported to Treblinka. There was no indication that those "persons" were Jews.[15]

The prolonged evasive silence of the *Times,* an appalling dereliction of journalistic responsibility, did not begin to abate until 1944, when the newly established War Refugee Board focused attention on Jewish extermination. Only then, with the imprimatur of the American government providing patriotic protection, did the newspaper begin to run front-page stories on the plight of the people chosen for annihilation. An editorial even urged abrogation of the impending termination of Jewish immigration to Palestine under the British White Paper – not, however, because of the desperate predicament of Jews but to protect "our vital concern in peace and order in this strategic region."[16]

In justification, Sulzberger explained to a friend: "In our editorial we chose to think of Jews as human beings instead of any particular religious group, and apparently Zionists don't like that." Several weeks later he offered a "very simple" statement of his position: "It is my belief that Judaism is a faith and that, therefore, Jews as such should not be involved in political issues such as Zionism." Recognizing that "Something must be done for the poor fellows who are Jews," he suggested that we "work for that as Americans and humanitarians and not as Jews." Insisting that "Persons of Jewish faith should be permitted anywhere they elect to dwell," he concluded: "That ... is infinitely more vital than that a 'homeland' should be secured for them."[17]

Near the end of the war a *Times* editorial urged the American government to do "everything it can to rescue innocent and persecuted people in Europe," pointedly adding: "It is not any man's religion or any man's race that matters." Reliable reports from Europe that two million Jews had been murdered in an "extermination campaign" were printed on an inside page. The horrors of Auschwitz never made the front page. The liberation of Dachau did, without any indication that most victims were Jews.[18]

In retrospect, half a century later, Max Frankel (a German-born Jewish refugee who joined the *Times* in 1952 and rose to become editorial page editor and executive editor) described its "staggering, stunning failure" to depict the Holocaust as "a horror beyond all other horrors." Only six times between 1939 and 1945, he noted, were Jews mentioned on the front page as "Hitler's unique target for total annihilation." Only once "was their fate the subject of a lead editorial." The plight of Jews never qualified for the daily *Times* ranking of important events.[19]

Sulzberger was sufficiently agitated by Zionist advocacy to become actively involved with the American Council for Judaism, an anti-Zionist breakaway group of Reform rabbis organized in 1942 to oppose the prospect of Jewish statehood. "My job," he wrote to its founding leader Rabbi Morris Lazaron, "is to show all and sundry that I do not subscribe to the thesis that 'all Jews are brothers.'" The *Times* printed the Council's Statement of Principles, filling three columns, proclaiming: "We oppose the effort to establish a national Jewish state in Palestine or anywhere else as a philosophy of defeatism. ... Jewish nationalism tends to confuse our fellow men about our place and function in society and diverts our own attention from our historic role to live as a religious community wherever we may dwell."[20]

Sulzberger enthusiastically embraced Judah Magnes's alternative to Zionism: the "union of Jews and Arabs within a binational Palestine." The *Times* published a lengthy letter from Magnes and an interview with him; Sulzberger offered to pay Magnes for a visit to the United States to publicize his ideas. Between 1930 and 1948 he was more prominently featured in the *Times* than all Zionist leaders combined. Within a week of its coverage of Magnes's binational solution the Times published a five-column summary of Sulzberger's speech at Rabbi Lazaron's Baltimore temple. Criticizing "Zionist extremists" who advocated a Jewish army in Palestine, the *Times* publisher linked Zionism to "the Nazi connotation that we are a racial group apart." Sulzberger urged that the Holy Land not become "merely another nation, jealous of its own national rights, heedless of those who for the past two thousand years have lived within its borders." He was convinced that "the Jew and Arab can live side by side in peace and work out a common destiny in a commonwealth," thereby obliterating any need for Jewish statehood.[21]

Responding to sharp criticism in the Jewish press, Sulzberger acknowledged: "It is perfectly true that ... we chose to think of Jews as human beings instead of any particular religious group, but apparently Zionists don't like that." Subsequently amplifying his explanation, he wrote that Jews had "missed their great opportunity of merging their cause with other assailed people. ... Judaism can, with entire propriety, link itself with the democratic faith, and ... can be saved through democracy." The destruction of American democracy, Sulzberger asserted, "is much more serious than the destruction ... of all Jews" because "America is a greater faith."[22]

In 1943 Cyrus Sulzberger, the publisher's nephew and a *Times* foreign correspondent, wrote a cluster of articles about "the turbulent question of Palestine." He was convinced that Zionists posed an "embarrassing" problem for the Allied war effort. Their activities stirred Axis allegations that Roosevelt was "a Jew working for the Jews" and "Americans are going to take over the Middle

East and give it to the Jews." Although "most Arabs have little feeling against Jews" and their "reputable leaders have none," Sulzberger concluded (two years after the Grand Mufti had taken refuge in Nazi Germany and received Hitler's blessing), they disliked Zionism as "a foreign land-grabbing device."[23]

Until 1944, and then only sparingly, the *Times* virtually ignored the Holocaust. A report of the murder of 180,000 Dutch Jews was placed beneath the story of a sleeping American soldier who was awakened by the British King and Queen. The slaughter of Polish Jews was buried in a Page 4 article about the budget of an international refugee committee (while gangster Louis Lepke's efforts to stave off his execution received front-page coverage). Right-wing Zionists received a vastly disproportionate – and hostile – share of minimal *Times* attention. In the closing months of 1944, following the assassination of British Secretary of State for Colonial Affairs Lord Moyne in Cairo by two members of the Stern Gang (Lehi), the *Times* focused on Jewish terrorism. In the Irgun, the military wing of Revisionist Zionism (which had nothing to do with the Moyne murder), "boys and girls are trained in accordance with methods reminiscent of those used in totalitarian states." Bracketing Jews with Nazis, it cited the "astounding paradox" that "the most mercilessly tortured of all European minorities comes to imitate ... some of the practices invented by its persecutors."[24]

With the war in Europe nearing an end, the *Times* paid closer, and increasingly critical, attention to Zionism. Pulitzer Prize winning foreign news correspondent Anne O'Hare McCormick wrote a cluster of articles revealing her fascination with Palestine and displeasure with Jewish nationalism. Charmed by Tel Aviv, a city "so completely Jewish" that it did not reflect British-ruled Palestine or its Arab majority, she was delighted to discover a "cosmopolitan and international" oasis. But Zionists were "intensely self-absorbed," displaying "surprisingly little comprehension of or sympathy for the feelings of their neighbors."

McCormick acknowledged that Zionist "colonizers" had achieved "spectacular results." Given "the campaign of extermination waged on a helpless people," and "the shame of the civilized world" that did nothing to prevent "this inexplicable crime against humanity" (Jews were not explicitly identified), "the pressure for the Zionist case becomes almost irresistible." But the "forgotten partners" in the conflict were Jews "who are passionately devoted citizens of other countries." Among "all places on earth," she concluded hopefully, Palestine "seems destined by history, geography and spiritual predilection to be inter-religious, interracial and international."[25]

Two weeks later the *Times* printed another lengthy letter from Magnes, echoing McCormick and reiterating his advocacy of a bi-national Palestine. "Any answer to the Palestine question," he wrote, "must have inter-religious and international character." He urged a solution that would be "reasonable to the ordinary Jew and Arab and to Christians everywhere." With Switzerland as his multinational model, Magnes recommended limiting Jewish immigration "to parity." Comprising no more than half the population, Jews would not "upset the political balance in Palestine."[26]

Sulzberger reiterated: "I do not believe Jews are a race. I do not believe that they are a people." There was, he insisted, "no more reason to reconstitute the Jews as a nation than the Angles, the Celts or the Saxons." He expressed his "very firm conviction that Judaism should be restricted to the religious ethical life, and that politics, or racialism, or nationalism have no part in it." Rejecting their "clamor for statehood," he accused Zionists of "coercive" economic pressure and "character assassination." A visit to Dachau did not moderate his hostility. To be sure, he conceded, Jewish refugees had "suffered beyond all others." But with Jews comprising "a minor percentage" of all displaced persons (because so many of them had been murdered in Nazi extermination camps) he blamed Zionists for focusing exclusively on their plight. Sulzberger believed that "thousands now dead might be alive, and in Palestine as well," had Zionists not put "statehood first."[27]

Six months after the war in Europe ended, a *Times* editorial finally recognized "Hitler's war of extermination against the Jews" as "one of the ghastliest crimes of all history." Noting "the sufferings and present predicament of these innocent people," it awaited the recommendations of the Anglo-American Committee for assisting homeless survivors. But, the editorial cautioned, "there is no indication that the solution will be found in mass immigration to Palestine."[28]

During the early months of 1946 *Times* coverage came from several correspondents who sojourned briefly in Palestine. Clifton Daniel, covering hearings conducted by the Anglo-American Committee, quoted David Ben-Gurion's firm assertion: "This is and will remain our country; we are here as of right." But for Daniel the undisputed star of the hearings was Judah Magnes. No other witness, Arab or Jew, generated enthusiasm until he urged that Palestine become a bi-national state with eventual numerical equality between Jews and Arabs. With "quiet rhetoric and conviction," Daniel wrote admiringly, his "compromise" proposal, which effectively doomed Jewish statehood, "visibly stirred" Committee members.[29]

Reporting from Palestine three months later, Julian Louis Meltzer described a "taut" political atmosphere, riddled by "explosions of ill-tempered violence." But he discovered abundant evidence of "the unchanging Arab-Jewish friendship," with Arabs and Jews "rubbing shoulders" in cafés, movie theatres, and restaurants. "The rank and file of both peoples," he concluded, "really like each other" and were "bound together by … ties of economic propinquity and good neighborliness." Days later, Daniel described massive British raids in "a country-wide campaign to root out the leadership of the Haganah, the Jewish community's underground army," after it exploded ten bridges linking Palestine to neighboring countries. Sweeping British military retribution, launched on what Zionists identified as the "Black Sabbath," placed the entire Jewish population under "virtual siege." Jewish Agency officials were arrested and dispatched to detention camps.[30]

In the most spectacular attack (and worst tragedy) of the Mandatory period, Irgun fighters, with tacit Haganah approval, retaliated by dynamiting the King David Hotel in Jerusalem, where British government offices were located. Nearly one hundred British staff members, along with Arab and Jewish workers, were killed. Labeling them as "fanatics" who "do not balk at jeopardizing the rescue of the victims of Hitlerism in whose name they have launched this second terror," Anne O'Hare McCormick identified the Irgun as "the greatest enemy of Zion." It had transformed the Holy Land into "a place of hate and terror." She called for a world where "all Jews and all other minorities are safe from persecution." A *Times* editorial deplored "indefensible" acts of terrorism while favoring the "immediate admission" to Palestine of 100,000 "harassed refugees," without identifying them as Jews.[31]

In a follow-up article five days after the bombing Meltzer reported a split in the Yishuv. "Execration of this kind of indiscriminate violent action" by "sober, responsible Jewish public opinion" was challenged by "younger elements." Resenting the "authoritarian administration" of Mandatory rule, a majority of Jewish teenagers and young adults held British policy responsible for the King David tragedy. Lacking "political education," these young Zionists declined to blame the "fiendish efficiency" of the Irgun, led by "thin, hawk-faced" Menachem Begin, the "skilled technician" who was responsible for "daring coups." Meltzer noted that Irgun fighters "live outwardly respectable" lives, but many were "swarthy Yemenite Jews or Oriental Jewish types." Only the Haganah, he concluded, had the support of "responsible" Jews.[32]

The *Times* focus on Jewish "terrorists" in Palestine, in conjunction with its repeated reiteration of Magnes's bi-national alternative to Zionism, revealed its acute discomfort with the prospect of Jewish statehood. By then, however, Sulzberger had become increasingly isolated in the American Jewish community. Early in 1946 he attempted to organize a fund-raising dinner to support Magnes's anti-Zionist activities. When only three invited guests accepted the publisher's invitation the event was cancelled. But Sulzberger remained resolute. Addressing a Chattanooga congregation he blamed Zionists for the plight of Jewish refugees, "helpless hostages for whom state-hood has been made the only acceptable ransom." Zionist political aims, he asserted, had "obscured the human problem." Proclaiming his dislike for "the coercive methods of Zionists," he criticized them for focusing "the attention of the world upon the question of the Jewish refugee instead of using their great moral strength to plead the cause of all displaced persons."[33]

By 1947 the *Times* had begun to notice David Ben-Gurion. His demands for Zionist unity and an end to "terrorism" were favorably reported. But Jewish "terrorism" remained the core of the *Times* narrative. Palestine's "regime of terror" was governed by "primitive ancient rules," wrote S.J. Gordon, which honored "an eye for an eye." According to Julian Meltzer, a veteran reporter from Palestine since 1921 for the *Palestine Post* and various British newspapers, the Jewish "terrorist underground intended to stop at nothing in its indiscrimi-nate warfare against anything British." But "like a voice crying in the wilderness, but a voice which is gradually growing in volume and gaining a hearing," Judah Magnes remained "a fervent opponent of any kind of chauvinism" (namely Jewish statehood). Meltzer admired Magnes for "his humanness and his way of shunning the limelight" (except, to be sure, in the *Times*) – and for his convic-tion that "Palestine as a land of three monotheistic religions is no place for an exclusively nationalist state."[34]

The return of Jews to their ancient homeland was not a narrative that the *Times* wished to emphasize. Its primary focus in the "Palestine Powderkeg" remained the militant Zionist groups. Irgun leader Menachem Begin was described as "an ingenious terrorist tactician." Nathan Friedman Yellin, leader of the Stern group following Avraham Stern's assassination by the British, was "less ambitious than Begin, but perhaps more dangerous because he teaches his men to be killers."[35]

The *Times* reported the "spectacular defiance" of British martial law by "Jewish terrorists" who targeted British army and police headquarters. In a stunning attack that "blasted open the ancient and formidable walls" of Acre prison, "Zionist terrorists" freed 251 prisoners, including "some of the eighty convicted terrorists" who were confined there. "One of the biggest jail breaks in history," Clifton Daniel reported, it was the "pay-off" for the recent British hanging of four convicted (Jewish) "terrorists." With discernible respect, Daniel noted that the assault, planned and executed "with the usual dash and precision of the terrorists ... broke down the walls that Napoleon had not been able to reduce."[36]

Daniel's counterpoint to Zionist terrorism was the "shadow government" represented by the Executive Committee of the Jewish Agency. "If it were in fact a government," he acknowledged, it would "unquestionably be the most talented, most capable, most progressive and most democratic in the entire Middle East." Led by Ben-Gurion, it already possessed "all the essential aspects of a sovereign government except the most essential of all – sovereignty."[37] But its state-building efforts received little attention in the newspaper whose publisher's fervent wish was that no Jewish state would ever arise.

Daniel's reports were the fairest, indeed most laudatory, to appear in the *Times*. Covering travels through Palestine by members of the United Nations Special Committee on Palestine (UNSCOP) in the early summer of 1947, he noted that "every hillock provided contrast between the Arab and Jewish ways of life." Committee members confronted "a vivid contrast between the traditional and almost unchanging life of the nomadic desert Arab and the pioneering enterprise of the Jewish colonists." Zionists showed them "pink gladioluses and giant onions growing in the wasteland south of Beersheba that Abraham knew." In kibbutz Revivim, the furthest southern settlement, they observed "date palms and fruit trees" adjacent to "the tattered tents of Bedouin tribesmen."[38]

But anti-Zionist criticism was unrelenting. The *Times* provided a two-column summary of a pamphlet signed by Lessing J. Rosenwald, president of the American Council for Judaism, claiming that the Balfour Declaration had effectively sustained the "anti-Semitic racialist lie that Jews the world over were a separate, national body." Urging Jews to seek "maximum integration" in the countries they inhabited, Rosenwald advised the United Nations to prevent the establishment of a Jewish state. Any claim to "Palestinian" citizenship by Jewish citizens of other nations would raise the question "whether citizens in this position could give complete allegiance to their country." The pamphlet denounced references to the "historic connection" of Jews to Palestine, which ignored "the equivalent connection with Palestine of Christians and Moslems."[39]

Among the most dramatic events in postwar Palestine was the story of the battered ship *Exodus*. Arriving in Haifa harbor under British military escort on July 19, 1947, it carried more than 4,500 Jewish refugees who had boarded in southern France nine days earlier. Attacked at sea by British destroyers, the *Times* reported that a "naval boarding party" had engaged in a "bloody and vicious" battle with defiant passengers (three of whom were killed) before seizing control. The *Exodus*, Gene Currivan wrote in his front-page account, was a "sorry sight" when it arrived in Haifa with "the largest contingent of unauthorized immigrants ever to reach Palestine." The "tired refugees" were "searched and sprayed with DDT" before their transfer to British ships, presumably bound for Cyprus. "Their fighting spirit seemed to have gone," Currivan wrote; they sang *Hatikvah* "with tears streaming down their faces."[40]

In fact, as Currivan subsequently reported, the *Exodus* refugees, "quartered on the caged decks of the ships," were being returned to their original point of departure in France. There they remained, refusing to disembark, for twenty-five days. The thwarted immigrants, according to a Reuters report in the *Times*, were "cheerful." Relying on Associated Press and Reuters reporters in Paris, the *Times* did not deem the refugees worthy of coverage by its own journalist. Focused on record holiday travel for the Labor Day weekend, it only sparingly reported their plight until the British government announced its intention to transport them to Germany. Once there, following a "fierce, bloody three-hour battle," they were relocated to former Nazi detention camps and confined "behind barbed wire and under heavy military guard." For the first time, the *Times* paid editorial attention to their "tragic Odyssey."[41]

During the weeks preceding the United Nations vote on Jewish statehood the *Times* braided various themes revealing its discomfort with the prospect. Conceding that "nothing could be worse than the continuation of the present turmoil in the Holy Land," Anne O'Hare McCormick nonetheless asserted: "Partition is not a good solution." The Palestine problem "must be settled in the interests of the world"; any settlement required "a universal sanction." United Nations enforcement, with an "international force" to police it, offered the only viable solution.[42]

Gene Currivan remained preoccupied with the "terrorist" Irgun. There was "a civil war" brewing in Palestine, he wrote; its eruption depended on whether "Irgun nationalism or common sense prevails." Committed to "terrorism to oust the British and make all Palestine a completely Jewish state," the Irgun threatened a "fratricidal war." Its leaders "want all or nothing immediately"; like the Stern Gang, "it favored outright violence, assassination and other disregard for human rights." A News of the Week summary held "a small minority of Jewish extremists" who had "launched a campaign of terror against the British" responsible for the spreading carnage in Palestine, resulting in "open war."[43]

Only Daniel challenged the prevailing *Times* narrative. Confronting "seemingly unmovable" Arab opposition to a Jewish state, he wrote, Zionism had become "an apparently irresistible force." Living "without natural fortifications on a political island in a hostile Arab sea," Jews in Palestine had demonstrated "a remarkable degree of self-confidence" while remaining "one or two steps ahead of the Arabs in their planning." With the Haganah prepared for war and a "shadow administration" assuming the reins of Zionist government, a nascent Jewish state "on Western democratic lines" was emerging.[44]

With the United Nations vote for the partition of Palestine into Jewish and Arab states, Currivan noted the "stunned silence" of Arabs and the "restrained joyousness" of Zionists. Ben-Gurion anticipated "an independent Jewish society which will express the great ideals of the prophets of Israel." (A "dissenting note," predictably, came from Judah Magnes, who expected "trouble.") The next day Currivan again balanced his report of "thousands of jubilant Jews [who] jammed the streets singing and dancing" with a concluding wish from Magnes: "Would that with God's help an opportunity should be given to us to cooperate in all spheres of life with our Semitic neighbors."[45]

Noting that "history was written" with the United Nations partition vote, a *Times* editorial acknowledged: "Many of us have long had doubts ... concerning the wisdom of erecting a political state on the basis of religious faith." But the General Assembly decision should command "the acquiescence, the respect and the loyal support of all nations and all peoples." *Times* editors expressed the hope that it offered a solution for "the Holy Land's tragic and heart-breaking problems."[46]

The next day the *Times* reported "a violent Arab retort" to the UN vote in a warning from Dr. Hussein Khalidi, chairman of the Palestine Arab High Committee, that if the partition plan was enforced Arabs would wage "a holy war," a "crusade," against the Jews. Within days "the Jews' right to sovereignty" was challenged, the *Times* noted, by "the sword of repeated Arab threats" to obliterate the nascent Jewish state. But any reduction in inter-communal tension, wrote Sam Pope Brewer, "seemed destroyed" by Irgun "terrorist bombings." Barely noticed by the *Times* was an Arab Legion attack on a bus convoy near Tel Aviv that killed fourteen Jews.[47]

During the waning months of British rule in Palestine the *Times* alternated reports of increasing violence between Arabs and Jews (invariably incited by Jewish "terrorists") with dire warnings from the American Council for Judaism against the perils of Jewish nationhood. At the opening of its annual conference in January 1948, expansively covered by the *Times*, Rabbi Morris Lazaron called for "an uncompromising fight to stem Jewish nationalism." American Jews must decide whether being a Jew means "a new devotion to, or even a link with, a separate nation" or "a steadfast maintenance of the eternal truths of the religion of Judaism." A special committee identified Jewish nationalism as "a misinterpretation of the spirit of the Jewish faith and a tragic reversal of the historic process of emancipation." The United States, it asserted, is "our homeland" and "we reject the concept that Jews are homeless unless they live in Palestine."[48]

Welcoming support for the Council's position, the *Times* published a letter from New York lawyer Joseph M. Proskauer, president of the anti-Zionist American Jewish Committee, asserting: "There can be no political identification of Jews outside of Palestine with whatever government may there be instituted." American Jews, he wrote, "suffer from no political schizophrenia. . . . We are bone of the bone and flesh of the flesh of America." One week later the *Times* published Lessing Rosenwald's endorsement of Proskauer's statement, warning of attempts by the fledgling Jewish state "to manipulate the political attitudes and loyalties of Americans." American Jews, he insisted, "cannot have, as a group, a foreign policy of their own. . . . In our religious adherence, and in that alone, we are of the Jewish faith."[49]

Amid rising violence in Palestine during the early months of 1948, *Times* reporters and editors offered variations on anti-Zionist themes. It greeted the new year with a report that two Jewish immigrant ships bearing 12,000 "visaless Jews," and "full of potential 'fifth columnists,'" were arriving. Its passengers were "believed" to be "mostly hand-picked Communists or fellow travelers, with links to the Stern Gang." The following day the Jewish Agency labeled the report "a malicious slander."[50]

Reporter Sam Pope Brewer, who had joined the *Times* in 1944 and was assigned to Palestine three years later, contributed a cluster of articles describing "fanatical determination" on both sides "because both the Zionists and the Arabs want Palestine." (He failed to mention that only the Zionists were willing to accept its partition into Jewish and Arab states.) Brewer found it difficult to identify the combatants because they did not wear uniforms and "Jews from the Yemen often are indistinguishable from Arabs." But he recognized that "a dream of nearly 2,000 years" neared fulfillment. Jews were "firmly bound together by common memories of persecution." (Memories of Jewish national and religious history in the Land of Israel were ignored.) Their "task" was to convince non-Jewish residents "that they will not be proselytized or squeezed out of their livelihood by Jewish immigrants." A *Times* editorial ten days later, once again echoing Magnes, lamented that "the homeland of three great religions is having its fate decided by expediency without a sign of the spiritual and ethical considerations which should be determining."[51]

With the impending departure of British forces from Palestine the *Times* clung tenaciously to Magnes's advocacy of a UN trusteeship in the Holy Land rather than partition and Jewish statehood. Otherwise, Palestine might "set off a conflagration which could destroy a large part of mankind." According to Magnes, Jews and Arabs alike "yearn for the opportunity of building up their common country, the Holy Land, through labor and cooperation." Only "a bi-national or federal Palestine with two equal peoples, Jews and Arabs, with neither dominating the other," could achieve this worthy goal. With partition "a false and dangerous course of action," leading inevitably to "the perpetuation of hatreds and hostilities" (and, to be sure, Jewish statehood), sovereignty depended on the willingness of Arabs and Jews "to live together."[52]

Anne O'Hare McCormick returned to Palestine to add her voice to the rising chorus of *Times* apprehension over the imminence of Jewish statehood. Focusing on the Old City of Jerusalem, "a shrine for both contestants in the deadly struggle in the Holy Land," she asserted that it "can never be possessed by either." If partition had legal force, she gratuitously advised Zionists, then the internationalization of Jerusalem "also has the force of law which they are bound to respect." Arabs, she wrote, were no match for "the burning zeal and determination of the Zionist fighters."[53] Two weeks later the triumphant Arab Legion swept through the ancient Jewish Quarter, expelling residents and destroying their synagogues. The *Times* preference for internationalization was silenced.

In mid-May McCormick confronted the indisputable fact that with Israel's Proclamation of Independence "the shadow and the dream outlined in the Balfour Declaration had become a reality." Ironically, the nation that "was born and grew to the fighting age with British aid and under British protection" had rejected the guiding hand of its mentor. That left the "grim prospect" of Jews and Arabs on their own "to slug it out." But she took some solace from fantasizing that if partition succeeded, "it is easy to see that the two states would be bound in time to something approaching the bi-national system that men like Dr. Magnes have long advocated."[54]

For nearly twenty years, ever since Joseph Levy had propelled the Hebrew University pacifist to prominence in the pages of the *Times*, Adolph Ochs, Arthur Hays Sulzberger and a bevy of reporters had deferentially deferred to Magnes. They elevated him to stature vastly disproportionate to his marginal influence in Palestinian Zionist circles, where he had virtually no following

beyond the tiny circle of intellectuals in Brit Shalom and its political successor Ihud. The *Times* embraced his bi-national fantasy ever more stridently the
more irrelevant it became.

As Arab attacks compelled a Zionist response for national survival, resulting in territorial gains in Jerusalem and Jaffa that crossed UN partition lines, the
Times blamed Zionists for their successes. Extending their boundaries, under
attack to be sure, "Jews seemingly ran the risk of weakening the 'legal' position
of partition that they claimed to embrace." Palestine, according to the *Times*
(again echoing Magnes), was "a symbol of the struggle for peace with justice
and justice with peace ... a test of the ability of mankind to settle its quarrels
without bloodshed." It pleaded for "firmness and justice, mercy and understanding."[55] Four days before the British departure, the *Times* still could not
bring itself to mention, no less deplore, the evident Arab intention to destroy a
Jewish state within any borders.

Disregarding the exultation of Jews in Palestine over the Proclamation of
Independence signed on May 14, 1948 in Tel Aviv, *Times* foreign correspondent Dana Adams Schmidt focused on "a tendency to authoritarianism in the
nascent Jewish state." It was likely to be strengthened by the "influx of Oriental
Jews, who are the rank and file of the dissident organizations" (the Irgun and
Stern group). In this "land of extremes," he wrote, ranging "from Zionist dyna-
mism to Arab fatalism," Jews display "the aggressiveness of the pioneer" rather
than the "defensive aggressiveness" of diaspora Jewry. But they confronted
"an ancient [Arab] society whose forefathers have lived here for 1,300 years,"
which resents the presence of "foreign intruders." Framed within his inversion
of history, ignoring more than a millennium of Jewish national and religious
life in the Land of Israel preceding the Muslim conquest, he sorrowfully concluded that "peace between the Arab and the Zionist worlds is not in sight."[56]

One day later the *Times* prominently reported a statement by Lessing
Rosenwald, president of the American Council for Judaism, lamenting the
United Nations partition vote as "a sordid story of pressuring and high-handed
methods." He insisted that "the problem of the Jews who live in many nations of
the world must be solved throughout the world," not by Zionism. The following
week the palpably anxious *Times* reported the Council's insistence that "Israel can
in no way represent those of Jewish faith who are citizens of other nations." Israel
"is not the state or homeland of the Jewish people." To "Americans of the Jewish
faith it is a foreign state. Our single and exclusive national identity is to the United
States." Although the *Times* supported American government recognition of the
fledgling Jewish state, it nonetheless asserted that Israel "cannot hope to exist and

prosper without economic unity of the whole of Palestine," thereby offering its own version of bi-nationalism. Sulzberger's "attitude toward Israel," the publisher told the Newark *Jewish News*, "is the same as my attitude toward Indonesia."[57]

One week after Israeli independence the *Times* published a *Magazine* article entitled "Man with an Obsession." After thirty years of "dreaming and scheming," this leader displayed "remarkable decisiveness and tenacity" in pursuit of his nationalist goal: "title to Palestine." Clifton Daniel was not describing Prime Minister David Ben-Gurion, but King Abdullah of Trans-Jordan, interviewed more than a year earlier in his winter palace. Clearly fascinated by his royal presence, Daniel described him as "a master of that elaborate and ceremonious double talk with which Arabs evade embarrassing direct questions." But the King had made clear his claim to "Palestine and the surrounding lands."[58]

Two weeks later, Gene Currivan glowingly profiled Ben-Gurion, the "Key Man in Israel" rarely noticed by the *Times* during his pre-state years of Zionist leadership. Hailing "Israel's wartime Churchill," and comparing him as commander-in-chief to Franklin D. Roosevelt during World War II, Currivan praised his "age-old intuition," "overwhelming personality," and "indomitable strength." Citing Ben-Gurion's "tremendous ... will power," he identified the new prime minister's appearance with that of "a poet or of one whose thoughts transcend the material."[59]

The *Times* sporadically reported the war launched by five Arab states to annihilate Israel. But a front-page article by Sam Pope Brewer, one of three *Times* journalists covering the battle for the Old City of Jerusalem, described the surrender of a "haggard and dazed" Israeli garrison to the Arab Legion after a fierce eleven-day battle. "Two aged rabbis, carrying white flags, walked out through the clouds of dust and smoke hanging over the Jewish Quarter." To their religious Orthodox followers, Currivan wrote, the Jewish Quarter "meant the whole religious world and all it symbolized." At their "Wailing Wall ... they prayed, crying out their hopes and aspirations." Historians, he concluded, "may chronicle it as one of the world's most valiant last stands." Dana Adams Schmidt, writing under the headline "Surrender is a Relief," described the loss of the Old City as "the hardest blow, morally and psychologically, that the Jews have suffered." But the surrender had "some positive effects": Jews would have "less reason to fire mortars into the Old City and danger to Christian and Moslem holy places will be diminished."[60] The fate of Jewish holy places was ignored.

Covering a story that would reverberate among Israelis (and in the *Times*) more than six decades later, Gene Currivan reported the strategically vital battle for Lydda, an Arab village located on the road between Tel Aviv and Jerusalem. Currivan noted that "Lydda had offered considerable resistance at first and suffered heavy casualties as a result." He described "armored cars of both sides darting back and forth and mortar fire crashing about." With the Arab defeat assured, civilian residents had suddenly fled. Because of the "seeming hopeless position of the Arabs, there appeared to be little hope of anything better for them than a disorderly retreat." There was no mention of an unprovoked Israeli massacre of innocent Arab civilians, propelled to notoriety by *Haaretz* journalist Ari Shavit sixty-five years later in his book, glowingly reviewed in the *Times*, about "the triumph and tragedy of Israel."[61]

Tel Aviv, relatively unscarred by war (and a safer place for journalists), remained the primary focus of *Times* attention. "Imagine any large beach resort in midsummer and you have Tel Aviv," Currivan wrote, where people "know that a war is going on ... but are not greatly affected by it." (During the early days of the war, unnoticed by the *Times*, Egyptian Dakota transports refitted as bombers had attacked Tel Aviv with impunity.) He was impressed by the "courageous nonchalance" of Tel Aviv residents. Although "one gets the impression of people huddled together as if protectively," normal life seemed uninterrupted. Residents of "the first Jewish state since the time of Agrippa" still gathered every morning in cafés to drink coffee and consume "large quantities of fancy cakes."[62]

Sidney Gruson (identified as the *Times* correspondent in "Palestine," not Israel) noted "a curious mixture of cockiness and jitters" that pervaded Tel Aviv during a brief truce. His wife Flora Lewis contributed a glowing tribute to Chaim Weizmann, "President and 'Conscience' of Israel." He speaks, she wrote, "with the detachment of a sage"; aloof from politics, he was "not a man of violence, but of reason." As "the conscience of the Jewish state," he realizes that "peace must be the ultimate objective of the Israeli policy ... and perhaps Weizmann keeps his eye farther toward the horizon than Ben-Gurion."[63]

Five months after the birth of the Jewish state the *Times* reported the death of Judah Magnes. Both the *Times* obituary and a tribute entitled "Magnes of Mount Scopus" downplayed his unrelenting anti-Zionism, focusing instead on his efforts to build "a great university" in Palestine that would "enable Judaism to carry on its historical role as an interpreter and mediator among nations." Magnes might have become "a great political figure in the new State of Israel," the *Times* speculated, but for his refusal to compromise on his commitment to a bi-national Palestine.[64]

In late October the *Times* briefly noted "the flight of 80 per cent" of the "500,000 Arabs" (a number that it would subsequently, and repeatedly, vastly inflate) who had inhabited territory now held by Israel. Their departure "astounded the new state but it also greatly simplified its internal problems." More intriguing was the identity of the Jewish state that the newspaper had so resolutely opposed. With its "contradictions and paradoxes," Gruson wrote, it "defies description in ordinary political and economic terms." For Israelis, the "miracle" was that "a state was born, flourishes and promises to survive, not with the perfection of a utopia, but with all the faults and credits of the Western world with which they want to be associated." Puzzled by the influence of religious parties, Gruson noted their opposition to a constitution in the belief that "the state has a ready-made one in the Old Testament."[65]

From Hitler's rise to power to the birth of the State of Israel fifteen years later the convergence of Reform Judaism and American patriotism guided *Times* news coverage and framed its anti-Zionist editorial advocacy. Minimizing the Nazi menace, it suppressed the annihilation of six million Jews and viewed the Zionist struggle with unrelenting discomfort. *Times* coverage of the State of Israel would be constricted and distorted by its embedded anti-Zionist legacy.

CHAPTER 4

Democratic Allies:
1949–1957

Between 1946, when the Anglo-American Committee began to consider the future of Palestine, and 1949, after the fledgling Jewish state had repulsed invading Arab armies and held its first national elections, the *Times* dispatched a bevy of journalists to report the story of a people decimated by the Holocaust struggling to restore national sovereignty in their historic homeland. No correspondent offered a more penetrating (and self-revealing) depiction of the complexities of the Israel story, and the ideological framework within which it was so often reported, than Anne O'Hare McCormick, who had joined the *Times* editorial staff in 1936, winning a Pulitzer Prize for foreign reporting the following year.

In a *Times Magazine* article nine months after the State of Israel proclaimed independence McCormick described "the drama of conflict and creation being played out against the scriptural landscape of the Holy Land." The transformation of Palestine, she wrote, had been achieved "at the cruel price of the exile of at least half the former inhabitants." In Orientalist mode she lamented: "Gone are the brown-cloaked natives that used to drive their sheep and goats along the roadside." They were replaced by "a strange new people from Northern and Eastern Europe" – in a word, Jews. She described the fledgling state as "a huge kindergarten of healthy, well-fed and happy youngsters." Her "happy" Israelis "belong to a movement rather than a race"; and "the mystique that animates this movement is not religion, memory of the past, or homesickness for the promised land." Rather, it was "a new and intense" nationalism – with the potential danger, McCormick anticipated, that Israelis would develop "a superior-race complex" as an "advanced people in what they consider a back-ward area."[1] Israelis, by invidious insinuation, might become the new Nazis. The war-ravaged nation that had lost 1% of its population, including 2,000

Holocaust survivors, during its birth struggle against Arab invaders had no place in her narrative.

A *Times* editorial the following day was more welcoming. The convening of the Knesset, it noted, fell on "The Feast of Trees" (Tu B'Shvat). Now "the new state, the first independent, predominantly Jewish regime in Palestine since the time of the Maccabees ... is to be planted." Extending "our good wishes," the editors anticipated "growing pains" as the fledgling state struggled to enact "just and democratic" laws while extending "the helping hand of friendship to its recent enemies, particularly to the Arab refugees." "In making its own desert bloom," the editorial concluded optimistically, Israel could "help to bring peace and plenty to the whole Near East."[2]

As Israel struggled to absorb a flood of new immigrants from war-ravaged Europe and the Arab Middle East, *Times* coverage veered from awe to despair. It described 4,000 Yemenite Jews wandering through the streets of Aden, "weary, hungry and homeless." Then "a plump woman with gray hair began putting them on a magic carpet. Now they all have landed in Israel and are living there happily." The "plump woman" was Dr. Olga Feinberg, who had spent the war years in India before departing for Aden where she managed a rescue camp for Jews displaced by pogroms. Yemenite Jews, the *Times* cheerfully reported, "took to flying like ducks to water."[3]

Four months later Gene Currivan described a far bleaker picture. He had received a letter from the *Times* Foreign Editor suggesting that he report on "the Israeli housing problem" due to the "influx of immigrants." An unidentified "informant" had suggested that Jews in Arab countries be permitted to immigrate to Israel, leaving their homes and businesses to be exchanged "for the homes and businesses of Palestinian Arabs." The editor "would like to see our readers informed on these points." He suggested that Currivan also investigate "the police problems of the new state" – specifically: "How has the recent tide of immigration affected the general level of crime."[4]

Currivan's subsequent visit to three Israeli immigrant camps revealed a reality that was "not pleasant": "The general bitterness and appalling living conditions ... are almost beyond belief." Despite "almost superhuman" efforts to ease their absorption, the newcomers confronted months of "discomfort, idleness and disillusionment." Their preconceived ideas of "ideology, patriotism or love for Zion" had yielded to questions about "why so much had been promised and so little given." Filled with "sullen humanity," with "nothing to do but eat, sleep and gripe about conditions," he imagined that the camps were becoming "fertile grounds for the seeds of communism."[5]

On the first anniversary of independence the *Times* made its peace with the existence of a Jewish state with an editorial celebrating the "Birthday in Israel." It cited "a year of impressive achievement," with free elections, a "stable and representative" government, armistice agreements with neighboring Arab states and the successful absorption of "a remarkable flow" of immigrants. Israel's future was "bright with hope" and the editors, urging its admission to the United Nations, congratulated the fledgling state for "an impressive first year."[6] The *Times* finally seemed reconciled to the Jewish state that its publishers for so long and so adamantly had opposed.

The armistice concluded between Israel and Syria in July, a *Times* editorial proclaimed, was "good news in itself" and "a considerable triumph" for the United Nations, whose mediator Ralph J. Bunche had presided over the negotiations. With agreements now reached with all its Arab neighbors, the *Times* expressed optimism about resolution of the remaining "large and serious problems": Arab refugees and the status of Jerusalem (both of which would remain sources of contention seventy years later). With military issues resolved the *Times* enthusiastically, if prematurely, anticipated that "a new era may be ready to dawn throughout the Middle East."[7]

In three perceptive *Magazine* articles, Gertrude Samuels (who had joined the *Times* staff as a photojournalist six years earlier) illuminated the arc of Jewish immigration from displaced persons camps in Germany to fledgling kibbutzim in the promised land. It was, she wrote, "a miracle born of years of longing." Guided by a twenty-year-old Polish woman who had survived Auschwitz, Samuels took up residence in a camp. She then accompanied nearly nine hundred refugees on the two-day train ride that transported them from "the country of their persecution" to the ship that would bring them to "*their* country." It was, she noted, an "all-Jewish" ship. No one saluted anyone, and the Captain danced the hora with his passengers every night of their five-day journey from Munich to Haifa. Arriving in port, there was "a long, aching silence" among the passengers; then, in "a swelling symphony" that began with children's voices, everyone sang *Hatikvah* – "as though they had been storing it like some treasure and were now showing it to all" in "an emotional purge." With tears flowing, "their role as Israeli citizens had begun."[8]

Two months later Samuels described "the three great challenges" for Israel: political, spiritual, and economic. "Politically and spiritually the state exists," she wrote, describing the "ebullient" national mood. But "the question of economic survival looms over Israel." Despite the proliferation of new industries, reclamation of roads, farms and homes, kibbutzim that were "turning fighters back into farmers," and two dozen new settlements in the Negev desert "where once the Patriarchs and their descendants pastured their flocks," the country confronted a looming economic crisis. Especially in the Arab towns of Nazareth and Akko, youngsters displayed "the thin, shabby, undernourished appearance of neglected children." The Arab minority presented "a complex of political, economic and psychological problems": "a 'nation' almost the size of Israel itself, is in exile."[9]

Israelis, Samuels wrote, clung to Theodor Herzl's credo: "If you will it, it is not a dream." In her final report, from kibbutz Dafne in the northern Galilee region "immortalized in Solomon's Song of Songs," Samuels described life among the residents with whom she had briefly resided. She was intrigued that members, sharing "a philosophy of social justice," worked "for the common community good instead of for profit or individual gain" while their children were "under community control." Embracing the motto "yesterday nothing – tomorrow all," kibbutzim, Samuel concluded, "are able to meet the needs of Israel's ever-changing society."[10]

Even as the *Times* accepted the reality of Jewish statehood it continued to provide a welcoming forum for the increasingly marginal anti-Zionist American Council for Judaism. The smallest and least influential of the major American Jewish organizations, it remained Sulzberger's undisputed favorite. The *Times* reported that Council member Alfred Lilienthal, speaking during Sabbath services at Temple Israel in Manhattan, insisted that American Jews must choose between "universal Judaism and nationalism." Israel, in turn, must "return to the original concept of the refugee and the haven" and "renounce its claim on world Jewry."[11]

Sporadic reports from Israel remained favorable. Citing preparation for a "joyous Passover," Currivan wrote: "There have been few times in the long span of Jewish history when Passover … has meant so much to the Jews of the world, and especially to those of Israel." With the Jewish diaspora substantially reduced by the Holocaust, "those who formed the exodus from the dispersion can now pray in the Holy Land instead of praying that they might be here." Even 80,000 recent refugees living in transit camps realized that "despite the temporary hardships, they are settled in their own land." On "Israel's Second Birthday" a laudatory editorial asserted that "this little country has earned its place in the world through the courage, endurance and devotion of its people." Despite military threats and a struggling economy, forcing it "to live almost from one crisis to another, and in a bitterly hostile environment," the Jewish state was "unquestionably a shining outpost of democracy in the Middle East."[12]

With evident fondness for biblical analogies, Currivan compared the flight of Jews from Iraq to Israel to its ancestral precedent 2,500 years earlier, when King Cyrus freed the Jews who had been exiled from Jerusalem. But the burden of absorbing 200,000 newcomers annually, primarily from Morocco, Yemen, Algeria, Tunisia, and Libya weighed heavily on the Israeli economy. Sydney Gruson reported that their "primitive capabilities" were slow to adapt to Israel's "modern industrial needs." And a new immigrant's life in a "rudimentary hut or tent camp" was exceedingly difficult. But Israeli political parties, "moved as much by moral principles as political considerations," welcomed them.[13]

The *Times* remained concerned about the loyalty issue that Israel might pose for American Jews, and for the newspaper. It was reassured when American Jewish Committee president Jacob Blaustein returned from Israel with a statement from Prime Minister Ben-Gurion affirming that "Israel speaks only on behalf of its own citizens." Indeed, Ben-Gurion continued, Israel was "anxious that nothing should be said or done which could in the slightest degree undermine the sense of security and stability of American Jewry." Although there were occasions when it was necessary for the *Times* News Department "to refer to the State of Israel as 'the Jewish state,'" a representative of the American Council for Judaism was reassured that there was strong resistance to "seeing it so designated on our editorial page."[14]

The *Times* continued its expansive coverage of the annual conference of the Council, whose leaders remained agitated over the existence of a Jewish state. President Lessing Rosenwald warned that "Zionist influence was aimed at implementing Jewish national policies among American Jews." He urged the American Jewish community to adhere to "the basic principles of complete identification with American national life." Executive Director Elmer Berger insisted that American Jews must not become "mere appendages to Israeli national interests." Asserting that it betrayed "a sacred, personal trust to camouflage with religion worship of a foreign state," he urged the conference to redouble its efforts "to repudiate Zionist claims that "Jews are 'one people'" and that Israel is "the 'Jewish State.'"[15]

With Israel's third anniversary of independence approaching, Prime Minister David Ben-Gurion made his first official visit to the United States. The *Times* provided generous coverage, reporting his meeting with President Truman; a pilgrimage to West Point to place a wreath on the grave of Colonel David ("Mickey") Marcus, who died fighting for Israel's independence in 1948; a joyous rally at Madison Square Garden where he pledged that Israel would be "a fortress of democracy in the Near East"; and his foray into

Brentano's bookstore, where he satisfied his eclectic interests with volumes of classical Greek literature, Chinese philosophy and George Bernard Shaw's plays. In a glowing *Magazine* article, London *Observer* correspondent Flora Lewis described him as "the fighter, the frontiersman ... [who] placed his faith in action, not in tact and talk." Citing his "electric energy ... of will," she identified him as truly "the founder of the state."[16]

Once again, however, the *Times* gave the last word to Lessing J. Rosenwald. In a lengthy letter to the editor he rejected Ben-Gurion's recent claim that Zionism "embraced all Jews throughout the world." If unchallenged, it would "give tacit acquiescence to a program calling into question the single-minded national attachment of American Jews to the United States of America." Judaism, Rosenwald insisted, is "a historic religious faith, not a nationality." Zionism is "a distortion of our faith, reducing it from universal proportions to the dimensions of a nationalistic cult." Six months later he responded furiously to a *Times* article quoting Ben-Gurion's allegation that American Zionist leaders were "bankrupt" for not moving to Israel. Repeating the phrase "Americans of Jewish faith" ten times to make his point, he asserted: "Israel is a foreign state like any other foreign state, and Americans of Jewish faith have no national attachments to it." He insisted: "The roots of Americans of Jewish faith are deep and firm in the soil of America."[17] With Judah Magnes's bi-nationalism consigned to oblivion, Rosenwald's anti-Zionism filled the void.

But by then *Times* editorial policy had shifted significantly, with three editorials in four months strongly supporting Israel. One cited "the natural bond of friendship that exists between one of the world's oldest democracies and one of the world's newest." Another supported a Congressional allocation of $50 million for refugee assistance that demonstrated the "friendly feeling" of the United States toward Israel as "a genuinely democratic nation that can be a force for stability and progress in the Middle East." The *Times* even located the Middle East problem in "the dark and fiery recesses of Arab emotionalism." Arab governments were "so driven by hatred and fear of Israel that they have deliberately and callously used [Arab refugees] as instruments of politics." Still missing was "the Arab will to face the facts and make the best of a decisive setback."[18]

Times reporter Dana Adams Schmidt, who had covered Europe, North Africa and the Middle East since 1943, provided updates on Israeli domestic politics. He contributed dramatic accounts of rioting in Jerusalem by "a mob of 1,000 adherents of the extreme right-wing Herut party" ("surly looking men") over Israeli negotiations with the West German government for war reparations.

During a mass protest in Zion Square, Menachem Begin (invariably identified as leader of the dissolved Irgun "terrorist organization") had inflamed the crowd by asserting that police were armed "with grenades made in Germany" containing "the same gas that was used to kill your fathers and mothers." The crowd "stormed through police barricades" surrounding the Knesset to become a "howling mob," fueling "an irrational demagogy that could lead to dictatorship." More poignantly, a Knesset member reported that his six-year-old son, over-hearing a discussion of German reparations, asked: "What price will we get for grandma and grandpa?"[19]

In a nuanced editorial the *Times* considered "the most explosive" problem to be "Arab refugees" who were "crowded in squalid camps along Israel's borders." Comprising "a living, heaving mass of humanity," they were "prey to the demagogues that swarm around them thick as flies." Until this problem was resolved, "no real peace" was possible between Israel and the Arab states. The *Times* proposed their "reintegration" in Syria, Iraq and Jordan as the only "feasible and economically practicable" solution that could demonstrate "a willingness to recognize realities for what they are" – a proposal that Arab states still showed no inclination to accept seven decades later.[20]

The *Times* continued to devote more attention to the increasingly marginal American Council for Judaism than to Israeli issues. It published a laudatory review of *A Partisan History of Judaism* written by Rabbi Elmer Berger, executive director of the Council. Carefully distinguishing Jewish history from "nationalistic folklore" (Zionism), Berger urged Jews to remain "universal men." Claiming that any notion of Palestine as the ancestral home of Jews was "a forgery of history," he preposterously asserted that "the distinguishing features of incipient totalitarianism were 'screamingly apparent' in Zionism."[21]

In daily reports from the Council's annual convention Irving Spiegel, who had covered Jewish news for the *Times* since 1942, revealed its consuming concerns over Zionism and Israel. Rabbi Morris Lazaron claimed that Judaism had "deteriorated" once "the primacy of its universal religious ideas" was superseded by "a nationalist faith" that elevated "the primacy of the Jewish people" above individual dignity. In a rousing conclusion, convention delegates voted unanimously that "no Jew and no organization of Jews can speak of all Americans of Jewish faith," thereby implicitly marginalizing themselves.[22]

Although the *Times* continued to provide the Council with disproportionate coverage far in excess of its support or influence among American Jews, its publisher's fervent support for the organization no longer determined editorial policy. The newspaper celebrated Israel's fourth anniversary of statehood, citing it "as an outpost of living democracy in the Near East." Despite "extreme difficulties," the Jewish state had "stuck to their principles" by "opening wide the doors to an immigration program unique in human history." It deserved "encouragement and best wishes."[23]

Correspondent Dana Adams Schmidt was considerably less laudatory. Reporting from Israel on Independence Day, he concluded that material concerns had become less harrowing than its "moral and psychological problems." Primary among them was the challenge of "integrating cultures of disparate elements, whose only common bond appears to be that they are Jews." "Old-timers," he wrote, were "appalled by the low standards of achievement and sloppy working habits of many Oriental and some recent East European immigrants." They worried that with kibbutzim losing their "pre-eminent position as cultural centers," Israel could become "an East European-Oriental slum." Second-generation Israelis "lack the extraordinary professional, intellectual and artistic qualifications that distinguished their fathers."[24] Only four years into statehood, Schmidt implied, Israel's best years were in the past.

Yet Schmidt (like Joseph Levy before him) found biblical analogies compelling. Israelis, he wrote, drew meaning from "Biblical history and prophecy," deriving "not only spiritual inspiration but physical guidance" to chart their future. As Ben-Gurion frequently reminded them, "the Bible is a practical guide toward realizing Israel's destiny." The discovery of copper and iron in the Negev desert, where King Solomon's mines were located, had prompted the fledgling state to secure the "cradle of the Jewish people, where Abraham dwelt 4000 years ago." Israelis were inspired by "the grand vision of recreating the glories of the ancient past."[25]

But admiration for Israel was constrained by criticism. The mourning period for President Chaim Weizmann, who died in November 1952, was a time for "taking stock." Although the Jewish state was firmly identified with the West, it "must find the way to peace with her Arab neighbors even at the cost of sacrifices." An editorial cited "850,000 Arab refugees" (a considerably inflated number, repeated several days later) as a continuing source of Middle East instability. "Wisdom as well as humanity" required cooperation between Israelis and Arabs to relieve "this really desperate refugee situation."[26]

Biblical analogies remained favorite tropes for *Times* reporters. Describing the construction of a pipeline through the Judean hills to provide Jerusalem residents with water, Irving Spiegel cited David the Psalmist: "my flesh longeth for thee in a dry and thirsty land." When completed, Spiegel anticipated, "the thirst of the Holy City will be slaked." Dana Adams Schmidt, reporting from Israel's first sheep ranch and its southernmost Negev settlement, described the determination of a small group of former members of a Negev patrol unit to restore an ancient Nabataean irrigation system to provide water for their kibbutz.[27]

The *Times* closely monitored the deteriorating relationship between Israel and the Soviet Union, resulting in a break in diplomatic relations early in 1953 when it became "the avowed enemy of the Jewish national homeland." Schmidt reported that the Soviet Union had developed "its own brand of anti-Semitism," with political trials and purges reminiscent of the 1930s. Consequently, Arab states had become more threatening toward Israel, "feeding on … [Soviet] anti-Jewish propaganda" and emboldened to consider a "second round" against the Jewish State.[28]

Two days later an editorial reported the appeal of forty-nine distinguished Americans to President Eisenhower on behalf of three million persons, identified as members "of Jewish faith," then living in the Soviet Union. In the familiar *Times* language of Jewish identity circumlocution, the editorial asserted: "They might have been of any faith or of any race, for it is their situation, not their creed, that claims our attention. They are human beings in dire peril." Condemning Soviet prejudice the editorial concluded: "Now the men who began by giving lip service to the brotherhood of man are preaching the doctrine of Cain."[29]

On Independence Day in 1953 the *Times* celebrated five "eventful" years of "constant struggle" yet "heroic achievement" for Israel, an "outpost of democracy in the Middle East." It had confronted military, political and economic challenges that "might well have proved too much for a people of lesser faith and resolution." If "Arab neighbors would make peace" it would assure a prosperous and peaceful future for the Jewish state, the renewed birthday wish "from one of the world's oldest democracies to one of the world's youngest."[30] It marked the pinnacle of *Times* praise for Israel.

Barely two weeks later the newspaper once again provided an expansive forum for its publisher's favorite Jewish organization. Three days of coverage reported the continuing anxieties provoked by the Jewish state among leaders of the American Council for Judaism. Lessing Rosenwald alleged that Zionist activities separated "American citizens of Jewish faith" from "Americans of other religious beliefs." The Provost-emeritus of the University of California implored the American government to demand that Israel repudiate the notion that Jews outside its borders were "living in exile." Council founder Morris Lazaron berated American Jewish organizations for not lifting their voices on behalf of "800,000" Arab refugees. "Does Jewish nationalism," he asked, "crowd out every feeling of sympathy for any other group than Jews?"

Executive Director Elmer Berger abhorred the "Zionist-Israel axis" embracing the "fantastic medieval logic" that promulgated a misguided view of Jews as "an exclusive fraternity."[31]

Months later the *Times* published nuanced accounts of the "Arabs' Case vs. Israel" and the "Israel Case vs. Arabs." The former focused on "the banishment of 870,000 persons – Palestine's Arabs – from their homes, lands and livelihood." It deplored the acquiescence of the United Nations in this tragedy, designed "to assuage Western conscience toward persecuted Jews." Arabs believed that continuing Israeli cross-border attacks into Jordanian territory were "part of a terrorist campaign similar to that exemplified in massacres that frightened the present refugees from their homes." For Israelis, however, the armistice agreements of 1949 had failed to hinder the Arab governments in "their economic war designed to strangle the young state by boycott and blockade after they had failed to throttle her by force."[32]

In mid-October, after cross-border raids from Jordan killed thirty Israelis, including a mother and her two children murdered in their home, Prime Minister Ben-Gurion authorized a forceful response. Unit 101 of the Israel Defense Forces (IDF), commanded by Ariel Sharon, attacked the Jordanian village of Kibya, killing fifty-three civilians and provoking international outrage and a resolution of censure in the United Nations. Unquestionably, responded an initial *Times* editorial, the "tragic raid" had been "provoked by a long series of Arab incursions on Israeli villages." Editorial criticism was reserved for the Jordanian refusal to engage in discussions with Israel over border issues.[33]

But international condemnation of Israel for the Kibya attack prompted the *Times* to recant its initial focus on cross-border Arab incursions. After the UN Security Council censured Israel by a 9–0 vote Anne O'Hare McCormick referred to "the holocaust at Kibya." The *Times* stiffened its criticism of Israel, acknowledging that the UN had "a moral obligation to condemn an outrage which no amount of provocation can justify" (although the *Times* had already justified it). Indeed, the UN censure of Israel "does not go far enough." The "root problems" – provisional borders and "a mass of [Palestinian] refugees who have lived for four years in a state of unspeakable squalor and misery" – must be confronted "firmly and without delay."[34]

Five years after Gertrude Samuels had accompanied Holocaust survivors on their journey from European refugee camps to the fledgling Jewish state she returned to Israel. Samuels reconnected with Marysia Mamelok, now married with a ten-month-old child and living in Tel Aviv, who marveled: "I have everything today." Dr. Sigmund Binder, who had endured a first-year "nightmare" in a displaced persons camp, lived in a "gracious, high-arched" apartment in Jaffa. Having learned Hebrew, he reported: "I am no stranger here." "Life is not easy," Israel Weisse told her, "but the feeling of freedom is here." Samuels tracked down ninety-year-old Szulim Lederman, the oldest passenger on board the *Galilah,* "still reading his prayer book" in the housing-project apartment that he shared with his granddaughter and her family. "I like it here," he told her. "I want to die here on my soil. I want to be buried in Israel." Samuels concluded, with evident admiration, "the gates stubbornly stand open to all seeking sanctuary or to help build the new state." Peace might remain "a mirage," but "audacity" had inspired remarkable achievements: "with the reclamation of Israel as a land has gone the rehabilitation and strengthening of her people."[35]

Several months later Moshe Brilliant reported increasing government sensitivity to the cultural mores of immigrants from "oriental" countries. "The 'pressure cooker' method" of Westernizing these newcomers had receded. Rather than mixing them among strangers they were gathered by country or village of origin. Medical personnel, along with union officials and educators, demonstrated greater sensitivity toward their "traditions and prejudices"; nurses no longer stripped amulets from Oriental patients, recognizing their psychological benefits. "The ethnocentric attitude of the dominant [Ashkenazi] community" had subsided.[36]

Amid rising Cold War tension in the mid-Fifties the rumblings of renewed conflict between Israel and its Arab neighbors punctuated *Times* coverage of the Middle East. Relying on inflated United Nations Relief and Works Agency for Palestine Refugees in the Near East (UNRWA) figures, it continued to grossly exaggerate the number of dispossessed Palestinians. Syria, Lebanon, Jordan, and Egypt, sheltering "900,000 refugees" according to an article in late November, insisted that they must be "repatriated" to Israel. Two months later, Cyrus Sulzberger referred to "almost one million Arabs who were driven out" of Palestine amid "butchery and war," as the British Mandate ended. Townsmen, villagers, farmers, and Bedouin herders all dreamed of the day when they will "wrest back their homes." So "Palestine assumes its Biblical role as the land of milk and honey" for displaced Arabs yearning to return.[37]

On the American Jewish front, the *Times* continued to report lamentations from the American Council for Judaism over the implications of Jewish statehood for American Jews. At its annual convention in 1955 the Council criticized the American Zionist movement for attempting to influence American government policy in Israel's favor. Any such effort, its chairman warned, must rest on the principle of "what is good for America." An American citizen must not claim that "a certain foreign state is the only friend that America has in the Middle East and that such foreign state is the only bastion of democracy in that area." Criticizing Jewish "tribalism," the Council expressed support for "high religion, worthy of the history and destiny of both Judaism and America."[38]

During the summer of 1955 *Times* reporters in Israel and Egypt switched places when Kenneth Love replaced Harry Gilroy. Love described Israel as "a new nation trying to set its often broken roots into the past as well as into the land." The "common cause" of Israelis was "reconquering and redeeming what they feel is a heritage promised by God." Like his predecessors Love was drawn to the Negev desert, where Israeli development in the midst of an ancient biblical landscape was alluring to Western reporters. Visiting Nahal Oz, a kibbutz founded two years earlier along the Gaza border, he was struck by the youthful energy of its members. An accompanying photograph showed a twenty-year-old nurse, proudly displaying her rifle, identified as a "Minutewoman" (favorably identified with colonial American fighters for independence in Lexington and Concord).[39]

In a series of articles in late 1955 Cyrus Sulzberger analyzed the Arab refugee problem, Israeli immigrant absorption, and looming conflict between the Jewish state and its Arab neighbors. The "Palestine dispute," he concluded, was "a conflict of refugees," with Israel having absorbed more than one million Jewish "fugitives from terror" whose resettlement had "inspired the flight of almost a million Palestinian Arabs." In that (erroneous) symmetry, he wrote, "lies the problem of peace in the Middle East." He recognized that Israel "cannot afford to admit back the displaced Arabs," who would create "an impossible fifth column" endangering the nation. Arab intransigence, he concluded, "is influenced by fanaticism and fears of political assassination," while Israel, "made cocky by battlefield victories and confidence in its own energies," was in "no mood to compromise."[40]

As a symbol of Israel's emerging "multi-racial" culture Sulzberger cited a northern Druze village on the crest of Mt. Carmel. Its young Arab men served in the IDF, where they were "renowned for their courage." They enjoyed kosher food rations while studying Hebrew and learning about Zionism. Indeed, the army was "the cocktail shaker of this little country"- like the United States, "an immigrants' haven." To be sure, there was "snobbery" from "middle-class townspeople with Western antecedents" toward Asian and African newcomers, some of whom did not know how "to eat with knife and fork." As in the United States, there was "incipient race prejudice" and little intermarriage between "light-skinned" European Jews and "their darker fellow citizens." But "a new nationality" was emerging to produce "a tough, lean, new Israeli type."[41]

A *Times* editorial, repeating the inflated number of "nearly 906,000" Palestinian refugees, identified "a homeless nation, threatening Middle Eastern peace." But it recognized that "not all came from what is now Israel and a considerable number of them are not technically 'refugees.'" Calling on Israel to accept "a few thousand" as a humane gesture, it suggested that "It would not be hard for the Arab states to find land within their own borders for these unfortunates."[42]

By the mid-1950s, in its reporting and editorial policy, the *Times* had moved away from the resolute anti-Zionism that had guided pre-1948 coverage. The most discernible remnant of its once pervasive anti-Zionist bias remained its continued elevation to prominence of the tiny and increasingly marginal American Council for Judaism. In December 1955 Council President Clarence Coleman, Jr. received ample space to reiterate that "in the historic traditions of Western democracy Judaism has been recognized as a religious faith." Efforts by the Israeli government and the Zionist movement "to construe Judaism as a nationalism" remained "repugnant to the vast majority of American Jews," while impeding "successful implementation of an American policy of impartiality in the Middle East."[43] By then, however, the Council was crying in the American Jewish wilderness; but the *Times* still publicized its lamentations.

Sustained Arab hostility fed the potential for renewed conflict, but *Times* editors held Israel to strict standards. Early in 1956 it supported United Nations condemnation of the Jewish state for its retaliation against Syrian attacks on Israeli fishing boats on the Sea of Galilee along the Syrian-Israeli border. Given fifty-six Syrian deaths, "the moral reasons for condemning Israel's actions are obvious." Although Israel was "an embattled, besieged nation" that "still reacts from fear," its reprisal policy was "morally and practically bad."[44] The editorial ignored Syrian aggression that provoked the Israeli response.

Times reporters provided more balanced judgments. The bond between modern and ancient Israel, a favorite *Times* trope during the early statehood years, signified an implicit acceptance of the Zionist narrative. Citing "nearly 1,000,000" Palestinians living within "the grim confines of refugee camps," Osgood Caruthers noted that Arab states "have not done much to ease [their] plight." The *Times* printed a two-column letter from James G. McDonald, former United States ambassador to Israel, endorsing the suggestion by former President Herbert Hoover that large numbers of Palestinian refugees could be resettled in Iraq, Jordan, and Syria as "a solution by engineering instead of by conflict" with "both honor and wisdom." Such a resettlement program, McDonald believed, "would advance, decisively, the cause of peace in the Middle East."[45]

In the Spring of 1956 war once again loomed ominously over Israel. David Ben-Gurion, who had returned to national leadership after a brief retirement, was generously praised in the *Times* for his "extraordinary capacity to look Dickensian and sound Churchillian." With "his sense of history, his erudition and eloquence," he was "particularly qualified to use either books or bullets" to secure national independence. "An Old Testament quality of prophecy" filled his speeches, while "fanatical determination motivates his actions."[46]

Even amid the prospect of war, wrote reporter Homer Bigart, it was "impossible to keep a free people in a constant state of fright." During the Passover holiday Israelis were "enjoying their Seder feasts with traditional cheer" and "the bogey of another Egyptian bondage does not lie too heavily here." Comforted by the retelling of their ancient exodus, they displayed "calmness and confidence" despite the absence of Western military assistance and American reluctance to be drawn into the looming conflict. Perhaps, Bigart speculated, Ben-Gurion will "prove another Moses." He visited kibbutz Nahal Oz, on the edge of the Gaza strip where "you can see danger with the naked eye." Fortunately for its residents, Egyptian mortar fire was unimpressively random: one week earlier, he reported, "two Hereford cows were injured, one seriously." Most "settlers" were Sabras, who resembled "dirt farmers anywhere." After arduous harvesting of wheat and barley, they found entertainment by playing chess and, "naturally," enjoying TV Westerns that evoked the ruggedness of their own lives.[47]

A *Times* editorial criticized the "reluctance of the Arab states ... to admit that the State of Israel legally exists and give up, for good and all, their ambition to drive the Israelis into the Mediterranean." Embracing the Zionist narrative, it chastised Arab spokesmen in the United Nations who had failed to demonstrate "the slightest understanding, or desire to understand, the urge that drove so many abused and harassed individuals into the ancient land of Palestine, to set up a new commonwealth and labor for a new hope." Despite its linguistic preference for "individuals" rather than Jews, and the "land of Palestine" for the Land of Israel, the editors offered an unusually strong statement of support for the Jewish state.[48]

In editorials one month apart, the *Times* endorsed Israel's "policy of restraint" despite civilian deaths from Jordanian cross-border attacks during a mutually agreed upon cease-fire. It sharply criticized Egyptian President Nasser for trumpeting his seizure of the Suez Canal as "a rallying point for all the stirrings of the Arab world." The *Times* noted that Arab nationalism, "purblind" in its hostility to the creation and growth of Israel, "is not always rational." As cross-border tension mounted, *Times* editorial criticism of Egypt sharpened. Citing Nasser's boastful plan "to head an 'empire' of the Moslem world from the Atlantic to the Indian Ocean," the *Times* identified the prospect of a "reasonable settlement" with the Egyptian leader as unlikely as it had once been with Hitler. "Appeasement," it firmly declared, "is no answer."[49]

But Israeli "reprisal" raids (for Jordanian attacks) were nonetheless "deplorable." In September, after four Israeli archeologists at work in Ramat Rachel were killed during a cross-border attack, a harsh Israeli response caused the deaths of fifty Jordanians. Such "devastating acts of retaliation," the *Times* editorialized, failed to halt border "incidents," while turning "otherwise sympathetic people in many lands into critics." To be sure, Jordanians were either "criminally negligent or woefully weak" in permitting such attacks. But this was "a case for the United Nations and not for unilateral punitive raids" by Israel.[50]

Israelis, the *Times* reported, were determined to "fight fire with fire." In yet another comparison linking Israeli struggles to the American frontier experience, Joseph Haff observed that Israelis living in border settlements "are not warlike." But these "frontier settlers" carried loaded rifles into their fields for protection against "attack by hostile Arabs" – just as American "frontiersmen" had once protected themselves against "hostile Indians." While relying on the moral teachings of the ancient Hebrew Prophets to provide "the basis of a model world order," wrote Moshe Brilliant, Ben-Gurion would not hesitate to use force to protect Israeli interests.[51]

Near the end of October Israel confronted renewed cross-border attacks from Egypt, Jordan and Lebanon. Arab leaders, proclaiming "a war of destruction," placed their armies under unified Egyptian command. With Israel encircled and endangered, the Israel Defense Forces responded by powering deep into the Sinai peninsula to within twenty miles of the Suez Canal, which had been closed for months to Israeli shipping. It was not merely "a retaliatory raid" to be followed by prompt withdrawal, cautioned a *Times* editorial: "It could jeopardize the armistice system" in place since 1948. But Israel, unwilling to endure continuing Arab "belligerency," seemed committed to the policy of never initiating war while asserting "the right of self-defense."[52]

Once the Israeli assault in Sinai was coordinated with the imminent arrival of British and French paratroopers in the Canal Zone, reported Dana Adams Schmidt, American relations with Israel reached "an all-time low." Israeli explanations could not overcome "a bitter feeling" among American officials that the Jewish state had "not only flouted" President Eisenhower's "earnest entreaties" for a peaceful resolution of the conflict but had rewarded American "generosity and understanding by embarking on an irresponsible adventure." Adding insult to injury it had done so with British and French, not American, collaboration.[53]

"Continued Arab violence against Israel and continued Arab refusal to make genuine peace," a *Times* editorial pointedly asserted, "does not justify the Israeli incursion into Egypt," which posed "a grave situation." Strongly endorsing President Eisenhower's policy of "non-involvement," it blamed Israel, Britain and France for having "embarked on a military solution of their problems in the face of open disagreement with the United States" without United Nations approval. Military force, it asserted, was "neither a wise nor proper instrument for the settlement of international disputes." Yet, the editorial noted, if there was "any one man guilty of aggression" it surely was Egyptian President Nasser, whose forceful seizure of the Suez Canal in disregard of treaty obligations evoked the moment when "Hitler marched into the Rhineland."[54] In the end, however, Israel was expected to turn the other cheek.

Editorial approval for Israel was reserved for Ben-Gurion's reversal (under intense international pressure) of Israel's "belligerent policy," accompanied by its "wise and constructive" decision to accept a cease-fire and prepare to withdraw military forces from Sinai and Gaza. Israel's backtracking eased Arab concerns that Western powers were "in league with" the Jewish state. But even frustration of Nasser's "dream of annihilating Israel" could not soften the "blow" to the United Nations of a war launched by Israel. Its commitment to peace had been "flouted," while the "conviction of the Arab-Asian world that imperialism and colonialism are still alive" had been strengthened.[55]

C.L. Sulzberger exulted that within "one brief week ... Ben-Gurion's moment of transcendent glory vanished," erased by "political reality." Israel stood "alone and isolated. It has no ally." The United States, he noted, was "appalled" by Israel's "adventure into Egypt" and was now "cooler to Jerusalem's cause than at any moment since the Zionist state was founded." Ben-Gurion's "great audacious challenge was ventured" and – to Sulzberger's evident satisfaction – it failed."[56]

The Sinai war thrust Israel into prominence in the *Times* that it had not experienced since its birth. Beyond sporadic local coverage provided by various Jerusalem-based journalists, it even began to attract attention from Washington columnists whose primary focus was rising Cold War tension between the United States and Soviet Union. Pulitzer Prize winning correspondent Arthur Krock was blunt: Israel, he declared, had "precipitated the Middle East crisis by a desperate resort to preventive war."[57]

The view from Israel differed sharply. To be sure, as Moshe Brilliant reported ten days later, Israeli-American relations had been buffeted by the Sinai war. But once Ben-Gurion had acceded to President Eisenhower's demands for the withdrawal of Israeli military forces there was hope for "rapprochement" with the United States. Israelis believed that their "spectacular victory" had earned them respect as a force to be reckoned with, placing them "in a position of greater strength to induce their Arab neighbors to negotiate peace."[58]

Whatever the Sinai war may have accomplished, a subsequent editorial declared (yet again), the problem of "900,000" Palestinian refugees remained unresolved. It carefully parsed blame for their plight. "Part of it goes to Israel, which will not accept even small Arab repatriations." Most, however, was the responsibility of Arab states that permitted refugees "to rot" in Gaza, Jordan, Syria, and Lebanon. Their "resettlement" must become "part of any permanent solution of the Near Eastern problem."[59]

Even as the American Council for Judaism slid into irrelevant obscurity, the *Times* continued to provide a sounding board for its anti-Zionist tropes. After a week-long visit to Israel, former President Lessing Rosenwald remained convinced that "Zionism was wrong." In an expansive gesture, he declared: "We accept Israel as a sovereign state and we wish her well, but we do not recognize that there is a Jewish people as such." He reiterated: "America is our home and we are not seeking any other."[60] It remained the message that Arthur Hays Sulzberger, like Adolph Ochs before him, wished his newspaper to convey.

Editorial pronouncements swung like a pendulum. Israel, the *Times* declared, was "in the wrong in seeking to entrench itself in the Gaza Strip," which provided "a semblance of validity to Arab charges of Israel's expansionist ambitions." Three days later it affirmed that Israel was "fully justified in asking for guarantees against exposure to a national catastrophe." The Jewish state rightly demanded that Egypt renounce belligerency before completing its withdrawal: "What Israel seeks is peace. Is it to be punished for this?" State Department insistence that an Israeli withdrawal precede Egyptian action was "unrealistic and even dangerous."[61]

A subsequent editorial insisted that "sacrifice and risk" were required of the Jewish state, whose future depended on "the preservation of peace and on the friendship of ... the civilized world." (No such "sacrifice and risk" were required of its Arab enemies.) To be sure, Egypt – like Israel's other Arab neighbors – had "an abominable record of provocation and aggression." But Israel must stand "unequivocally on the side of international law and order, which means compliance" with UN resolutions. Egypt must not be permitted to resume its "gangster tactics"; nor could Israel "be rewarded for violating the United Nations Charter" by invading its Arab neighbor.[62]

Columnist James Reston emphasized Ben-Gurion's "mulish determination ... to overplay his hand." The Israeli prime minister had the temerity to demand enforcement of a Security Council resolution, passed in 1951, instructing Egypt not to block Israeli ships from the Suez Canal. But a *Times* editorial castigated Egypt for its guerilla attacks and blockade of the Canal and Strait of Tiran, amounting to "a state of war" against Israel. Because the Eisenhower administration had been "unwilling to use any kind of pressure," the West "is forced to bow to the Egyptian dictator." Such was "the price of appeasement."[63] It was a sharp turn-around from the blame-Israel-first policy that *Times* editors had previously embraced.

One *Times* journalist was not convinced. In his April report on the Middle East Sam Pope Brewer, who had served as chief Middle Eastern correspondent for the *Times* between 1947 and 1949, concluded that Israel is "at the heart of the Middle Eastern crisis." To be sure, "there is no sign of relenting in bitter hatred" toward the Jewish State in the Arab world. But one of the "greatest potential trouble sources," Brewer asserted, "is the existence of more than 925,000 Arab refugees from the territory now held by Israel."[64] Festering Middle Eastern instability, by implication, was Israel's fault.

Times United Nations correspondent Kathleen Teltsh elaborated on Palestinian refugees as the "peace key." Their predicament provided "one of the most explosive issues in the Middle East" (although not one, she noted, that any Arab state cared to alleviate). Her primary source was Henry R. Labouisse, head of the UN aid program "now caring for 925,000 Arab refugees," the substantially inflated number that had become the staple of *Times* reports. Labouisse suggested that the "wisest course" would be to provide refugees with the choice between returning to Israel or financial compensation.[65] No responsibility for easing the refugees' plight was assigned – by UNRWA or the *Times* – to the Arab states that confined them in miserable camps, refused to grant them citizenship, and callously used their plight to stoke hostility against Israel.

Publisher Arthur Hays Sulzberger continued to worry about having a "Jewish specialist" posted in Jerusalem – although Irving Spiegel was assigned to cover the American Council for Judaism, to which Sulzberger remained deeply loyal. Reporting expansively on its thirteenth annual convention, the *Times* devoted two columns to the presidential address claiming that American Jews became "anesthetized" whenever Israel was scrutinized. Their "myopia" deprived them of the objectivity expected of responsible American citizens, "a tragedy directly attributable to Zionism."[66]

Sulzberger's Jewish discomfort was expressed with the assignment of men with "unmistakably Anglo-Saxon" names – Turner Catledge, James Reston, Arthur Krock – to editorial positions. He preferred to "never put a Jew in the showcase" lest the *Times* be devalued "in Gentile circles." Reporters named Abraham – Raskin, Rosenthal, Weiler – still had bylines only with the initial "A." Not until 1976, fifteen years after Sulzberger relinquished control to his son, would the *Times* have a Jewish editorial page editor: Max Frankel, the child refugee from Germany who confessed that he was "much more deeply devoted to Israel than I dared to assert."[67]

CHAPTER 5

Conquest and Occupation: 1960–1979

The decade of relative calm following the Sinai war enabled Israel to focus on the daunting challenges of immigrant absorption, economic development, and state-building. For hundreds of thousands of Jewish refugees who fled from Arab countries, as for a younger generation of Israelis, the Holocaust belonged to another time, another place. But on May 23, 1960 Prime Minister Ben-Gurion stunned the nation with his announcement that a Mossad team had captured Adolf Eichmann, smuggled him out of Argentina and brought him to Israel to stand trial.

Israelis, *Times* foreign correspondent Lawrence Fellows wrote, responded with "elation" to news of Eichmann's capture, expressing "satisfaction that ran deeper than a simple desire for revenge." The trial of the notorious Nazi "by due process of law in a Jewish State, seemed to be unsurpassable ironic justice." Eichmann, an editorial declared, would "undoubtedly receive as fair a trial in Israel as anywhere on the globe." But *Times* editors "share the opinion widely held outside of Israel that Israel is not the place for Eichmann to be tried." His crimes, after all, "were committed against humanity ... not in Israel but in Europe." A trial in Jerusalem would "do Israel more harm than good." It was, therefore, in the interest of "all civilization ... not in the interest of Israel alone," that Eichmann be tried by "an international tribunal representing the conscience of the international community."[1]

The preferred *Times* location for Eichmann's trial was Germany, where "a people who will have those crimes on their collective conscience for all time" would stand in judgment. Whether by an international or German tribunal, it "would be a far more impressive demonstration of retributive justice" than if Eichmann were to be tried in Israel.[2] Either alternative would undermine any claim by Israel to speak on behalf of world Jewry, whether dead or alive, a claim the *Times* resolutely opposed.

Eichmann, Fellows wrote, "was never a personality like Hitler, Goebbels or Goering." Anticipating Hannah Arendt's subsequent characterization of him as "a desk-level bureaucrat" who exemplified "the banality of evil," he identified Eichmann as merely a "bureaucrat ... who headed the Gestapo's Jewish department." Indeed, it would be difficult to document Eichmann's actions because "he was a cautious, unglamorous civil servant." But Israelis had turned "deaf ears" to suggestions that they had "no right to try a man who committed neither crimes against Israeli nationals nor crimes on Israeli soil."[3] Embracing Eichmann's bureaucratic "banality," the *Times* once again averted attention from the Holocaust horrors that it had previously consigned to its inside pages, when it even noticed them.

Prime Minister Ben-Gurion was provided with an opportunity to respond to critics. In a *Magazine* article he insisted that Hitler's brutality offered "a unique case" of an attempt to exterminate "an entire people." Evidently familiar with the sources of *Times* discomfort, he declared that "only a Jew with an inferiority complex" could claim that "ethically" Israel should not try Eichmann because his crimes were "against humanity and the conscience of humanity." It was "foolish" to assert (as the *Times* insisted) "that these Jews were not part of our people but merely shared the same religious beliefs." Eichmann's victims "were not murdered because they were international people," Ben-Gurion pointedly observed, "but only because they were Jews." Therefore, "it is historic justice that he be tried by a Jewish state."[4]

The Eichmann trial touched sensitive nerves at the *Times*. Sulzberger complained to Managing Editor Turner Catledge that the newspaper had referred to the Jewish "race." Jews, he wrote, "are not a race; they also are more than a religion." The word "people" would be "least offensive" to the publisher, who advised Catledge: "Watch out in all cases when you're talking about the Jewish race or the Israelis." Several days into the trial the *Times* reported an allegation by the American Council for Judaism that "Zionism" was "exploiting" it "in an effort to link all Jews to the State of Israel." The Council claimed that "Israeli-Zionist officials" were referring to "'the Jewish people' to imply automatic nationalistic relationship to the State of Israel," which the Council resolutely denied.[5]

Israel, wrote Homer Bigart (who covered the trial for the *Times*), "set out to prove that Eichmann was a fiendish arch-killer of Jews – the chief butcher." But he was, in reality, "a dull and completely predictable witness" who displayed "the image of a petty bureaucrat." In sharp contrast Bigart described witness Zivia Lubetkin, one of the leaders of the Warsaw Ghetto uprising (and among the postwar founders of kibbutz Lohamei HaGeta'ot), as "a thin woman with a sharp, embittered face ... livid with hate." The trial, Fellows suggested, was intended to teach young Israelis who did not feel Jewish about "their heritage of suffering." Another "undercurrent," he conjectured, and "a particularly unpleasant one," was the tendency "to fix blame of a sort for the whole Nazi chapter on Christianity." It might have been better, he suggested, if charges against Eichmann had been restricted to "transport officer."[6]

Between Eichmann's conviction for war crimes and crimes against human-ity and his punishment by hanging, Sulzberger reflected at length on his own Jewish identity. Tracing his American ancestry to "around 1700," when mem-bers of his mother's family had arrived from Holland, he disavowed any sug-gestion that Judaism "plays a large or important part of my life." Defining it as "a religion plus," he hastened to add: "I am not a political Jew. I don't feel any affinity for the State of Israel but only sympathy with those who, being home-less, made it their refuge." He mentioned his resignation from Shearith Israel, the former Spanish-Portuguese Synagogue (where one of his maternal ances-tors was the rabbi during the colonial era), "because at one of their gatherings they chose to sing Hatikva ... and bracketed it with the Star-Spangled Banner."[7]

In May 1967 the *Times* reported increasing tension along Israel's bor-ders with Syria and Egypt. The "persistent painful pinpricks of Arab guerilla raids jabbing into Israel from Syria," followed by "blunt Israeli threats of stern and sharp reprisal," prompted a concerned editorial. It warned that the "war of nerves," including "sword rattling, the troop movements, the military alerts and the assorted alarums," might yet trigger "a major conflict that none of the parties want."[8]

Assessing the situation, veteran *Times* military analyst Hanson W. Baldwin concluded that the primary objectives of Egyptian President Nasser were "Yemen, Aden and oil," not war with Israel. Zionism and Israel were merely his pretext "to forge a superficial appearance of Arab unity." Yet the chance of "accidental" war remained, especially if Egypt blockaded the Strait of Tiran, shutting down Israel's only southern port in Eilat. But the Arab "army," Baldwin wrote dismissively, was nothing but a "mob" of "fellaheen," lacking "the cement of discipline." Israel, however, enjoyed the "intangibles of military power": pro-fessional leadership and skills, mobile and air warfare, and "élan." He concluded that "neither side has enough superiority to court all-out war."[9]

But amid its increasing likelihood, veteran correspondent Terence Smith arrived to supplement *Times* coverage. In Tel Aviv, "a city under siege," he focused on the "economic threat" to Israel from maintaining a mobilized army. In Jerusalem he found "a deliberate calm" as its residents prepared for the worst. At night, homes were "shrouded in blackout curtains." Even on the Sabbath Orthodox Jews were digging trenches. Long lines stretched outside blood donation centers. Roman Catholic nuns, replacing sanitation men called to military service, cleaned the streets.[10]

From a less endangered location, Washington columnist Tom Wicker proposed that Nasser be granted the sovereignty he desired over the Strait of Tiran; "in return, he might agree to bar the Strait only to Israeli-flag vessels." To Wicker, if not to Israelis, that seemed an acceptable compromise. Writing from Paris, C.L. Sulzberger airily observed: "Chicken as played in Palestine" was "in the hands of hotheads." Nasser had demonstrated "remarkable acumen and derring-do," while insisting on the destruction of Israel and return to the *status quo ante* preceding Jewish statehood. War seemed inevitable, to be fought over "mankind's most insane incentives to kill – race, religion and ideology."[11]

On June 5, following Egyptian military mobilization along the Sinai border, Israeli jets launched a preemptive strike that virtually destroyed the Egyptian air force. A massive Israeli ground attack forced Egyptian military evacuation from the entire Sinai Peninsula. Reporting from Tel Aviv, James Reston wrote of Israelis: "These people have gone to war with remarkable calm and kindliness to one another." Detecting "a curious combination of sadness and determination," he was struck by "the thoughtfulness of simple people caught in a common predicament." Their "discipline and spirit" were "admirable." He imagined Israeli soldiers "smoking and singing like Hemingway's heroes at the start of the Spanish Civil War."[12]

Other *Times* reporters preferred biblical analogies. J. Anthony Lukas observed that "the descendants of Isaac and the descendants of Ishmael are fighting for the Land of Canaan" in a "tangled, emotion-laden dispute." As the Israel Defense Forces surrounded the Old City of Jerusalem, Seth S. King anticipated the imminent "return [of] the site of King Solomon's temple to the control of a Jewish state after nearly 2,000 years." Once Israel fended off foreign criticism and demands for a cease-fire, Reston discerned a sharp change in mood among its citizens: "Relieved of last week's fear and now cock-a-hoop with military success, Tel Aviv is in no mood to go back to the old, dangerous frontiers." Noting that "the Arabs can lose a war and live, but Israel cannot," he braided praise and warning: Israel "can outfight the Arabs. But they cannot outbreed them."[13]

On June 7, the third day of fighting, Israeli soldiers triumphantly returned to the Old City of Jerusalem, where Jews had lived for millennia before their expulsion in 1948. Ecstatically singing Hallel prayers, they "wept and prayed" at the "Wailing Wall." *Times* reporter Terence Smith vividly described the scene as soldiers, submachine guns "slung over their shoulders," were "trembling with emotion." Chief Military Rabbi Shlomo Goren, who arrived with a Torah scroll and joyously blew his shofar, declared: "We are entering the messianic era. We shall never leave this place." On the Temple Mount above, Smith reported, Israeli soldiers "lounged in the sunlight" and an Israeli flag "flapped from the golden crescent atop the mosque."[14]

The Israeli capture of Gaza and Jordan's "West Bank," wrote *Times* foreign correspondent Seth S. King, "suddenly left her with the responsibility for many of the 900,000 refugees" who had fled Palestine nineteen years earlier. "Israeli victories have reopened the painful problem of what should be done with these unhappy people." King suggested that Israel would assume a "tremendous burden ... if she kept very much of what she had taken." Its captured Jordanian territory, he opined, "is among the least desirable on earth" with "no ready assets" – other than its (unmentioned) identity as the biblical homeland of the Jewish people; and the historic Jewish Quarter of Jerusalem's Old City, demolished nineteen years earlier.[15]

Writing from London Anthony Lewis, awarded a Pulitzer Prize for his coverage of the Supreme Court, made his debut as a commentator on Israeli affairs. Reporting urgent British government efforts to persuade Israelis "to halt their military sweep" to the Jordan River lest King Hussein be driven from power, he quoted "an informed diplomatic source" claiming that it was "very short-sighted of Israelis to risk that kind of political change in Jordan for a few more miles of territory." Columnist James Reston wrote a more admiring summary. "Israelis are not only a nation but a family," he observed during the war. They demonstrated "what can be done by an intelligent and courageous people with a common purpose," behaving "as if the life of the nation was everything and their personal lives were incidental." It was, Reston concluded, "a plain case of survival, and they worked together in that quiet and selfless way men and women do when everything is at stake."[16]

The next day Reston reported a split in the Israeli government over the retention of wartime territorial gains. Prime Minister Levi Eshkol and Foreign Minister Abba Eban "understand" the "holy row" in religious communities worldwide should Israel retain exclusive control over the Old City, with its Muslim and Christian holy sites. But Defense Minister Moshe Dayan and his military colleagues were willing to concede control over the Temple Mount, site of the ancient Jewish Temples, to Jordan. Perceiving the "extraordinary influence" of the military in Israeli public affairs, Reston suggested that "one of the mysteries of the past twenty years" was how Israel had "avoided being taken over by some popular military dictatorship," as though the democratic Jewish state was indistinguishable from its Arab neighbors.[17]

In a torrent of postwar editorials and unsigned commentaries within the space of four days, the *Times* analyzed the dramatic transformation wrought by the Six-Day War. In "Bind Up the Wounds," the first editorial comment insisted that "the interests of the world community in avoiding nuclear war must take precedence over local quarrels, important as they may seem to the nations involved." It urged that "a serious effort must be made to redress the legitimate grievances of the Arab world, none more important than the resettlement of Arab refugees." Regarding Israel's "legitimate grievances," including two decades of unremitting Arab hostility, terrorist attacks, and war, *Times* editors remained silent.[18]

The following day, in an unsigned exploration of the "Mideast Upheaval," the *Times* acknowledged the Israeli demonstration that "force and determination can eliminate the unbearable." But it cautioned that "these qualities cannot evoke the wisdom and charity now needed to produce the desirable." In a nearby editorial, pleading "Let There Be Peace," *Times* readers were reminded (yet again inaccurately) that during Israel's war for independence "nearly a million Palestinian Arabs were dispossessed" and now constitute "a growing source of danger and reproach." Although Israel had just won "a great victory with skill and bravery," the Jewish state "must be prepared to help the Palestinian refugees" and, bolstered by foreign aid, "bring about their absorption into the economy and politics of their region."[19] There was no mention of any responsibility by Israel's Arab neighbors to absorb and grant citizenship rights to their Palestinian residents, who had been confined to miserable refugee camps for two decades.

Two days later *Times* editors recognized that a divided Jerusalem had been "a monstrosity." Conceding that "the emotional, historic and religious importance of the city to Judaism for thousands of years is undeniable," it nonetheless asserted that "Israel's true interest lies in a lasting peace settlement if obtainable rather than in territorial gains." At least in the short term, a Swedish proposal to place holy sites under UN supervision could be implemented.[20]

Times discomfort over the stunning Israeli triumph quickly intensified. Israel, wrote C.L. Sulzberger one week after the war ended, must show "more tolerance and generosity" than was evident in Moshe Dayan's "paeans of triumph." Calling on the government to "bridle" the defense minister, he urged it to "influence a suddenly overconfident and resurgent Israel along the path to wisdom." (Sulzberger ignored Dayan's order to withdraw IDF paratroopers from the Temple Mount and forbid Jewish prayer on that holiest Jewish site.) Three days later, a *Times* editorial proclaimed the necessity for Israel, "the lightning conqueror, to show magnanimity to her victims" – indeed, "seek to heal their wounds, not inflame them further." For eighteen years Israel had "refused to repatriate substantial numbers of Arab refugees without a stable peace settlement." With its conquest, however, the refugee problem "has been transferred to Israel's hands"; it must find "a solution ... [and] explore formulas for gradual reconciliation."[21]

Three months after the war ended, delegates from eight Arab states met in Khartoum to frame policy toward the Jewish state. Affirming "the unity of Arab ranks," they unanimously proclaimed: "no peace with Israel, no recognition of Israel, no negotiations with it." For *Times* editors, who imaginatively spun Arab obduracy into an editorial entitled "Positive Notes at Khartoum," this unequivocal rejection of Israel represented "a modest first step toward peace in the Middle East." Less than a year later the Charter of the newly formed Palestine Liberation Organization (PLO) eerily echoed long-standing *Times* anti-Zionist precepts, proclaiming: "Judaism, being a religion, is not an independent nationality. Nor do Jews constitute a single nation with an identity of its own; they are citizens of the states to which they belong."[22]

By then the *Times* had begun to pay attention to some consequences of the stunning Israeli military victory in Hebron, the ancient biblical city (and King David's first capitol) twenty miles south of Jerusalem. With a dateline reading "Hebron, Jordan," James Feron described "Occupation Frictions." In accordance with the terms of compromise reached between local Arab leaders and the Israeli military, an Israeli soldier had turned Jews away from prayer in "Haram el Khalil" (using its Arab name rather than the Hebrew "Me'arat HaMachpelah") to permit Arabs to take their turn. But "a different aspect" emerged several minutes later when another soldier chased and caught an Arab peddler, "threw his fabric to the ground, punched him in the face, [and] kicked him." That was "a harsh language," Feron wrote, "but one that seems to be coming into increasing use on the West Bank." Indeed, Hebron Arabs expected "a brutal occupation" in revenge for their 1929 massacre.[23]

Returning to Hebron nine months later, Feron reported the presence of eighty "ultra-Orthodox Jews" (in fact, some were secular Israelis) who had moved into the Park Hotel to celebrate the Passover holiday – and remained there to reestablish a Jewish presence in the city. In an action likely to "infuriate"

Arab leaders, the Israeli government had authorized the military governor to "attend to the defense and housing needs" of the newcomers. Hebron Mayor Ali Ja'abari insisted that "Israelis should not be allowed to settle in Hebron," where "the people" did not want them.[24]

A new postwar threat confronted the Jewish state. *Haaretz* columnist Amnon Rubenstein reported in the *Times* a series of deadly Palestinian terrorist attacks against Israeli civilian targets. Launched in the Central Bus Station in Tel Aviv, the Mahane Yehuda outdoor market in Jerusalem, and the entrance to the Machpelah shrine in Hebron, they had been designed "to meet one criterion: killing the maximum number of people." But the greatest success of these "fedayeen terrorists" had been "virtually to kill any prospect of a peaceful settlement" and to strengthen Israeli resolve to maintain military control over the West Bank. Rubenstein noted that any Israeli retaliation triggered "an almost reflexive denunciation by world opinion and by the U.N.," which only made Israelis "more contemptuous of the world outside."[25]

The massacre of eleven Israeli athletes at the Munich Olympics in 1972 was extensively covered in the *Times*. Describing "an invasion of the Olympic village by the Arabs," reporter David Binder referred to "Arab commandos" who broke into Israeli team headquarters and inflicted murderous carnage. There was no mention of the Palestinian Black September group, the faction of the PLO (founded eight years earlier) that was responsible for the attack. Describing a "murderous assault" by "Arab fanatics," which "plumbed new depths of criminality," an editorial blithely asserted: "Arab terrorists made it plain that their real target was civilized conduct among nations, not merely Israel or the Israeli athletes captured and killed yesterday."[26] The editors failed to explain why, if that was true, only Israelis were targeted for murder.

Its concluding editorial praised Deputy Prime Minister Yigal Allon, standing before the coffins of the murdered athletes, who "cautioned his outraged countrymen that the crimes of extremists do not warrant extremist reprisals." After the "human tragedy," according to *Times* editors, the "next saddest result" was the setback it provided to "those forces inside Israel who have been advocating a more conciliatory policy toward the Palestinian Arabs." The Black September "movement of gangsters" who perpetrated the Munich attack should not claim "to be considered leader of the Palestinian cause."[27]

In early October 1973 Terence Smith reported the eruption of "heavy fighting ... between Israeli and Arab forces" that began when "Egyptian forces managed to cross the Suez Canal" while "a large-scale Syrian force ... supported by Syrian war-planes launched a simultaneous attack on a broad front" in the

Golan Heights and northern Israel. Two *Times* editorials followed the outbreak of what became known as the Yom Kippur War. "Neither Arabs nor Jews," it admonished both Arab attackers and their Israeli targets, "have anything to gain through force of arms." The most urgent task was "to call off the fighting and use this clash of tension as a somber catalyst for starting real negotiations toward a long elusive peace settlement." The following day it acknowledged that "the aggression perpetrated by Egypt and Syria … cannot be condoned or justified."[28]

But the primary editorial focus quickly became the necessity for Israeli restraint. The "inescapable lesson" of the Six-Day War was that "military victory offers no road to enduring peace, whatever the gains in territory." Israeli strategists must recognize "the dangers of long-term warfare and political unrest which such action could bring down upon themselves – and the rest of the world." Israelis would "repeat the initial blunder of the Arab states if they attempted to cross the 1967 lines in the misguided expectation that this would give them a more secure political future."[29]

Upsetting *Times* strategy, Israeli military forces led by Ariel Sharon boldly crossed the Suez Canal and established a beachhead within twenty miles of Cairo, while in the north IDF soldiers recaptured the Golan Heights and moved within artillery range of Damascus. The *Times* warned against continued Israeli air attacks on Damascus and near Cairo, which marked "an ominous escalation." It was "a dangerous delusion" for combatants to expect that continued fighting would yield "diplomatic as well as military dividends. … Nothing that either side can possibly expect to gain on the battlefield can justify that risk."[30]

From New York the *Times* provided a previously unknown professor of literature at Columbia University with an opportunity to expound on the larger meaning of the conflict. Identified as a "Palestinian Arab," Edward Said (who had grown up in a wealthy Cairo family) described himself as an "intellectual of secular persuasion." No Jew, he asserted, can "immerse himself in his ancient tradition and so lose the Palestinian Arab … and what Zionism has done to him." He supported the Palestinian alternative to Israel: "a secular democratic state for … Jews *with* Arabs."[31] With the *Times* imprimatur, Said's career as a prominent Palestinian advocate was launched.

As the Yom Kippur War entered its third week the *Times* critique emerged with sharper clarity. Correspondent Terence Smith noted that "hard-line" Israeli groups were bolstered by the Arab attack. Right-wing leader Menachem Begin could now argue that the war "demonstrated beyond a doubt that the Arab territories acquired in 1967 were crucial to Israel's basic security interest." But an American freelance writer researching a book in Israel reported his conversation with a wounded Israeli soldier who believed that "we should be ready to give back territories for peace." An *Al Ahram* correspondent in Cairo concluded that "Israel's invincibility has been shattered beyond repair." American government support for Israel, he asserted, now meant "support of the continued occupation of Arab territories." Nothing less than full Israeli withdrawal of military forces to pre-1967 lines was acceptable.[32]

But *Haaretz* columnist Amnon Rubenstein, dean of the Tel Aviv University law school, informed *Times* readers that following the Arab attacks "there are no more doves left in Israel." The Yom Kippur War had taught Israel "the realities of the unfathomable Arab hatred which she is facing." Every Israeli, he wrote, "can visualize the impact of a surprise attack if launched along the pre-1967 armistice lines." Even his left-wing newspaper advocated an Israeli military crossing beyond the armistice lines and "taking over strategically important territory – 'to cut not merely the fingers but the hand which was raised against us.'" A "definitive change in the Israeli mood," Rubenstein observed, had eased the way for a new "hard-line policy."[33]

Rubenstein's cogent analysis demonstrated what the *Times* conspicuously lacked: a correspondent in Israel who could write informatively about its society, politics, culture, and strategy. Instead, the *Times* continued to rely on an array of reporters, at times as many as half a dozen, who were inclined to repeat conventional pieties based on little knowledge derived from limited sources. During the Yom Kippur War they were reduced to offering second-hand summaries spiced with trivial clichés, exemplified by the correspondent who described an Israeli soldier with "a Biblical face and beard."[34]

Once again, as in 1967, Arab armies had been routed. After three weeks of fighting a cease-fire left Israeli military forces in control of half the land area west of the Suez Canal, with the elite Egyptian Third Corps of 20,000 fighters completely encircled and main routes to Cairo severed. The Israel Defense Forces had regained the Golan Heights and controlled a bulge to the east that brought it within twenty-five miles of Damascus. But *Times* reporter Terence Smith found an Israeli soldier who insisted: "We have got to learn to live with them. If we do, this war will have been worth it." A *Times* editorial criticized "hard-line Israelis" for their angry response to American pressure for a cease-fire "short of total humiliation of the Arab armies." Such "short-sighted intemperance," the *Times* hoped, might be offset by questioning "whether Sparta is really the most desirable model for modern Israel."[35]

Two years later the United Nations General Assembly branded Zionism "a form of racism and racial discrimination." *Times* editorials labeled the resolution "offensive, spiteful and futile – and stupid as well," deserving of "infamous oblivion." While attributing the UN resolution to "plain old anti-Semitism" and "the incitement of hatred against Jews," Anthony Lewis believed that it was also necessary to say "a word … about Israel's responsibility." Its policy "made it easier for the Arabs to push through an extremist resolution." Indeed, Israel "persistently refused to make a real commitment to return the Arab territories won in the 1967 war," as though it would be more secure if it retreated to the 1949 Armistice lines that had invited Arab aggression. For Lewis, Israel's "diplomatic line" was "so hard that moderate Arabs are given no encouragement and extremism thrives."[36]

In an article entitled "Zionism and Racism," A.M. El-Messiri, UN adviser from the League of Arab States, proclaimed that from his perspective as an "Afro-Asian" it was "not difficult to see Israel as yet another manifestation of a racist form of colonization – namely, settler colonialism." Zionist "visionaries," after all, had arrived in Palestine "under the aegis of British imperialism." (In fact, they began to arrive during late nineteenth century Ottoman rule.) It had been nothing less than "moral myopia," El-Messiri continued, "to try to solve Auschwitz by Deir Yassin" and concentration camps with Palestinian "dispersion." Concluding with a trope that had long been embraced by *Times* publishers and editors, he offered reassurance that condemnation of Zionism did not "imply any condemnation of Judaism. … To insist on the identity of Zionism and Judaism is to insist that all Jews are Zionists."[37]

Ten days later the *Times* published an essay by a journalist who early in his career had been advised by an editor (not at the *Times*) to change his recognizably Jewish name. Isidor Feinstein became known as I.F. Stone, appearing in an array of left-wing publications including *The Nation* and his own *I.F. Stone's Weekly*. An enthusiastic supporter of Jewish statehood between 1947 and 1948, he subsequently became an advocate of a bi-national Jewish and Palestinian state. The best way to blunt the UN "propaganda attack," Stone suggested in his *Times* article, would be "a mediatory peace initiative from the American Jewish community" that would "recognize the Palestinian Arabs as a people" and "relinquish the occupied territories to them." Three weeks later the *Times* published an analysis of Zionism by Harvard sociologist Nathan Glazer claiming that its identification with racism was "simply a lie," nourished by "an almost unreduced hatred" of Israel by Arabs.[38] But Lewis, El-Messeri and Stone had already preempted the conversation.

By then the *Times* had begun to pay attention to Jewish settlers, led by Gush Emunim, who were determined to restore a presence in the biblical homeland of the Jewish people. An editorial identified them as "expansionist-minded squatters" who would harm relations between Israel and the United States. The editors approvingly cited "a young New York-based organization called Breira," which had gathered "wide support among influential Jewish intellectuals" for its critique of Gush Emunim. The fledgling group was "overcoming ... the misapprehension of many Jewish Americans that criticism of Israeli policies would be seen as a rejection of Israel."[39]

On July 4, 1976 Israel temporarily regained favor in the *Times*. In a "daring night-time raid," Terence Smith reported, Israeli commandos landed at the Entebbe airport to free more than one hundred hostages held by "pro-Palestinian hijackers" of an Air France airliner. The "spectacular rescue operation," ending "seven days of terror" for the captives, had "electrified" Israelis. For his colleague Drew Middleton, Israel's "strategic and tactical surprise, achieved through deception," was the key to its stunning rescue in an operation "with no precedent in military history." A *Times* editorial hailed its "courageously conceived and brilliantly executed rescue." Israelis had demonstrated that "the criminal terrorist practice of holding the lives of innocent civilians for ransom to achieve political ends can be successfully thwarted by ... resourcefulness, determination – and guts."[40]

Between the Yom Kippur War and Menachem Begin's election as prime minister four years later *Times* editorial commentary about Israel veered from occasional praise to frequent criticism. Hailing Israel as "one of the most democratic countries of the world," it challenged the "almost morbid zeal" of the United Nations for finding "ever new pretexts" for condemning the Jewish state while evading "the lunacy of terrorism" that Yasser Arafat embraced. It nonetheless criticized Israel for its "rigid stance" in shunning the PLO. It was "simple to recite reasons of history, law and morality" to refuse contact with Israel's sworn enemy, but *Times* editors expressed confidence that negotiations would moderate the hostility of Palestinian "terrorist ideologues."[41]

Jewish settlements increasingly became a prime target of *Times* editorial ire. "Colonizing selected regions in the occupied territories" may have offered "strategic merit" in 1967, but Israeli policy had come to resemble "deliberate territorial expansionism." It might rank among "the most benign military occupations of modern times," but occupation was nonetheless "a festering irritant" for Israel. Condemning "the hardline Gush Emunim bloc," editors once again praised Breira for rallying "influential Jewish intellectuals" in opposition to settlement efforts. Israel, an editorial warned with patriotic fervor, "cannot go it alone diplomatically without sooner or later undermining other American interests in the Middle East."[42]

In May 1977 the *Times* confronted a transformative moment in Israeli history: the election of Menachem Begin as its first right-wing prime minister. Unlike *Time*, which memorably identified Begin with the name that "rhymes with Fagin," the *Times* was more restrained. But Begin confronted *Times* editors with a distinctive challenge to their assimilationist values. He was – by background, language, and religious observance – Israel's first "Jewish" prime minister. His predecessors had been secular socialists for whom the religion of Judaism was a Diaspora ghetto relic. But the murder of Begin's family during the Holocaust framed his responses to Arab attempts to annihilate Israel; he perceived Yasser Arafat as another Hitler.

William E. Farrell, newly identified as the *Times* "Correspondent in Israel," carefully scrutinized Begin's political career. He described a "firebrand orator – a hero to some, a demagogue to others, with still a touch of the pariah about him because of his Irgun days." During twenty-nine years in the Knesset Begin had thrust "his unavailing shafts against the Government" while enduring "the dislike and derision" of successive Labor Party prime ministers. "A friendly man, an artful politician with a bag of parliamentary skills," he was "an unabashed fundamentalist in his views on Judea and Samaria." His position, Farrell noted, had been stated in a 1948 radio broadcast: "The homeland is historically and geographically an entity. Whoever fails to recognize our right to the entire homeland does not recognize our right to any of its territories." Menachem Begin, Farrell concluded, "says what he means."[43]

CBS News Diplomatic Correspondent Marvin Kalb contributed his impressions of Israel in a historic moment of transition that was "electric with political activity, gossip and speculation." At the Western Wall during a Friday evening visit, Kalb was approached by a "well-dressed" Israeli who told him: "No Israeli government can, or will, give up Jerusalem." Visiting Masada, the ancient desert fortress site of the desperate last stand of Jewish Zealots against Roman conquerors in 73 CE, Kalb wondered whether contemporary Israelis were "more like Samson" (presumably inclined to destroy their own state rather than make peace). But in the Galilee mountain town of Safed he encountered a Moroccan Jew who proudly defended his vote for Begin, "a man of principle" who "says what he means."[44]

Conservative columnist William Safire, the solitary *Times* defender of Israel on the Opinion page, also identified Begin as "a man of principle" who had recently rejected an offer from "superpowers of the media" to enter into negotiations with PLO "terrorists." Speaking with "unabashed passion" during a press conference, the newly elected prime minister had reviewed "the lessons of the holocaust ... to show how some Jews feel about negotiating with those who threaten Israel with extermination." Safire described Begin as "a waspish Jew, to use an oxymoron." At a time of "weathervane leadership" in the United States (under Jimmy Carter), Begin was truly an "Authentic" who did not "wet his finger, hold it up to the breeze, and then point the way."[45]

As President Carter attempted to nudge Begin and Egyptian President Anwar Sadat toward peace negotiations the issue of Jewish settlements became more salient in *Times* coverage. Begin had caused consternation in Washington after his election when he referred to "occupied" territories in the West Bank as the "liberated" homeland of Judea and Samaria. Reporter Moshe Brilliant identified the fledgling settlement of Elon Moreh in "occupied Jordan." But Beverly Bar-Illan, wife of internationally acclaimed Haifa-born pianist David Bar-Illan, recounted her husband's recital in the settlement of Kedum. After the performance, an audience member told her: "It's been nearly 3,000 years since music was heard in these hills. ... The musician then was called David, too." She wondered: "Was it possible that the West Bank was to be like Kuwait, Abu Dhabi, Jordan and Saudi Arabia, where no Jew is allowed to live?"[46]

The appointment of Max Frankel as the first Jewish editorial page editor seemed to mark a significant milestone for the *Times* no less than for Frankel, capping his twenty-five years as foreign correspondent, Washington bureau chief and Sunday editor. A decade earlier, following the Six-Day War, Frankel, claiming "affection for Israel," had become its sharp critic when "it refused to use its military triumph to offer the Palestinians honorable terms." Concerned that the new Begin government "favored a Greater Israel not just for security but for biblical ideology," he spoke boldly in an editorial "to America's Jews *as* a Jew," criticizing American Jewish organizations for "spending their influence uncritically on behalf of every twist and turn in Israeli policy." Subsequently claiming that most *Times* editorials about Israel during the 1980s were written by "a proud, defiant Jew," Frankel chose to "escape the irrationality of the herd" while remaining "sentimentally faithful to the tribe whose genes I carry."[47] It proved to be a difficult balancing act.

After months of diplomatic maneuvering, William E. Farrell reported, the Begin-Sadat negotiations were jeopardized by continued Jewish settlement in the West Bank and Begin's insistence that Sinai settlements must remain in place even after the return of the peninsula to Egyptian sovereignty. His "sagacity and sincerity," Farrell reported, were being questioned as the result of his "apparent determination" to maintain Israel's settlement policy. His writings, Farrell suggested, shared the perspective of Jabotinsky (and Herzl) in their "almost total absence of recognition of the fact that Arabs were living there."[48]

A spate of articles explored the political consequences of settlements. Correspondent Charles Mohr cited issues of international law and Israel's unwillingness to relinquish the "biblical 'Palestine'" that it won in 1967. Farrell examined the "borders-equal-security" debate within Israel. Noting the "great psychological meaning for a small but powerful nation" surrounded for thirty years by "hostile neighbors," he relied on critical analysis from left-wing *Haaretz* and Uri Avneri, once an Irgun fighter who had migrated to the political left and called for "a leap of faith" to surmount Israel's reluctance to relinquish land for promises of peace.[49]

As Jewish settlements multiplied editorial criticism increased. "Friends of Israel," the *Times* suggested, should oppose the efforts of "a few thousand emotional pioneers" who acted "with and without the connivance of Israeli authorities." *Times* editors were prepared to disregard "the juridical merits of Israeli claims," asserting that "the legalities, and the generally benign nature of Israeli occupation" were of "relatively modest weight" because settlements constituted "a serious obstruction to Middle East peace." Conceding that Israel "may well have a firmer title to Judea and Samaria than any of its enemies," its assertion of these claims "may make real peace impossible." The *Times* dismissed Prime Minister Begin's avowal of Israeli sovereignty there as "a position of historical bad faith and tactical folly."[50]

In advance of Begin's first White House meeting with President Carter, Farrell focused on his domestic political critics, including Defense Minister Ezer Weizman and former Foreign Minister Yigal Allon. He also noted a letter to the prime minister from three hundred army reservists expressing unprecedented public criticism of Begin's "hard line," which was "jeopardizing peace efforts." Several weeks later the *Times* reported that 25,000 Israelis had gathered in Tel Aviv to support the reservists' call for Israel's return of land to the Arabs. Many of them signed a "Peace Now" petition addressed to Begin, asserting: "Don't endanger peace for the sake of settlements."[51]

Considerably less attention was given to a far larger public rally to support Begin and express disapproval of the military officers' campaign for Israeli concessions. In an unsigned three-paragraph article the *Times* reported that an estimated 40,000 Israelis had rallied outside City Hall in Tel Aviv to demonstrate their support for a "Secure Peace." Speakers warned that "unwise concessions to the Arabs for the sake of a quick settlement would endanger Israel's survival."[52] The disparity of coverage for the rallies left little doubt about the *Times* preference for peace now.

In his Op-Ed debut Harvard doctoral student Leon Wieseltier located Begin's "firm politics" in "the lachrymose history of the Jews in exile." He belonged to a "damned and glorious generation" that had learned from Auschwitz the need for "bitter and unslackening vigilance, distrust, [and] self reliance." The precocious graduate student, soon to launch his career in journalism, suggested that "the trauma of the Jews must be honored" – but he cautioned: "the lesson of Auschwitz is not that Jews should conquer." Auschwitz was "a mandate for peace"; Israelis needed "a new heroism – not the heroism of the Warsaw Ghetto." Pragmatism, he claimed, "has its own nobility."[53]

Two days later the *Times* reported that fifteen Palestinian terrorists (including two women) had landed by boat south of Haifa, seized a public bus heading toward Tel Aviv, and murdered thirty-seven Jewish passengers (including a five-year-old girl and an American photographer). The bus hijacking and murders, Moshe Brilliant wrote, constituted "the bloodiest attack on Israel by Arab guerillas" since the Six-Day War, plunging the nation into "gloom, grief and anger." In the same issue, coincidentally, columnist Tom Wicker, irritated by criticism of President Carter's Middle Eastern policy, complained that "some Jews think the only 'square deal' for Israel is to give Israel what it wants." But, he concluded, any suggestion that the American government or American Jews "should merely acquiesce in Israeli policy falls of its own weight."[54]

A *Times* editorial condemned "the senseless terror against Israelis" – while noting, with the moral equivalence soon to become its preferred trope, that "in their torment Israelis also hate." It called on Israel's Arab neighbors to demonstrate "their acceptance of the Jewish state ... and stand with Israel against Palestinian wrongs." Another editorial, two days later, supported Israel's temporary military seizure of a six-mile zone in south Lebanon as a demonstration of its "need for elementary security." But A.M. Rosenthal notified the foreign editor that *Times* reporting of Israeli retaliatory action, including the death of three Israeli soldiers, had "unwittingly slighted the deaths of Arabs. ... We look indifferent."[55]

A more anguished response came from writer Cynthia Ozick, whose fourteen-year-old cousin Imri, the son of concert musicians, had been killed in the recent terrorist attack. Responding to a Palestinian military spokesman who justified the carnage, she poignantly identified the youth as "a fallen soldier in the army of clarinets" and a member of "the army of civilization." Columnist William Safire defended the Israeli military response: "Not only will the murder of its citizens not be tolerated," he wrote, "but no place from which such attacks are planned and staged can be inviolate," even in "today's blame-Israeli atmosphere."[56]

The *Times* allotted substantial space for exculpation of Palestinian terrorism. The Syrian ambassador to the United States explained in an

Opinion column: "the Palestinians are resorting to violence because they are desperate and still deprived of a homeland." He predicted: "Until they have one, conflict between those deprived of a homeland and those who have usurped it is inevitable." Several days later Egyptian President Anwar el-Sadat suggested that "psychological barriers blurred the vision of millions [of Israelis] … and rendered them totally incapable of thinking of peace, let alone working for peace." He asserted that "there is no alternative to conceding to the Palestinian people their right to self-determination" as "masters of their destiny in their own homeland."[57]

Bolstering the mantra of Israeli culpability, Anthony Lewis criticized American Jewish leaders for their "posture of total, uncritical support for Israeli government policy." Their response was "an insult to the intelligence of American Jews." Jewish tradition, Lewis claimed, was characterized by "the greatest diversity and intellectual independence." Therefore, American Jews, who are "contentious," not "conformist," should not blindly support the pro-Israel views of their organization leaders.[58]

One week later Lewis, emerging as the *Times'* incessantly hectoring Jewish critic of Israel, lamented the loss of hope that followed Sadat's historic visit. Begin "did not seem aware of, or sensitive to, the scale and risk" of that effort. In his Knesset response the Israeli prime minister had failed to display "the barest gesture of awareness that Arabs, too, have suffered." Lewis dismissed Begin's assertion that UN Resolution 242, which called for Israeli withdrawal "from territories," not "the" territories or "all the territories" that it won during the Six-Day War, as merely "a legalistic argument" (curious criticism from the *Times* legal authority). Comparing Begin unfavorably to De Gaulle for his inability "to put aside nationalist ideology for the sake of his country's true peace," Lewis implicitly identified Israel's retention of its biblical homeland with French colonization of Algeria.[59]

Protracted Israeli-Egyptian negotiations over land for peace tested the patience of *Times* editors and disclosed the source of their unease: "The idea that a Government of Israel might be diplomatically unwise or chauvinistically greedy sticks in the throat of American Jews, and for good reason." Israel, they wrote, was "a moral creation, atoning for the slaughter of millions of European Jews, the embodiment of a humane, ethical society." Confronting the tension between Jewish liberalism and Israeli national interest, the editors expressed concern that Prime Minister Begin's "grudging response" to President Sadat's peace initiatives would undermine Israel's moral credibility. They lauded several dozen prominent American Jewish intellectuals and rabbis for signing a petition (circulated by liberal *Moment* editor Leonard Fein) sharply critical of Begin for his intransigence. Their public expression of "anguish" over his "dream of a Greater Israel" legitimized "the very idea of criticism of Israel in our political life." Such criticism, according to *Times* editors, "ought to strengthen support for Israel."[60]

Menachem Begin puzzled, and more frequently infuriated, the *Times*. When four hundred members of Peace Now picketed his home, William Farrell wrote, Begin castigated his Knesset critics "with the not inconsiderable oratorical skills he honed" during nearly three decades as leader of the Herut opposition. "It was very indecorous but not dull," Farrell observed, as Begin displayed "tenacity" in proposing "civil autonomy" for Palestinian Arabs while retaining an Israeli military presence for security and grounding his claim in "the Old Testament." The *Times* indicated its political preference by granting Labor Party leader Shimon Peres four columns to critique Begin's position. In an adjacent column European diplomatic correspondent Flora Lewis noted the "striking irony of history that at the time when Israel's most important Arab opponent at last offers peace, the leader of Israel should be a man dedicated to the Biblical concept of the holiness of land."[61]

While peace negotiations between Israel and Egypt continued, columnist Russell Baker imagined a letter from the Nobel Prize Committee to Begin requesting the return of the award given to him "by mistake." Reviving a centuries-old calumny against Jews, Baker impersonated Begin's response: "After I pay expenses for a trip to Oslo to pick up the Peace Prize, you want it back? And not even any mention of reimbursing me for the expenses, much less my time? Some nerve."[62] Baker was dismayed that the legalistic, avaricious Shylock of his imagination presided over a Jewish state.

"In the Middle East today," an editorial declared one month later, "we can think of no more important principle than Israel's respect for the human rights of the Arab population of the occupied West Bank." When negotiations between Begin and Sadat seemed to falter, the editors caustically inquired: "Is it for the safety of Jerusalem and Tel Aviv that Israel bargains, or for ancestral rights in Hebron?" Once again the solitary dissenting voice came from William Safire, the Jewish conservative who had joined the *Times* staff in 1978 after a stint as President Richard Nixon's speechwriter. Accusing President Carter of seeking "to jam an 'iffy' peace treaty down Israeli throats," he suggested that the administration lift its "heavy-handed pressure." With the successful culmination of negotiations even Anthony Lewis relented, praising Sadat, Begin and Carter for getting "the fundamental decisions right." Given domestic political pressures in Israel against relinquishment of the entire Sinai and the handful of Jewish settlements located there, Lewis acknowledged, "Begin played a difficult hand with great skill."[63]

On March 26, 1979, the morning of the historic signing of a peace treaty on the White House lawn, a *Times* editorial referred to Begin and Sadat as "the odd couple" who were "exchanging their most precious gifts: recognition and territory." Sadat accepted Israel as "a legitimately sovereign neighbor" while Begin yielded "land, resources and even settlements to the Arabs." But for the *Times* that was insufficient: Israel must "distinguish its security needs from territorial ambitions on the Arab-populated West Bank."[64] There was no hint that Israel might have legitimate historic claims and international legal rights to its ancient homeland.

Comparing the Israeli and Egyptian national leaders, columnist Flora Lewis identified Begin as the embodiment of "the politics of extremism and opposition," who "fed the flames of uncompromising faith in the vision of biblical Israel being restored." Displaying "the formality and pride of wordsmanship of Warsaw's prewar Jewish bourgeoisie," Begin "knows exactly what he thinks and never tires of repeating it, but that leaves no impression of candor or spontaneity." Sadat, by contrast, displayed a "rush of feeling that ... gives him his charm." Struck by the coincidence of Israel signing a peace treaty with its ancient oppressor while celebrating Passover and the exodus from Egypt 3,200 years earlier, Anthony Lewis claimed to discern "the legitimizing of Palestinian nationality in Israeli psychology." But for reasons he did not explore, "no Palestinian of note ... is ready to join in the negotiations."[65]

Preoccupied with Jewish settlements, the *Times* barely noticed a vicious Palestinian terrorist attack in the northern Israeli coastal town of Nahariya, inside Israel's recognized borders. Folded into an article about Cabinet approval for two new settlements, Bernard Gwertzman merely indicated that members of an Israeli family were assaulted in their home by Palestinian attackers. The husband and four-year-old daughter were dragged away and murdered; her two-year-old sister was accidentally smothered to death after their mother sought refuge in concealed crawl space.[66]

It was, however, among the ghastliest terrorist attacks in Israeli history. Four members of the Palestine Liberation Front had come ashore from Lebanon. After killing a police officer they raided an apartment building, took Danny Haran and his daughter hostage, and brought them to their rubber boat on the beach for the return trip to Lebanon. Instead, leader Samir Kuntar shot Haran in the back while his daughter watched; then he killed the girl by smashing her skull on the rocks. The *Times* provided brief coverage of their funeral. An editorial accused Israel of "exploiting the outrage" by resuming settlement construction, which would "inflame passions" and "make accommodation more difficult."[67]

It gave more expansive coverage, three weeks later, to the planting of vines and olive saplings near Hebron. "A group of liberal Jews" organized by Peace Now wished to demonstrate "sympathy and support" for local Arabs (who responded to their benevolent gesture by uprooting the plantings lest they constitute a Jewish claim to the land). It also noted, in passing, that a group of Jewish women from the nearby settlement of Kiryat Arba (accompanied by their thirty-five children) had begun a "sit-in" at the former Hadassah medical building in Hebron "to demonstrate their determination to strengthen their settlement."[68] It marked the return of Jews to Hebron half a century after the 1929 massacre.

Anthony Lewis was livid at the prospect of renewed Jewish settlement. He condemned Israeli Cabinet approval of a plan by "Jewish zealots" from Gush Emunim to build the Shiloh settlement near Nablus, "a town intense in its Arab feeling, a center of Palestinian nationalism" (first identified in the book of Samuel [3:21] as a sacred site of Jewish worship). It sent the message that "Israel intends to continue the occupation of the West Bank ... indefinitely." Lewis claimed that the hearts of "many Israelis ... cry out at what is happening to the country." Was this the Israel, he asked, "for which thousands gave their lives ... [and] Theodore Herzl dreamed?" For the *Times* columnist "the character of Israel" was at stake; and he was the self-appointed arbiter of its morality.[69]

Israel's peace treaty with Egypt marked a critical turning point in *Times* coverage. Relinquishment of the entire Sinai Peninsula and a commitment to destroy all Jewish settlements located there whetted its appetite for further Israeli concessions. The refusal of any other Arab state, to say nothing of the Palestine Liberation Organization ruled by Yasser Arafat, to negotiate terms of recognition of Israel that could secure "land for peace" was ignored. In the *Times* Israel was to blame for Arab intransigence.

CHAPTER 6

Arabs and Jews:
1979–1984

In May 1979 A.M. Rosenthal informed Moscow correspondent David Shipler that his next assignment would be in Israel. He was chosen, Rosenthal explained, "because we feel the need there of a correspondent who can not only write well, but who is sensitive and mature, who understands the diplomatic forces that will be at work in the next year or two, and who has the sensitivity to track the delicate peace process" – adding "what I hope will be a peace process."[1]

Shipler would become fascinated by the struggle between "Arab and Jew," the title of his Pulitzer Prize winning book following five years of reporting from Israel. There, he wrote, he developed "affection and distaste for those mounting the struggle, sympathy for the personal lives that were wrenched by the conflict, revulsion over the zealous intolerance that fueled the strife." He came to view both Palestinians and Israelis as victims: "Each has suffered at the hands of outsiders and each has been wounded by the other." But he also understood that the "hardships of the Palestinian Arabs in modern history bear no resemblance in scope or depth to those of the Jews. ... Their sense of distinctiveness as a Palestinian people has come not from an ancient source but largely in reaction to the creation and growth of Israel on part of the land where they lived."[2]

Soon after becoming Bureau Chief Shipler visited the settlement of Elon Moreh, "deep in Arab territory," where fifteen Jewish families had arrived to "nourish ancient Jewish claims." He was an attentive listener, noting that speaking with settlers was "to step from raging political debate outside into a circle of certainty and quiet logic." For them, he understood, "the motivation is biblical." They found their authority in Genesis 12, where God told Abraham: "I give this land to your descendants." He listened to Gush Emunim leader Benny Katzover explain: "For all our roots, this is a connection. This is the heart of Israel."[3]

In a lengthy interview with Moshe Dayan, Shipler asked: What had twelve years as "an occupying power" done to Israeli society? Dayan's succinct reply: not much. "There is no reason to establish a Palestinian state," Dayan continued. "It would just cause troubles." Eventually, he predicted, Jordan (with its Palestinian demographic majority) would become that state. Israelis, Shipler wrote one week later, displayed "the ambivalence of wishing to be both secure and just, of seeking both firm Jewish roots in ancient soil and peaceful relations with Arab neighbors. Sadly, these remain irreconcilable goals."[4]

During his early months in Israel Shipler focused on the polar extremes of conflict. Hebron Mayor Fahd Kawasmeh, who supported the PLO, expressed his willingness for Jews to return to the houses they lost in 1929 – if Arabs could return to their lost homes in Jaffa and Haifa. In the adjacent settlement of Kiryat Arba, Rachel Klein explained the necessity for the exercise of Jewish power. "I'm afraid I sound very intransigent," she conceded, "but in our history that's how we've managed to stay alive for 2,000 years." In the Jabaliya refugee camp in Gaza, Shipler introduced readers to a twelve-year-old boy whose parents and grandparents had joined "the flood of Palestinian Arabs" who fled in 1947 and 1948. These refugees, "held hostage by their dreams," desperately yearned "to go home." But their poignant wish, Shipler understood, implanted among Israelis "the fear [that] ... the goal is to return – and to annihilate Israel." Returning "home," he realized, was double-edged: debate in Israel had "flared," only a week earlier, when "militant Jewish nationalists called for a return to formerly Jewish homes" in the "exclusively Arab city of Hebron." Palestinians yearning to return were dreamers – but Jews who shared that dream were, for Shipler, "militant."[5]

One month after the murder of a twenty-three-year-old yeshiva student in Hebron, the Israeli government approved the restoration of Jewish habitation there. *Times* editors were dismayed by the return of Jews to their ancient capitol city, the burial site of their biblical patriarchs and matriarchs. "By one ruse or another," an editorial declared, "Jews are encroaching on the region's Arabs." Condemning Jewish "claims to ancestral homes," *Times* editors berated the Israeli government for its "provocative policy," warning that "colonizing" the West Bank was "bound to injure American interests."[6]

The return of Jews to Hebron aroused Anthony Lewis's ire. He criticized Israeli settlements in "occupied Arab territory" – "even in the heart of an Arab city." To be sure, he acknowledged, the "hills and stones" of the West Bank "have echoes of the Bible." But if Jews returned to live on "Arab land," they "would now be imposing on themselves a new kind of spiritual bondage." Labeling Hebron "a center of Palestinian national sentiment," he fancifully compared restored

Jewish settlement there to "a Moslem mission being installed by armed force in the midst of a Jewish community in, say, Brooklyn."[7]

In a lengthy *Magazine* article following his settlement visits Shipler offered a more nuanced perspective. He discovered "a special breed – young, conservative, idealistic, mistrustful of the peace accords." He understood that the Israeli "passion" for Judea and Samaria was grounded in "the Jewish connection to this land through the Bible, a deeply idealistic drive to return to religious-national roots." Recognizing that Israeli "national security" had been enhanced by Jordan Valley settlements previously authorized by the Labor Party, he found "newer hilltop settlements near Arab towns and cities … more difficult to justify." Resembling "lower-class, garden-apartment suburbs," they were inhabited by Jews who "tend to be skeptical" about the commitment of the United States to the defense of Israel.[8]

Shipler's analysis seemed to augur a new era of *Times* coverage in Israel. He offered readers a close-up view of West Bank geography in language that would enable any New Yorker to instantly grasp Israel's security concerns. Superimposing Jerusalem on Central Park, he indicated that its northern boundary would begin near Yankee Stadium, slicing westward to New Jersey near the Holland Tunnel. He noted among Israelis the "consensus of abiding fear" at the prospect of such proximity to their enemies. Demonstrating deeper understanding of Menachem Begin than was customary in the *Times*, Shipler observed (without reflexively mentioning "terrorist") that since his days in the "radical Irgun Jewish underground" Begin's unyielding determination had been "to keep the Jewish people proud and free, the antithesis of compliant and oppressed."[9]

Shipler visited the Machpelah shrine in Hebron where, for seven centuries, Moslems had forbidden Jews to enter. Summarizing the Genesis narrative of Abraham's purchase of the site for Sarah's burial place, he described it as "the ancient intersection of Islam and Judaism, for both Arabs and Jews believe they are descended from Abraham." Shipler reported interviews with Rabbi Moshe Levinger, founding leader of the restored Jewish community in Hebron, who unequivocally asserted Jewish rights to the site; and with Moslems who complained that Jewish soldiers and visitors did not remove their shoes before they entered the massive Isaac Hall. Jews, he noted, were pained to be deterred by their own government from rebuilding their destroyed community.[10]

Two weeks later the *Times* published an op-ed by Dov Ronen, a child Holocaust survivor and self-described "Israel dove" who, as "a liberal and a humanist," had relocated from the Jewish state to Harvard. Rejecting any "biblical right" to sovereignty in Judea and Samaria, he opposed Jewish settlements and even the opening of a yeshiva in Hebron. But he conceded that he had never heard "a clear statement ... even from a single Palestinian," that the establishment of a Palestinian state "would not be the first step toward the elimination of Israel."[11]

The next day Shipler reported a brutal attack in Hebron by Palestinian "terrorists" who murdered six Jews and wounded sixteen others. The victims were returning from prayer in Machpelah for Sabbath dinner in Beit Hadassah, the former medical clinic (identified as a "Jewish owned building" that was "occupied by militant settlers"). In a more detailed account of the horrific assault a day later, Shipler noted that two of the murdered Jews and four wounded young women in their twenties were native-born Americans. Reporting the political consequences of the attack, he revealed that Defense Minister Ezer Weizman, describing "a battle for the land of Israel," had ordered deportation of the mayors of Hebron and nearly Halhoul, who had "close ties" with the PLO. The expulsion order, Shipler wrote, "satisfied some recent pressure from Gush Emunim, a movement of militant, ultranationalist Jewish settlers."[12]

In his third consecutive daily report, with the conspicuous presence of American victims doubtlessly propelling *Times* coverage, Shipler wrote: "The unwritten rules, the tacit understandings, the silent code that kept the smoldering hostility from flaring into guerilla warfare has been swept away." But his focus had shifted from the Arab murderers (about whom virtually nothing was written) to "Arab and Jewish extremists," especially the latter. In retaliation for the Hebron attack Rabbi Meir Kahane and his followers had launched "rampages" through Arab towns, while "angry Israeli soldiers" assaulted Arab protesters.

The Hebron massacre, Shipler concluded, "broke the long immunity that had seemed to envelop the Jewish settlements." It targeted "the most controversial segment of the Jewish population, those regarded by many as too militant, too dogmatic and too provocative." He claimed to detect among Israelis "some sense, hard to capture," that the Jewish victims "were not wholly innocent." He returned to Hebron for the funeral of Eli Hazeev, an "ultranationalist" murdered in the Beit Hadassah attack, who had served in the American and Israeli armies and told friends "the only good Arab is a dead one."[13]

Anthony Lewis used the murder of Jews in Hebron to fuel his reflexive critique of Jewish settlers. Ignoring the Jewish victims he cited journalists covering the West Bank, especially from *Haaretz*, who "express alarm about the consequences for Israel of continued occupation." A *Times* editorial published the following week claimed: "Many Israelis concluded wisely in their grief that such violence is the inevitable fruit of a policy of provocative settlement."

It praised Eli Hazeev's father, attending his son's funeral, for refusing "to accept a rabbi's assurance that his son had died in a holy cause."[14]

Shipler was riveted by the odyssey of Hazeev, an American-born Christian who died as an Israeli Jew in Hebron "during his unfinished, violent search ... for a victory that always eluded him." Formerly James Eli Mahon, Jr. of Alexandria, Virginia, he had served two tours of duty in Vietnam where he suffered near-fatal wounds. He then worked as an FBI informant penetrating radical antiwar groups in Washington. Forty-eight hours after the Yom Kippur War ended he arrived in Israel, where he spent several months on a kibbutz and in a yeshiva, returning to Virginia to convert to Judaism. The following year he became an Israeli citizen, served in the elite Golani Brigade, joined Rabbi Kahane's Kach movement, left his Jerusalem home to live in Kiryat Arba, and spent eight months in prison for breaking into Arab homes in Hebron. He was, Shipler wrote, "a warrior who never won a war." Attending Hazeev's funeral in the ancient Jewish cemetery in Hebron, Shipler reported Chief Rabbi Goren's assurance to his parents that their son would be remembered among the "heroes of Israel." The rabbi was shocked when they expressed regret for their son's actions.[15]

Times editors seized on Hazeev's story, but not the Palestinian massacre that killed him, to reinforce their condemnation of an Israeli "policy of provocative settlement and annexation of the region." His biography affirmed the necessity of unrelenting opposition to Jewish settlements. While many heard "only a call to violent vengeance" from those who mourned his death, the editors were "deeply indebted" to Hazeev's parents for their "graveside wisdom"; his mother had said: "We keep honoring the dead. But they were dead wrong."[16]

The *Times* editorial was sharply criticized by New York Rabbi Ralph Pelcovitz, formerly a student at the Hebron Yeshiva in Jerusalem, who labeled it "a terrible distortion of the truth." Its focus on Hazeev, he wrote in a letter to the editors, was "a calculated attempt ... to discredit the Jewish settlers in Judea by creating an image of extremists and fanatics" who provoked "peaceful Arab inhabitants into counter-violence." He wondered why the *Times* had not applied similar scrutiny to the two innocent yeshiva students who were also murdered. Instead, the rabbi wrote, the *Times* had assaulted the character of "hundreds of decent, peace-loving Jewish families who reside on the West Bank," while desecrating the memory of "wonderful, gentle, God-fearing Talmudic scholars."[17]

The Hebron massacre, followed by a retaliatory attack from right-wing Israeli extremists that crippled two prominent Palestinian mayors, focused

Shipler's reporting on Jewish settlers. Mostly young married adults with children, they were "well-educated, lean and strong, articulate, bright, multilingual, pleasant and friendly." Describing them as "militant idealists" and "dreamers," yet "coldly logical," he perceived them as "a force that no Israeli government ... can ignore." He recognized that only a minority were "fervent ideologues"; most were "reverent Jews and devoted Zionists" whose beliefs "have surged through Jewish consciousness for thousands of years." Benny Katzover, leader of the Elon Moreh settlement (located, according to the Biblical narrative, where God had promised the land of Israel to Abraham and his descendants), told Shipler: "This is the beginning of all our connections to this land.... This is the heart of Israel."[18]

In June 1981 Israel shocked the world by launching a stunning bombing raid that destroyed the Iraqi nuclear reactor at Osirak. The attack, Shipler wrote, was intended to eradicate an imminent danger. But a furious *Times* editorial, claiming that Prime Minister Begin had embraced "the code of terror" of his "weakest enemies," condemned the "sneak attack ... [that] was an act of inexcusable and short-sighted aggression." Israel, the *Times* asserted, "risks becoming its own worst enemy." To editorial page editor Max Frankel it seemed "to be invoking an impermissibly aggressive right of 'self-defense.'" But in his memoir, published fifteen years later, Frankel identified the editorial among his "major mistakes."[19]

Most *Times* editorials on the Middle East between 1977 and 1986, Frankel subsequently wrote, were written by a "proud" Jew (himself), "defiant of the majority of American Jews who believed that a people so horrendously victimized could never do wrong." He contrasted himself with *Times* publishers who feared that Zionism "would exacerbate doubts about every Jew's ultimate loyalty." (Its evasion of the Holocaust, he would write in the newspaper's 150th anniversary issue, was "the century's bitterest journalistic failure.") Claiming that he was "much more deeply devoted to Israel than I dared to assert," he rejected Menachem Begin's "hawkish policies" while hoping that Israel "would find the confidence to recognize the Palestinians' Zion-like aspirations." Frankel insisted that his criticism of the Jewish state was driven by "affection for Israel."[20]

Columnist William Safire fulsomely praised Israel for its enormous "favors" to the world. He noted sardonically that not only had Israel denied to "an aggressive dictator the ability to inflict atomic terror"; it had "enabled the rest of the world to indulge in an orgy of hypocrisy" by lacerating the Jewish state. Israel, Safire wrote, "had the legal right and moral obligation to deny Iraq's dictator the capacity to bring about instant holocaust." As it had done at Entebbe, Israel "rescued its people from threatened slaughter by a bellicose dictator."[21]

Times editors remained adamant critics of the Osirak attack. Their second editorial within a week identified its "terrible price": further inflaming the Arab world and generating "heightened distrust of America in the Middle East." It labeled Israel's defenders as "romantics who think that daring and determination can devise a military fix for every danger." Israel must "run more risks for accommodation, encouraging especially Palestinians to trade steps toward peace for hunks of territory." Applause for Israel's "martial spirit" would only erode America's "moral obligation" to support it.[22]

But for *Maariv* columnist Jacobo Timmerman, "The World Demands Too Much From the Jews." Until the Osirak raid, Israelis – "isolated in the world" – had "found nothing strong enough to put at ease what we Jews call our 'historic memory.'" The "question of survival" was "the distinguishing sign of the Jewish psyche." Israel, he observed, is "trapped between … isolation and fear of a second holocaust." American journalist Sidney Zion, a committed Zionist and religiously observant Jew, mocked Israel's critics: "The world is outraged and the world will not forget. … It is angry with Menachem Begin, it is impatient, it is at wit's end. And so history becomes intolerable."

But history mattered to Zion. A decade earlier King Hussein had killed 10,000 Palestinians and driven the PLO out of Jordan. Israel's bombing of PLO enclaves in Beirut and invasion of Lebanon in 1978 were "minuscule" compared to what the Arab nations, especially Syria, had wrought there. "Yet the world sees Palestine," Zion wrote, "as wherever the Jews live." He wondered: "Why are we continuously advised that Begin is the obstacle to peace?" It was a question for which the *Times* had no answer. Instead, it excoriated Israel for its "aggressive militancy" when it needed "aggressively offered peace terms that promise more than the endless occupation of land bearing a million hostile Arabs."[23]

During Prime Minister Begin's re-election campaign Shipler focused on the political chasm between Israelis who were sounding "urgent alarms about anti-democratic trends" and those who displayed "a rising chauvinism that sees criticism as disloyal, treacherous and unpatriotic." Amid their acrimonious debate over "the vigor or fragility of democracy in Israel," the views of Begin's critics predominated in the *Times*. Shimon Peres, Begin's Labor Party challenger, described the election as a battle over "Israel's democratic soul." Jerusalem Mayor Teddy Kollek accused the Likud party of fostering "a hysterical personality cult which arouses fears of the growth of fascism." Hebrew University political scientist Yaron Ezrahi, a Peace Now activist who believed that settlers were "destroying Israel," criticized the elevation of Zionist "tribal" values over liberal democratic ideals. The *Times* responded to Prime

Minister Begin's election victory with a declaration that Israelis needed to be rescued from their "Masada complex" and diverted from their reliance on "military prowess."[24]

Begin's re-election prompted another laudatory column from William Safire. The prime minister, he wrote pointedly, makes "ultra-assimilated American Jews uncomfortable." Begin can seem "belligerent, rigid, didactic" – but, Safire added, "I like him." He might describe himself as "a simple man and a simple Jew," but Safire cited his remarkable foresight: he presciently anticipated the establishment of a Jewish state and warned of Hitler's holocaust; he realized the necessity of force in persuading the British government to keep its word on Palestine. He opposed assigning the West Bank to Jordan, "and now we see how right he was." He believed, despite eight election defeats, that he would become prime minister, and he did. Accused of being a war-monger, he made peace with Egypt. Safire identified Begin as "the most consistently under-estimated man in the world."[25]

On the eve of Begin's first meeting with President Reagan in September 1981 Shipler was skeptical. He cited a "contradiction between Israel the American asset and Israel the American burden." The close tie between the two nations "interferes with building the American-Arab relationship." But Israelis, he observed, "feel too vulnerable to adjust their defense policies to American convenience." Begin's style might be "prickly," but Shipler understood that he enjoyed a "broad public consensus" for his policies on the West Bank and deterrence of PLO terrorist attacks from Lebanon.[26]

An editorial focusing on Begin's Palestinian policy identified Israel as "the occupying master of 1.3 million Palestinians." High among the "anxieties" of Americans was "the fear that Israel is needlessly isolating itself by ever-bloodier reprisals" for Palestinian terror attacks. "Without a genuine grant of political rights to the West Bank Palestinians, Israel plays into terrorist hands." Another editorial the following week, entitled "Merchants at the Summit," dismissed the Begin-Reagan meetings as nothing more than "public declarations of mutual esteem and dependency." They did not "get serious" about the primary item on the *Times* agenda: "an early answer to the Palestinian question." The editorial concluded: "Two merchants have got what they could from each other; there were no statesmen in the room."[27]

Columnist Flora Lewis took umbrage at the flood of letters from readers who were "mostly irate and in some cases shrilly insulting and even menacing" in their responses to recent editorial criticism of Israel. Detecting "a tone of desperation," she concluded that "frenzy" had replaced "reason." Suggesting "orchestration" among "automatic-reflex supporters" of Prime Minister Begin, she lumped PLO terrorism with the pre-state actions of the Irgun and Stern Gang. Israel's survival, Lewis concluded, "can only be sustained by coming to terms with the Palestinian Arabs and the neighboring Arab states."[28] She ignored any responsibility they might have to come to terms with Israel.

The *Times* barrage continued with a contribution from Eqbal Ahmad, a Fellow at the Institute for Policy Studies in Washington. He aligned himself with "many thoughtful Americans" who considered Israeli settlements "an impediment to peace" that "strike at the roots of Arab communal life." Yet "throughout the world, especially in the United States," he claimed, "Zionist 'pioneers' were being recruited as settlers." His conclusion, increasingly fashionable among critics of the Jewish state, was that "Israel is pursuing 19th century colonization."[29]

From the Sinai, where Israel would soon abandon a handful of remaining settlements in compliance with its peace treaty with Egypt, Shipler focused on the humanity of the residents. To be sure, "militant Jewish settlers" opposed the impending destruction of their communities. He recognized the possibility of "a messy, perhaps even violent confrontation" with the soldiers dispatched to evict them. But such threats, he noted, were expressed "in calm terms, ... in the eerie quiet and tranquility of people at peace with their convictions." Shipler listened to a woman assert that settlement expressed "one of the ideals of the Zionist movement." Abandonment, she explained, is "almost like committing suicide. On top of it being a defense disaster, it's a moral disaster. It's like killing your values."[30]

In mid-December Prime Minister Begin abruptly announced Israeli annexation of the Golan Heights, under its control since the Syrian attack in the Six-Day War. Ratified by the Knesset without prior consultation with the United States, Begin bluntly declared: "We shall continue to be allies, but no one will dictate our lives to us, even the United States of America." The next day Harvard professor Nadav Safran, born in Cairo and an Israeli officer during the Independence War, warned in the *Times* that the Golan annexation undermined "the credibility of Israel's quest for peace." He considered it a "serious mistake" to imagine that Syria, despite insistent reiteration by President Assad, was "fundamentally and immutably opposed to peace with Israel." The American government, he proposed, should reject Israel's action and open "discreet" talks with Syria to demonstrate its intention "to advance an equitable peace."[31]

But Shipler recognized Begin as a "Master Politician." His "old guerilla-warfare tactics of surprise, practiced so skillfully when [he] led the Irgun ... have been elevated to principles of state policy." Begin's decisive actions, including the Golan annexation no less than his previous decisions to bomb Iraq's nuclear reactor and PLO headquarters in Beirut, displayed "sleight of hand" designed "to keep everyone off balance – Arab enemies, American friends, Israeli political rivals." The prime minister was infuriated by criticism from the Reagan administration. "What kind of talk is this, 'punishing Israel'?" Begin fumed. "Are we a vassal state of yours? Are we a banana republic?"[32]

Times columnists were sharply divided over the fracas. William Safire described suspension of the American strategic cooperation agreement with Israel as "the most stinging slap in the face administered to any U.S. ally in recent history." Begin had responded by giving President Reagan "a piece of his mind and I say good for him. ... The scale of the Reagan insult made the heartfelt blast understandable." The United States, Safire concluded, "must never succumb to the temptation of bullying an honorably stiff-necked ally." But Flora Lewis declared that it was "all the more disturbing" that Begin chose to annex the Golan Heights during the season of joy and renewal (Christmas) – as though Israeli policy must conform to the Christian calendar. James Reston concluded dismissively that Begin was "a wonderful but bad-tempered old man" whose Golan annexation was "political, ephemeral and almost meaningless."[33]

Several months later BBC Correspondent Michael Elkins, based in Israel, authored a *Times Magazine* article questioning the morality of the Jewish state. Israelis, he suggested, might not be worthy of the teaching of their ancient sage Hillel: "That which is hateful to you, do not unto others." It seemed to Elkins that they had "forgotten the ethics of their sages and remember only the exploits of their warriors." Citing the Osirak attack, the bombing of PLO headquarters in Beirut and annexation of the Golan Heights, he wondered whether Israel was "in danger of losing its soul in its quest for security." For Elkins "the existential question remains: What has happened to the Zionist dream?"[34]

From Washington Anthony Lewis berated Israel for its "suicidal folly" in attempting, "by force, to bring a million Palestinians under its permanent control." For Lewis, citing Rhodesia, Israeli tactics were "exactly those that have been used by colonial powers against fractious natives." Several weeks later he presented "other Israeli voices" to bolster his criticism of government policy. An Auschwitz survivor teaching at Tel Aviv University told him that no nation "can keep its moral spirit, its self-respect for long ruling a million people against their wish under occupation." A Bronx-born kibbutznik believed that "occupation is destroying the character of this country." To be sure, Lewis conceded, two men constituted a rather minuscule sample of Israeli public opinion. But those "who want peace and security more than territory deserve a hearing."[35]

Flora Lewis focused on Menachem Milson, who had taught Arabic literature at the Hebrew University before becoming head of the Israeli Civil Administration in Judea and Samaria. His "transformation from sensitive scholar to blinkered oppressor reflects what happens when compromise is ruled out." Many Israelis, she wrote, consider him "an extremist, the man who is preparing annexation." With the *Times* penchant for catchy derogatory headlines, her contribution was devilishly entitled "How to Grow Horns."[36]

Shipler, more nuanced, was more perceptive. He identified Begin's "strategy of brinkmanship," which had brought peace with Egypt no less than war in Southern Lebanon against the PLO. The prime minister grounded his policy in "a terrifying sense of loneliness, always the affliction of the Jewish people, particularly the burden of their modern nation." As defense minister Ariel Sharon insisted, justifying the growing conflict against the PLO in southern Lebanon: "A nation must defend its sons," especially following the recent murder of an Israeli diplomat in Paris (for which the PLO denied responsibility), a Gaza grenade attack that killed an IDF sergeant, and a bomb discovered outside a kindergarten in the Israeli town of Holon.[37]

Without lofty moral judgments from the security of Washington (Anthony Lewis) or Paris (Flora Lewis), Shipler recognized that the withdrawal from Sinai, an area twice as large as Israel, had been a "deep" concession, "probably more extensive than any ever made by a country in a comparable position of military strength." But given Middle Eastern realities, "the ancient hatreds are too virulent, the suspicions too entrenched, the dream of peace too dreamlike still." Sharon's order for the bulldozing of Yamit, the last remaining Sinai settlement, to seal the peace with Egypt was "a searing wound" for Israelis, symbolizing "a slow dying of the most ambitious dreams." Few believed that their country "will ever again remove settlements voluntarily from anywhere."[38]

Yet Shipler detected "a latent revulsion" in Israel "over the occupation, especially in its current heavy-handed form." Some Israelis "fear the erosion of their own society's democratic processes and human values." He turned to despairing leftists for documentation. Peace Now leader Tzali Reshef described its members as "constructive Israelis" whose "moral views" framed their opposition to "the oppression of another people." A German immigrant whose parents and sister were murdered in Nazi death camps compared "good" Germans with "'good Israelis' who keep quiet when they see injustice done." Felicia Langer, leader of the Israel Communist party, described occupation as a "disaster" for Israel, "corrupting" and leading to "immorality." Shipler's cohort hardly comprised a representative sample of Israelis. Even "dovish Israelis," wrote

Knesset member Amnon Rubenstein from the secular liberal Shinui party the following week, would "justly" reject Israeli withdrawal to 1967 borders and creation of a Palestinian state on the other side of the line.[39]

Early in June 1982 the simmering conflict between Israel and the PLO erupted into war. Israeli air strikes on Palestinian bases in southern Lebanon, in retaliation for the shooting of Ambassador Shlomo Argov in London (questionably blamed on the PLO), provoked intensive Palestinian shelling of northern Israeli communities. Civilian life, Shipler wrote, "disintegrated" under the severity of the Palestinian attack. Begin was strongly supported, he noted, by political opponents Yitzhak Rabin and Shimon Peres, who provided the prime minister with "the political consensus that he had lacked before."[40]

Shipler offered a careful analysis of Israeli strategy and deepening internal conflict over an expanding war. Its "smallness, its intimacy, its 'people's army' of musicians, teachers, farmers and auto mechanics, cannot withstand the gradual erosion of a prolonged conflict." Soldiers, he observed, "leave behind a population gripped thoroughly by their absence. It is as if an entire small town were mobilized; literally every Israeli knows someone on the battlefield." But concern mounted once Ariel Sharon expanded the destruction of a Palestinian military presence in Lebanon into the shattering of Lebanon as "the center of world terrorism."[41]

From Morningside Heights, Harvard Square and Washington the *Times* critique of Israel was unremitting. Columbia professor Edward Said, by then a member of the Palestine National Council, accused Israelis of "an apocalyptic logic of exterminism." Begin's version of Zionism, he wrote, "reduces Palestinians either to the pacified inhabitants of 'Judea and Samaria' or to terrorists." For Harvard professor Stanley Hoffmann, Israel's hope of "cowering the Palestinians in the occupied territories ... is as absurd as ever." The United States must find "a solution of the Palestinian problem" that satisfied the "legitimate Palestinian demand for a nation."[42]

Times columnists joined the academic critics. To be sure, James Reston wrote, Israel had achieved another military victory "but didn't know what to do with the rubble" it left behind. Begin must be "prepared to deal more generously with the problem of self-determination for the Palestinians, which is the heart of the problem." Once again the Lewises responded with complementary critiques on the same day. To Flora Lewis "Israeli violence has scrambled the pieces of the tragic puzzle once again." Israel must use its military advantage "to promote ... a real possibility of Palestinian self-determination." Anthony Lewis conceded that the "moral and political position" of the PLO would be stronger if it endorsed "the idea of living in peace with Israel." But Israel, he concluded, was dominated by "military opportunism": Begin spoke as prime minister "but the hands are the hands of Arik Sharon."[43]

The Israeli invasion of Lebanon ignited editorial criticism. Imagining that the dispute between Arabs and Jews dated from "biblical time," editors insisted: "The strong are required to be farsighted, in the hope that the weak will find the courage to reduce their ambition." Israel must suspend "colonization" of the West Bank and Gaza and its military action must lead to "a place in the sun, a homeland, a national voice for Palestinian Arabs." But a subsequent editorial wondered why Israel should be held "to higher standards of moral conduct" when Arab states deprived it of "even the lowest attributes of nationhood: safe borders and legitimacy." Accusing the PLO of "the biggest hijacking in history – half of Beirut is the hostage," it nonetheless urged the United States to "pressure Israel for major concessions to Palestinian nationalism."[44]

The Israeli consensus that initially supported the war as a necessary response to Palestinian terrorism proved to be short-lived. It was "a different kind of war," Shipler wrote, in which Israel's "actual existence was not threatened." After two weeks of fighting, Israel was "wrestling with its conscience." Writer Amos Elon assured him that Israelis "didn't feel guilty." Yet *Davar* journalist Teddy Pruess asked skeptically: "Was it necessary?" To Peace Now leader Janet Aviad, it was "an imperialistic war."[45]

As the Israeli military barrage in besieged West Beirut reached its climax in late June so did *Times* criticism. Its new Beirut Bureau Chief, twenty-nine-year-old Thomas Friedman, relayed the harsh response to the Israeli assault from Lebanese politicians, Western diplomats, the PLO press agency, and Yasser Arafat. On the Opinion page Middle East scholar Fouad Ajami referred to the Israeli invasion as "a great delusion" by "dreamers and maximalists" who believed that "if you could pound men and women hard enough, if you could bring them to their knees, you could make peace with them." Ajami blamed Israelis for disregarding support for compromise from "within the Palestinian community" – although, he conceded, "the will to state it openly was never there."[46]

From Paris Flora Lewis cited "blind, stubborn brutality" by Israelis and Palestinians alike. Begin's primary goal, she wrote, was to remove the PLO as "the main obstacle to getting disheartened West Bankers to submit to Israel's version of autonomy." From Washington Anthony Lewis asserted that Israel's Lebanon invasion was "a war to exterminate Palestinian nationalism." He detected a growing American sense that Israeli interests in the Middle East, as defined by Begin and Sharon, were "not the same as American interests."[47]

Shipler increasingly relied on critics who were "not entirely convinced of the justice or the unavoidability of the war." He cited Peace Now advertisements and a Tel Aviv protest; a Hebrew University professor who anticipated that "Lebanon is likely to become our Vietnam"; and the mother of a soldier killed in the battle for Beaufort Castle who insisted "we must make sure that our sword is clean and drawn only in defense." "Many Israelis," Shipler concluded, feared that "intensive air and artillery bombardment" would "stain the national honor." He cited the danger that an expanding war would penetrate the Israeli conscience as "a mark of shame." From Beirut, Thomas Friedman described Israeli bombing as "indiscriminate," which *Times* editors deleted as unacceptable editorializing. He was instructed by A.M. Rosenthal never to "pull a stunt like that again, or he would be fired."[48]

In mid-September 1982 Lebanon's President-elect Bashir Gemayel and twenty-six other Christian Phalange officials were killed when a bomb exploded their Beirut headquarters. It was "unclear," Shipler reported, whether the retaliatory Phalange massacre of hundreds of Palestinian inhabitants in the Sabra and Shatila refugee camps was "coordinated or planned jointly" with Israel. He carefully tried to sort out who knew what and when they knew it. *Times* editors were less restrained, proclaiming: "no military reason can cover Israel's responsibility for the crimes in Sabra and Shatila." They called on Israel to begin "the long journey from horror and shame to peace."[49]

Amid the Israeli search for culpability, Shipler understood that "to a people who remember that six million Jews were slaughtered as others turned their backs, the standards of behavior are more exacting, the questions more troubling." He cited "two conflicting impulses": "a siege mentality, easily activated as a reflex to the Jewish people's long history of aloneness and persecution"; and "an instinct for self-criticism, an introspection so intensive that it can inflict wounds as well as cure afflictions." Disgusted by "the government's impulse to cover up" the massacre, Israelis responded with "a powerful surge of outrage." Prime Minister Begin, Shipler conjectured, would end his career "in bitter symmetry, stained by the Beirut massacre, as he began it stained by Deir Yassin." Yet with the announcement of an inquiry led by Supreme Court Chief Justice Yitzhak Kahan, he concluded, "Israel proved again … what a vigorous democracy it is."[50]

Times editors and columnists castigated Begin. According to James Reston, the prime minister "began by terror and he's being destroyed by it in Lebanon." Reston found "something sad, even tragic," in Begin's "quoting selectively from the Bible about Judea and Samaria." The prime minister "has been unfaithful to the honorable memory of Israel." Anthony Lewis chastised Begin for his "offense to Jewish values" and evasion of "the knowledge of evil" during "the holiest week of the Jewish year" between Rosh Hashanah and Yom Kippur. In his self-appointed role as defender of Jewish values, Lewis proclaimed: "The character of Israel will not permit this mockery of Jewish tradition to stand." But *Times* editors acknowledged that the PLO, refusing to recognize "the reality of Israel," seemed "incapable of turning a frustrated nationalism into constructive political action."[51]

Shipler discovered among Israelis the moral conscience that his Washington-based colleagues condemned them for lacking. Amid soaring public demand for a commission of inquiry to investigate possible Israeli complicity in the Lebanon massacre, Shipler asked: "Are there people of comparable honor and courage in the Arab world who can appreciate Israel's revulsion?" He wrote pointedly of Israelis: "By their shame, they shame the killers of their own children. By their revulsion, they expose the hypocrisy of many of their critics." Announcement of the Kahan commission of inquiry mollified *Times* editors, who praised "cries of conscience" from anguished Israelis in "a society that refuses to let its leaders avert their eyes from the blood of innocent Palestinians."[52]

Israel's moral failure and quest for redemption framed *Times* coverage. When the Kahan Commission report found Israel indirectly responsible for the Sabra and Shatila massacre, assigning personal responsibility to Defense Minister Sharon for not taking necessary steps to prevent it, even *Times* editors acknowledged: "How rare the nation that seeks salvation by revealing such shame." But Commission findings, they segued, carried "prophetic meaning for the West Bank and Gaza, whose absorption by Israel will surely lead to rebellions and repressions of Palestinians." The editorial urged Americans to "support and encourage the many Israelis who want to avoid a brutalizing dominion over Palestinians."[53]

After a peace marcher was killed by a grenade during an anti-war demonstration, Shipler wrote, Israelis confronted the question: "what is happening to the fabric of their society." The government had permitted "a climate of hatred to build over the years along the ethnic and class lines of Israeli Jews," while tolerating "vigilantism" against West Bank Arabs. But now it was "purging itself" by popular demand and with the "reasoned voice" of Kahan Commission members. With publication of its report, Israel stood "at the conjunction of honor and tragedy," where "healthy democracy crossed with dangerous intolerance."[54]

Fascinated by internal Israeli conflict, Shipler explored the contrast between the cohesiveness with which the country once faced "a common enemy outside" and its divisiveness over "new dangers from within." He perceived a "sense of doing wrong," especially "callousness to human life – to Arab life," that sharpened "the long struggle between humanism and nationalism" in the Jewish state. The core Israeli belief that the IDF would only fight "no-choice" wars had disintegrated in Lebanon. According to a kibbutznik paratrooper (one of the founders of the anti-war protest group Soldiers Against Silence) the refusal of unprecedented numbers of Israelis to fight, or even to perform military service there, challenged "the basic agreement of collective life in this country." Liberal Israeli civilians, Shipler wrote, had joined the protest against militarism and amorality that had replaced the "ethical, noble and pure" values of traditional Ashkenazi culture.[55]

That culture, Shipler subsequently suggested, had been undermined by the arrival of Jewish immigrants from Arab countries. The old Ashkenazi Israel of "communal kibbutzim and humane impulses" had humiliated them in primitive transit camps before dispatching them to isolated development towns. Poverty, discrimination and ethnic tensions had created "a gulf of misunderstanding, and often bigotry." Shipler compared Ashkenazi hostility to the "white backlash against blacks" in the United States. Yet Begin's "emphatic Jewishness," he noted, drew the new Sephardi immigrants into Israeli society. His Likud party represented "the anti-establishment impulses of an alienated and impoverished group," while expressing the "anti-Arab reflexes of those who suffered as Jews in Arab countries."[56]

Once the Lebanon war subsided, Shipler's coverage broadened beyond internal Israeli conflict. He was moved by the nationwide observance of Remembrance Day, when sirens wailed and traffic halted to honor the nation's war dead. At the dedication of a new settlement on the thirty-fifth anniversary of independence he interviewed Elyakim Haetzni, one of the founders of the restored Hebron community and the adjacent settlement of Kiryat Arba, who asserted that the torch of Zionist idealism had passed from kibbutzniks to settlers. Visiting the cease-fire line between Israel and Syria, Shipler was assured by an Israeli soldier: "It is less dangerous here than in Central Park at night."[57]

As Shipler's criticism of Israel sharpened, so did criticism of his coverage. He described a "mass sickness" among hundreds of Palestinian teenage girls in the West Bank, for which a recently deposed Arab mayor accused Israel of poisoning the students. (The *Times* published a correction for printing the false accusation.) He relied on a solitary American-born soldier on reserve duty in the West Bank for allegations of the mistreatment of Nablus residents, including beatings of teenagers in "a routine of petty violence and humiliation."

His source, a Yale graduate, accused soldiers "from the margins of Israeli society" of "working out their fantasies of violence" on innocent Arab residents.[58] No corroborating evidence was provided.

In August 1983 Prime Minister Begin unexpectedly announced his resignation. Ever since the death of his wife the previous November, Shipler wrote, Begin had been "reclusive and lonely." His decreasing public appearances indicated that he retained "little taste for the political and diplomatic combat that he had enjoyed all his life." A *Times* editorial, recognizing Begin as "a fighter of integrity," concluded that he had "avenged the slaughter of his family and brethren in Europe and the terrorism of Arabs." But by "wile and violence," he had pointed the way to "absorption of what he deems the promised land ... irrespective of the Palestinians living there."[59]

Begin was Israel's first self-consciously and proudly *Jewish* Prime Minister. Asked by the *Times* whether he intended to annex the West Bank, he had responded sharply: "You annex foreign territories, not your own country. ... A Jew has every right to settle in the liberated territories of our Jewish homeland." Even Anthony Lewis recognized that Begin embodied qualities that many Israelis found to be "heroic": a "vision of Jewish destiny" and "defiance of the external world." But Begin's "war of choice" in Lebanon, which Lewis compared to Bar Kokhba's futile second-century rebellion, exemplified "the dangers of unrealism" – and "the result was disaster." His "biblical vision" marked an era "when zealotry and fantasy raised new dangers for Israel." Conservative columnist William Safire disagreed. Under Begin, Israel had become "a bastion of strength and a center of controversy, making peace with Egypt and breaking the power of the P.L.O."[60]

Shipler analyzed the "Begin era" as "a time of historic evolution in Israel." Begin had initiated "a political revolution, overthrowing the entrenched socialist, Labor elite," while offering "a voice" to Sephardic immigrants from the Middle East and North Africa who, like Begin himself, had previously fallen "outside the mainstream of Israeli political life." With the Osirak attack, Golan annexation, peace treaty with Egypt and seeding of new settlements he had "infused Israel with a sense of nationalist grandeur backed by a new ideological fervor and a faith in the power of armed force to cut through the complexities of the Middle East."[61]

In his final months as Bureau Chief Shipler focused on "A Land Divided." In four lengthy articles he previewed the theme of "Wounded Spirits in a Promised Land" that would frame his *Arab and Jew*, published two years later. The most distinctive attribute of Israel, he concluded, was the prevalence of "ancient patterns of distrust." It "is not a melting pot, and neither Arabs nor Jews wish it to be." Living in separate neighborhoods, Arab and Jewish children attended separate schools; their points of contact were "relatively few, and far from intimate"; there was virtually no intermarriage. Indeed, they "remain stooped in mutual aversion."[62]

Guided by two American volunteers from Interns for Peace, Shipler explored feelings of "rejection and suffering" by both Arabs and Jews. In the Dheisheh refugee camp near Bethlehem he encountered "a hatred of the Jews of Israel [that] seethes quietly." In their "ghetto" Arab residents "relish the opportunity to turn the language of Jewish suffering against the Jews." He was charmed by an eleven-year-old girl whose dream was "to get back our land" – by demonstrations and with guns. In Jaffa, adjacent to Tel Aviv, Shipler described Israeli Arabs as "aliens in their own land," whose children suffered from a "confused identity." He recognized that an Arab Israeli, existing "in a twilight zone between citizenship and suspicion," was "freer than he would be in an Arab country, but not as free in Israel as he would be if he were a Jew."[63]

Shipler's four-part series was sharply criticized by the Director of the Israel Press Office. The American journalist, wrote Morton Dolinsky in a letter published by the *Times*, resorted to "armchair psychoanalysis" in ascribing the anxieties of Israelis about the safety of their women and children to "sexual fears and fantasies" rooted in "racism." He located Shipler among journalists "dedicated to the trendy proposition that Israel is to be unremittingly flogged and condemned for the crime of not being paradise." At war with Arab states ever since its founding, Dolinsky reminded Shipler that Israel's treatment of its Arab citizens compared quite favorably to the incarceration of 120,000 Japanese-American civilians by the American government during World War II.[64]

Writing to Executive Editor A.M. Rosenthal shortly before leaving Jerusalem, Shipler recalled: "I had to struggle to preserve a description of Israel as a Jewish state" and was told that it would be included as "'an exception' to a longstanding rule barring such a characterization." He asked: "Why the rule?" But "none of the editors who routinely enforce it seemed to know. They could only repeat rumors that after '48 the Publisher had certain attitudes about Israel." Shipler was puzzled. "You can imagine how bizarre it must seem to anyone sitting in, and reporting from, Israel ... to find that Israel cannot be described as a Jewish state in his newspaper." But "it *is* a Jewish state. ... Saying so is not an endorsement and is not a criticism, but merely a statement of reality."[65] Yet nearly four decades after its birth, the reality of Israel as a Jewish state still remained too discomforting for the *Times* to acknowledge.

Shipler's posting in Jerusalem concluded with his inadvertent, but pivotal, role in another Israeli crisis. In April 1984 four Arab terrorists seized an Israeli bus transporting thirty-five passengers from Tel Aviv to Ashkelon. Armed with grenades, bombs and explosives, they forced the driver to speed south along the coastal highway toward Gaza, where they planned to enter Egypt and use their Israeli captives to negotiate the release of Palestinian prisoners. They permitted a pregnant woman to leave the bus; she flagged down a truck whose driver notified the police. Crashing through border blockades the bus crossed into Gaza, where pursuing Israeli soldiers forced a halt by shooting out its tires.

According to "reporters on the scene," Shipler's account revealed the following day, two of the terrorists had been killed "in a barrage of gunfire from both sides of the bus"; the other two were captured alive. But the caption beneath the photo of a dead terrorist on the bus stated that "Israeli troops retook the bus and killed all four terrorists." A reporter from *Hadashot,* a new left-wing newspaper, showed Shipler a photograph of one of the terrorists being led from the carnage by "two men in civilian clothes." Accumulating evidence, Shipler wrote, suggested that the hijacker was "captured alive and killed later," by Israeli soldiers. An IDF spokesman flatly denied the allegation.[66]

Several days later Shipler was informed by the Government Press Office that he "had been in violation of military censorship." His press credentials were not revoked only because his posting in Jerusalem was nearing an end. Before his departure he reported that two of the bus hijackers "were captured alive and then killed by security men." Once the *Times* violated the censor's restrictions, Israeli newspapers were free to highlight the story. By then, as Shipler would write in *Arab and Jew,* "the cover-up began to spread like a stain, tainting a broad spectrum of high-level Israel political figures" and resulting in the appointment of an Israeli commission of inquiry. Anthony Lewis, praising his colleague for revealing the truth about the hijacking episode, was inclined to blame "the habit of censorship," not terrorism, as "a cause of what went wrong." Lewis, like Shipler, focused on Israeli malfeasance, not Palestinian hijacking of a civilian bus.[67]

In his final article from Jerusalem Shipler focused on Israel's failure to resolve its most fundamental issues of identity: "religious or secular, nationalistic or humanistic, Western or Middle Eastern, absolutist or pluralistic." His perspective reflected the views of three Israelis who had guided his understanding of the Jewish state, and its deficiencies. Prominence was given to Rabbi David Hartman's concern that "the land, as an object of the Zionist dream, has become an idol." Hartman emphasized the need to elevate "rebuilding Judaism" above "settling the land." Political scientist and Peace Now advocate Yaron Ezrahi lamented the warping of national priorities by "a war of survival against enemies" that strengthened Israeli chauvinism. According to Meron Benvenisti, Deputy Mayor of Jerusalem, the power of "militant messianism" among Jewish settlers had fatefully molded the national psyche.[68]

As Shipler explained in *Arab and Jew,* his primary focus in Israel was on "the strife" between two peoples in "the promised land." He oscillated between feeling that "in their mutual hatred, both sides deserved each other" and "a sense that both sides were right." Absorbed by the drama of conflict, the damning paradox that he found most compelling was the "free society" of Israel as an "occupier." Settlements became convenient targets for all that was wrong with the Jewish state. "The messianists who arose after the 1967 war," he had learned from Rabbi Hartman, "were a new breed of fundamentalists who created a dangerous synthesis of religion and nationalism." As Rabbi Hartman taught him, a "deep moral decay" of "religious and national fanaticism" had accompanied Israel's return to its biblical homeland in 1967, undermining its moral integrity.[69] An eager student, Shipler had evolved from a fascinated explorer into a stern critic of the Jewish state.

CHAPTER 7

Moral Equivalence: 1984–1988

In June 1984 *Times* editor A. M. Rosenthal transferred Thomas Friedman from Lebanon to Israel, succeeding David Shipler as Jerusalem Bureau Chief. According to Friedman, Rosenthal "wanted to dispense with an old unwritten rule at *The New York Times* of never allowing a Jew to report from Jerusalem."[1] Evidently neither Rosenthal nor Friedman knew about Joseph Levy. Nor could they have anticipated the irony of yet another Jewish reporter posted in Jerusalem whose coverage of Zionism (and now Israel) would reveal – indeed, reinforce – the enduring Jewish problem embedded within the Ochs-Sulzberger newspaper.

Raised in what he described as "a rather typical middle-class American Jewish family" (in Minnesota), Friedman had identified himself as a "three-day-a-year Jew" who experienced boredom or embarrassment during his boyhood years of Hebrew school and summer camp. But with the outbreak of the Six-Day War, CBS News anchorman Walter Cronkite introduced him to "my Jewish identity." During his first trip to Israel with his parents the following year, "something about Israel and the Middle East grabbed me in both heart and mind." He began to feel "more Middle East than Minnesota." Friedman described his high-school years as "one big celebration of Israel's victory in the Six-Day War." During three summers as a volunteer in Kibbutz HaHotrim (located on the site of a former Palestinian village) his identification with Israel, he confessed, became "insufferable."[2]

While a Brandeis undergraduate Friedman made a stopover in Cairo on his way to a semester at the Hebrew University. Enchanted by the mosques and minarets, fresh pita bread, and the Gezira Sporting Club golf course, he was smitten by Arab culture. Friedman returned to Brandeis with his identity transformed. His previously passionate embrace of Israel yielded to sharp criticism of the Jewish state. He belonged to the steering committee of a "Middle East Peace Group" comprising the Hillel rabbi, several left-wing faculty members and a handful of students. It published a statement in the student newspaper, co-signed by Friedman, discounting recent PLO terrorist attacks against Israelis as "clearly not representative of the diverse elements of the Palestinian people" and supporting "Palestinian self-determination."

The Peace Group vigorously opposed the rising storm of protest among American Jews over Yasser Arafat's impending appearance before the UN General Assembly (where he would infamously link Zionism with racism). Co-steered by Friedman, the group joined Breira ("alternative"), an organization of left-wing rabbis and Jewish intellectuals that endorsed Palestinian national aspirations while blaming Israel and the United States for Middle East instability.[3] Recounting his undergraduate infatuation with Israel in *From Beirut to Jerusalem,* Friedman would omit any mention of his role in the Peace Group, its embrace of Breira, or the implications for his nascent political identity as a critic of Israel.

During post-graduate Middle Eastern studies at Oxford, Friedman published several newspaper articles and discovered his "calling as a Middle East correspondent." He was hired by United Press International in 1978; the following year he was posted in Beirut. Given the evident perils that confronted a Jewish reporter in the Arab Middle East, Friedman adopted a "maze of defenses" to conceal his identity. Lest religion become an issue that would "get in the way of my reporting," he identified himself as "American." If pressed, he would cite his grandparents' origins and identify his family name as "Romanian." "The name of the game," he quickly learned, "was keeping on good terms with the PLO."[4]

Hired by the *Times* in 1981, Friedman returned to Beirut following the Israeli invasion of Lebanon. He covered the massacre of Palestinians by Christian Philangists in the Sabra and Shatila refugee camps. The experience, he subsequently confessed, "was something of a personal crisis for me. The Israel I met on the outskirts of Beirut was not the heroic Israel I had been taught to identify with." The massacre was "a blot on Israel and the Jewish people." Friedman "worked out" his fury by writing the articles castigating Israel that earned him a Pulitzer Prize. He was driven, he subsequently confessed, "to nail Begin and Sharon – to prove, beyond a shadow of a doubt, that their army had been involved in a massacre in Beirut." Conceding that "an 'objective' journalist is not supposed to have such emotions," he self-defensively claimed: "the truth is they made me a better reporter."[5]

Friedman focused "on the role played by the Israeli army" in the massacre that he acknowledged was executed "by Christian militiamen." He interviewed senior Israeli commander Maj. Gen. Amir Drori, who claimed to have had no "specific information" of the massacre until it was over. Recounting the interview Friedman confessed: "I must admit I was not professionally detached. ... I banged the table with my fist and shouted ... 'How could you do this? How could you not see? How could you not know?'" But "what I was really saying, in a very selfish way," he realized, "was 'How could you do this to *me*, you bastards? I always thought you were different. I always thought *we* were different.'" The next morning, consumed with fury, "I buried Amir Drori on the first page of *The New York Times*, and along with him every illusion I ever held about the Jewish state."[6]

One month after his arrival in Jerusalem Friedman reported to A.M. Rosenthal that Israel was "fascinating." His "only frustration" was that "I don't have the instant feel and grasp of the place that I had with Lebanon. ... It leaves me feeling a bit incomplete every time I file a story." Several days later he proudly referred Rosenthal to an article by *Jerusalem Post* correspondent Wolf Blitzer citing Friedman's Jerusalem posting as evidence that the *Times* "has finally recognized ... that Jews, like their Gentile colleagues, are fully capable of reporting on Israel thoroughly, objectively and fairly."[7]

The trauma of Beirut lingered. In a *Times Magazine* article published three months after his arrival in Jerusalem Friedman explored "the power of fanatics." In both the Arab world and Israel "the political center ... is being hijacked by extremists determined to go to any length to pursue their causes." He linked the recent "maiming of West Bank mayors by Jewish terrorists" (at the fringe of Israeli society) to state-sponsored massacres in Lebanon and Syria and "utterly ruthless repression" in Iran under Ayatollah Khomeini. He lumped the terrorist demolition of his Beirut apartment building and the blowing up of the United States Embassy and Marine compound in Beirut with the election of Rabbi Meir Kahane, "an anti-Arab racist," to the Knesset. Noting the arrest of twenty-seven members of a Jewish underground for violence against West Bank Arabs, he claimed: "anyone who says the Jewish terrorists in Israel are a fringe element is fooling himself." But he conceded that the refusal of Arab states to recognize Israel and negotiate with it strengthened "Israeli fanatics." Friedman's primary cited sources were Peace Now activists and an Israeli friend who reported a discussion with his Moroccan maid.[8]

Israel's "dirty war" in Lebanon continued to draw Friedman's attention and focus his coverage. In a *Magazine* article he explored the two-year conflict that had claimed the lives of more than six hundred Israeli soldiers and imposed prison sentences on nearly 150 young men for refusing military service. He was guided by Avraham Burg, a peace activist who subsequently enjoyed a distinguished career in Israeli politics before becoming an outspoken critic of his country as "the last colonial occupier in the Western world." Friedman provided other disillusioned Israelis with a forum for the criticism that pervaded his article. Writer A.B. Yehoshua interpreted the Lebanon war as "a kind of divine punishment ... for the West Bank" by bestowing territory "which you will beg to return and cannot." Rabbi David Hartman, who would become Friedman's moral mentor, explained that "the grandeur that started in 1967 was exploded" in Lebanon. If the Six-Day War was "an overdose of fantasy," the war in Lebanon provided "an enormous overdose of reality."[9]

With a final withdrawal from Lebanon looming, the Israeli government stunned the nation with the announcement that 1,150 convicted Palestinian terrorists would be exchanged for three Israeli prisoners captured during the war. With the exchange, Friedman wrote, "Israel can finally disengage from Lebanon physically and psychologically." But he saw "vengefulness" in "a widely shared desire to get even for this 'humiliating' exchange" when the government released twenty-seven Jews on trial for acts of terrorism against Arab civilians. The "cycle of violence has scarred many Israelis," he concluded, some of whom "no longer see any wrong in taking the law into their own hands so long as it is against Arabs."[10] For Friedman, the Israeli release of more than one thousand convicted Palestinian terrorists was commendable; but releasing twenty-seven Jews accused of terrorism was abhorrent.

By then Rabbi Hartman had become Friedman's interpreter of Israeli culture and politics, "my own rabbi" as the journalist would proudly identify him in *From Beirut to Jerusalem*. Friedman, like Shipler before him, became an eager student of the charismatic rabbi whose blend of religious Orthodoxy and political liberalism was their guiding standard for critical judgment of Israel's deficiencies. Friedman learned from Hartman that "secular Zionists built a nationalism without reclaiming Judaism"; religious Zionists from Gush Emunim offered "a politics of fantasy"; and ultra-Orthodox Jews defended "a politics of regression." No one, Friedman acknowledged, "taught me more about Israel and the Jewish people than he did."[11] And no one cultivated credulous *Times* reporters more skillfully than Rabbi Hartman.

West Bank Palestinians gradually replaced the PLO in Lebanon at the core of Friedman's narrative of Israeli malfeasance. The destruction of the PLO as a military force, and Israel's "refusal to negotiate with credible Palestinian leaders over the future of the West Bank," had plunged young Palestinians into "a new mood of despair" that propelled them into "increasingly, and brazenly, taking the military initiative." The murder of two Israeli couples, and targeted shootings of Israeli soldiers and shoppers in West Bank towns "at point-blank range in broad daylight," demonstrated (according to Friedman's primary source, Meron Benvenisti) "a real sign of despair" among Palestinians. But Israeli leaders were to blame for their unwillingness to acknowledge the presence of "another political community here."[12]

Amid the surge of Palestinian violence Friedman's designated Israeli villain was Rabbi Meir Kahane, the Brooklyn-born founder of the militant Jewish Defense League whose Kach Party advocated the annexation of occupied territory and expulsion of its Arab residents. Friedman found guidance for understanding Kahane's extremism from Alouph Hareven of the Van Leer Foundation, who attributed the groundwork for Kahane's political ascent to the Knesset to the "increase in right-wing nationalist ideology" inspired by Menachem Begin: "Kahanism is the ultranationalist logic played out to its final conclusion." Friedman was fond of such pithy analogies. In *From Beirut to Jerusalem* he would write that Begin "always reminded me of Bernhard Goetz, the white Manhattanite who shot four black youths he thought were about to mug him on the New York subway" – adding caustically that Begin "was Bernhard Goetz with an F-15."[13]

Vigorous Israeli responses to Palestinian terrorism troubled *Times* editors. Conceding that an attack on the PLO base in Tunis in which fifty Palestinians were killed "may avenge" the recent murder of twenty Israelis, an editorial nonetheless complained that "such humiliation of the United States does not seem to matter much in Israel's calculations." Ostensibly concerned that the raid might have killed Arafat, creating a martyr who would further inspire Palestinian nationalism, the editors identified the challenge to Israel "not to prove it can bomb a target many miles away, but to practice restraint and bear the risk of negotiations that might bring it many years of peace."[14]

In the waning months of 1985 two dramatic events stunned Israelis. In October four Palestinians hijacked the cruise ship *Achille Lauro* and headed for the port city of Ashdod to capture Israeli hostages and exchange them for imprisoned Palestinians. Friedman reported that "an American passenger" who was "singled out from among a group of American and British tourists" had been killed by "apparently panicked hijackers." A *Times* editorial that day referred to "the murder of an ailing American passenger." Neither Friedman nor the editors identified the murdered passenger, confined to a wheelchair, as an American Jew named Leon Klinghoffer.[15]

The following day Friedman recounted a "surgical strike" by United States Navy jets that resulted in the capture of the hijackers. It was, he suggested (in editorializing mode), "the best means for combating terrorism," in contrast to the "ferocious retaliation that kills terrorists and civilians alike." It demonstrated that "Western democracies can combat terrorism without having to discard their values and adopt the attitudes of the terrorists themselves." Klinghoffer's murder, Friedman acknowledged, "was particularly disturbing for Israelis because they believe he was singled out as a Jew." He concluded that the *Achille Lauro* tragedy was caused by "the unresolved Palestinian-Israeli conflict" – not Palestinian terrorism.[16]

Friedman's focus quickly shifted to the political damage inflicted on PLO leader Yasser Arafat (who claimed that Klinghoffer probably died from a heart attack) and on the Israeli peace movement, whose dreams were being undermined by a "cycle of violence," unidentified as Palestinian terrorism. With the *Achille Lauro* hijacking and the murder of Klinghoffer (once again identified as "an American," not a Jew), Friedman concluded, Peace Now had "clearly lost some of its edge" in a time of "increasing fear and hatred."[17]

Near the end of November Jonathan Pollard, a civilian employee of the United State Naval Intelligence Service, was arrested and charged with espionage for passing secret documents to Israeli agents. With potential to seriously rile American-Israeli relations, Pollard's betrayal raised the menacing issue of dual loyalty that had long agitated *Times* publishers. *Times* editors suggested that "Israel's policy of never spying on the United States is a policy only never to be caught at it." Israel "stutters in embarrassment, but not much regret," they concluded, secure in the knowledge that the United States "surely observes the same policy" of spying on friends whenever possible.[18]

Once the shock of Pollard's espionage receded, Friedman's focus shifted to varieties of Palestinian nationalism, and terrorism. A lengthy profile of Abu Nidal, who had planned recent massacres in the Rome and Vienna airports that killed twenty passengers and wounded nearly 150 people waiting to board El Al flights, was followed by a report from Nablus, "a center of Palestinian nationalism" in the West Bank. Relying once again on Benvenisti, who condemned occupation as financially profitable to Israel, he cited Palestinian complaints that Israeli economic benefits were designed merely to better integrate occupied territory into the Jewish state. As Rabbi Hartman explained, "the anger and frustration of the deprived give them the right to destroy all moral boundaries."[19]

Israel, for Friedman, seemed little more than a seething cauldron of problems, internal no less than external. In a *Magazine* article he explored the growing challenge to Zionism from the "bounty, pluralism and endless opportunities for Jews and other minorities" that the United States afforded. As Israel became "more like America," he concluded, "it lost some of its distinct identity." The United States became more enticing, especially for Israelis (mostly secular and liberal) who resented "the extraordinary pressures of everyday life, from Army service to the increasing inroads of religious extremism." Friedman imagined that younger Israelis, increasingly drawn to the United States by "the full range of opportunities open to them," might decide to remain at home if Israel rejected the influence of "ultra-Orthodox messianic Jews" and "right-wing extremists such as Rabbi Meir Kahane."[20]

Two years after his arrival in Jerusalem Friedman still clung to memories of the Lebanon war. In a four-column article he reported the production of an Israeli military training film intended "to prepare soldiers for fighting in a country so torn by war that not even the law of the jungle seemed to apply." He described the "paradox" of "a highly critical feature movie produced by the Israeli Army about a war it conducted," without considering whether such rigorous self-scrutiny might be an Israeli military virtue. He complained that the film "reflects and caters to the Israeli attitude that Lebanon is just a crazy place – while ignoring how the [Israeli] occupation might have made it crazier."[21] The Lebanon war still offered Friedman an opportunity to blame Israel.

A flare-up of religious-secular tensions provided yet another fulcrum for criticism. The conflict between "Orthodox militants" and "secular Jews" (not secular "militants") erupted with a fire set in a Tel Aviv synagogue to protest the defacement of scores of bus shelters plastered with posters (displaying women in "skimpy bathing suits") that had offended ultra-Orthodox Jews. Vandals also invaded a nearby yeshiva, shredding prayer shawls, tearing prayer books and smashing the ark. Depicted by Friedman as a "secular offensive," the eruption of violence expressed "a basic and unresolved tension: whose law is supreme in the State of Israel?" The answer, predictably, came from Rabbi Hartman, who asked pointedly: "Are the religious ready to live in this country, accepting that there will be a permanent value disagreement with other Jews?"[22]

Nothing focused Friedman's attention like conflict, whether between Arabs and Jews or among Israelis. He noted that Shiite attacks inside the Israeli security zone along the Lebanese border had prompted Israeli retaliation. A "casual observer," he wrote, might wonder why Israel risked widening the conflict (although not, apparently, why Shiites provoked it). Conflict among Jews was also riveting. The election of Leah Shakdiel, an Orthodox woman, to the religious council of a Negev development town provoked a polarizing controversy over "delicate boundaries ... between feminism and Jewish law." In a lengthy interview, Shakdiel explained to the evidently sympathetic Friedman her determination "to get Judaism to adapt itself to modernity."[23]

These seemingly disconnected episodes were pieces in the larger Israeli identity puzzle that intrigued Friedman. Exploring its "leadership problem" after right-wing Yitzhak Shamir replaced left-wing Shimon Peres as prime minister in a national unity government, he lamented that a generation of political leaders had failed to produce "a solution for the most pressing dilemma facing the State of Israel – coming to terms with the Palestinians." What younger Israelis needed, Friedman asserted, was "an Israeli Anwar el-Sadat, ready to throw caution to the wind and grasp the core issue of two communities wanting the same land."[24]

Evaluating the transfer of political power, Friedman praised Peres for securing "an Israel that is much more subdued, and with a better international standing, than the one he inherited" from Likud leaders. But according to "Israeli analysts" (primarily a left-wing Knesset member and a columnist for *Haaretz*), "the most emotional issue of today – what to do with the occupied territories" was placed on "a back burner." Friedman succinctly described Shamir as "a man with a reputation for saying no," whether to the Camp David accords, the peace treaty with Egypt, or the military withdrawal from Lebanon. Shamir's amiable exterior, he concluded after an interview, "masks a steely character underneath that is capable of the most brutally tough decisions."[25]

Two months later Friedman wondered: "Has there been a decline in the rule of law in Israel?" His answer was a foregone conclusion. According to legal scholars, "there was pressure to cut corners and bend the rules" – although "some kind of justice," even if limited, was eventually administered by the Israeli legal system. Explaining these deficiencies, Friedman cited the majority of Jews who had immigrated to Israel from (Arab) countries "with no democratic legal traditions." And decades of conflict had "numbed many Israelis when it comes to strictly interpreting the law as it is applied to Arabs." His primary cited sources for these gloomy conclusions were Hebrew University Professor Ruth Gavison, a prominent civil liberties lawyer and founding member of the Israel Association for Civil Rights, and her colleague Joshua Schoffman, who looked to "a strong coalition of the free press, intellectuals and lawyers" to defend the rule of law. If there were defenders of the Israeli legal system in the solitary democratic nation in the Middle East Friedman could not locate them.[26]

"The challenge of the Israeli occupation" in conjunction with the ascent of the PLO, Friedman wrote, had combined "to forge a Palestinian national consciousness among West Bank youth." Belonging to the "post-1967 generation, having spent all their lives under Israeli rule," they had become increasingly assertive – often, to be sure, with knives, axes, screwdrivers, and stones that targeted Israeli soldiers and civilians. As a Beir Zeit University student revealed, "We want any means of getting back at the Jews." Without hope for a solution to the conflict, Friedman explained, "theirs is simply a politics of revenge." Neither Palestinians nor Israelis, he concluded, "can stand the symmetry of acknowledging that there is another legitimate collective on the land."[27]

Friedman was drawn to Arab subtexts within Israeli society. In an interview with Anton Shammas, an Israeli Arab writer whose recently published novel *Arabesques,* written in Hebrew, had "set the Israeli literary world on its ear," Friedman reveled in the complexities of the author's identity. A Palestinian Christian (whose mother was Lebanese), Shammas did not focus on who is a Jew, the issue that frequently roiled Israeli society, but "who is an Israeli?" Friedman seemed delighted to discover that Shammas wanted to prove that "there is something called 'Israeli' that is not necessarily Jewish," but a product of both Arab and Jewish cultures.[28]

Friedman wrestled with questions that had engaged him ever since his arrival in Jerusalem: "Why are so many people fascinated with Israel?" "Why is Israel so often," and so disproportionately, "the focus of news"? It was, he concluded in a *Times Magazine* article, "fed by the biblical tradition, the role of the Jew in the Christian world, guilt over the Holocaust, and yes, probably also some traditional anti-Semitism." Israel also needed "to satisfy a deep longing to be accepted and a need to prove its worthiness to those upon whom it is most dependent" – especially, by implication, the United States. Consequently, the Jewish state often behaved like the stereotypical pushy Jew, demonstrating "an uncanny ability to inject itself into the news."

Once again Friedman was guided by his favorite sources – and, by then, trusted friends – Peace Now advocate Yaron Ezrahi and Rabbi Hartman. The Bible, Ezrahi suggested, provided "the controlling myth of Western civilization, history, and religions." Friedman concurred: "One must begin at the beginning – with the Bible." Israel's newsworthiness had ancient origins: "Little David beating Goliath – that is news." But there was a downside. As Ezrahi explained: "When the Jews, with their moral record of preaching and advocacy, after so many years of vulnerability, behave cynically, now that's news." In a self-revealing aside Friedman wrote: "for some people, there is something almost satisfying about catching the Jewish state behaving improperly. It is a bit like catching one's Sunday school teacher in an indiscretion."

Not only the Hebrew Bible but the early American experience had transformed Israel into the "super-story" that engaged Friedman. Seventeenth-century Puritans, after all, were determined to build a "New Jerusalem" in their own promised land in America. Just as ancient Israel was "deeply ingrained in the imagery, memory and rhetoric of Americans," so the State of Israel, "with its image as a pioneer democracy, only reinforces the bond." Rabbi Hartman cited "expectations and demands" that Israel would "mirror its long moral history," linked to traditions rooted in its ancient history and homeland. Intrigued by the web of analysis spun by his favorite Israeli sources, Friedman concluded by blaming the Jewish state for its failure to adhere to its own "biblical-moral tradition that has helped to shape Western civilization."[29]

Friedman seldom missed an opportunity to highlight criticism of Israel, especially by Israelis. He was intrigued by "a trend in Israeli theatre and art, particularly on the left, to reexamine the past and get beyond all of the myths and troubles of today." He visited a West Bank site north of Jerusalem where film producers who were "heavily involved in the peace movement" and "staunchly opposed" to Jewish settlements were recounting the story of Zionist pioneers in pre-state Palestine. But the actors were predominantly Palestinian; as the Gaza refugee who designed the set explained: "What I like is that this film shows that when Jews arrived there were already Arabs living here." In a subsequent article about four anti-war Israelis on trial for violating Israeli law by participating in unauthorized meetings with PLO representatives in Romania, Friedman relied on Meron Benvenisti's assertion that "both sides provide ample examples of real terroristic behavior"; each claims that "the other side is demonic."[30] Guided by Ezrahi, Hartman and Benvenisti, moral equivalence was embedded in Friedman's narrative.

The trial of John Demjanjuk, extradited to Israel from the United States for his war crimes at Treblinka, provided Friedman with another opportunity to publicize the views of left-wing Israeli critics. He reported their complaints that the trial fed "a certain Israel self-perception as 'victim,'" which strengthened "a certain tendency in Israeli society to feel that the world owes it something, and that Israel does not have to feel accountable for its actions" because of "what was done to the Jews." These "liberal Israeli experts on the Holocaust," Friedman wrote, were concerned that the trial "distracts attention from pressing domestic Israeli issues, such as Israeli power in the occupied territories."[31] Jewish settlements, in Friedman's narrative, overrode justice for Holocaust perpetrators.

Friedman's focus often shifted to Palestinian culture, whether in the West Bank or inside Israel. In a six-column report from Umm al-Fahm, an Israeli Arab village north of Tel Aviv, he described a "surge in Islamic fundamental-ism" that left a visitor "feeling at times that he is in Saudi Arabia, not Israel." Friedman was persuaded that an Islamic revival inside Israel, emulating the American civil rights movement, embraced a "non-violent approach." But in the West Bank, he conceded, the primary source of inspiration for university students was Ayatollah Khomeini's religious revolution in Iran (not Martin Luther King, Jr.).[32] Intrigued by the Islamic surge, Friedman paid considerably less attention to the religious Zionism of Jewish settlers, who remained little more than a shadowy threatening presence in his narrative.

No facet of Israeli life captivated Friedman more than Arab-Jewish rela-tions. He was fascinated by a popular Israeli disc jockey, born in an Arab coun-try, whose program on the Israeli Arabic radio service offered "new wave" music "in which Hebrew words are sung to jazzed-up traditional Arab melodies." The disc jockey "caresses his listeners" with "a flowing, honey-like Arabic." His pop-ularity, Friedman suggested, "underscores the degree to which Israel is slowly becoming a Middle Eastern country." Sephardic Jews, he noted, had arrived in Israel with "the echo of Arabic music in their ears." Despite "the curtain of conflict separating Arabs and Jews," he concluded hopefully, "a certain cultural mixing is taking place on an uncontrolled popular level."[33]

But in the struggle over "who will determine the Jewish religious charac-ter of Israel," Friedman wrote, ultra-Orthodox Jews who believed that Jewish statehood must await the coming of the Messiah were locked in a struggle with Israelis who believed that "Judaism can flourish in a modern state." "We have one flag," a rabbinical leader proclaimed: "The Torah." But Rabbi Hartman warned ominously that "once these ultra-Orthodox have finished off the reli-gious Zionists, they are going to take on the non-religious Zionists ... and make this state an uninhabitable place." One week later Friedman reported the concern of disquieted American Jewish leaders, determined to protect "American values of religious tolerance, democratic education and pluralism," who believed that "Israel is too important to be left to Israelis."[34]

Paralleling the religion-state conflict was the unrelenting struggle between Arabs and Jews. In a *Times Magazine* article entitled "My Neighbor, My Enemy," Friedman recounted Meron Benvenisti's personal experience to illuminate the entwined complexities of the conflict. The son of one of Benvenisti's Arab neighbors had planted a bomb in the garden of a nearby Jewish home. After his release from prison four years later his family invited Benvenisti to his wedding, raising the question: "Are we enemies or are we neighbors." Friedman was fascinated by that ambiguity. The "Palestinian-Israeli twilight war," he concluded after conversations with a representative sample of Israeli left-wing opinion (Professor Ezrahi, sociologist Janet Aviad, writer David Grossman and Rabbi Hartman), was a "war without a front," compounded by "the physical similarities between Arabs and Jews." Israelis and Palestinians alike, he wrote, "try to avoid seeing the conflict for what it really is: two equally legitimate communities fighting a war over the same home." But "as long as your neighbor is your enemy, your house will never be home – it must be a fortress."[35]

Among the Israeli complexities, paradoxes and conflicts that Friedman delighted in exploring, only Tel Aviv culture sparked his unabashed enthusiasm. Guided by journalist Zeev Chafets, a fellow mid-Westerner who made aliya and became director of the Government Press Office during the Begin years, he described the migration of "young, secular and educated Jerusalemites" who had abandoned "the holy world of Jerusalem" for the "freewheeling and proudly secular Tel Aviv." Those cities, a young Israeli observed, were separated "by a 45-minute drive and a 2000-year-old state of mind." Tel Aviv, Friedman discovered, enjoyed a vibrant nightlife long after Jerusalem had "rolled up its sidewalks and gone to bed." As Chafets quipped, "This is what Theodor Herzl had in mind when he thought of the Jewish State."[36]

Friedman was inexorably pulled back to the Arab-Israeli conflict. He turned to Professor Sari Nuseibeh of Bir Zeit University to answer the question: "Has Israel already become a Jewish-Arab state in all but name?" Friedman described Nuseibeh as a political moderate who favored "the South African model of resistance" over the more violent "Algerian" experience. Israelis were not "imperialists to be driven out," the professor conceded, but "a deeply rooted population with a monopoly over power and resources that could be gradually taken over from within." Indeed, "the two societies are becoming so integrated that a bi-national state has already been created in daily life." The reality of integration, Nuseibeh asserted, would inevitably require "equal rights as citizens" for the Arabs of Gaza and the West Bank.[37]

Everyone, it seemed to Friedman, was justifiably unhappy with Israel. Surveying the work of Israeli artists, songwriters and film makers, he discovered "exhaustion" with "what seems to be an endless war and an overwhelming desire to escape, to shut out the world and emotionally disengage." Painters and sculptors raised questions about "the problems the West Bank occupation had bequeathed their country." From "antiwar and protest art," artists had retreated to a "refuge in the abstract." The Six-Day War, twenty years earlier, was "the last war Israelis wrote songs about – or at least songs they could all sing together." Disillusioned song writers had recently replaced "stirring lyrics about the quest for peace or the building of a nation" with "frivolous pop tunes" and mournful nostalgia for the time when, as the lyrics of one song proclaimed: "We had a dream and now it's gone/I am so sad." Artistic expression, suggested the director of the Israel Museum, had shifted to "a sense of lost life and lost innocence."[38]

Nor was Israeli malaise confined to artists, songwriters and film-makers. Friedman noted the irony that "the nation descended from Moses the lawgiver ... could never produce a constitution of its own." But "the increasing power of religious forces who want to impose Jewish law on the secular majority," in conjunction with the "rise of right-wing elements who reject equality for Arabs," had prompted a group of liberal legal scholars to draft a model constitution and bill of rights. They would try to convince "an Israeli public that has come to despair of politics and politicians into believing that they can actually change the system."[39] Like artists and songwriters, legal critics attracted Friedman's attention with their disparagement of Israel for its deficiencies.

By the summer of 1987 Friedman found seething conflict throughout Israel: among Jews and between Israelis and Palestinians. Weekly Friday night clashes in Jerusalem involving Orthodox and secular Jews occurred outside movie theatres that violated a local ordinance prohibiting public showings on the Sabbath. Orthodox Jews gathered at the Western Wall and in the streets surrounding their Mea Shearim enclave to demonstrate opposition to Sabbath violations. Friedman repeatedly identified the protesters as "rigorously" Orthodox; their "secular" adversaries were never as "rigorous" in their convictions as their religious protagonists.[40]

For Israeli-Palestinian relations Meron Benvenisti remained Friedman's primary source. Sharply critical of the Israeli Ministry of Defense for creating a computerized data bank of personal information about Palestinian residents, Benvenisti identified it as a potential "Big Brother" operation that enhanced Israeli control over the West Bank and Gaza. Friedman publicized his West Bank Data Project conclusion (and implicit warning) that "the suburbanization or 'yuppization' of the West Bank [by Jewish settlers] is gathering momentum." One month later Friedman returned to Benvenisti for an explanation of the "sense of dead end" in Israeli-Palestinian relations. "It just means," Benvenisti suggested ominously, "that there is a very long fuse that is burning slowly."[41]

Demographic warnings provided Friedman with additional leverage for criticizing Israel. Visiting the Gaza Strip he learned that Palestinians were creating a "demographic bomb." Large families, with ten or more children, were building a future in which, Friedman wrote, "in 12 years Israel and the occupied territories will be, in demographic terms, a binational state." He heard a similar message from Haifa University demographer Arnon Sofer, who declared that unless Israel "withdraws soon" from the West Bank and Gaza, Israelis would confront the "calamity" of an Arab majority. Then Israeli Jews "will either have to extend voting rights to the Arabs in the occupied territories and risk their taking over the state, or systematically deprive them of their rights and turn Israel into a South Africa-like nation."[42] It did not happen. Israel would relinquish control over Gaza in 2005; a decade later twice as many Jews as Arabs inhabited the territory west of the Jordan River comprising Israel and the West Bank.

Friedman persistently scrutinized the "intercommunal war between Israelis and Palestinians," exacting its toll from "the damage to people's souls and in the erosion of norms of behavior." A government investigation of Shin Bet, Israel's security service, focused on the methods, some illegal under Israeli law, that were used to extract confessions from Palestinians suspected of planning or committing attacks against Israeli soldiers and civilians. Friedman noted that most Israelis, whether civilians or government officials, "seemed ready to condone the Shin Bet's behavior as a necessary war against militant Palestinian nationalists." He acknowledged that "many" of the suspects who were harshly treated by security agents "were guilty of planning or carrying out armed violence against Jews." But Rabbi Hartman criticized Israel's "unwillingness to examine the underlying political reality and the occupation of the West Bank, which create the conditions for attacks against it." He told Friedman: "We have to stop looking at our great moral past and start looking at ourselves as we behave in the present."[43] For Rabbi Hartman and *Times* journalists who eagerly embraced his moral judgments, Israel invariably was the source of Middle East problems.

A cross-border attack from Lebanon that killed six Israeli soldiers provided Friedman with yet another opportunity to chastise Israelis for ignoring the plight of Palestinians. Ever since the Lebanon war, he wrote, "Israel has been slowly wrapping itself in a cocoon, both in security terms and emotionally." Craving "stability, order and a sense of normality," Israelis were "taking a break from the anxiety of constantly living at war." But it was "impossible," argued left-wing Knesset member Dedi Zucker, for Israel "to ignore or delegitimize the Palestinian national cause by dismissing it and its advocates as terrorists," even after suffering a deadly terrorist attack. Friedman concluded by quoting the prophet Amos: "Woe to them that are at ease in Zion."[44]

Early in December 1987, following a traffic accident in Gaza that killed four Palestinians in a collision with an IDF truck, a wave of rioting erupted in the Jabalia refugee camp. Within two weeks, Friedman reported, more than twenty Palestinian "youths," mostly teenage boys, had died in "demonstrations against the Israeli occupation." But neither major Israeli political party, he asserted, would recognize the presence of "another legitimate national group on the land, the Palestinians, that will not rest until its quest for national self-determination has been satisfied." Israelis could not acknowledge what Friedman grasped: the riots were "spontaneous acts of a people frustrated by being occupied by another people," with "real political grievances that must be addressed politically." His primary quoted source was Rabbi Hartman, who lamented the elevation of "a politics of reaction" over "a politics of vision."[45]

Friedman described the intifada, as the Palestinian uprising became known, as "a civil war." Locating it within an American historical framework, he cited the battle of Bull Run in 1861 as the appropriate historical analogy. "It is a war," he wrote, "between two communities who share the same land." The dispute, he asserted, was not over the West Bank and Gaza but "all of Palestine." At a psychological level Friedman interpreted the uprising as "a story about Palestinian fathers and sons." The fathers, who grew up under Jordanian or Egyptian rule, had been acquiescent under foreign authority. But their sons, "ready to bare their chests at Israeli soldiers, . . . have known only a dead-end life under Israeli occupation." These youngsters "only seem to know the dialogue of the stone and the politics of rage." According to his friend Yaron Ezrahi, neither Israel nor the PLO possessed leaders who were capable of diagnosing or solving the problem. Palestinian rioting expressed "a desire for freedom, dignity and to escape from the humiliation of depending on strangers who control your fate." But Israeli leaders refused to acknowledge that "a popular and spontaneous uprising" was underway.[46]

Responding to Palestinian rioting, Friedman wrote, Israeli soldiers found themselves "increasingly less able to resist the image and role of an occupying power." There was, consequently, "increasing dissent" within the IDF over the morality of occupation. Meeting in Nablus with soldiers who viewed themselves as "police officers trying to preserve order" rather than "occupiers," Friedman heard them describe their own fathers who, by contrast, had been "clear-cut soldiers in clear-cut wars of survival against clear-cut enemies in uniform." If Palestinian sons rebelled against paternal passivity, Israeli sons yearned for the moral clarity that had guided their heroic fathers.[47]

The only unity that Friedman could discern among Israelis was their national unity government, comprising Likud Prime Minister Shamir and Labor Foreign Minister Peres and Defense Minister Rabin. To his evident dismay they agreed on an "all-stick and no-carrot approach" to the Palestinian uprising. Once again, the shadow of Lebanon framed his analysis. That war had required flexibility from Israeli leaders, who found themselves unable to impose their will on another country. "But the West Bank is not Lebanon," he conceded. "Many Israelis see it as an integral part of their country."[48]

Returning to Washington early in 1988 Friedman cast himself as moral arbiter of the Israeli-Palestinian conflict. Once again framing it within biblical analogies he concluded that it was not a war between David and Goliath, "with one side exclusively victims and the other exclusively victimizers." Rather it was "a war between Abraham and Ishmael" that "returned to its primordial tribal origins." He found "the rage of Israeli soldiers" to be especially shocking for an army that "always prided itself on maintaining civilized norms." Now, however, it had adopted "a policy of beating and breaking the bones of Palestinian men and women demonstrators."

The "tragedy," for Friedman, was that "neither side seems capable of transforming the heat and the suffering generated by this confrontation into a light at the end of the tunnel." Instead, the conflict had become "a way of life." Perhaps Palestinians and Israelis "still have not come to terms with each others' legitimate national claims, and never will." As he so often did in his embrace of moral equivalence, Friedman gave the final words to Rabbi Hartman, who deplored "a rage that is so ugly and fierce that it has the power to destroy the identity" of Israelis and Palestinians alike.[49]

The PLO, Friedman subsequently wrote, was still living in 1947, believing that statehood was achievable without recognition of Israel's right to exist. Israelis were mired back in the day before the intifada began, believing that Palestinians would "continue to acquiesce in Israeli occupation." Neither delusion was credible. For Friedman the choice was clear: Israelis must decide "Who is an Israeli?" Was it someone "who believes that Israel must occupy the West Bank and Gaza Strip because the Bible or Jewish nationalist ideology says so," or someone who accepts "whatever lines and security arrangements will produce a stable peace with its Palestinian neighbors?"[50] His preference was evident.

In *From Beirut to Jerusalem*, published a year after his return to Washington, Friedman recounted his Middle East experiences. Its subtext, Israel's "occupation" of "Palestinian" land led inexorably to its moral decline, was the embedded conventional wisdom among Israel's liberal *Times* critics. Israel's moral golden age, for

Friedman, preceded the Six-Day War, when it was the Jewish and democratic state that David Ben-Gurion had envisioned. Surrounded by Arab countries sworn to its annihilation, it won the stunning victory in 1967 that posed the moral dilemma framing Friedman's coverage two decades later: to "keep all the land of Israel ... could be done only by curtailing Israeli democracy."[51]

The Lebanon war, for Friedman, had been Israel's crucial turning point (as it had been for him). Would the Jewish state become "a Jewish South Africa, permanently ruling Palestinians in West Bank homelands"? A "Jewish Prussia, trying to bully all of its neighbors"? Or "a secure, democratic, and Jewish society at peace with its neighbors" – as though peace with its Arab neighbors had ever been for Israel alone to determine. But the deeper issue was "the tragedy and irony of the Zionist revolution": its failure "to eradicate the collective self-image of the Jew as victim." Apprehension over another Holocaust during the weeks preceding the Six-Day War, followed six years later by the trauma of the Yom Kippur War, had frozen Israelis with fear. With the Holocaust "well on its way to becoming the defining feature of Israeli society," Friedman concluded sardonically, "Israel today is becoming Yad Vashem with an air force."[52]

In Friedman's inversion of history, "the biggest victors" in the Six-Day War were the Palestinians, for whom "nation-building and identity-building" were "the direct result of the Israeli occupation." To be sure, waves of Palestinian terrorist attacks on Israeli buses, restaurants and public spaces, supplemented by airplane hijackings and the Olympic massacre, posed a "constant challenge – like a continual poke in the ribs" to Israeli civilians. Friedman seemed surprised that "Palestinian" and "terrorist" were "fused together in the minds of people the world over." And he found "tiresome" the "self-delusions" of Israelis that their "legal and morally upright ways" contrasted with the actions of "vile terrorists beyond the pale of civilization."[53]

During twenty years of occupation Israel's "repressive and humiliating treatment" had provided Palestinians with "a common experience of bitterness to reinforce their historical and cultural ties." Friedman admired how the intifada, "an irrational primal scream of rage" among Palestinians, had developed into "a complete liberation strategy." He celebrated their emergence as "a people" and a "nation." As he wrote admiringly, "the unity and courage Palestinians demonstrated in challenging fully armed Israeli soldiers with stones" gave them "a sense of dignity and self-worth that they had never previously enjoyed." By "daring to challenge the Israelis the way David challenged Goliath" they had (as Benvenisti suggested) transformed Israelis into "Goliaths with David's guilty conscience." Throwing stones, not shooting bullets, Palestinians engaged in what Friedman ponderously labeled "massive, relatively non-lethal civil disobedience." But a fifteen-year-old Palestinian, imprisoned for stone-throwing, told Friedman that he threw a stone only because he did not have a grenade. And the land he wanted back, he added, was "the land Jews took in 1948," not 1967.[54]

Friedman identified the intifada with the American civil rights struggle. Many Israelis, he wrote, viewed Palestinians as "niggers" who were "suddenly getting uppity and saying that they would not accept their second-class status any more." They wanted "Palestinian maids and waiters to be put back in their proper places." The fault, as always, lay with Israelis who possessed "too much power and paranoia to ... crate the conditions for a territorial settlement."[55] To Friedman, by implication, they were virtually indistinguishable from Southern racists.

Friedman pondered why Israel, a tiny country compared to world powers, commanded such disproportionate media attention. The reason, Yaron Ezrahi helped him to understand, was the prominence of ancient Israelites in the "biblical super story." News from Israel was "uniquely compelling," Friedman concluded, "because of all the historical and religious movements to which Israel is connected in Western eyes." Jews became "the yardstick of morality and the symbol of hope" by which Israel was judged – and invariably found wanting by Jewish journalists, columnists and editors at *The New York Times*.

But this "unique double dimension," as Friedman described it, might be better understood as the double standard that the *Times* routinely applied to the Jewish state. As he acknowledged: "When Israelis were indirectly involved in the massacre of Palestinians" (by Lebanese Christian Philangists) in Sabra and Shatila, it became "front-page news for weeks" – largely due to Friedman's coverage. He claimed that when Israel no longer was subjected to unique scrutiny, judged by standards applied to no other country, it "can only be a sign that something very essential in Israel's character and the character of the Jewish people has died."[56] As a prominent chronicler of its moral failings for the newspaper that had long been wary of Zionism and critical of Israel, he implicitly claimed to be helping Israel to preserve its moral integrity.

In *From Beirut to Jerusalem* Friedman vividly recounted how his encounter with Israel in Lebanon prompted his repudiation of the "heroic" Jewish state embedded in his teenage fantasies. But with the burial of "every illusion I ever held about the Jewish state," Friedman also buried any claim to journalistic objectivity.[57] Like Joseph Levy more than half a century earlier, his discomfort with Zionism and Jewish statehood framed news fit to print about the struggle to restore and preserve Jewish national sovereignty in the ancient homeland of the Jewish people.

CHAPTER 8

Occupation Cruelty: 1988–1989

The Palestinian uprising known as the intifada erupted in the Jabalia refugee camp in Gaza in December 1987. After four residents were killed in a traffic accident rumors spread among Palestinians that it was a deliberate act of revenge for the fatal stabbing of an Israeli shopper the previous day. Amid mass rioting in the camp, a seventeen-year-old boy was killed by an Israeli soldier after throwing a Molotov cocktail at an army patrol. Over the next week rock-throwing and tire burnings erupted throughout Gaza, the West Bank and Jerusalem, launching a four-year spiral of violence in which more than one thousand Palestinians and nearly two hundred Israelis were killed.

In his first column about the Gaza violence Anthony Lewis articulated his guiding principle: "Ruling someone as a subject people, without political rights, requires the use of force and more force – and corrupts those who rule." Blaming the Israeli government for refusing to negotiate with Palestinians, he declared: "Occupation requires repression" and "repression breeds hate." With the invidious comparison that became a recurrent theme of his critique of Israel, Lewis identified Palestinians in Gaza with "South African blacks" (thereby converting Israelis into their racist oppressors). Israeli military occupation, he warned, "insures the corruption of its own democratic ethic."[1]

Surely with unintended (but revealing) irony, *Times* editors chose Christmas, when "the mind seeks ageless thoughts of peace," to reprimand Israel. Its values were being "defiled," they wrote, and "friends of the Jewish state agonize over the wave of Palestinian unrest." The editorial called on Israel to freeze or roll back "highly provocative settlements" in Gaza. Two days later, editors identified Palestinians in Gaza with Shylock, lamenting "If you prick us, do we not bleed?" Professing to see "guilt on all sides," Israel was nonetheless blamed for "its blunt, clumsy use of lethal force to control the disorder."[2]

Executive Editor A.M. Rosenthal was not persuaded. Israel, he noted, was judged by a double standard: its Arab neighbors "preach death and hate and slaughter in the name of God" while Israel, asserting "pride and duty" to its "biblical roots" and "principles of decency," was castigated. Attentive to "the tragedy of Israel as occupier," he nonetheless asserted that the "tragedy of Gaza" resulted from the refusal of Arab states to recognize Israel's right to exist.[3]

The *Times* reported that liberal American Jews were deeply troubled by Israeli military responses to the eruption of Palestinian violence. Rabbi Alexander M. Schindler, president of Reform Judaism's Union of American Hebrew Congregations, warned that perpetuation of the status quo of Israeli occupation "corrodes the Jewish and democratic nature of the state." Predicting that an Arab demographic majority west of the Jordan River would eventually transform Israel into a "bi-national" state, he anticipated that Israel's "Jewish and democratic nature will be disfigured and the Zionist dream betrayed."[4]

After weeks of violence in Gaza spread to the West Bank, *Times* editors found "guilt on all sides." But Israel alone was to blame for "the blunt, clumsy use of lethal force to control the disorder." Flora Lewis depicted the Israeli dream of nationhood as a nightmare. She learned (from Meron Benvenisti) that "Jews have failed to remember their purpose to build a democratic, healthy home-land." Instead, Israel had adapted to the surrounding hostile environment: "to compromise ideals, to learn to hate and to oppress." Edward Said joined the chorus of criticism, berating Israel for its brutal treatment of young Palestinians and portrayal of them as "terrorists, as subhuman, barbaric people."[5]

Writing from Jerusalem one week later Anthony Lewis discerned "a genuine popular uprising" by Palestinians. Stone-throwing youths were not "terrorists"; nor could Israel justify its harsh response as "a war on terror-ism." To combat Palestinian protests, he warned, Israelis might be forced to sacrifice "their own values of democracy and human rights." Dependent on the familiar *Times* cohort of Israeli critics of Israel, he cited Meron Benvenisti's gloomy expectation that the "emotions of nationalism" were likely to overcome "rational judgments about the cost of the occupation." Yaron Ezrahi warned that "the cost of suppression may exceed the point of tolerance in Israeli soci-ety." In the end, Lewis concluded, Israel "must take account of the reality of Palestinian nationalism."[6]

"When a democratic government turns to thuggery as a policy," a *Times* editorial warned, "it risks losing far more than control." By "resorting to brazen brutality and betraying its own values," the editors concluded, "the state that once promised deliverance to the oppressed has truly lost its way." They dealt

Israel the familiar *Times* insult: as "a truly humane country with a democratic government," it might yet "invite parallels with South Africa." Anthony Lewis embellished that invidious analogy. In an article from Ramallah he discerned "chilling similarities" between the West Bank and South Africa: "people suffer humiliation without recourse, without voice or vote. … Law is manipulated to serve the rulers, until justice is eaten away."[7]

The *Times* published excerpts from interviews conducted by Lewis on "the consequences of occupation." His array of sources hardly was random; some were familiar to *Times* readers from their frequent appearances in articles written by Shipler and Friedman. Benvenisti perceived "a new phase of Palestinian resistance" but predicted that Israeli military action, like the application of armed force in Sharpeville, Soweto and Northern Ireland, would succeed. Professor Ezrahi blamed Israel for "destroying" Palestinian moderates. Peace Now spokesman Tzali Reshef lamented that "we've aroused so many reasons for hatred." Among Lewis's ten respondents only Defense Minister Yitzhak Rabin and his predecessor Moshe Arens defended Israeli military action against violent Palestinian rioters. Lewis was convinced that "the occupation is untenable."[8]

The *Times* was attentive to growing unease among liberal American Jews over Israeli military responses and the rising number of Palestinian civilian casualties. David Shipler discovered "a deeper disquiet" among Jewish community leaders, citing Reform Rabbi Alexander Schindler who had cabled Israeli President Chaim Herzog that military beatings of Palestinian civilians constituted "an offense to the Jewish spirit" that "betrays the Zionist dream." The *Times* published a letter from prominent American Jews (including Irving Howe, editor of *Dissent*, and Rabbi Arthur Hertzberg, president of the World Jewish Congress) expressing shame over Israeli military responses and urging American Jews "to speak out in criticism."[9]

The *Times* effectively functioned as the sounding board for American Jewish critics of Israel. Steven Erlanger (a future Jerusalem Bureau Chief) reported the "anguish" of Jews in Teaneck (New Jersey) over Israel's "tactics and the safety of its moral standing." A bizarre climax to the cascade of criticism came from humorist and film director Woody Allen, not previously known for his Middle East expertise. A self-identified "uninformed coward," he was "a supporter of Israel" who had been "outraged at the horrors inflicted on this little nation by hostile neighbors, vile terrorists and much of the world." But he was "appalled beyond measure by the treatment of rioting Palestinians by the Jews."[10]

Although public opinion polls indicated that most Israelis supported "a tough line to control the Palestinians," *Times* coverage virtually ignored them.

Instead, it persistently and prominently featured the "moral indignation" of Israel's left-wing critics. In an article about Israeli "doves," Janet Aviad of Peace Now claimed that the "average" Israeli was "repulsed by the beatings"; her colleague Galia Golan described Israelis as "galvanized" in opposition. An American-born member of Israelis by Choice declared: "We did not come to Israel to participate in the oppression of another people."[11]

Two months after the intifada erupted there still was no *Times* coverage of the silent majority of Israelis who supported the "tough line." In its succinct editorial narrative: "Predictably, Palestinians without hope started rioting." Then, "surprisingly, Israel responded with excessive force." And, "inevitably, world opinion erupted against Israel." Another editorial cited "ever more ugly evidence that the use of brutal force is brutalizing." Israel, once a "symbol of human decency," had discovered the "harsh consequences of its occupation" and "behaves unreasonably." In the judgment of the *Times*, the exchange of land for peace was "the surest way to preserve Israeli democracy, decency – and safety."[12]

In another cascade of columns, the *Times* critique of Israel sharpened. Anthony Lewis once again relied on Benvenisti, who blamed his country for insulting Palestinian honor and pride while practicing "creeping annexation: taking the land, building settlements, treating the Palestinians as a subordinate population." His "gloomy view," Lewis concluded, was confirmed by reality. "Everyone can see that Israel holds the West Bank and Gaza by force alone, and that force has evil consequences."[13]

In an ostensible gesture of balance the *Times* printed companion articles on the "Palestinian" and "Israeli" views of the conflict. Beir Zeit University philosophy professor Sari Nusseibeh was paired with Hebrew University political scientist Yaron Ezrahi, identified as "active in the Israeli peace movement since 1973." Not surprisingly, they were in virtual agreement. Nusseibeh advocated "mutual recognition by the two nations of one another," with Palestinians and Israelis enjoying their own "collective political identity and national rights" in their "common homeland." "To be an Israeli these days," Ezrahi lamented, "is, for many of us, to live with the sense that our world has begun to crumble, that our deepest beliefs and most cherished dreams are being shattered." He warned that the elevation of "military over democratic values" would "subvert the Zionist vision and betray fundamental Jewish beliefs."[14]

On the adjacent page the *Times* published a letter from four prominent (left-wing) Israeli literary figures – Yehuda Amichai, Amos Elon, Amos Oz, and A.B. Yehoshua – who cited "more than 20 years of shortsighted Israeli policies." Insisting "there is no military solution," they advocated partitioning the land west of the Jordan River between Palestinians and Israelis. Convinced that the status quo "will further corrupt Israeli society," they urged American Jews (and "all friends of Israel") to "speak up." By their silence, they were supporting "the tragically wrong side" – Israel.[15]

The *Times* also published a letter from Eugene V. Rostow, Under Secretary of State under Lyndon Johnson, who had played a significant role in drafting UN Resolution 242 following the Six-Day War. Asserting that media coverage of the intifada was "shockingly superficial," with repeated depictions of the "heroic protests" of "a people suffering under foreign occupation," Rostow noted that after World War I the League of Nations Mandate for Palestine, "an international trust for the Jewish people," brought the West Bank and Gaza under their jurisdiction. Israel's presence there, he wrote, was "entirely legitimate" pending the willingness of Arab states to make peace.[16]

Even *Times* editors conceded that "until the P.L.O. summons the courage and wisdom to accept peace with Israel for some kind of Palestinian homeland, it would be folly for Israel to bargain." Its columnists were divided. For Anthony Lewis the Israeli military response to the Palestinian uprising made it "increasingly difficult for friends of Israel to remain silent." But A.M. Rosenthal rejected comparisons of Israel to "Fascists and South Africans" as "not only false but odious." He bluntly suggested that the cause of conflict was "40 years of Arab refusal to accept the existence of Israel," exemplified by "40 years of furious hostility and military attempts to destroy her." Israel's occupation of the West Bank and Gaza, he noted, was "a result, not the cause of aggression – Arab aggression."[17]

Following a Palestinian terrorist attack on an Israeli bus, Lewis asked: "How can we hope for a negotiated way out of the conflict when the P.L.O uses the tactic of murderous assaults on civilians?" But he devoted the remainder of his column to the views of retired Israeli general Yehoshafat Harkabi, former chief of Israeli intelligence, who urged "accommodation" with the Palestinians by recognizing "the folly of trying to rule over lands inhabited by an antagonistic people." Lewis praised Harkabi's "realism" for accepting "the mortal danger" of "trying to rule the West Bank and Gaza forever."[18]

Although conservative columnist William Safire suggested that Israel's "secret weapon" was "the strength of being a democracy," Lewis was not persuaded. Yet again identifying himself as a "friend" of the Jewish state (the better to criticize it), he hectored the Israeli government for Prime Minister Shamir's refusal to embrace the land-for-peace formula, relinquish territory or negotiate with the PLO. Palestinians, for Lewis, had become the new Jews, "struggling, as Jews struggled, for statehood on a piece of that land." Reiterating his favorite derogatory analogy, he referred to Israeli tactics – detentions without trial and restrictions on press coverage – that came "right out of the South African book." He anticipated the possibility of an Israel "so dominated by religious-nationalist fervor" that it "loses its own values in order to suppress another people."[19]

As the intifada raged and Israeli military responses hardened, the *Times* critique of Israel increasingly focused on Jewish settlers. Berating "religious-nationalist fanatics" and "settler justice," Lewis was certain that his idolized Justice Brandeis "would look at where Israel is going today and be heartsick." In a *Times Magazine* critique Reform Rabbi Albert Vorspan, declaring that "the moral equation has changed," depicted Israelis as "oppressors," revealing their country as "a nation like all others" that "has lost its moral compass." Worse yet, for Vorspan (and, doubtlessly, for the *Times*), American Jews were implicated: "It's about us."[20]

A.M. Rosenthal disagreed. The path to peace, he wrote, lay in "acceptance … of the permanent existence of Israel as a nation among nations in the Middle East, place of its birth and roots of its religion." But "Arabs rejected that road and chose Holy War." Yet "brave little Israel suddenly became 'arrogant and intransigent'" – words, Rosenthal pointedly noted, that "seem reserved for people of a certain persuasion." The intifada had persuaded Israelis, "who may be embarrassed by the violence but not to the point of suicide," that Palestinians "still live in the dark dreams of Israel's death."[21]

In mid-May 1988 Joel Brinkley, awarded a Pulitzer prize eight years earlier for international reporting from Cambodia, published his first article as Jerusalem Bureau Chief. He noted that Jerusalem Day, celebrating the reunification of the city following the Six-Day War, was a "catastrophe day" for Palestinians. His early articles skimmed the surface of current events, reporting a "sudden drop in tourism," especially among American Jews who constituted Israel's "largest source of foreign capital"; a "stern letter" from the Israeli government to a State Department legal adviser, warning him not to remove archeological artifacts from the country without a permit; and the first Peace Now demonstration in the West Bank in three years.[22]

When the Center for Media and Public Affairs found *Times* coverage of the intifada filled with "negative spin," most of it "anti-Israel," Anthony Lewis was furious. "Unchallenged facts," not biased reporting, he responded, "hurt Israel in American eyes." The problem was "Israel's attempt to exercise permanent dominion over territories inhabited by another people." According to Lewis, most press criticism was not "anti-Israel"; it merely targeted "Israeli Government policy" that "many Israelis think is harmful to their country."[23]

Lewis remained unyielding in his support for the Palestinian struggle. He was impressed by the tone of "mutuality and respect" from a PLO press spokesman, who claimed that Palestinians wanted "lasting peace and security for themselves and the Israelis." It was, he wrote enthusiastically, "the most explicit and articulate statement so far by the Palestinian mainstream of a two-state solution," with a Palestinian state "living in peace alongside Israel." Yet again citing Justice Brandeis, Lewis warned that Israel cannot be "a humane and democratic state" if it chooses "permanent domination" over peace.[24]

William Safire, the self-described "libertarian conservative," thought otherwise. The intifada, he wrote, was "totally misconceived outside Israel's borders." It must be understood as part of "the 40-year war against the Jews," whose objective was "to drive the Israelis out once and for all." Palestinians, he predicted, would have their own state some day – "in the land on the East Bank of the Jordan," where a Palestinian majority population was ruled by King Hussein and his Hashemite minority. Safire chastised American supporters of Israel who "have been reduced to handwringing anguish at the sight of a democratic nation defending itself against a new form of guerilla warfare in which the attacker assumes the role of victim."[25]

But Lewis continued to badger Israel for trying "to suppress any meaningful expression of Palestinian identity." It "must get over the illusion that it can destroy the legitimacy of Palestinian nationalism by bannings and detentions." He acknowledged "hideous" Palestinian terrorist attacks and the failure of Palestinian leaders to express their willingness to "give up terror and settle for a small Palestinian state alongside Israel." But many Israelis, he claimed to know, perceived Palestinians "only as a threat, not as human beings with their own sense of national identity."[26]

The pending Israeli deportation of a Palestinian physics professor for incitement further provoked Lewis's ire. Conceding that "from a distance, one cannot know all the facts," he nonetheless knew (from the professor's lawyer) that the deportation proceeding was "a mockery of justice." It "offends the Jewish sense of justice. It offends Jewish honor. It offends the moral and political premises of a Jewish state." And, predictably, it offended Justice Brandeis's insistence on due process.[27]

The analogy between Palestinian and Jewish suffering was a favorite *Times* trope. Editorial board member Karl E. Meyer linked Palestinians to pre-state Zionists, planting trees and organizing youth movements. But Israel, "reluctant to disregard its British nightstick," responded to the Palestinian drive for statehood with "the same hated laws": curfews, censorship, detention without cause and deportation. Consequently, Palestinians experienced "a sense of despair and powerlessness" – not unlike that felt by displaced Jews after World War II who were unable to reach their homeland.[28] In the *Times,* Palestinians were the new Jews, abused by their cruel (Israeli) rulers.

As the Israeli voice of the morally compromised Jewish state, Meron Benvenisti contributed a *Magazine* article recounting the years following the Six-Day War when, "alone and unarmed," he had wandered everywhere in Jerusalem. He built his home overlooking the Temple Mount in the only mixed neighborhood, where Arabs and Jews lived in "a twilight world … torn between our affinity to our respective tribes, and our kinship as human beings." Benvenisti finally realized that "my brand of Zionism – secular, humanistic, peace-loving – never really took firm root in Jerusalem." It was "strangled by the exotic growths of fundamentalism and chauvinism, Jewish and Arab alike." The conflict, he sadly concluded, was "primordial, irreconcilable."[29]

On the eve of Israeli elections in November 1988 the potential victory of right-wing prime minister Yitzhak Shamir vexed *Times* reporters, columnists and editors. For Bureau Chief Joel Brinkley, it would determine "whether Israel is to be a conciliatory nation of the left, an assertively hardline nation of the right – or a people … incapable of defining itself." Returning for a visit, Thomas Friedman rediscovered "visceral, almost primordial attitudes" among Israelis that resulted from "100 years of intimate contact and conflict between two communities wrestling over the same few miles of land." The goal of Israelis (echoing Benvenisti) should be "to turn my enemy who never allows me to feel at home in my own house into a neighbor with whom I can live comfortably side by side." The next day the *Times* reported that an Israeli mother and her three children were killed in a Palestinian attack on a bus near Jericho. It was the most devastating terrorist act since the beginning of the intifada.[30] Nothing was written about "primordial attitudes" of Palestinians.

To the evident dismay of *Times* editors, preliminary Israeli election results indicated a likely governing alliance of Likud and ultra-Orthodox religious parties under the continuing leadership of Prime Minister Shamir. "Once again," the editors lamented, "the hard-liners and bitter-enders have triumphed in the Holy Land." Both Shamir and Arafat were "extremists" who "flower" amid terrorism. Should Shamir respond to the Palestinian uprising with "full and vengeful force and no hope, he risks tearing his divided nation apart – Arab from Jew and Jew from Jew." The editorial anticipated that a Likud alliance with religious parties would "ignite unease among Jews elsewhere" – especially, if left unspoken, at *The New York Times.*[31]

"There will be no peace," Anthony Lewis lamented. With Israel ruling "by force" over the West Bank and Gaza, "resistance will continue and terrorism increase," leading Israel to respond "with greater repression, spending ... its moral capital to keep the occupied territories." The cycle would continue: "outrage breeding Israeli fear, fear breeding hate." Israelis need to hear "the truth: that the cost of ruling another people ... is destroying Israel." Another post-election *cri de coeur* came from Flora Lewis, perceiving that "the old Zionist dream is eroding in favor of a warrior-priestly state" in which the strength of "theocratic and messianic" forces was especially alarming.[32] Like her Lewis namesake and *Times* editors, she was aghast at the prospect that Jewish religious parties might share political power in governing a Jewish state.

The election results, according to Brinkley, portended "a right-wing theocracy ... dominated by religious fundamentalists." Those on the political left were shocked "at the sight of rigorously Orthodox rabbis in streimels and long black coats parading into the prime minister's office" to present their demands. Shulamit Aloni, leader of the left-wing Citizens Rights Movement, feared that the religious parties would transform Israel "into a Khomeinistic country, into a fascist country." Many Israelis, "not to mention Americans," Brinkley wrote alarmingly, "worry that Israel could become another religious fundamentalist nation, a Jewish version of Iran."[33] Even the poisonous South African analogy no longer sufficed as sufficient condemnation.

With religious parties winning eighteen Knesset seats, Brinkley wrote two days later, their "unexpected surge in power" alarmed secular Israelis – and, to be sure, the *Times*. To assure their support Prime Minister Shamir embraced their definition of "Who is a Jew?," excluding converts by non-Orthodox rabbis from entitlement to Israeli citizenship under the Law of Return. Brinkley reported "growing anger" of American Jews over the prospect that Israel would no longer recognize their Jewish identity. "Anguish and anger have gripped American Jews," wrote John Kifner. Flora Lewis was outraged by the prospect of a redefined Jewish identity. The issue of "Who is a Jew?," she asserted, was "a matter of Israel's relations with the Diaspora, especially American Jewry." Although only a miniscule number of American Jews would be affected by Israeli legislation, the underlying issue was about "the nature of Israel and Zionism, about the meaning of Jewishness." In Israel she claimed to witness a "combination of fundamentalist power and the banalization of brutality."[34]

In December 1988 Yasser Arafat, confronting mounting international pressure amid the lagging intifada, declared his acceptance of UN Resolution 242 and willingness to engage in direct negotiations with Israel. Anthony Lewis was euphoric that Arafat and the PLO had "voiced a new moderation on the question of peace with Israel." The PLO, he believed, had finally accepted "the reality of Israel." But "regrettably, striking changes in the P.L.O.'s historic position" had been brushed aside by Israeli leaders of both major parties with "hostile contempt," indicating that "the current state of Israeli politics is inhospitable to diplomacy."[35] As always, Israel was to blame.

A.M. Rosenthal was scathingly critical of American recognition of the PLO as a negotiating partner. The American turnabout, transforming Arafat into "a victorious international hero," had placed Israel at risk of becoming "a vulnerable sliver," like Czechoslovakia after the Munich pact fifty years earlier. He was joined by William Safire, who suggested that "the way to induce Israeli risk-taking is not for America to pressure its ally but for Arab nations to recognize and directly reassure their neighbor." Palestinian "terrorcrats," he wrote, "make no secret of their goal: the taking of the West Bank as the first stage in a two-stage war of extermination."[36]

Writing from Washington, Thomas Friedman perceived "shock and numbness" in Israel following the American decision to talk with the PLO. The overriding question, he anticipated, would soon become "Who is an Israeli?": someone who believed in occupation "because the Bible or Jewish nationalist ideology says so" – or someone who prefers borders that will produce "a stable peace with its Palestinian neighbors?" Israel, Yaron Ezrahi asserted, "has been jarred into reality." Rabbi Hartman compared Israel to a long-battered child needing assurance that his parent had indeed been cured. Friedman optimistically (and, as it turned out, erroneously) anticipated "even more self-confidence and expressions of moderation" from the PLO, "producing words and deeds that even a majority of Israelis will find believable."[37]

Several days later Rev. Jesse Jackson, not noted for his Middle East expertise, contributed a column praising the American decision to engage in discussions with the PLO. Citing the "non-violent protest and suffering of young Palestinians," he called on Israeli leaders "to indicate their recognition of the Palestinian claim for self-determination." Anthony Lewis wondered "what is in the mind of Israelis who want to continue the occupation, and their conservative American supporters." The choice, to Lewis, was clear. If Palestinians become citizens of a "Greater Israel" it would no longer be a Jewish state. But if Israel continued to deny them "elementary rights," it "will be a kind of South Africa ... denying the equal humanity of another people."[38]

Amid the cacophony of voices from columnists and contributors over the consequences of Arafat's pronouncements, *Times* editors were stunned by the restoration of the Likud-Labor coalition government with Yitzhak Shamir remaining as prime minister. With Israeli politicians unwilling "to heed the seismic shift of attitude elsewhere, especially the United States," the *Times* anticipated "a continued tilt toward repression in the occupied territories."[39]

Israel's "decidedly hardline stance," noted John Kifner, was a direct response to the American decision to talk with PLO representatives. A "triumph" for Arafat, it was "one of the most shattering events in Israel's recent political history." *Times* editors acknowledged that Israelis had "every reason to be skeptical" of Arafat's "words and motives" and "every right to be worried about being drawn into a negotiating process that could bulldoze them into risky concessions." Americans, in turn, had "little hope that either the P.L.O. or Israel will make the real concessions needed to achieve peace in the Middle East."[40] It was a rare expression of editorial even-handedness, braided, to be sure, with moral equivalence.

Early in 1989 Brinkley reported from Jerusalem that the Palestinian uprising "still rumbles steadily along, barely deterred by Israel's ever-changing tactics for suppressing it." Despite an intensified Israeli military response, Palestinian resistance "has not flagged." Israel, he wrote, "remains alone," confronting "an uncommon chorus of disenchantment" from friends and opponents alike as it adamantly refused to talk with the PLO. Interviewing Israeli soldiers at an army base in Bethlehem, Brinkley concluded: "None likes fighting the intifada. Most curse when they get their assignment notices." One revealed poignantly: "I've lost my basic beliefs. . . . I've lost my basic human feeling."[41]

Focused on the plight of suffering Palestinians, the *Times* published three articles (including an editorial) in a single issue exploring life in the town of Beit Sahour, near Bethlehem. A once-thriving community of "merchants and entrepreneurs," its "middle-class nature" and Greek Orthodox majority had convinced Israelis that it was "an unlikely candidate for anti-Israeli militancy." But after four days of interviews, Youssef H. Ibrahim, regional Middle East correspondent who frequently reported from the West Bank, concluded that among local Palestinians "the legacy of the intifada . . . is a bitterness that verges on hatred" toward Israel.

The editorial described Beit Sahur as a town where "people are angry for reasons ranging from rage to despair," driving young Palestinians to wage "an uncompromising revolution against 21 years of Israeli occupation." An older resident admitted that "we are committing suicide, but we cannot retreat. Our children want an end to the occupation and they are running the show."

A biology professor who had spent five months in jail without charges complained: "It's dehumanizing"; Israelis "reduce you to a number. Slowly you begin to change."[42]

A.M. Rosenthal sharply rebuked Israel's critics. Ever since independence it had tried to coax Arab neighbors into negotiations, but for thirty years the response was "rejection and war." In the decade since its treaty with Egypt, "not one Arab state has had the will or the courage" to make peace. Yet the struggle is "seen simply as a contest between a brutal Israeli state and a single, rock-throwing Palestinian liberation movement." Rosenthal identified the West Bank as "a symptom, not the cause" of the continuing crisis, which was "40 years of Arab rejectionism." For Israel to relinquish it, he concluded, "would be self-destructive idiocy."[43]

Months later Anthony Lewis wrapped himself in the Jewish holy days to frame his criticism of Israel. At a time "when Jews are supposed to look into themselves … and commit themselves to what should be," he wrote, they needed "honest thinking about the future of Israel." If it continued to evade peace negotiations with the PLO, Israel would become a Jewish state in which Arabs comprised nearly half the population but with "no vote or other political rights." That would transform it into "a garrison state," a "brutalized state," relying on "increasing military force and increasing abandonment of the rule of civilized law."[44]

In an adjacent column the *Times* printed the critique of a European Jewish journalist posted in Israel. "Not a day goes by in Gaza or on the West Bank," Hal Wyner wrote, "without new cases of wanton brutality" by Israeli soldiers who were violating, "with nearly complete impunity, all accepted norms of civilized military behavior." But reports of this "appalling human rights situation" were understated in the media lest a Jewish journalist be "censured for 'self-hatred'" or a non-Jew be accused of anti-Semitism. Even more disturbing to Wyner, the Israeli government "purports to be acting in the name of the Jewish people" – thereby, presumably, implicating him. The *Times* ran three articles in a single issue with variations on the theme of Israeli responsibility for a lost opportunity for peace. Jack Rosenthal, its Tel Aviv-born editorial page editor, identified Israeli settlements as the primary obstacle to peace. "Israel does not need the occupied territories," he wrote, warning that "the more settlements, the more Israelis desensitize themselves to the odious idea of dominating others, and to the harsh means required to maintain such dominion."[45]

Joel Brinkley reported yet another interview with Benvenisti, whose West Bank Data Project provided "the vital statistics of Israel's occupation." Identified as an Israeli liberal who had scathingly referred to Israel's "master race democracy," Benvenisti anticipated "the gradual, inexorable intertwining of Israeli and Palestinian societies" that would "almost certainly destroy the original Zionist vision of Israel as a country populated and run by Jews." Anthony Lewis cited an affidavit describing Israeli abuse of a Palestinian human rights worker to illuminate "the Kafkaesque reality of life" in the occupied territories. Israel, he alleged, "does not live up to minimum standards of humanity." But *Commentary* editor Norman Podhoretz, the solitary defender of Israel among *Times* critics, insisted that Israelis had "no choice" but to resist "with all their might the establishment of the Palestinian state that so many people are now hectoring them to accept." With the PLO charter still committed to the destruction of Israel, the status quo was preferable to an extension of the "Hobbesian hell" that it had already inflamed in Lebanon.[46]

One week later, relying primarily on a telephone conversation with an Israeli computer programmer, Lewis concluded that the Israeli army had "systematically harassed and humiliated" the people of Beit Sahour. For Lewis, the town illuminated "the oppressive reality of the occupation." In seven months since Youssef H. Ibrahim's first report, no Israeli city, town, kibbutz or settlement, nor all of them together, had received anywhere near the coverage afforded by the *Times* to Beit Sahour.[47]

As the intifada neared its second anniversary Joel Brinkley reported in the Sunday *Magazine* from the Palestinian town of Husan, the Dheisheh refugee camp, and the tiny village of Kafr Malik. He witnessed "youths" from Husan, near Bethlehem, preparing and launching their twice daily attack with "baseball-sized" stones on a "settlers' bus" transporting three "long bearded Jews" from a nearby settlement. In Dheisheh he was told that "the life of animals is better than the life of refugees." From Kafr Malik, where the nearest road suitable for stoning Israeli cars was a mile distant, shebab (militant young Palestinians) slept in caves to escape Israeli military retaliation. They were fighting, one claimed, "the same way George Washington fought" and for the same goal: liberty.[48] Once again Brinkley's narrative was framed by beleaguered (but heroic) Palestinians resisting oppressive Israelis.

Editor Jack Rosenthal refocused attention on Beit Sahour, whose residents, in "the newest battle against Israeli occupation," refused to pay taxes. As the intifada dragged into its third year, he anticipated that "fear and fury will harden in the dark-eyed boys of Beit Sahour." But Israelis "pay a painful price for containing the uprising – a price that abrades the army, hobbles the economy and corrodes democracy." Occupation, Anthony Lewis wrote two weeks later, "requires force, lawlessness and increasing corruption of one's own moral standards." Israel "wounds itself by its continued occupation of land inhabited by another people."[49]

Observing the second anniversary of the intifada, Brinkley selected four Palestinians and four Jews "for their interesting points of view and representative experiences." The Palestinians, including a twenty-two-year-old who had been in prison seven times in eight years and a homeless family living in a tent, in Beit Sahour, were victims. Among the "representative" Israelis were a civil liberties advocate who understood that "democratic freedoms often take a back seat to the nation's security concerns" and a religious settler from the United States who made mezuzah scrolls, carried an Uzi machine-gun as a "holy duty" while driving his children to school, and believed that when the Messiah arrived – in twenty years – all the Arabs would be gone.[50]

In a subsequent front-page article about the arrival of an unprecedented number of Soviet immigrants, Brinkley emphasized the ambivalence of Israelis toward the newcomers. After years of higher emigration than immigration, the Russian influx "would enhance Israel's sense of national identity." But given unemployment levels and scarce housing, "many Israelis" resented the newcomers, who "have little if any Jewish identity." Observing the arrival of a planeload of immigrants, Brinkley noted that they "looked startled, even a bit disturbed" when yeshiva students welcomed them with "chanting, clapping and singing traditional Jewish songs the Russians had never heard." They even had to be "prompted to stand" for Hatikva.[51] Their Jewish alienation, not their decision to make aliya, drove his narrative.

As the decade ended the central theme of *Times* coverage was expressed by Flora Lewis. Israel's approach to the Palestinian problem, she wrote, was "a dead end, … degrading into endemic, endless communal strife." No less disturbing, Meron Benvenisti expected the struggle to "go on and on, neither escalating beyond the point of bearability nor fading away." The generation of Zionist founders had envisioned the state as "a Jewish homeland where the question of identity would be solved in what seemed a normal, national cultural way." But "the demands of theocracy have grown to challenge the secular idea."[52]

In 1967 neighboring Arab states had forced Israel into a war for survival that within six days expanded its boundaries into East Jerusalem, the West Bank and Gaza. For more than two decades, with infrequent exceptions, *Times* coverage of the Jewish state – whether from Jerusalem, Washington or New York – had been relentlessly critical. So it was that the Palestinian intifada was framed in its news reports, columns and editorials as the story of an oppressed people whose heroic freedom fighters confronted an Israeli Goliath determined to suppress their yearning for independence and statehood.

CHAPTER 9

Illusions of Peace: 1990–1996

The new decade began with harbingers of a massive flow of immigrants from the Soviet Union. With one thousand new arrivals weekly, Bureau Chief Joel Brinkley focused on forty Russian families in the West Bank settlement of Ariel. The "stream" of newcomers, according to a *Times* headline, "Disturbs the Occupied Territories." Although it actually was "just a trickle," as Brinkley acknowledged, it "created a tempest" that prompted complaints from government officials in Egypt, Jordan and the United States. Speaking with a newly arrived Soviet couple in Ariel, Brinkley was reminded that "the territories are named Judea and Samaria," their biblical names. They asked: "Doesn't this tell you something?"[1]

Two weeks later Brinkley offered a gloomy demographic perspective. "As Israel grows wholly preoccupied with absorbing a mass of Soviet immigrants," he wrote, "far more Israelis who already have job skills, homes and deep familiarity with all aspects of life here are leaving." That imbalance posed a problem that "touches Israel's soul," with "many Israelis" taking it as "an even more eloquent statement that the state has failed to be a successful homeland." An editorial approved the "prompt resettlement of as many Soviet Jews as possible," which "rekindles Israel's founding spark." But Arabs were "upset" lest the newcomers "flood into the West Bank, and thereby prevent negotiated Palestinian control" of the territory. Instead, the *Times* advised, Israel should develop new cities in the Galilee and Negev: "an uplifting project, consonant with the original romance of the Jewish state."[2]

It was much ado about little. Brinkley reported that fewer than 1% of new Soviet immigrants chose to join 72,000 West Bank settlers. There was "little evidence" to indicate that Israel was making "special efforts" to steer them there. Although new apartments featuring "garden views" (as headlined in the *Times*) were under construction in the largest settlement of Maaleh Adumim, located between Jerusalem and Jericho, Brinkley noted that only "several dozen" Soviet newcomers had chosen to join its 14,000 residents. "For the most part," he concluded, "the Soviet Jews are not ardent Zionists interested in promoting the idea of 'greater Israel.'"[3]

President Bush's press conference statement that no new settlements should be built in the West Bank or East Jerusalem infuriated A.M. Rosenthal. Israel's stalwart *Times* ally condemned "the growing double standard routine of attacking the Israeli democracy and remaining mute about the Arab tyrannies." To Israelis, Brinkley reported, "the concept that Jews are 'settling' in East Jerusalem seems about as unbelievable as the idea that residents of Wyoming are 'settling' on disputed Indian territory." *Times* editors acknowledged that President Bush's statement gave "a thoughtless, unnecessary jolt" to Israelis but patriotically urged his administration to continue its "tough diplomatic pressure" on the Jewish state.[4]

On the evening of Good Friday, according to a furious *Times* editorial, "20 armed Jewish families, singing and clapping," moved into St. John's Hospice, a vacant building near the Church of the Holy Sepulchre in Jerusalem's Old City. By authorizing an "unprecedented Jewish settlement in a Christian or Muslim area of the Old City," instantly sparking Arab riots and international condemnation, Housing Minister David Levy and Prime Minister Shamir had "defiled Israel's unblemished record of support for freedom of separate worship in the Old City." (That freedom had not been even slightly impacted.) Brinkley reported the foreign ministry's defiant response: "It is the right of Jews to live everywhere, and to purchase or rent property in all parts of the land of Israel, and especially Jerusalem."[5]

Watching the Israeli government, Anthony Lewis wrote, was like watching as King Lear "destroys himself by acts of willful folly." He conceded that "Jews should be able to live where they want, in Israel or anywhere." But "the way this project was done, with what offense to tradition and the feelings of others," indicated that Israel had chosen "rejection and isolation" over "cementing friendship and trying to talk with Palestinians who are ready for peace." Ten days later he deplored "Israeli extremists" who believed that they can "permanently occupy Palestinian territory, if necessary expelling its inhabitants." In Israel Lewis noted, as in South Africa, "Trying to deny the existence of a people – to deny them the vote and ordinary human expectations – will not produce peace." He conceded that journalists judged Israel by a double standard, claiming in self-exculpation: "From its birth Israel asked to be judged as a light among nations."[6]

In early June, after Israel thwarted an attempted Palestinian terror attack on the Tel Aviv beach, an editorial brushed aside Arafat's claim that the attack came from a rogue faction. But "Israeli credibility" was also being tested. Would its government "deal with the realities of Palestinian nationalism and Palestinian rights"? Israel's security "cannot indefinitely be limited to being tough on Palestinians; it has to involve trying negotiations." Flora Lewis added: "The extremes have found each other in the Jewish-Palestinian conflict. ... The choice is narrowing to war and peace, builders and blasters, regardless of being Jew or Arab."[7]

In mid-October an outburst of violence erupted in the Old City of Jerusalem. Several thousand rioting Palestinians on the Temple Mount, Brinkley wrote, fearing the imminent arrival of "Jewish radicals" intending to desecrate Muslim holy sites, were "raining stones and bottles" on Jewish worshippers celebrating the Sukkoth holiday at the Western Wall below. Israeli "paramilitary police officers, unprepared and ill-equipped," responded by firing into the angry mob, killing twenty-one Palestinians. Based on investigations conducted by B'Tselem, an organization recently founded by left-wing Israeli activists to document Israeli human-rights abuses, and Al-Haq, a Palestinian human rights organization, Brinkley concluded that Palestinians had "initiated the violence" – but "both sides share blame."[8]

Times editors labeled the "bloody blunder" of the Israeli police "a startling use of deadly force" that "violates police policy throughout the civilized world." By doing so in "occupied territory," Israel had violated international law. "It was not paranoid," the editorial continued, "for ordinary Palestinians to worry about the designs that some Jewish fanatics have on the Temple Mount." And "even *assuming* flagrant P.L.O. provocation, it would not excuse opening fire on unarmed civilians."[9] The editorial ignored the hordes of Palestine stone throwers who triggered the disturbance and the stature of the Temple Mount as the holiest ancient Jewish site.

Anthony Lewis offered historical context and, predictably, criticism. "Attacked by its neighbors, ostracized, told it had no right to exist," Israelis "understandably became a hard-shelled people," determined to "go it alone." But they demonstrated "indifference to the suffering of others," treating Palestinians "without understanding or sympathy." In "a civilized country," not even "planned" and "outrageous" stone-throwing attacks could justify a response with live ammunition. Palestinians, after all, were "highly agitated" by the prospect of a "planned march" by Jewish "extremists" (which the Israeli government had prohibited). It was "not in America's interest," he concluded, "to help Israel inflict moral and political wounds on itself."[10]

But in columnist William Safire's recounting, 3,000 Arabs, many of them throwing stones at Jews praying at the Western Wall, had committed a "desecration of Judaism." The PLO "got what it sought: enough of its hapless followers sacrificed to call the tragedy a 'massacre.'" Meir Rosenne, former Israeli ambassador to the United States, challenged the *Times* editorial response. "Like the Jews," he wrote, Israel is "a pain in the neck, and the world would feel relieved without it." Or, if Israel "insists on persisting, let it at least have the good grace to be ... a victim." In the end, he wrote sardonically, "Israel is to blame, by its very being, for everything."[11]

During the waning months of 1990 the Iraqi invasion of Kuwait dominated Middle Eastern news coverage. For Israeli officials, Brinkley reported, Iraqi aggression "reaffirmed the correctness of their longstanding, hard-line foreign policy." After the first Iraqi missiles fell on Tel Aviv, thousands of terrified residents fled the city for safety elsewhere. Iraqi Scud attacks were "no threat to the security of the state," Brinkley wrote, but "they have shaken its people to the core." *Times* Jerusalem reporter Sabra Chartrand (Brinkley's wife) covered the Palestinian response. Morale "soared" when the air-raid sirens sounded. They "welcome the missiles, because they believe Israel deserves to be attacked, and because ... they think war will help create a Palestinian state."[12]

Israel was highly praised for its restraint, noted A.M. Rosenthal. But by not responding it was also "risk-taking on a historic scale." To be sure, the West had begun to understand "the daily danger in which Israel lives." Western minds, he wrote, might even begin to imagine the consequences for Israel of Scuds launched from a Palestinian state: "Tel Aviv would certainly have been awash in blood, choking with gas and piled with dead." For Israel's survival and Middle East peace, Rosenthal warned, "reprisal cannot be surrendered, ever again."[13]

Within two weeks more than two dozen Scud missiles had landed in Tel Aviv and Haifa, killing four Israelis and wounding hundreds. The homes of nearly one thousand Tel Aviv residents had been destroyed. In neighboring Ramat Gan, where dozens of houses were damaged or demolished, three elderly Israelis died of heart attacks. Brinkley reported that "tens of thousands" of Tel Aviv residents had left the city seeking safety elsewhere and "much of the nation is traumatized." For the first time, Israel was under attack and unable to respond lest it damage the American-led coalition that demanded restraint.[14]

Commentary editor Norman Podhoretz contributed a stinging op-ed entitled "Unleash the Israelis." Many Israelis, he wrote, "suspect that they are getting such a good press only because the world is more comfortable with Jews as passive victims than as feisty warriors." It was unclear why the United

States should give "tender consideration" to the wishes of Syria, Jordan, and other autocratic Arab states, "while treating a democratic ally like Israel as an embarrassment to be kept in the closet." By restraining Israel, he warned, "we are squandering a precious strategic asset."[15]

Two weeks after the first Scud missiles fell on Israel, *Times* editors with little to say about the plight of its endangered citizens focused instead on the arrest of Palestinian activist Sari Nusseibeh by Israeli authorities for allegedly informing "Iraqi targeters" of Scud site hits. "That looks less like justice than a vendetta," the editors wrote, reminding Israel that its "claim on American sympathies rests most solidly on its respect for law and democratic rights." Anthony Lewis, who had remained silent while Israel was under attack, attributed Nusseibeh's arrest to the unwillingness of Israel's right-wing government to negotiate with the Palestinians. Acknowledging that "Israel has done many good things, and its burdens are heavy," that could not justify "the folly of trying to rule another people by force – without even talking to them."[16]

In an op-ed entitled "Don't Strong-Arm Israel" Eugene V. Rostow, former Under Secretary of State who had played a major role in drafting UN Resolution 242 after the Six-Day War, reminded readers that Israel was entitled to administer the West Bank and Gaza "until peace is made." Indeed, Israel "has a stronger claim to the West Bank than any other nation or would-be nation" because the League of Nations Mandate for Palestine (never rescinded) gave it "the same legal right to settle the West Bank, Gaza Strip and East Jerusalem that it has to settle Haifa or West Jerusalem." A.M. Rosenthal concurred. A Palestinian state, he wrote a week later, "exists already, just across the narrow River Jordan, and one day will be known by its real name": Palestine.[17] But Rostow and Rosenthal were marginalized amid the barrage of *Times* criticism of Israel.

In May 1991 Israel temporarily gained *Times* approval after an emergency airlift (named Operation Solomon) transported more than 14,000 Ethiopian Jews to their promised land, causing "joyous celebration" among Israelis. Leaving their planes, Brinkley wrote, they "cheered, ululated and bent down to kiss the tarmac." Israelis, in turn, "watched them aglow, marveling at this powerful image showing that their state still holds appeal, even with all its problems." Operation Solomon was "a marvel of speed, efficiency and secrecy," a rare approving editorial acknowledged, that "touched chords of memory and tradition that connect ancient and modern Israel." Like the influx of Soviet Jews, "their safe passage reaffirms Israel's original mission as a haven for exiles."[18]

The "resounding victory" of the Labor Party in 1992 after nearly fifteen years of Likud domination, wrote Clyde Haberman (Joel Brinkley's successor), was "certain to gladden the Bush Administration" with its "stated willingness of land for peace." An editorial entitled "New Promise for Peace in Israel" enthusiastically praised Yitzhak Rabin for emphasizing "national interest and security guarantees" over "ideological and biblical claims to a Greater Israel." Anthony Lewis was euphoric over the "transforming" election results. For a decade Israel had been governed by "zealots" who were "determined to impose their ideology whatever the cost." Now there was an opportunity for "the mixture of idealism and practicality" that once defined "the Zionism of Weizmann, Ben Gurion and Brandeis." In a blunt response two days later, A.M. Rosenthal suggested that "under any government Israelis survive in a jungle of dictators hunting for Israeli weakness." Perhaps with his own newspaper in mind he warned against moral equivalence, a "political perversion" that ignored "the difference between democracy and dictatorship."[19]

By the end of 1992 the *Times* had a new Sulzberger publisher, the first non-Jewish family member since Adolph Ochs purchased the newspaper. Arthur Ochs Sulzberger, confirmed as a child at the St. Thomas Episcopal Church in Manhattan, was raised in his mother's religion. With multicultural sensitivity he declared: "We can no longer offer our readers a predominantly white, straight, male vision of events and say we're doing our job."[20] But there would be little discernible difference in its critical coverage of Israel.

One year later the Labor government approved a secretly negotiated agreement with the PLO that provided for Palestinian self-rule in the Gaza Strip and Jericho, with a projected five-year transition period to statehood. Two "bitter enemies," Thomas Friedman exulted, "would become mutually recognized partners for peace." During a century of "violence and delegitimization," Israelis and Palestinians "made sure that the other was never allowed to really feel at home in Israel." Describing the agreement as "nothing less than the Israeli Balfour Declaration for the Palestinians," he euphorically predicted that the Middle East "will never be the same." Friedman fantasized about Arafat and Rabin drinking "thick Arabic coffee" while chatting together in Jericho about "the modalities of self-rule."[21]

A *Times* editorial hailed the "diplomatic revolution" achieved by the "courage, vision and finesse" of Israeli leaders and "the Palestinian inner circle" that surrounded Arafat. To be sure, "Israelis are being asked to trust the P.L.O.," whose Charter proclaimed that Palestine between the Jordan River and the Mediterranean could only be liberated through armed struggle. Although fierce opposition came from "extremists on both sides," most Israelis and Palestinians "seem ready to give peace a chance." Clyde Haberman cited "the breathtaking change that has now swept across this land for which Jews and Arabs have fought and died across the last century."[22]

A.M. Rosenthal offered a more sober and, as events proved, more astute assessment. Israel was taking an "almost heart-stopping risk" in believing that Palestinians and Arab states were "ready to settle for a West Bank Palestine – and end the fight there." In an op-ed pointedly entitled "Peace in Our Time?," Likud party chairman Benjamin Netanyahu scathingly compared the agreement to Prime Minister Neville Chamberlain's capitulation in 1938. He described it as "a guarantee of increased tension, future terrorism, and, ultimately, war."[23]

The signing ceremony on the White House lawn, Friedman reported, sealed "the first agreement between Jews and Palestinians to end their conflict and share the holy land along the Jordan River that they both call home." He highlighted Prime Minister Rabin's declaration "Enough of blood and tears! Enough!" and Chairman Arafat's assurance that "Our two peoples ... want to give peace a real chance." With their historic handshake, two hands were "locked together for a fleeting moment of reconciliation."[24]

Three editorials within five days celebrated the Oslo Accords. The Middle East, "biblical land of miracles," had brought "these modern-day astonishments that almost defy belief," the editors exulted. Lauding Rabin and Arafat, the Times declared: "When lifelong enemies embrace ... peace has a rare chance." Israel had demonstrated its commitment to "the principle that the Palestinians are a distinct people entitled to negotiate their own destiny." Palestinians, in turn, accepted "the principle that their Israeli neighbors are on the land to stay, and are to be lived with in peace."[25]

Times euphoria was framed within its familiar embrace of moral equivalence. Israelis and Palestinians "have experienced decades of mortal conflict, but also share some experiences and dreams." Zionists "saw a national homeland as the only way to make the world's Jews safe from persecution, expulsion and extermination" while Palestinians, "herded into refugee camps" and "subjected to occupation," developed "similar aspirations." Israelis and Palestinians alike, David Shipler wrote, had defined themselves "as victims with no guilt for each other's suffering." But A.M. Rosenthal noted bluntly that Jews had been "ready to share Palestine with Arabs from the beginning. The Arabs refused."[26]

Within a month after the signing of the Oslo Accords two Israelis hiking in Wadi Qelt near Jericho were killed by Arab assailants. A Palestinian suicide bombing wounded thirty Israelis on a West Bank commuter bus. A prominent rabbi was wounded, and his driver killed, on their way to Kiryat Arba, adjacent to Hebron. In December a Soviet refusenik was murdered in downtown

Hebron. He died in the arms of Dr. Baruch Goldstein, chief medical officer for the Jewish community of Hebron.[27]

Three months later, on the eve of the Purim holiday, Goldstein went to the Machpelah shrine for the reading of the *Megillah* story of Esther and Mordechai. He was enraged by menacing shouts of "Etbach el Yahud" ("Kill the Jews") from crowds of angry Muslims, gathered outside awaiting entry for Ramadan prayers. Early the next morning, wearing his military uniform and armed with a Galil assault rifle, Goldstein returned to Machpelah where he murdered twenty-nine Muslims in prayer, and wounded more than one hundred, before he was beaten to death.[28]

As a Brooklyn-born Orthodox Jew who became a devoted follower of militant right-wing Rabbi Meir Kahane, and a Jewish settler who ended his life as a mass murderer of Moslems at prayer, Goldstein touched deep nerves at the *Times*. The day after his horrific massacre it published three front-page stories, an editorial and an op-ed. Clyde Haberman speculated whether Goldstein's rampage was motivated "by revenge for recent attacks against Jews" or by "calculated political terrorism … that would cause the peace accord to unravel." Although the attack was widely condemned throughout Israel, he noted that in Hebron and Kiryat Arba "costumed parades for the festive Purim holiday continued as though nothing had happened."[29]

A *Times* editorial referred to "the unspeakable atrocity" in Hebron that "appears to have been the work of a deranged and fanatical individual." Yet the "right response" would be to "quickly and credibly investigate charges of a wider conspiracy." Calling on Israel to be "as generous as it can be in its negotiating stance," it recommended an accelerated "transfer of civil authority in the territories into Palestinian hands." In an op-ed column left-wing activist Michael Lerner, editor of *Tikkun* Magazine, declared that Goldstein's "craziness mirrors a climate of hatred nurtured by right-wing Jews." Identifying himself with "the Jewish religious peace movement," he urged American Jews "to feel shame … over the systematic misuse of Judaism and Jewish suffering to justify racist and oppressive treatment of another people."[30]

For David Shipler, Goldstein was not the "lone, demented criminal" that Prime Minister Rabin had identified. He was "the product of an ideology" that is "an amalgam of anti-Arab bigotry, religious certainty and nationalist zeal," abetted by Israeli governments across the political spectrum that "permitted, even encouraged, settlers to carry guns and use them in their defense." Indeed, Shipler wrote, "A violent symmetry emerges in which extreme settlers become the mirror image of Hamas." No less disturbing was "the disproportional presence of Americans" among the "more militant" settlers. Yet Shipler recognized that most settlers were not "ideologues" who endorsed terrorism and yearned for "a mighty Jewish state on biblical land"; they were "commuters to Jerusalem and Tel Aviv."[31]

Times conservative columnists responded. William Safire described Goldstein as "the fanatic bigot who shamed his people and betrayed his religion." But Jewish settlers were "embattled pioneers, often attacked and necessarily armed to protect themselves." Goldstein, wrote A.M. Rosenthal, "committed a monstrous act of terrorism that cannot be softened by talk of his rage or sense of injustice." But he warned against "the offense of moral equivalence, the curse of Western society," which had become "shield and weapon for those who oppose the existence of Israel." He insisted that "the worth of Israel as a democratic nation, set alone among the dictatorships of the Middle East," must be affirmed.[32]

Times editors, concerned lest American Jews be implicated in Goldstein's murderous rampage, noted: "Especially chilling for Americans, perhaps, is the fact that Dr. Goldstein and many of his fellow settlers began their odyssey in the United States." An American Jew, originally from New York, had committed a horrible crime. Goldstein's "dark legacy" must not be nourished by "American dollars" or "Americans' moral support." The conspicuous presence of American Jews among the more militant settlers remained a source of *Times* unease.[33]

The euphoria that had accompanied the Oslo accord disintegrated amid devastating Palestinian terrorist attacks. In April 1994 a Hamas suicide bomber killed eight Israelis in Afula. Six months later a bomb exploded in a crowded Tel Aviv bus traveling along Dizengoff Street, killing twenty-two Israelis and exacting the highest death toll since the 1978 coastal highway bus hijacking. In a country "familiar with terrorism," Clyde Haberman reported, Dizengoff "became a ribbon of horror, with corpses scattered on the ground, body parts blown into treetops and the copper-like smell of blood thick in the air." He quoted two wounded survivors who expressed their continuing support for the peace process. He also cited a Hamas leader who compared the bus bombing to Baruch Goldstein's Hebron massacre.[34]

A *Times* editorial urged Israeli leaders and Arafat "to reassure a frightened and angry Israeli public by cracking down hard on the elusive Hamas terror network." But Israel must do "all it can to dry up the sea of sympathizers in which these killers swim by responding to the legitimate political claims of the Palestinian population." (In translation, Israel shared responsibility with Palestinian suicide bombers for terrorist attacks against Jews.) A.M. Rosenthal declined to mitigate the responsibility of terrorists for their atrocities. Israel, he wrote, was a proxy for Western values of freedom. The Dizengoff massacre framed his warning that the West must decide "to stop the bus before it gets to Madison Avenue."[35]

Three months later, in what Haberman described as "a grim scene that has become steadily more familiar to Israelis," two Palestinian suicide bombers exploded themselves at a bus junction in central Israel killing eighteen Israeli soldiers and a civilian. "One of the deadliest terrorist incidents in Israeli history," it was the fifth major suicide bombing in nine months. Haberman reported "signs that a growing number of Israelis have had enough" and demand a halt to talks with the PLO. "This is not the peace they were promised in the glow of the famous White House handshake."[36]

Times editors were resolute in their insistence that peace talks remain "on track." Praising Prime Minister Rabin for reaffirming "his commitment to peace diplomacy," they asserted that "the worst response would be to surrender to the cruel logic of the terrorists, lumping all Israelis into one camp and all Palestinians into another." Israelis "must make clear distinctions" between Palestinian terrorist groups and "a P.L.O that has forsworn terrorism."[37]

On November 4, 1995, following his speech at a massive peace rally in Tel Aviv, Prime Minister Yitzhak Rabin was murdered. Yigal Amir, his twenty-five-year-old assassin, was a Bar-Ilan University student who had been active in right-wing political causes, defending Jewish settlements and opposing the Oslo Accords. After his arrest he was quoted as saying "I acted alone on God's orders." *Times* reporters cited right-wing militancy as the source of Amir's action. Joel Greenberg noted that "many students" at Bar-Ilan University, where Amir had studied, "are Orthodox Jews who oppose the policies of Mr. Rabin's Government and are sympathetic to Jewish settlers."[38]

Paying tribute to Rabin for recognizing that "the P.L.O. was ready to turn its back on its terrorist past and agree to compromises that would assure the survival of the Jewish state," the lead editorial described the "unthinkable": "a Jewish Israeli citizen is accused of striking down the nation's leader." With linkage that pervaded *Times* coverage of the assassination, the editors noted that Rabin's "program of peace was violently opposed by Palestinian and Jewish extremists."[39]

Thomas Friedman embellished that theme. Rabin had pursued peace "because he believed Israelis would never be able to feel at home unless the Palestinians did as well." But "Jewish and Muslim fanatics" were determined to thwart the peace process by engaging in "acts of violence so unspeakable" that they would "unravel the new relationship between Israelis and Arabs." These "lunatics" had "tried their best – with suicide bombings" and "killings in a mosque." Now, however, "instead of killing each other, ... they have begun to kill their own" to stop the peace process. Friedman, who had interviewed Rabin ten days earlier, recalled that he "was sure in his soul that what he was doing was best for Israel and the Jewish people." And, the columnist preened, "I know he was right."[40]

Three days later Friedman rejected any identification of Amir as "a lone gunman from outside the pale of Israeli political life." That was "wrong – all wrong." Likud leader Benjamin Netanyahu was "doing his best to present Yigal Amir ... as a lone gunman. ... No, no, no." Amir, Friedman wrote, was not "deranged." His politics, Friedman claimed, were "virtually identical" with those of Likud and its right-wing allies. He "is just your average religious right-wing hard-liner" who took Likud's "verbal attacks" on Rabin to their "logical extreme." Netanyahu "wants to disguise his connection" to Amir, but they shared "the idea of stopping the peace process."[41] With the Likud party cast as the venal source of Amir's action, Friedman implied that its leader was a virtual accomplice to murder.

Netanyahu promptly responded to the "political vilification" and "barrage of calumny" that was directed at Likud following Rabin's assassination. It was, he wrote in the *Times* two days later, "a classic case of guilt by association." The "most outrageous charge" (perhaps with Friedman's column in mind) was the allegation that Likud shared in Amir's guilt because both opposed the Oslo agreement. That, Netanyahu asserted, "is McCarthyism at its purest." Israeli democracy can survive "a horrible assassination." But he warned that "it may not be able to survive the delegitimization of honest debate."[42]

A bevy of *Times* journalists and contributors covered the assassination and its aftermath, contributing reports from the West Bank and Gaza, Brooklyn and the Lower East Side. Anthony Lewis lacerated "the Israeli right," settlement leaders and "extremist rabbis" for branding Rabin a traitor and murderer. He cited "the awful danger of treating political ideas as religious commands." While religion could "inform" political views and "shape" moral premises, "that is a very different thing from saying that God has drawn the boundaries of a state." Israel would fail, he predicted, "if its territorial ambitions require it to rule by force over another people."[43]

Israeli writer and left-wing activist Amos Oz described Rabin's assassination as "an attack on Israel as a lawful, democratic society and on the most sacred values of Judaism." He warned that Jewish "fundamentalists" were "keen on turning Israel into an Iran-like theocracy." In his own formulation of moral equivalence, Oz was convinced that "the crucial battle in the Mideast is no longer between Jew and Arab. It is a battle against violent zealots – on both sides."[44]

Journalist Ze'ev Chafets normalized Yigal Amir to broaden his critique of religious fundamentalism. Amir, he wrote, "is not a deranged outsider." He was the "boy next door" from "a stable, religious family." But he was "no lone gunman." He was "inspired by the fundamentalist ideology" that is shared by "perhaps tens of thousands of Israelis," including "a number of the country's most prominent Orthodox rabbis" who advocate "replacing democracy with theocracy." For its own survival, Chafets concluded, "democratic Israel must knock the fundamentalist rabbis off their pedestals and lock up their violent disciples."[45]

Writing from Hebron, foreign correspondent Alan Cowell discovered "a subdued and confused mood among Israeli far-rightists" who confronted "the killing done by a professed ideological associate." But they refused to acknowledge that their "vituperative onslaughts" against Rabin and perception of his betrayal "might have inspired Mr. Amir to murder." (Cowell offered no evidence to support his speculation.) Among Hebron "hard-liners," Cowell detected "little sorrow" over Rabin's death.[46]

New Jerusalem Bureau Chief Serge Schmemann targeted "the bellicose settlers of Hebron," who "spew the violent religious ideology that fired Yigal Amir." Even more disturbing, American Jews, most notoriously Baruch Goldstein, "figured prominently among the militant religious nationalists in Hebron." Feelings of "humiliation … of being thrust aside in a new, secular Israel" formed "the crux of the settlers' angst." It was "the fears and passions of the settlers," Schmemann conjectured, that were "at the heart of the bitter dispute that has severed the nation" – and bore responsibility for Rabin's death.[47]

Guilt by association also penetrated the editorial page, where Jewish settlers were implicated in Rabin's assassination by an Israeli from the Tel Aviv suburb of Herzliya. Although Yigal Amir was not a settler, his identification with the settlement movement was woven into *Times* coverage, which used settlements to contextualize his action – and fix blame for it. In Kfar Tapuach, home to followers of Rabbi Meir Kahane (who had been assassinated in Manhattan five years earlier), Middle East correspondent John Kifner found "unrepentant reactions from settlers and far-right activists."[48]

Times editors, hailing Rabin for having "embodied Israel's modern history," echoed the eulogy of Jordanian King Hussein praising the slain leader for his "contribution as a pioneer of regional peace." But they could not resist another swipe at Jewish settlers. Israelis, they admonished, "must take a hard look at those who would press their case through weapons rather than words. This applies especially to the extremist wing of the West Bank settlers' movement."[49] In the pages of the *Times*, Yigal Amir, Rabbi Kahane, Baruch Goldstein and Jewish settlers bore the identical mark of Cain. The entire Israeli political Right was implicated in the heinous deeds of two lone murderers.

In the assassination aftermath the themes of guilt and remorse – and guilt by association – punctuated *Times* coverage. Former *Times* theatre critic Frank Rich, who had recently become an op-ed columnist, described the assassination as "a crime of biblical size" that could not be dismissed as "the aberrational act of a lone nut." For Rich, Amir's deed spoke for "a discernible fringe movement among Jews" who "can hold their own with the rest of the world's fanatics." Joel Greenberg described mourners who "felt guilty for not speaking out earlier" against "the swell of hatred" that led to the assassination. Many were "young, liberal, nonreligious Israelis" whose voices of support for Rabin "were often drowned out in the streets by opposition protests." Now the "Song for Peace," sung by Rabin along with thousands of supporters who attended the rally preceding his assassination, had become their "anthem of grief."[50]

Like the political right in Israel, A.M. Rosenthal noted, left-wing opponents had "also used invective and insult," condemning their critics as "enemies of Israel, cancers, pariahs." But Israelis were asked "to give up territory that all of its leaders, Labor and Likud, insisted for decades was essential to Israel's existence." He called on Prime Minister Peres to respond to critics of his peace policy with "as much attention, courtesy and flexibility as Labor has given to the talks with the Palestinians."[51]

Yossi Klein Halevi, whose recently published *Memoirs of a Jewish Extremist* recounted his attraction to, and subsequent rejection of, Rabbi Kahane, offered a nuanced perspective. Religious Zionists must admit that "the evil in their midst has grown well beyond a lunatic fringe." But "for the sake of Israeli democracy," critics of the peace process "need to be able to raise legitimate security and religious concerns" without secular Israelis identifying them with Yigal Amir. Memories of Rabbi Kahane, a Brooklyn Jew, haunted the *Times*. Former Jerusalem Bureau Chief Clyde Haberman claimed that Yigal Amir had acted "in an atmosphere of hate nurtured in New York, with some Jews feeling that they were free to vilify Israel's leader as a traitor, a murderer, a Nazi."[52]

Times coverage of the Rabin assassination and its aftermath concluded with John Kifner's perceptive profile of Amir. Born into an Orthodox Yemenite family, he was "a studious Jewish boy" who entered the *hesder* yeshiva program combining advanced Torah study with military service, which he fulfilled in the elite

Golani Brigade. He was not a "crazed pariah," but he viewed the peace accords with Palestinians "not as a blessing, but as a curse, not just wrong, but a sin." Claiming justification for the assassination under the Jewish legal principle of *din rodef,* Amir believed that when a Jew "gives over his land and people to the enemy, he must be killed." The Rabin-Arafat handshake "spelled the end of the world that Yigal Amir believed God had given the Jews."[53] Kifner, rather than assign blame randomly to Jewish settlers, Orthodox Jews and their rabbis, or Likud leaders as his *Times* colleagues had insistently done, searched to understand the assassin. No moral equivalence was drawn between innocent Israelis on the political right and Rabin's murderer, nor were 140,000 Jewish settlers blamed for the act of a solitary Israeli who was not a settler. Yigal Amir and Baruch Goldstein had committed horrific murders. Kifner understood that each had acted alone.

During the early months of 1996 the surge of optimism that had accompanied the signing of the peace accords, only to be overwhelmed by the tragedy of the Rabin assassination, was undermined by a wave of Palestinian suicide bombings in Jerusalem and Tel Aviv. The terrorist rampage began when a bus approaching the Jerusalem terminal just before 7 a.m. was "pulverized" by the explosion from a suicide bomber that killed twenty-six passengers and wounded dozens. Within eight days terrorist attacks killed fifty-eight Israelis.

Reporting the massacre, Jerusalem Bureau Chief Serge Schmemann devoted most of his coverage to the potentially "profound" implications of the horrific attack for the peace process and forthcoming Israeli elections in May. Schmemann cited, but did not explore, "Israeli rage and grief over the deadliest day of suicide bombing the country has known." Instead, he focused on Prime Minister Shimon Peres's "tough tone" in a Knesset speech, insisting "Murder will not kill the peace process." *Times* editors were convinced that the terrorists' purpose was "not just to kill people but to destroy the peace agreement." They commended "political leaders on both sides" – Peres, Netanyahu and especially Arafat – for remaining "admirably steadfast in their pledges to resist terrorism."[54] There were no articles about Israeli victims.

"In the fury of the moment," Schmemann reported, Israelis "reverted to their basic instinct: that war against terrorism must be constant and total." He acknowledged that "Hamas has done terrible things, that terror is an integral part of its mystique." Indeed, since the peace agreement was signed it had launched fourteen attacks inside Israel that caused 102 deaths. Yet armed struggle was "only a small fraction of its activity," he hastened to add, which also included "social work, politics, indoctrination." Was Hamas "an irreconcilable enemy of peace that has to be destroyed, as the Israelis insist," he wondered, or "a political and social movement that ... may be enticed to reject its radical fringe?"[55]

An answer came the day his article appeared. In what Hamas claimed was its "final act of retaliation" for the Israeli assassination of its bomb maker Yahya Ayash a month earlier, a bus traveling through the heart of downtown Jerusalem was bombed. Nineteen fatalities included Israelis, Arabs, Romanian laborers, and an Ethiopian tourist. Although the suicide bomber, like his predecessor a week earlier, came from the Hebron area, local Arabs, unlike Hebron Jews after the Goldstein massacre, were not held guilty by association. "Outpourings of frustrated rage" from Israelis suggested that Prime Minister Peres's "tough talk" was insufficient to offset "the obvious political damage" to his forthcoming election campaign.[56] Peres's dimming political future, not Israeli casualties from Hamas terrorism, loomed over *Times* coverage.

One day later another suicide bomber killed thirteen Israelis when he blew himself up outside Dizengoff Center, the largest Tel Aviv shopping mall. The explosion, Schmemann reported, "sent victims sailing through the air" and injured more than one hundred, many of them children. "Mounting public rage" prompted the Cabinet to declare "all-out war against the new terrorism." Israeli military forces sealed off West Bank cities, towns and villages in areas that only recently had celebrated the "lifting of Israeli occupation." Protests erupted in Jerusalem's "low-income district of Katamon," where both bombed buses in that city had begun their final journeys and many of their victims lived.[57] There were no interviews with family members or residents.

The Oslo peace process, Anthony Lewis lamented, had become "a frail hope." Told by an Israeli friend that Arafat "should have his own Altalena," Lewis implicitly identified Hamas with the "right-wing terrorist" Irgun, led by Menachem Begin. He blamed Israel, which "helped to build Hamas and the spirit of rejection" with its "burdensome and corrupting" occupation, for the disintegrating peace prospects.[58]

Times editors insisted that "only courageous leadership and decisive action by Israel and the P.L.O. can keep the hope of peace alive." Peres, Arafat and "the supposedly nonviolent wing of Hamas" must "act boldly" to regain the initiative. In the war between "a small group of fanatics" and "the millions of Israelis and Palestinians who want to live side by side in peace, prosperity and security," the fanatics "must not be allowed to prevail." Peres could not win the forthcoming elections "unless he can make Israel safe." But he must do so "without abusing the rights of innocent Palestinians."[59]

On the eve of Israeli elections the *Times* declared an American interest in "a secure and stable Israel that continues on a path to negotiated peace." The Labor government's "historic" agreements with the PLO and Jordan had "ended Israel's long diplomatic isolation and strengthened its relations with the United States," of no small concern to *Times* editors. Their preference was evident: Netanyahu emphasized "Israeli strength" but Peres was "prepared to remake the map and mind-sets of the Middle East to put Israel in peaceful partnership with its neighbors."[60]

Thomas Friedman believed it "inconceivable" that Palestinians or Arab states would negotiate with a Netanyahu-led government that would freeze the peace process, build settlements and permit security forces to operate throughout the West Bank and Gaza. He advised Netanyahu to "adjust" to the new reality, not rely on "nostalgia and rhetoric," lest he "crash on the rocks of reality." Covering the election from Jerusalem, Serge Schmemann understood that "the vision of a new Middle East fades before the bloody reality of suicide bombings – especially with Mr. Netanyahu there to drive the message home."[61]

Netanyahu's 1996 victory by an exceedingly narrow popular majority raised concerns at the *Times*. The "big winners," Anthony Lewis wrote sorrowfully, were "terrorists": Yigal Amir and Palestinian suicide bombers. Warning against Israeli "adventurism in the West Bank," he anticipated that settlement growth would place relations with the United States "under stress." Israeli writer and peace activist David Grossman, confessing that "today a great anguish lies on my heart," lamented election returns that revealed an Israel "more militant, more religious, more fundamentalist, more tribal and more racist."[61]

The "rising power of the Orthodox as lawmakers," wrote religion correspondent Joseph Berger (guided by the director of the liberal New Israel Fund), "is sure to constitute a setback for the small Reform and Conservative movements" in Israel. With Netanyahu combining "American packaging and native ruthlessness," Serge Schmemann concluded, the election returns "do not look favorable either for the future of the Palestinian peace or the internal unity of Israel." With "a sharply divided Israel," chief diplomatic correspondent Steven Erlanger wrote, the peace process was "effectively dead."[63] In the *Times*, fault invariably lay with Israel.

Thomas Friedman wrote bluntly: "The bad guys won." Citing Yaron Ezrahi's conversation with a taxi driver as proof, he concluded that what Yigal Amir had begun "from the Jewish fringe" Palestinian suicide bombers "finished off from the Muslim fringe." Since "fear always trumps logic," Israelis could not be blamed "for reaching out to the tempting, but illusory, appeal" of Netanyahu. An editorial, commending the new prime minister for emphasizing "national reconciliation and a continued quest for peace" in his post-election statements, urged him to minimize his "dependence on extremists" and pursue "compromise" over the future of Jewish settlements and Palestinian statehood.[64]

After horrific Palestinian suicide bombings that claimed more than fifty Israeli lives within a week, the voter shift to the political Right erased post-Oslo euphoria. Once again, as during the Begin-Shamir years between 1977 and 1992, a right-wing Israeli government stirred deep concern at the *Times* over Jewish identity and loyalty.

CHAPTER 10

Realities of Conflict: 1996–2001

In June 1996 the *Times* welcomed Benjamin Netanyahu as Israel's new prime minister. A hopeful editorial praised him for "sensibly reaching for the center in Israeli politics ... with an eye to minimizing the role of hawkish ideologues and religious fundamentalists." His "conciliatory language" pleased secular Israelis, who were "uneasy" over the strength of religious parties in the governing coalition. Other than "a few questionable appointments" of militant ministers, he made "a sensible and sensitive start."[1]

Editorial approval lasted three months, until the opening of a tourist tunnel adjacent to the Western Wall triggered a violent Palestinian response. The tunnel, dating from the Herodion era, had attracted British explorers in the mid-nineteenth century and Israeli archeologists ever since the Six-Day War. For *Times* editors, however, "there was no need for Israel suddenly to resume a construction project near the Temple Mount." The Palestinian response, they conceded, was "extreme and equally rash." With dozens of Israelis and Palestinians killed in the rioting, the *Times* identified Netanyahu as "the pivotal figure" who must demonstrate Israel's commitment to the peace effort, without "the luxury of hesitation or delay." Since there was "no urgent need" for the new tunnel entrance, Israel "should terminate the construction work in the old city of Jerusalem that provoked the Palestinian rioting."[2] Its location in the Jewish Quarter, adjacent to the holiest Jewish site, was ignored. Nothing was demanded of Palestinian leaders who incited the rioters.

After three days of violence claimed the lives of fifty-three Palestinians and fourteen Israelis the *Times* launched a barrage of criticism at the tunnel opening. Adam Goodheart, editor of *Civilization* magazine whose specialty was the American Civil War, blamed Netanyahu for insisting on "sole Jewish control of Jerusalem." No group should have "exclusive control," a principle Goodheart did not extend to Muslim control over the Temple Mount. Thomas Friedman offered "free advice" to "Bibi": "Close the tunnel down" and focus instead on "building a secure peace." Palestinian advocate Rashid Khalidi, accusing Netanyahu of an "archeological-propaganda juggernaut," condemned the tunnel opening as "the latest calculated insult to Palestinian aspirations and rights in Jerusalem."[3] The tunnel remained open, attracting thousands of visitors.

Three months later, under intense American pressure to placate aggrieved Palestinians, Netanyahu signed the Hebron Protocol. The ancient city was divided into Arab and Israeli zones, with its 450 Jewish residents confined to a tiny ghetto. Before the agreement was implemented an Israeli soldier with a history of mental problems fired into the crowded Hebron vegetable market, wounding six Palestinians. Like Yigal Amir, wrote Serge Schmemann, Pvt. Noam Friedman wore "the black skullcap of an Orthodox Jew," claiming religious justification for his action. And like Baruch Goldstein, he "turned his hatred on Palestinians."[4]

Anthony Lewis transformed Pvt. Friedman into a symbol of "how dangerous the mixture of religion and nationalism" had become – for Jews, not Moslems. Blaming "nationalist rabbis" and "ultra-Orthodox Israelis who do not accept the authority of the democratic state," he echoed Schmemann in bracketing Friedman with Amir and Goldstein. They were not "isolated loners," Lewis insisted, but "ultra-Orthodox believers who see divine authority in territorial claims." He warned that the mixture of "religious visions" with "territorial claims" was "dangerous for Israel." Amos Oz declared that Hebron (the most ancient Jewish city) "is not part of our planet," where a "pragmatic solution" should transcend "biblical mysticism."[5]

The *Times* seized on Netanyahu's capitulation as a prelude to fulfillment of the Oslo agreement. The editors hailed "the makings of a consensus on peacemaking with the Palestinians." Describing "the softening of the hawk," Schmemann viewed Netanyahu as "indistinguishable" from Shimon Peres. To Thomas Friedman, the prime minister wanted to be "half-pregnant," withdrawing from Hebron but unwilling to make further military deployments that could lead to Palestinian statehood. Once again A.M. Rosenthal was the solitary *Times* dissenter. Noting that Netanyahu was taking a "great political risk" by relinquishing Israeli control over Hebron, he suggested that the prime minister was too deferential to American demands.[6]

Six months later Schmemann concluded that the peace talks were "moribund," and Israel was to blame. Its development plans for East Jerusalem neighborhoods, primarily on land owned by Jews before 1948 or purchased since 1967, had aroused Palestinian fury and triggered a new wave of terrorism. In an explosion that "created a huge fireball and a shower of bodies, limbs, fruit, fish, plaster and plastic roofing panels," two Palestinian suicide bombers affiliated with Hamas killed thirteen Israelis and wounded nearly two hundred in the popular Mahane Yehuda outdoor food market in Jerusalem.[7]

Schmemann focused on the damaged peace process, not Jewish victims of the deadliest Palestinian terrorist attack in more than a year. Amos Oz, his primary cited source, described a conflict between those who wanted peace and "extremists on both sides … wanting to eradicate the national existence of the other." Schmemann hastened to add that Oz was not suggesting "a moral equivalence between mass killings and appropriating occupied land for a settlement" – precisely what Oz had implied. In his own reformulation, Schmemann concluded that "extremists on both sides seem to take a perverse moral comfort in these predictable acts of terrorism."[8]

Times editors emphasized Netanyahu's responsibility for making peace, not Palestinian responsibility for murdering Israelis. They cautioned him to "resist the understandable temptation to freeze the peace effort," advising that "the only way to make Israel secure" was to resume negotiations with the Palestinians. Asserting the familiar *Times* mantra of moral equivalence, Thomas Friedman linked "Palestinian and Israeli extremists who will never reconcile." Israelis, he claimed to know, realize "there is no military solution," but "they have no leaders to show the way." About Palestinian leadership, and its embrace of terrorism, he remained silent.[9]

One month later three Palestinian suicide bombers exploded themselves on the pedestrian promenade of Ben Yehuda Street in the heart of downtown Jerusalem, killing four Israelis (including a twelve-year-old girl) and wounding nearly two hundred. Israeli-Palestinian tensions, Schmemann explained, had "mounted steadily" with "mutual accusations and recrimination" following an Israeli decision to build new housing for Jews in East Jerusalem. Once again, Israelis were blamed for Palestinian terrorism. The *Times* editorial response focused on "the cycle of violence" with Israel and the Palestinian Authority "locked in their own destructive spiral of hostility and punishment."[10] The editors would not condemn Palestinian terrorism without finding a reason to blame Israel.

Anthony Lewis branded Netanyahu "a failed leader" for the "abysmal failure" of his anti-terrorism policy and hesitant moves toward peace. Palestinians, confronting their confinement in a "handful of bantustans" (his favorite South African apartheid analogy for Israel), "felt they had no stake in the peace process." Responsibility for mitigating terrorism rested entirely with the Jewish state: "Only a serious political initiative by Israel has any hope of ending the climate of Palestinian despair that nurtures terrorism."[11]

Analyzing the sources of Israeli-Palestinian conflict, Schmemann blamed Netanyahu's "combination of reluctant concessions to the Oslo process and expansion in the West Bank," which "undermined ... partnership with Mr. Arafat and the Palestinians' faith in the peace." He prominently cited the response of the Israeli mother of one of the murdered teenagers, who described terrorist attacks as "products of continued oppression of the Palestinians by the Israeli Government." She lamented that "My Government betrayed me" with its "megalomania – for their need to control, oppress, dominate."[12]

Ever since 1948, A.M. Rosenthal noted, "it has been the Israelis who have been offering peace and the Arabs who have been answering with acts of war." Whenever an Arab bomb exploded in an Israeli marketplace or bus, he observed, "the world reacts as if it were the first. How terrible; ... Israel must make more concessions." Perhaps with his own newspaper in mind, he noted that Arab bombs, attacks and "anti-Jew propaganda" were barely mentioned, or ignored, "as if history had no meaning." So it was, he concluded, that "the myth continued that if only Israelis would make enough concessions to Palestinians peace would come to the Mideast."[13]

On the fifth anniversary of the Oslo Accord, new Jerusalem Bureau Chief Deborah Sontag (who had previously covered immigration and housing issues in New York) plunged into the Israeli-Palestinian cauldron. She quickly adapted, noting that the killing of two "Islamic militants" near Hebron by Israeli soldiers "had thrown a wrench" into peace negotiations. Visiting the Mahane Yehuda market site of the recent terrorist attack, she emphasized that Israelis and Palestinians alike had "vehemently accused the other of intransigence."[14] It had not taken long for her to embrace the familiar *Times* refrain of moral equivalence.

Times editors despaired over the faltering peace process, noting sorrowfully that the Oslo five-year timetable had been "all but obliterated." They, too, blamed the failure on "Palestinian terrorism and Israeli intransigence." With an impending meeting at the White House, the *Times* sternly admonished Netanyahu and Arafat that "it would be helpful if both parties refrained from provocative statements or decisions." But with Ariel Sharon's appointment as foreign minister to "placate the far right," according to Sontag, peace prospects dimmed. She relied on Yaron Ezrahi, the familiar left-wing source handed down from one Jerusalem Bureau Chief to the next, to explain that Sharon's appointment revealed Netanyahu's inability "to carry out the big decision" of ceding land "on his own."[15]

After two dozen Israeli soldiers were wounded in a Hebron grenade attack, Sontag was drawn to the ancient city. In "the hellish heart of the old city" she discovered "poles of antagonism" between Jews and Arabs. Displaying little familiarity with Hebron's conspicuous place in Jewish history, she ignored the tombs of the biblical patriarchs and matriarchs to focus on "a carefully tended shrine" for Baruch Goldstein. Amid the "daily dance of violence" in Hebron, "a magnet for firebrands on both sides," she described "an almost ritualized series of nasty tangos" between hostile adversaries.[16]

In October 1998 Netanyahu and Arafat signed the Wye Accord at the White House. It provided for a phased Israeli withdrawal from 13% of the West Bank and the release of hundreds of Palestinian prisoners in return for Palestinian promises to fight terrorism and amend their Charter calling for Israel's destruction. "God bless him," exulted Thomas Friedman over Netanyahu, for compromising with Arafat and agreeing to a deal "based on what most Israelis wanted (a better Oslo), not on what most Jews wanted (no more Oslo)." *Times* editors hailed Netanyahu and Arafat for "great courage in changing their positions." Netanyahu, if belatedly, had embraced "Oslo's formula of land for peace" while Arafat (the editors wishfully assumed) "finally closed the door on any return to confrontation and violence." Both leaders agreed that "the time to break free from the politics of stalemate had clearly arrived."[17]

Six months later, with peace negotiations dormant and support for Netanyahu waning, the Knesset voted for new elections. According to optimistic *Times* editors, Palestinian leaders seemed ready for peace: they had altered their Charter, removing the goal of destroying Israel; "worked to arrest suspected terrorists"; and, under American pressure, withdrawn their threat to declare Palestinian statehood. But Anthony Lewis warned of "a culture of illegalism" in Israel as "Orthodox rabbis and their followers" prepared to subvert democracy with "a theocracy, ruled by rabbis." Several days later A.M. Rosenthal reminded readers that "Arabs never produced a democratic society." Any Palestinian state, he predicted, "will be a dictatorship – ranging from stifling to murderous." There was only "one Mideast democracy," yet "American journalists who proclaim their love for Israel screech that its ethics, morality, and legal system are collapsing."[18]

On the eve of elections Joel Greenberg concluded that Israel was defined by its "divisions." Israelis "view each other as members of ideological, religious or ethnic sub-units, rather than one society of shared values." He depicted a "tribal trend" that was "graphically evident" among religious groups, whose men wore a "yarmulke at all times." Rising ethnic tension between Russian immigrants and Sephardi Jews suggested the "splintering of Israeli society." *Times* editors took note. "At a time when Israelis have generally embraced conciliation with old enemies, it is startling that the nation is more fragmented than ever on ethnic and sectarian lines." Expressing concern over "feuding tribal divisions," they conceded that "the squabbling among subgroups represents a certain healthy maturing of Israeli democracy." But they implored Israelis to reinforce "the values of tolerance and inclusion," urging that "no one form of Judaism should dictate to others, and Jews must learn to be sensitive to those of different backgrounds."[19]

In May 1999 Ehud Barak, whose distinguished military career preceded his ascent to Labor Party leadership, became prime minister. An editorial acknowledged that Netanyahu had been "a tough and eloquent defender of Israeli security needs," but he lacked "a larger strategic vision" of Palestinians as "Israel's partners." Barak's challenge was to "heal his nation and reawaken the dormant peace effort." Thomas Friedman applauded Barak's victory for providing "the overwhelming sense" in Israel of "a national nightmare having ended." Yearning for "peace at home and peace abroad," Israelis "wanted differences healed, not exploited."[20]

As a former kibbutznik and decorated general, Sontag wrote enthusiastically, Barak offered "the best path to internal and external peace." A "dovish hawk," he presented himself as "a calm, almost bland voice of reason and integrity." An editorial declared that Barak's victory "created an encouraging new atmosphere" for peace talks with Palestinians, and even with Syria. But a skeptical A.M. Rosenthal anticipated, at best, "a temporary peace" with Palestine emerging as "one more Arab dictatorship." He remained convinced that "Arab tyrannies can hardly be trusted to let the Jewish, and only, democracy in the Mideast live in a permanent peace."[21] It was a prescient warning from Rosenthal, Israel's most persistent (and often solitary) defender, whose fifty-six-year career at the *Times* was ending.

After a year without discernible progress toward peace Thomas Friedman implored President Clinton to summon Israeli and Palestinian leaders to Washington. There, he fantasized, they would participate in "one last cards-on-the-table, in-your-face, put-up-or-shut-up summit to finally, finally put an end to this conflict." After all, Barak "understands what Israel will have to give for a secure peace." And Arafat has "the stature, and the interest … to make the hard concessions for his own people." Never, Friedman insisted, would there be "a better alignment of the stars for making a deal."[22]

With negotiations imminent, the Op-Ed page welcomed peace advocates as cheerleaders. British writer Karen Armstrong, a former nun who had
embraced Islam, rejected Israel's claims to Jerusalem. For Middle East peace,
she wrote, a solution for the Holy City must "satisfy not only the Palestinians
and the Arabs, but also the whole Muslim world." After all, Jerusalem had been
"sacred to Muslims ever since the Prophet Muhammad" – but, she erroneously
claimed, it "only became central to Judaism ... after its destruction" (six centuries earlier). For Palestinians, Jerusalem was "a symbol of their own beleaguered identity" as "they watch their holy city slipping daily from their grasp."[23]

Leah Rabin, recalling her husband's handshake on the White House lawn
with Arafat that "broke down the barriers of mistrust and fear" and "set the
peace train on its track," contributed an emotional appeal for peace. She reassured Barak: "We trust ... your flexibility and creativity." She reminded Arafat:
"You have the power ... to fulfill the dream of your nation and mine." She hailed
them both as "brave and courageous leaders who can make peace happen."[24]

Believing that "a historic peace agreement" was within reach, *Times*
editors called for the "creativity and courage" required to make it possible.
Neither Barak nor Arafat "wants to walk away from the chance of ending a half-
century of destructive conflict." Reducing negotiating complexities to clichés,
Friedman proclaimed that in "the real world" everyone knew that Jerusalem
is "a multi-ethnic city" where "both sides know that they won't be able to take
their shoes off and relax until the other is secure in his own space." John Kifner
wrote that "resentment and reasons for distrust" were evident "on both sides."
His primary source was an Israeli paratrooper who had fought in Jerusalem in
the Six-Day War but now claimed that "in the euphoria of 1967 ... we did all
the most stupid things."[25]

The collapse of the Camp David negotiations in July 2000, an editorial
lamented, was "a wrenching setback for Israel, the Palestinians and the cause
of Mideast peace." The "larger burden" of responsibility fell on Arafat, who
was not prepared to compromise on Palestinian sovereignty over parts of East
Jerusalem. But Barak "must persevere in his efforts to enhance Israeli security
through a fair and defensible peace." Dismissing "tough talk" from Palestinian
"radicals" about another intifada, Friedman offered "free advice": "The days of
the intifada are over."[26] Two months later the second intifada erupted.

On the first anniversary of the Camp David failure Jerusalem Bureau Chief
Deborah Sontag offered a 5,000-word explanation. Echoing the sharply critical
and widely publicized analysis by former Clinton adviser Robert Malley, who
had sought to deflect blame from Arafat for the collapse of peace negotiations,

she assigned primary responsibility for their failure to Israel. Even *Times* editors disagreed. Columnist William Safire, by then Israel's solitary, if occasional, defender on the editorial pages, concluded that Arafat "gave up nothing," while Barak, "prodded" by Clinton, "gave away too much too soon." His concessions – virtually the entire West Bank, including the strategically vital Jordan Valley; the uprooting of 40,000 Jewish settlers; the right of return for thousands of Palestinians; and shared sovereignty with a new Palestinian state in parts of Jerusalem – "broke pledges … made in his election campaign a year ago." As Safire noted, the "land for peace" that Arafat wanted is "the land of Israel."[27]

Two months later Ariel Sharon's visit to the Temple Mount provoked a violent clash between Palestinian stone throwers and Israeli police. Concluding that Sharon's presence "was meant to assert Israeli sovereignty," Joel Greenberg reported that the Israeli leader had "a provocative reputation among Palestinians"; he even flew an Israeli flag from the home that he owned in the nearby Muslim Quarter. But Sharon, "determinedly unapologetic," declared that Jerusalem "is under Israeli sovereignty and I don't need anyone's permission" to visit the Temple Mount. *Times* editors concluded that Sharon "did Israel no favor" by provocatively "asserting Jewish claims to the Muslim holy site," unidentified as the site of the ancient Jewish Temples. Even Avraham Burg, Labor Party Speaker in the Knesset and prominent peace advocate, affirmed that the Temple Mount "belongs to us as much as it belongs to the Palestinians."[28]

Within days after the Temple Mount confrontation violence erupted throughout the West Bank and Gaza. Palestinian funerals, Sontag wrote, "fed the rage that propelled fresh protests." While Palestinians saw Sharon as the "devil," their "angel" became a twelve-year-old Palestinian boy, Muhammad al-Durrah, "killed in the crossfire in Gaza while his father tried to shield him." His death was captured by a France 2 TV cameraman who had his camera "trained on them when a bullet hit the boy and he crumpled and died." As the graphic video spread worldwide, it became "the image that summed up the horror" that was felt by "many Israelis and Palestinians."[29]

Sontag's front-page account was supplemented by a report about the newest "young symbol of Mideast violence." Muhammad al-Durrah, wrote William A. Orme, Jr. (Sontag's husband), was "a boisterous, blue-jeaned Gaza fifth-grader" who was "fatally shot in the stomach" by bullets that his father claimed were fired by Israeli soldiers. The video showed a "terrified" boy, "trapped by Israeli gunfire and then slumping lifeless into his father's lap." That "enduring image of the violence," Orme wrote, "turned the 12-year-old boy into a potent new symbol of what angry Palestinians contend is their continued victimization by Israeli occupiers."[30] With his death disputed, an Israeli government investigation subsequently concluded that that the boy's "killing," staged by a free-lance cameraman from Gaza who worked for France 2 TV, was a "blood libel" on the State of Israel.

With forty-two Palestinians, including thirteen children, killed in less than a week, Orme (by then the *Times* de facto West Bank reporter) wrote that Palestinians and "some Israelis" believed Israeli soldiers "employed deadly force far too readily." He described "a self-perpetuating cycle of bloodshed, mourning and violent retribution" in which "the machinery of martyrdom gets into gear quickly." The new intifada, Sontag wrote, was "a battle of the teenagers," initiating yet another generation, propelled by "anger and hate," into "the ritual of Israeli-Palestinian bloodshed." She focused on a seventeen-year-old Palestinian who expressed his enthusiasm for "the idea of a David-versus-Goliath battle."[31]

Welcoming criticism of Israel, especially from Jews, the *Times* provided a forum for Allegra Pacheco, who had moved from New York to Jerusalem to work for Palestinian human-rights organizations. In a *Times* interview two years earlier, when she represented the families of Palestinian suicide bombers, she had stated her opposition to "the Israeli occupation." The Oslo process, she now wrote, "cannot succeed" because it "did not offer any guarantee of Palestinian self-determination, full equality and an end to the military occupation." Indeed, an "influx of 50,000 new Jewish settlers," along with the demolition of eight hundred Palestinian homes and arrest of 13,000 Palestinians, doomed peace prospects. Any Palestinian state under such circumstances would, in familiar *Times* rhetoric, "create a reality of apartheid; a Palestinian state as a Bantustan."[32]

A *Times* editorial cautioned that continued violence "could deny Israelis the opportunity they deserve to live at peace with their neighbors" and "deny the Palestinians the dignity, statehood and international assistance they were recently so close to attaining." It called on Israel, not Palestinians, to be "measured in its response." Rami G. Khouri, a Jordanian Palestinian syndicated columnist, blamed Israel for "a crisis of [its] own making." Sharon's visit to the Temple Mount was "taken by all Arabs and Muslims as a direct, predatory Israeli threat to the most powerful religious and nationalist symbols in Arab Palestine." Khouri warned that "where Israel continues to occupy Arab lands and act with colonial swagger, resistance persists."[33]

Two weeks after the Second Intifada erupted a widely circulated photograph of the mutilated bodies of two murdered Israeli reserve soldiers, thrown from a building window in Ramallah, united Israelis in revulsion and fury.

While the bodies were trampled on and beaten by a frenzied Palestinian crowd, one of the murderers appeared at a window to flamboyantly display his blood-ied hands to the exultant mob. The photo of a soldier "plunging head down into the mob," wrote Sontag, became "the Israeli counterpart of the Muhammad al-Durrah image." Both photos were "unequivocally horrifying" (although not, it turned out, unequivocally genuine). Anthony Lewis, yet again linking Israel to apartheid, noted that South Africans had "grievances at least as profound" as Palestinians under Israeli rule. But they had learned from Nelson Mandela that "patience and negotiation were the best way to vindicate their rights." He concluded that "both sides" should pursue "the search for peace."[34]

David Shipler amplified the theme of moral equivalence, citing the inability of Israelis and Palestinians alike to "see the other's legitimacy as a people." Relying on his favorite Israeli sources from two decades earlier, he cited Rabbi Hartman and Professor Ezrahi for their shared hope that "the current convulsions could force rethinking and introduce new fluidity into the peace process." But Jewish settlements, Shipler concluded, "seem destined to inflame Palestinians unless an Israeli government dismantles them."[35] He failed to notice that Palestinians had been "inflamed" by Zionism for decades preceding the first settlement.

At the end of October Thomas Friedman reported from Ramallah, where he and a Palestinian friend observed "a modern form of ritual sacrifice": a clash between "Palestinian youths" (some armed with rifles) and Israeli soldiers. Friedman knew the rules of the Palestinian game: "Wounded are OK, but mar-tyrs are better – because martyrs produce the media images that create the most pressure on Israel." Dismissing as "fatuous nonsense" Israeli "propaganda" that Palestinians ruled themselves, he insisted that there was "no hope for peace without a Palestinian state in Gaza and the West Bank." Marwan Barghouti, leader of the "street war" with Israel (soon to be convicted of abetting murders for which he received five life sentences), helped him to understand that the intifada was "true guerilla theater."[36]

Times editors were convinced that "there can be no satisfactory military solution." A "negotiated peace" was "the only realistic way out." For novelist David Grossman, it was "impossible to ignore the centrality of the settlements in the conflict" (which long pre-dated the first settlement). Settlers were respon-sible for depriving Palestinians of their state. For "a just and lasting peace," he concluded, "a large number of settlements will have to be uprooted."[37]

Israeli voters believed otherwise, electing Ariel Sharon as prime minister in February 2001 by a decisive margin. *Times* editors were palpably discomforted by his victory. His "staged walk" across the Temple Mount months earlier had "lighted the spark" for Palestinian violence. Now he would "need to show that he combines his customary toughness" with the flexibility required "to avoid aggravating an already combustible situation." The American government should "counsel" Sharon to avoid "the impulse to escalate military confrontations" with Palestinians.[38]

Two years earlier, Sontag noted, Sharon's vision had seemed "paranoid"; but after months of Palestinian violence his "bulldog determination" now seemed "more sensible" to Israelis. He personified "nostalgia" for "an era when Zionism was depicted more heroically and Israel was willing to use its might." Noting Sharon's "predilection to use force," she identified him as an appropriate leader for Israel's "middle age crisis." To Arabs, Orme wrote, Sharon had long been their "implacable enemy." The settlements he had authorized made it "almost impossible" for Palestinians "to create a viable contiguous state in the Gaza Strip and West Bank."[39]

On the Op-Ed page Dennis Ross, President Clinton's failed peace negotiator, asserted that Sharon could neither "turn the clock back" and reoccupy Gaza or West Bank cities nor "deter Israelis in their quest for peace." He "must work with the Palestinians" who, in turn, must realize that "violence does not work." Using a favorite *Times* trope, Ross asserted that "both sides must realize that peace is the only way." Only William Safire dissented from the *Times* consensus, identifying Sharon's election as "a reinvigoration of Zionism."[40]

Palestinian terrorist attacks continued. In early June, several hours into the Jewish Sabbath, a suicide bomber affiliated with Hamas blew himself up at the entrance to the Dolphinarium, a popular Tel Aviv beach club. In the deadliest attack of the Second Intifada he murdered twenty-one Israelis, mostly teenage daughters of new Russian immigrants. Sontag's front-page report described "a wide area covered with pools of blood, body parts and shattered glass." Joel Greenberg interviewed Israeli survivors of the Dolphinarium bombing and attended the funeral of murdered sisters, buried side by side, while their classmates "wailed in inconsolable grief."[41]

With his repetitive fondness for citing Brandeis, the better to criticize Israel, Anthony Lewis responded to the Dolphinarium tragedy by proclaiming that "occupation … has endangered the security of Israel" – as though the Tel Aviv beachfront was occupied territory. Jewish settlement "mocks the tradition of Jews as a people of law" (predictably personified by Brandeis) and deserved denunciation "with the force of an Isaiah." Condemning Israel for "colonizing" the "occupied territories," he had nothing to say about Palestinian terrorism or the tragic deaths of Israeli teenagers. Thomas Friedman, embracing (false) moral equivalence, equated Palestinian suicide bombers and Jewish settlers, both sharing a preference for maximum force "regardless of the inability to distinguish between civilians and soldiers."[42]

With the peace process in tatters, Deborah Sontag offered a 5,000-word analysis of its collapse. She rejected the "potent, simplistic narrative" among Israelis that Barak had offered Arafat "the moon" but the Palestinian leader "chose the path of violence." Her own (unidentified) diplomatic and government sources suggested that Arafat did not bear "sole responsibility" for the failure. Indeed, she concluded, the peace process had been marked by "missteps and successes by Israelis, Palestinians and Americans alike." Mentioning "intifada" only once, she evaded Palestinian accountability for "the cycle of violence" that had merely "started" or "erupted."[43]

A *Times* editorial two days later reiterated her conclusion that both Barak and Arafat "made political and diplomatic miscalculations" during the negotiations. Despite "months of violence" since their collapse, which had "shattered the faith of most Israelis and Palestinians in reaching a negotiated peace," the editors remained convinced that "both sides understand that there can be no military solution to their conflict."[44]

William Safire challenged his newspaper's penchant for equating Israel with its enemies. A self-described "house contrarian," he disputed as "an Arab spinmeister's notion" the front-page sub-head for Sontag's article declaring "All the Parties, Not Just Arafat, Were to Blame." Although "instant revisionism" held Sharon's Temple Mount visit responsible for the Camp David failure, Safire asserted that Arafat was to blame for the Palestinian murder campaign that followed. In an adjoining op-ed column, former Prime Minister Ehud Barak presciently concurred: Arafat, missing "every opportunity … to achieve a permanent peace for his people, … did not prove to be a partner for peace and quite probably will not be one in the future."[45]

An array of contributors and columnists chimed in to explain the failure of the peace process. Yossi Beilin, Barak's former justice minister, and Yaser Abed Rabbo, culture and information minister for the Palestinian Authority, collaborated in declaring their "faith that we do have partners for peace in each other and that a negotiated solution is still possible." They called for "two sovereign national states – Israel and Palestine … based on the 1967 borders, with both capitals in Jerusalem." Anthony Lewis, praising Sontag's "masterly article," blamed Israel for its repeated failure "to carry out promises and negotiated agreements," while "continuously building and enlarging settlements." Sharon's retaliation for Palestinian terrorism "increase[s] Palestinian rage" and "assures that there will be more suicide bombers." Then, Lewis anticipated, Israel would become a country that Theodor Herzl "would not recognize."[46]

Thomas Friedman echoed Lewis, blaming Jewish settlers for the conflict. If they "got their way" and Israel retained the West Bank and Gaza, it "would become either an undemocratic apartheid state ... or a non-Jewish state" amid a growing Palestinian population. The conflict, fed by "extremist minorities" on both sides (moral equivalency again), required American pressure to reduce their "strong emotional hold over the moderate majorities." An editorial conceded that Israelis were "understandably frustrated" with Arafat, whose "miscalculations are manifest" and "embrace of violence" was "inexcusable." In return for "more responsible behavior" by Arafat there must be "a renewed Israeli willingness" to recognize him as "the only realistic Palestinian negotiating partner."[47]

The next day a Palestinian suicide bomber exploded himself outside the Sbarro restaurant, a popular kosher pizzeria in the center of downtown Jerusalem. Fifteen Israelis, including Holocaust survivors, a pregnant American woman and the parents and three children of an Orthodox family were among the fatalities. It was, wrote former Bureau Chief Clyde Haberman, "equivalent to a midday attack in the heart of Times Square." At that time and in that place, he noted, the twenty-three-year-old Palestinian terrorist "made it inevitable that many of his victims would be young families, including small children." In a photograph released by his Hamas sponsor, the bomber held an automatic rifle in one hand and a copy of the Koran in the other.[48]

After one of the worst terrorist attacks in Israeli history Haberman focused on the "hardening of positions on both sides." In a "direct blow to the heart of Palestinian nationalism," he wrote, Israeli forces had seized nine Palestinian buildings in East Jerusalem, including Orient House, their "government house" and symbol of their "yearnings for a state." The Israeli message was clear: "they, and no one else, remained in control of all of Jerusalem." For Palestinians, the seizure was "intolerable." Fifteen paragraphs along, his focus shifted to Jerusalem's Jewish neighborhoods, where "grief" prevailed over "politics."[49]

The next day Haberman described the mutual targeting of symbols. The Sbarro restaurant symbolized "the strong desire among most Israelis to lead ... a normal life." But the Israeli seizure of Orient House was a "direct blow to the heart of Palestinian nationalism." Intended to demonstrate that Israel "controls all of Jerusalem," it might "prove the symbolic act with the most enduring consequences."[50] The consequences of dead Jewish children and decimated families were ignored.

A *Times* editorial acknowledged the Sbarro bombing as "one of the worst outrages" of the conflict. Israel's "swift retaliation against Palestinian Authority targets" might be "understandable," but it was "unlikely to calm the situation." Predictably, "both sides" must make "difficult political decisions." Arafat must be persuaded of the necessity of an "effective cease-fire," while Sharon should be encouraged "to resist more hawkish Israelis who dream of purely military solutions." Schmemann focused on the evident reality that repeated Palestinian terrorist attacks were "milestones to the steady shedding of the hopes and illusions raised by Oslo." There was, he concluded bluntly, "no longer a peace process to preserve."[51]

Haaretz columnist Tom Segev contributed an op-ed lauding the Israeli transformation to a "post-Zionist, post-national stage of development," sadly interrupted by Palestinian terrorism. Ever more "multicultural," with Tel Aviv as their symbol, (secular) Israelis no longer embraced "nationalist" ideas or "the abstract ideology of Zionism." Instead, "they live for life itself, as individuals," blending "Jewish and multicultural values." For them the Oslo peace accords were the crowning triumph. But, he wrote presciently, the Sbarro bombing was "one of the catastrophes that may turn post-Zionism into an illusion," as Palestinian terrorism returns Israelis to "the Zionist womb."[52]

The final words in the *Times* on the consequences of the Sbarro attack came from novelist David Grossman. Concluding that "both sides are in a mad, dizzy spiral of violence," he implored Israelis and Palestinians, who "continue to grip each other by the most repulsive means," to "get out of the sealed space of their deeds, outside their panicky, cringing consciousness." Only then could they achieve his wish for "the inevitable separation of their two peoples" into "separate sovereign states, Israel and Palestine."[53]

Amid the horrors of the Second Intifada, Israeli parents and children at restaurants, bus passengers and pedestrians, and teenagers at night clubs were murdered by Palestinian suicide bombers. But the *Times* resolutely held "both sides" responsible. Its reporters routinely visited the homes of Palestinian terrorists but only rarely the homes of Jewish victims. In its narrative of news fit to print, Israel shared blame for the failed peace process that Palestinians violently rejected.

CHAPTER 11

Blame Israel First:
2002–2006

With the intifada raging, Joel Greenberg reported in a front-page article that more than one hundred IDF reservists had signed a statement declaring their refusal to serve in the West Bank or Gaza. Launching their "campaign of defiance" in *Haaretz*, they condemned a policy that involved "dominating, expelling, starving and humiliating an entire people." Citing the precedent of army reservists who had protested against the Lebanon war two decades earlier, Greenberg quoted one of the drafters of the declaration: "You can't be both an occupier and moral. Zionism is not occupation."[1]

Greenberg's report had personal resonance – and professional reverberations. Writing in the *Jerusalem Post* (where Greenberg had been its West Bank reporter between 1986 and 1991), veteran Israeli journalist Uri Dan challenged his "grave indictment against Israel, its government, and army." Locating it within the critique of the "extreme Left" in Israel, Dan dropped a bombshell: Greenberg, an American-Israeli citizen, hardly was a disinterested reporter. He had referred to the Lebanon war resistance movement in his *Times* article without disclosing his own participation in it. Indeed, Greenberg had received a jail sentence in 1983 for refusing to serve with his IDF unit in Lebanon. Dan wondered whether *Times* editors, "who criticize Israel at every opportunity," knew that. They should have known: in a 1985 article Thomas Friedman had identified Greenberg (a fellow Brandeis graduate) as "a conscientious objector to the war [who] went to jail for refusing to carry out reserve duty there."[2]

But the *Times* was palpably eager for peace now. In an op-ed column Yasser Arafat condemned "the attacks carried out by terrorist groups against Israeli civilians," claiming that they "do not represent the Palestinian people or their legitimate aspirations for freedom." Peace required "a return to Israel's 1967 borders" and "the sharing of all Jerusalem as one open city and as the capital of two states, Israel and Palestine."[3] Arafat ignored his own rejection of just such a proposal, offered by Prime Minister Barak two years earlier at Camp David.

An editorial the next day praised the Arafat statement as "a powerful testament to the historic and moral cause of the Palestinian national movement." But the "wide gap" between his promise and performance revealed why the conflict was "on a march to catastrophe," with "hardening attitudes in an increasingly hawkish Israeli government." Indeed, the "growing harshness" of Israeli military action in the West Bank and Gaza was "creating thousands of potential suicide bombers and Israel haters." (In translation, Israel was responsible for future Palestinian terrorism.) Furthermore, "the endless growth of Israeli settlements" was "depriving Palestinians of hope." Israel "must help" Palestinians by demonstrating that "a genuine peace settlement awaits them," as if that had not already been tried, and rejected, at Oslo and Camp David.[4]

In role-playing mode Thomas Friedman impersonated President Bush to advise Arab leaders how to achieve peace. In return for "a complete Israeli withdrawal to the June 4, 1967 lines – in the West Bank, Gaza, Jerusalem and on the Golan Heights," twenty-two Arab States would offer "full peace." Signing his article "W," Friedman-as-Bush warned that otherwise "the Israeli silent majority will continue following Sharon into a dead end." Ten days later Friedman reported his personal quest for Middle East peace while dining with Crown Prince Abdullah in Saudi Arabia. Never reticent about telling government officials how to govern, he had suggested that the Arab League endorse a "total Israeli withdrawal" to pre-1967 lines and establishment of a Palestinian state in return for "full peace" with the Arab world. Remarkably, the Prince responded: "This is exactly the idea I had in mind," until Ariel Sharon "took the violence, and the oppression, to an unprecedented level." Publishing his plan with the approval of the Crown Prince, Friedman modestly noted: "I pass all of this along as straightforwardly as I can, without hype or unrealistic hopes."[5]

Times editors took the bait. Lamenting that "the violent cycle of Palestinian attack and Israeli reprisal grows deadlier by the day," they applauded indications that the Saudi Prince was "finally ready to lead the Arab world to normal relations" with Israel – following "a fairly negotiated peace agreement with the Palestinians." Although the Friedman/Abdullah plan went "considerably further" than Sharon had been willing to go, "both sides have an obligation to explore" the proposal.[6]

For indications of Abdullah's flexibility, the editorial touted an op-ed by "veteran Mideast analyst" Henry Siegman (former director of the liberal American Jewish Congress and a critic of Israeli settlements). So "dramatic" was the Saudi turnaround, Siegman wrote, that Israel might have been expected to "renew a diplomatic dialogue" with Palestinians. "Remarkably," however, the Israeli government had responded to the plan "with a yawn." Sharon's "lack of interest" suggested that his government "seeks pretexts to avoid a political process" that would deprive Israel of the West Bank and Gaza.[7]

William Safire was not persuaded by fanciful prospects for peace now. Saudi "posturing," pretending that the Israeli-Palestinian dispute was "the source of the Arab world's discontent," was nothing but "warmed-over whining." The Arab-Israeli war would only end once Arabs realized that "the will of Israel's people cannot be broken" and the United States "will not force a false peace." Two days later Dore Gold, former Israeli ambassador to the United States and adviser to Prime Minister Sharon, noted that Hamas and Islamic Jihad, with Arafat's permission if not collusion, had established "a vast infrastructure of international terrorism" in the West Bank and Gaza. Israel, he wrote, "must win the war imposed on it by Palestinian leaders."[8]

Times editors lamented the "dark days in the Israeli-Palestinian conflict, in some ways the darkest ever. Each side has convinced itself that the other understands only the language of force and is using it in horrible new ways." Equating "a near suicide cult" among Palestinians with "especially brutal" Israeli military reprisals, the editorial urged Prime Minister Sharon to "do everything he can to encourage and promote the gestures and substance of peace." Two days later, moral equivalence was obliterated in the deadliest attack of the Second Intifada. A Palestinian suicide bomber disguised as a woman exploded himself at a Passover Seder in the dining room of the Park Hotel in Netanya, murdering thirty Israelis and injuring 140. That month more than 135 Israelis were killed in Palestinian terrorist attacks.[9]

With nothing to say about Palestinian terrorism or Israeli victims, Serge Schmemann concluded: "The wild card now appears to be Israel and its responses to the attack" in Netanya. But "few doubted ... that Israelis would seek to avenge so many victims on so sacred a night." Columnist Bob Herbert, who had joined the *Times* a decade earlier as an expert on poverty and racism, universalized the attack. It could have occurred on Christmas or Thanksgiving in New York, he wrote, or at a "family gathering" in Saudi Arabia or Sudan. "Outrage" came from "a clear sense of the betrayal of our humanity," not the murder of innocent Jews, "that is inherent in all acts of terrorism."[10]

A *Times* editorial recognized the Park Hotel attack as "one of the most horrific Palestinian suicide bombings to date." Noting its occurrence "in the heartland of pre-1967 Israel," the editors finally seemed to comprehend that "some Palestinian terrorists are not interested in two states living peacefully side by side." They even cited the Palestinian "double game of unleashing war while talking peace." The next day the *Times* regained its imbalance. Claiming to "share Israel's rage," an editorial expressed reservations over "the long-range effectiveness of policies that rely heavily on the use of force." Israel "must look beyond its current fury to find a political solution to the conflict" by recognizing its "need to relinquish the bulk of the territories it took in 1967." To be sure, the editors conceded, there was "no guarantee" that this would end Palestinian terrorism.[11]

In his second year as a *Times* columnist Nicholas Kristof, winner of a Pulitzer Prize for his coverage of the Tiananmen Square democracy movement in China, expounded on "The Boomerang Syndrome" among Israelis and Palestinians. The intifada was Prime Minister Sharon's fault: his "killing of Palestinians and their hopes" only "creates more terrorists." By "aggravating" terrorism he had turned Arafat into "a Palestinian hero." Kristof's primary source was Knesset Speaker (and former Peace Now activist) Avraham Burg, who would soon predict "the end of Zionism."[12]

Palestinian lawyer Raja Shehadah, focusing on Jewish settlements as "a central blockage to the peace process," blamed Israel for its "pursuit of territorial objectives that are clearly illegal under international law." Only a "quisling government," he wrote in defense of Arafat's defiant leadership, would make peace "with a country in full occupation of its land and which refuses to stop its colonizing program." Thomas Friedman lamented the collaboration of "feckless American Jewish leaders" and neo-conservatives, which "has helped prolong a colonial Israeli occupation that now threatens the entire Zionist enterprise."[13]

Virtually ignoring Israeli victims of the worst ever wave of Palestinian terrorist bombings, causing 124 civilian fatalities, *Times* reporters blanketed Palestinian towns to report the reciprocal suffering inflicted by Israel. Joel Brinkley visited Tulkarm, home of the Park Hotel suicide bomber, where the bomber's brother reported: "Everyone's proud of him." Posters celebrating the deadly attack "hang proudly" from the living-room wall. From Gaza Brinkley described Hamas leaders who were "pleased and satisfied" with the horrific suicide bombings. "Clearly enamored" of suicide attacks, they were "almost welcoming" of Israeli retaliation, which "generate more recruits." He also visited Bethlehem, where 150 (Palestinian) "gunmen" remained barricaded in the Church of the Nativity, holding priests hostage. The priests, a Palestinian guard told him, "are happy to have us here."[14] Brinkley ignored the desecration of a Christian holy site.

Times reporters were also drawn to Palestinian refugee camps, the better to document Israeli responsibility for civilian suffering. James Bennet devoted six paragraphs to the death from Israeli shrapnel of a Palestinian boy in a Bethlehem camp where posters showing "the proud faces of the martyrs – Palestinian gunmen most of them … stared down on the wreckage." Brinkley focused on an 18-year-old Arab girl from Dheisheh who exploded a bomb at the entrance to a Jerusalem supermarket, killing seventeen-year-old Rachel Levy. In a farewell videotape the bomber described herself as "a living martyr," prepared to die for Palestine. From the Jabaliya camp in Gaza, Kristof described "young Palestinians" who wanted to become "shahid, martyrs, and to die blowing up a few Israelis." He was charmed by a "cute" 8-year-old boy who displayed a photo of himself clutching an A-47 rifle.[15] No *Times* journalists reported visits to Israeli families of terrorist victims.

In editorials two days apart the *Times* belatedly recognized "no moral equivalence between the indispensible evil of suicide bombings and Israel's military actions to defeat terror." Demanding "strong steps to expunge the nihilism" of suicide attacks, they deplored leadership that "allows this macabre, self-delusional act of ruin to pass without anguished condemnation." But moral equivalence inevitably intruded: Palestinians needed "real leadership, not overheated talk of victimhood"; Israel "must withdraw their military from the West Bank, stop humiliating their neighbors and accept that peace can only come from an end to occupation."[16]

After fifteen suicide bombings in March reached their horrific climax in the Netanya Passover attack, Israel launched Operation Defensive Shield throughout the West Bank. Following a week-long battle in the Palestinian stronghold of Jenin, in which fifty-two Palestinians and twenty-three Israeli soldiers were killed, PLO officials falsely charged that five hundred Palestinians, a number soon upgraded to thousands, were massacred during the Israeli "genocide." A *Times* editorial response offered familiar "musts" to each side: Palestinians "must abandon their twisted devotion to suicide bombing"; Israelis "must withdraw their military from the West Bank, stop humiliating their neighbors and accept that peace can only come from an end to occupation." William Safire, once again the solitary *Times* voice of support for Israel, praised Prime Minister Sharon for "decisively fulfilling the mandate Israelis overwhelmingly gave him: to turn back the tide of terror."[17]

Former Jerusalem Bureau Chief Serge Schmemann offered "a statement of the obvious: stop the killing, give the Palestinians a state." For suicide bombers, he concluded, "no authority, no agreement, no concession – can right the wrong inflicted on them and their people." But Israelis, to his evident dismay, remained convinced "that the goal of the Arabs is to drive them into the sea." His analysis was guided by Amos Oz, who reiterated the Peace Now solution: "We need to begin putting an end to the occupation, begin evacuating settlements that were deliberately placed in the heart of Palestinian territories." Thomas Friedman also echoed Oz, blaming the collapse of the Oslo process on Israeli settlements that were "shrinking the Palestinians' opportunity for their own state."[18]

Despite President Bush's demand that Israel "must withdraw" military forces, Schmemann concluded that Israeli government officials seemed determined "to clear the West Bank of terrorist infrastructure and terrorists." *Times* editors focused on "Ariel Sharon's Costly Defiance." Perhaps he "does not understand," they wrote caustically, that the American president "has asked him to withdraw 'without delay.'" Sharon's behavior, they complained, was an "insult" to Bush and the United States. "A wise Israeli leader" would defer to the president and demonstrate his "willingness to talk peace with any responsible partner."[19] The editors seemed uncomprehending that Israel might disregard presidential wishes, even when duly endorsed by the *Times*.

After thirteen Israeli soldiers were killed in an ambush in Jenin, and a Palestinian suicide bomber murdered eight Israeli passengers on a Haifa bus, the *Times* focused instead on (false) reports of an Israeli "massacre" of innocent Palestinian civilians. Relying on telephone conversations with Jenin residents, Schmemann and Brinkley claimed (erroneously) that "more than 100 Palestinians have been killed" in "fierce and constant clashes" with Israeli soldiers. Their inflated report doubled the actual number of Palestinian civilian deaths during the entire 10-day battle. They had nothing to say about Israeli military policy not to employ massive air strikes or artillery barrages that might harm civilians, choosing instead to engage in the house-to-house combat that cost the lives of twenty-three soldiers.[20]

The persistent *Times* story line was innocent Palestinian civilians encountering ruthless Israeli military power. Joel Greenberg described Palestinians arrested in Jenin, "stripped to their underpants" and suffering "the stinging indignity" of being photographed before their release, who described "harrowing days under Israeli attack." Nicholas Kristof equated "two dangerous delusions": Palestinian yearning for a "'universal' right of return" and "malignant" Israeli settlement policy. His "dream" was for Arafat and Sharon to leave politics and find their respective exile in St. Helena and Elba.[21]

In an unrelenting Opinion-page fusillade, the *Times* provided an opportunity for two Jewish women to criticize Israel. Once again castigating her adopted country, Allegra Pacheco (the American-born Israeli lawyer living in Bethlehem) cited "another stage of the human rights violations that the Israeli occupation has caused." Writing from Brooklyn, Susan Sachs (soon to become *Times* Bureau Chief in Baghdad) focused on an Israeli couple who left Israel "out of frustration with its rightward drift and lack of progress toward peace with the Palestinians." Israel was making the husband "ill"; his wife explained: "I don't want my children to live in a culture that is so destructive, so sad and so hard."[22]

From outside the Jenin refugee camp, Bennet reported that the "fortress of Palestinian resistance" had "crumbled before overwhelming Israeli force." Palestinians described "bodies cut in pieces, bodies scooped up by bulldozers and buried in mass graves, … people drinking out of sewers and people used by Israeli soldiers as human shields." His primary sources were a twenty-six-year-old Palestinian whose mother and brother were killed by Israeli helicopter bullets, and an UNRWA official who was "clearly angry" at the carnage.[23]

Conversations with Hamas "radicals" in Gaza persuaded Kristof that Sharon's "rash military solutions" created "incentives for terrorism [while] undermining Israel's long-term security." The only solution, he claimed, was "a political deal creating a Palestinian state." What Israel did in the West Bank, *Times* editors lamented, "cannot be justified by any compelling military need." To be sure, Arafat "bears much of the blame": not only had he "failed to oppose terrorism but has directly authorized it." But Prime Minister Sharon "needs to make it clear to his commanders that Palestinian civilians are not Israel's enemy and that their lives, livelihoods and property deserve respect."[24] No similar demand was directed to Palestinian terrorists who murdered Israeli civilians.

Amid its unrelenting criticism of Israel the *Times* published a column by IDF Colonel Nitsan Alon explaining the necessity for military action. The Passover suicide bombing, he reminded readers, ended a month when 130 Israeli civilians were murdered by terrorists, a proportion of the Israeli population twice as large as that of Americans killed on 9/11. The Israeli response was intended to demonstrate to Palestinians "the futility of armed struggle." Among those killed were six "senior Hamas terrorists," including the leader responsible for the Netanya bombing. Jenin, where the Israeli military response was widely excoriated as cruelly destructive, was a city of refuge for "hundreds of militants," commanded by three senior Islamic Jihad leaders who served as "a human shield, at great danger to the civilian population." To limit civilian deaths from air bombings, Israel had chosen a "house-to-house ground assault" that succeeded in "disrupting terrorist plans and degrading terrorist capabilities," while maximizing risk to its own soldiers.[25]

But the primary *Times* story line remained Israeli brutality and Palestinian suffering. Once journalists (led by local Palestinian guides) were permitted entry into the Jenin refugee camp, Bennet filed two consecutive front-page reports describing the devastation in that "ruined place." He speculated that "seeds of terror may have been planted" in "the bulldozed ruins" of Jenin by the overwhelming Israeli military operation, thereby blaming Israel for future Palestinian terrorist attacks. Bennet fondly recalled bygone days under the Oslo Accords, when Israelis gambled in Jericho casinos and played cards in Ramallah clubs, while Palestinians strolled Tel Aviv beaches. Now there was only the "isolated, angry, wrecked city" of Jenin, and Jerusalem, "where people are afraid to send their children to school or their spouses to the grocery store."[26]

David Shipler lamented the fate of the Oslo Accords as "a failure of deterrence" that "never gave Palestinians enough autonomy to outweigh Israeli occupation." Sharon was to blame for "further radicalizing the Palestinian population." With settlements as symbols of an "indefinite Israeli presence," Palestinians felt "deceived and humiliated." Writing from Khartoum, Kristof conceded that "Israeli brutality in the occupied territories ... is small potatoes by Arab standards." But the Arab world was nonetheless outraged because "Israeli repression of Arabs is seen not just as brutal, but also as humiliating."[27]

The chorus of *Times* criticism of Israel for its military response to repeated Palestinian terrorist attacks reached a crescendo in two editorials three days apart. "Real Israeli security will prove elusive," the editors proclaimed, repeating the familiar *Times* mantra, "until the occupation of the West Bank ends and Palestinians are permitted to ... establish their state." They suggested that "American power has not been enhanced by the spectacle" of an Israeli prime minister "brazenly ignoring" President Bush's call for the immediate withdrawal of Israeli military forces.[28] For the *Times,* always eager to assert its patriotic loyalty, an Israeli affront to American diplomatic efforts was reprehensible.

Seven months after the eruption of the Second Intifada, 319 Israelis had been killed in terrorist attacks. Joel Brinkley reported interviews with family members (while noting that "people are dying on both sides in large numbers"). Although "the trauma is excruciating," the father of a teenage daughter murdered in the Sbarro pizzeria attack and the son of parents killed in the Passover bombing "wholeheartedly" supported the Israeli military response. Clyde Haberman bracketed Palestinians and Israelis within the "imperative of faith, advanced by force," with each side "convinced that it is history's true orphan." But Israel's "occupation" had bestowed on Palestinians "a cause that to much of the world seemed legitimate." Thomas Friedman claimed to speak for "many Israelis" who felt that Sharon was "paralyzed by his obsession" with eliminating Arafat and "his commitment to colonial settlements."[29]

Following two months of relative quiet, Palestinian terrorist attacks resumed when a suicide bomber murdered nineteen Israelis on a Jerusalem bus, the largest Israeli death toll since the Passover bombing (and the seventieth suicide attack in twenty-one months). Bennet and Kifner could not resist noting that the bus began its final journey from the neighborhood of Gilo, "built on land seized by Israel during the 1967 war." The bomber's father told *Times* reporters that he was "very happy" to learn of his son's success, which left the bodies of three women still in their seats "but their heads were gone." Palestinian officials attributed the attack to "Israeli oppression."[30]

The next day another suicide bomber, an Israeli Arab, killed six Israelis at a bus stop across the street from the site of the Mahane Yehuda market bombing a year earlier. For Joel Greenberg, covering his funeral, his death highlighted the "predicament" of Israeli Arabs, "caught in a conflict between their country and their people." But his Arab sources did not seem conflicted. The bomber, Greenberg noted, "was celebrated by his family as a martyr who died in a sacred struggle." The Mayor of Bartaa, the village where the bomber lived, said: "We condemn the reason for his death, which is the occupation."[31] Greenberg did not cover the funeral of any Israeli victim.

Times editors repeated familiar tropes of blame. The crisis provoked by "delusional young Palestinians" could not be resolved by Sharon's settlement-building and his "failure to offer Palestinians anything beyond threats and humiliation." Nor by Palestinians "intoxicated with the idea of power through death," who suffer from "a severe failure" of leadership. In their customary refrain the editors noted that "each side ... is locked into a position in which it sees any concession as rewarding the misbehavior of the other." For the *Times*, "the solution remains clear": abandonment of "select settlements" by Israel and "imprisonment of terrorist leaders by Palestinians."[32]

The frenzied dynamic of Palestinian terrorism gained strength during the months that followed. Attacks in Jerusalem and Hebron killed thirty-seven Jews. By the end of 2002, 238 Israelis had been murdered in Palestinian terrorist attacks, which would claim 145 additional Israeli lives the following year. Each of Israel's major cities – Tel Aviv, Haifa and Jerusalem – had been targeted. During the first week of January 2003 two Palestinians from Nablus, standing five hundred feet apart, exploded bombs at a bus step and in a pedestrian mall in the heart of Tel Aviv, claiming twenty-two lives (including six foreign workers). Dexter Filkins, newly arrived from New Delhi where he was Bureau Chief, quickly accommodated to *Times* equivalency standards, noting that "Israeli forces have carried out numerous operations of their own."[33]

Times editors conceded that Prime Minister Sharon "has every right to respond swiftly and firmly to Palestinian terrorist outrages." They even assigned "primary responsibility for the cycle of terror and reprisal" to "fanatical Palestinian groups … and weak Palestinian leaders like Yasir Arafat who fail to crack down on them." But Sharon's actions "undermine the prospects for better Palestinian governing and an eventual end to the violence." Israel's goal "should be to marginalize Palestinian terrorists, not to advance their cause" by "destroying chances for a compromise peace."[34] Once again, Israel was held responsible for Palestinian terrorism.

Later that month Sharon's sweeping re-election victory frustrated *Times* editors. The outcome suggested that "in this time of insecurity" Israelis "feel safer" with his "hard-line leadership." But Israeli occupation was "catastrophic for both peoples." It was time, they insisted, for Sharon "to turn away from his exclusively military response to Palestinian violence" and halt settlement construction. In a nearby column Gadi Taub, Hebrew University professor and an ardent advocate of Palestinian statehood, condemned Sharon's "doublespeak: talk peace but build up the settlements." If settlers did not relinquish their homes, he predicted (erroneously), Jews would "soon be a minority in their own country" confronting the necessity to "relinquish either democracy or the ideal of a Jewish state."[35]

That summer more than fifty Israelis were killed by Palestinian terrorists in Haifa and Jerusalem. The most horrific attack occurred on a double-length Jerusalem bus crowded with Orthodox children returning from a visit to the Western Wall. A Hebron Arab, disguised as an Orthodox Jew, detonated himself and murdered twenty-three Israelis, including a father and son, a pregnant mother, a three-year-old girl, and eleven-month-old and three-month-old boys. That day, coincidentally, Amos Oz contributed an op-ed asserting that both "fanatic Arabs" and "extremist Jews" had ignited "the infernal cycle of violence and vengeance." His solution was for Palestinians to "disarm the rejectionists' terror organizations" and for Israel to remove, "by force if necessary – all the unauthorized settlements."[36] For Oz, Jewish settlers were the Israeli equivalent of Palestinian terrorists.

The Jerusalem bombing, James Bennet reported, seemed most significant for "opening a deep wound in the American-backed peace effort." He paid less attention to the physical and emotional wounds inflicted on Israelis. But he noted that "fireworks burst" in Hebron as Palestinians "celebrated the bombing by one of theirs." The terrorist, according to his wife, had long been saying "Oh God, I wish to be a martyr." Despite "illusions of progress," Bennet wrote the following day, "nothing fundamental has yet changed." Israel had not frozen settlement growth or dismantled settlement outposts while Palestinians had not dismantled their terrorist groups.[37] Implicitly, Israel was the provocation for which terrorism was the predictable response.

Times editors equated the "devastating suicide bus bombing" in Jerusalem with the retaliatory Israeli helicopter attack that killed the Hamas leader responsible for the suicide mission. Such action "seems counterproductive," serving as an "excuse" for Hamas "to rouse its faithful to more violence." Bracketing "settlement activity" with terrorism, the editorial asserted that Israelis and Palestinians had "failed to carry out their commitments." It insisted, predictably: "Both sides need to act now."[38]

Thomas Friedman embellished the venerable theme of moral equivalence, the embedded core of *Times* reporting and editorial judgment about Israel. Noting that suicide bombings had made Israelis "crazy," he segued to the security barrier authorized by the Sharon government to stifle Palestinian terrorist infiltration from the West Bank. With his penchant for folksy metaphors, Friedman acknowledged that "Good fences make good neighbors, but only if your fence runs along a logical, fair consensual boundary – not through the middle of your neighbor's backyard." He relayed the warning of Yaron Ezrahi, who anticipated that the barrier might "bite off chunks of the West Bank to absorb far-flung Israeli settlements." Then, Ezrahi anticipated, Jews would "be mourning the collapse of their dream of a democratic Jewish state."[39]

One month later Friedman explicitly bracketed Israeli settlement expansion with Palestinian suicide bombings. One hundred terrorist attacks in three years exposed "unquenchable" passions among Palestinians, while "relentless settlements" expressed "insatiable appetites" by Israelis for "Palestinian land." He called on Israel to "use its overwhelming strength" to take the initiative and "dismantle" settlements. With Rabbi Hartman once again serving as his moral pundit, he quoted the rabbi's question whether Israel wanted to be "defined by Torah and values – or by which hill and rock it controls" in the West Bank.[40]

A plausible answer came two days later, the day before Yom Kippur, when a Palestinian woman from Jenin blew herself up in a crowded Haifa restaurant killing nineteen Israelis. Primary *Times* coverage came from John F. Burns, its London Bureau Chief for international affairs. Ignoring the families of victims (and wounded survivors), he filed a six-column report of his journey to Jenin to visit the bomber's parents. There he encountered "careworn but proud gentility" and "elaborate courtesy" but "no overt grieving" for their daughter and "no sympathy for the Haifa victims." She had not done "a shameful thing," her mother said, but had acted "for the sake of her people." To her father it was a "justified" response to her brother's death during the Israeli siege of Jenin.[41]

Burns was sharply criticized for his blithe indifference to Israeli victims. "Some might say," he wrote five days later, that he had attempted to "dignify the killing by seeking some comprehension" of the murderer's outrage, thereby effectively providing "a form of exoneration." Burns responded: "To sojourn in the Holy Land these days is to be pitched into a miasma of mutual political recriminations." Palestinian terrorism was merely part of "a spiral of mutual dehumanization and violence" in which Israel must also be implicated.[42]

Times editors similarly bracketed "despicable Palestinian terror" with the "recklessly inappropriate" retaliatory Israeli bombing of a Palestinian terrorist training camp inside Syria. Conceding "the depressing frequency" of Palestinian suicide bombings, they nonetheless admonished Israel for crossing the Syrian border. In a nearby column, *Jerusalem Report* editor David Horovitz endorsed the familiar *Times* refrain that "unless Israel can separate from the 3.5 million Palestinians, it cannot remain democratic and predominantly Jewish."[43]

Palestinian bus-bombings continued to exact their gory toll. An explosion in Jerusalem killed ten Israeli Jews and an illegal Ethiopian immigrant. Noting that the victims included Israelis who had emigrated from Russia, Georgia, France, Canada, and Romania, Greg Myre chose to make the death of the illegal immigrant the most newsworthy. An AP reporter in Jerusalem before joining the *Times,* Myre had previously discerned a "perverse logic" that led "both sides to choose the irrational over the rational." He, too, was drawn to Israeli critics of Israel, among them Amos Oz, dissident soldiers who joined Breaking the Silence, a disgruntled former Shin Bet chief, and his landlord who believed the solution to be "a bi-national state."[44]

The next day Prime Minister Sharon informed *Haaretz* that he was considering the evacuation of Gush Katif, the cluster of Gaza agricultural villages that had become home for some seven thousand Israelis since 1970. Coming from Israel's staunch supporter of settlement construction and expansion, Sharon's stunning announcement of Israeli withdrawal was a political bombshell that delighted *Times* editors. It marked "a turning point" that injected "a vital degree of sanity … into Israeli political debate." The only problem (predictably) was that "he does not go far enough." A "viable" Palestinian state "will have to be made up of the entire West Bank and Gaza, with small adjustments."[45]

One month later two Palestinian suicide bombers from Gaza murdered ten Israelis in nearby Ashdod. Israel retaliated with a targeted missile strike that killed Sheik Ahmed Yassin, the founding leader of Hamas. *Times* editors could not comprehend "how his martyrdom will make Israel any safer." Ignoring Sharon's Gaza evacuation plan, they identified him as "perhaps the most inflexible Israeli advocate of the policy of an unflinching fist." Predictably, they anticipated that "both sides," each possessing a "sense of victimhood," would persist in their shared policy of "assassinations, suicide bombings and mutual demonization."[46] Once again, the *Times* drew no distinction between Palestinian terrorism and Israeli retaliation.

Sharon's evacuation proposal was quickly followed by a roadside ambush in Gaza by Palestinian "gunmen" who killed an Israeli woman (eight months pregnant with her first son) and her four young daughters. In familiar *Times* language Serge Schmemann wrote: "Each side thinks, We are the victims; they are the terrorists." Any suggestion that "the other side also has just grievances and just demands becomes a denial of one's own suffering and claims." After Israel launched a retaliatory attack to demolish the Hamas military infrastructure in the Rafah refugee camp, *Times* editors labeled it "a plan to unilaterally destroy the Palestinian territory." Conceding that Israel "indisputably faces a threat from Hamas cells within Gaza," they emphasized "Sharon's obsession with appearing characteristically tough, lest his desire to withdraw be taken for a sign of weakness." Kristof labeled him a "right-wing jingoist" who had "done more to undermine Israel's long-term security" than Arafat ever did. Both leaders, he concluded, "display a bloodstained obduracy" and "should be exiled together to St. Helena."[47]

In February 2005 Sharon and Mahmoud Abbas (Arafat's successor following his death the previous November) arrived in Sharm El Sheik to sign a cease-fire agreement. Israel announced its pullback of soldiers from five major West Bank cities, while Abbas proclaimed "the beginning of a new era." Erlanger perceived the "fragility" of a truce that Hamas immediately announced it would disregard. For *Times* editors, however, the agreement offered "much to be happy about." To be sure, "both sides" must make adjustments. Israelis "must be demanding, realistic and smart," with "smart" meaning "strengthening the hand" of Abbas by "moving quickly on freezing any further settlement activity." Abbas, in turn, must figure out how to "take on" Hamas, Islamic Jihad, and the Al Aksa Martyrs Brigades, all of whom opposed the agreement.[48] The next day Hamas launched a rocket and mortar attack against settlements in the southern Gaza Strip.

What had changed, Erlanger wrote, was the willingness of Abbas and Sharon "to challenge and even confront the extreme elements in their societies who are most opposed to a negotiated peace." The Oslo Accords had failed, he suggested, because "both sides" had refused to do so. The suicide bombings by Hamas and Islamic Jihad "made it clear" that they wanted Israel "wiped off the map." Israeli governments, in turn, "decided not to confront the most extreme and ideological" settlers, even after the Goldstein massacre. "This is not to equate the two morally or otherwise," Erlanger hastened to add. It was "merely to observe" that Hamas and Jewish settlers "represent the most ideologically committed and devout of the rejectionists and that both opposed the Oslo accords," thereby equating them.[49]

With the approaching expulsion of Gaza settlers an editorial expressed concern that "thousands of religious protesters," who had gathered as close to the border as Israeli police and military forces permitted, were "pledging to do whatever they can to hamper the withdrawal." By mid-August, after half of the nine thousand settlers had left voluntarily and the Israeli army had detained one thousand protesters, the largest settlement of Neve Dekalim became the site of the climactic finale. *Times* reporters described "an emotionally searing confrontation" between settlers, joined by their "young, devout" supporters from West Bank settlements, and soldiers who were berated by protesters for their willingness to "act like Nazis" and "expel Jews."[50]

Erlanger vividly described the forcible Israeli evacuation of the most resolute Gaza settlers, five hundred families who were carried "screaming from their Neve Dekalim homes in scenes that moved a number of the soldiers to tears." One settler described a "pogrom"; a family of parents and children left their home with their arms raised, all wearing an orange star redolent of Jews under Nazi conquest. It was, he wrote, "a historic defeat" for the settlement movement. But the Gaza withdrawal demonstrated that "democratic Israel" could "face down the settler lobby and its messianic form of Zionism." Israel had accepted the principle of "territorial compromise." But what was true for "tiny, peripheral Gaza," Erlanger cautioned, "may not be true" once large portions of the West Bank were at stake.[51]

Recognizing the "genuine grief" of the evacuated settlers, *Times* editors noted that Gaza never was part of the "Zionist state" authorized under the United Nations partition plan in 1947. But following the Six-Day War Israeli leaders had permitted settlers to "take over the best parts" of the newly captured land. With Gaza representing "the worst side of Israel's settlement," it was "past time … to give the Palestinians there a chance at a better life." Lavishly praising Prime Minister Sharon's "extraordinary accomplishment," the editors spotted "a flicker of sunshine" amid "too many dark days" of occupation and violence. But Gaza should only be the beginning: Sharon's "historic shift" on settlements must now be extended to the West Bank. Israel, editors cautioned, "will never find security until it makes peace" with West Bank Palestinians, who were rarely admonished to make peace with Israel.[52]

After the last Israeli soldiers left Gaza, young Palestinians launched what Erlanger described as "a carnival of celebration … and widespread scavenging." They burned the synagogue at Neve Dekalim and vandalized two dozen others, described by a Hamas leader as "symbols of Israel and the occupation." Thomas Friedman took a final swipe at Gaza settlers. The very idea of Jews living in Gaza was "utterly insane – disconnected from any strategic, moral, demographic, nationalist or religious logic." (Like *Times* editors, he failed to note that Jews had lived in Gaza for centuries until the 1929 riots). Urging a "final settlement" with the Palestinians, he dismissed defenders of the status quo as "extremists and messianists who are a danger to the future of Israel and the Jewish people." *Times* editors predictably insisted that "Israel's historic disengagement from Gaza … must be the start, and not the end, of Israeli withdrawal from the lands that will eventually make up a Palestinian state."[53]

With the Gaza evacuation completed the *Times* focus shifted to the West Bank. Erlanger described the "weekly tactical battle" every Friday in Bil'in, a tiny village two miles east of the old Green Line boundary that had separated Israel and Jordan before the Six-Day War. Split by Israel's new security barrier, built to prevent Palestinian terrorist infiltration, it became the site of weekly protests by local Palestinians and Israeli sympathizers in what Erlanger described as "one of the closest spectacles the region provides to Kabuki theater." Eager "to provoke the [Israeli] army and the police into overreacting," they fed the international media image of Israel (embraced by the *Times*) as "a country of victims transformed into oppressors" by their continuing occupation of "Palestinian" land.[54]

In January 2006 Prime Minister Sharon suffered a cerebral hemorrhage that required emergency brain surgery to save his life. Israeli politics, Erlanger reported, were "thrown into turmoil" with the sudden arrival of a "post-Sharon era," without "a warrior willing to take risks" in dealing with the Palestinians. *Times* editors suggested that Sharon "struck such a powerful chord with the Israelis' craving for security and stability that he might well have been able to bulldoze his people into the future as he saw it." Israeli historian Benny Morris identified Sharon as "the wily, bulldozing general" of the 1967 and 1973 wars who understood, as many of Israel's professed diaspora supporters did not, that Jews and Arabs could not "live together like a bunch of mindless lambs." Without him, "hopes for further daring steps ... have been dashed."[55] The *Times* narrative of Israeli domination and Palestinian victimization would remain intact.

CHAPTER 12

Israeli Goliath:
2006–2009

With Ariel Sharon incapacitated (until his death eight years later), his legacy was framed within the familiar *Times* narrative of Israel's moral decline ever since the Six-Day War. In his "finest and wisest hour," Thomas Friedman wrote of Sharon's decision to withdraw from Gaza, the Israeli leader had recognized that one of his "greatest projects," building settlements in the Land of Israel, "was wrong." He could "finally see" (as Friedman did) that "overbuilding settlements imperiled Israel's Jewish and democratic character." *Times* editors, in their swipe at Sharon, even blamed him for the "bankrupt, powerless and divided Palestinian Authority," which had been "systematically undermined" by Israeli military aggression.[1]

Citing *Haaretz* journalist Ari Shavit, hardly a neutral source, Friedman imagined that "Israelis have never been more dovish" or more willing to embrace a two-state solution. Conversations with Hamas officials in Gaza prompted his wishful prediction that Hamas would be "low-key and patient." Its majority in the Palestinian parliament, he imagined, had the potential "to open some new, intriguing possibilities for a long-term settlement, or truce, in Israeli-Palestinian relations." Israel, Friedman concluded, "has an enormous interest in testing Hamas's ability to evolve."[2] It would not be long before Hamas launched a new war against Israel.

Jerusalem Bureau Chief Steven Erlanger offered a more astute understanding of Hamas. Its recent electoral victory, he wrote, had "enormous resonance for radical Islam." It marked a telling defeat for Fatah, Israel's "chosen partner" for peace negotiations, and for secular Palestinian nationalism. To Hamas leaders, Palestinian Authority agreements with the Jewish state were nothing more than "a honey trap"; with their victory in Gaza the "land for peace formula" had been "blown apart." By deep religious conviction, Hamas was convinced that "all of Palestine," including Israel, is "Islamic Waqf land, belonging irrevocably to the world's Muslims." And the State of Israel, they asserted, "has no right to exist on Waqf land."[3]

Fanciful *Times* anticipation of an era of Palestinian-Israeli amity was abruptly shattered. Hours before the new Israeli government led by Ehud Olmert was sworn in, a Palestinian suicide bomber launched the deadliest terrorist attack in nearly two years, blowing himself up in a Tel Aviv falafel restaurant and killing eleven Israelis. A *Times* editorial cited Hamas's "monumentally cynical and dim-witted applause" for the attack. But its "support for terrorism" bolstered Prime Minister Olmert's strategy of "unilateral separation from the Palestinian people," which the *Times* vigorously endorsed.[4]

The *Times* was delighted with Olmert's pledge of new borders for Israel within four years. Tens of thousands of Israeli settlers living east of the West Bank separation barrier, Greg Myre reported, would become "candidates for eviction." A *Foreign Affairs* editor contributed a laudatory review of Gershom Gorenberg's narrative in *The Accidental Empire* of Israel's "inadvertent colonialism," praising it as "a mournful reminder of what happens when a democratic government acquiesces in the face of its own militants."[5]

An editorial analysis of Palestinian "peace politics" conjectured that "most Palestinians," recognizing "explicitly or implicitly, Israel's right to exist," favored a two-state solution. It responded favorably to a proposal by imprisoned Palestinian leader Marwan Barghouti to grant "only implicit, not explicit" recognition to Israel within its pre-1967 borders, while asserting the right of return for Palestinian refugees. Although unacceptable "even to dovish Israelis," *Times* editors imagined that it might represent "an initial bargaining position" that could be seen as "a step in the right direction" toward peace.[6]

Gaza continued to attract *Times* coverage. Steven Erlanger visited the former site of kibbutz Neve Dekalim, converted with funding from a United Arab Emirates sheik into a new campus linked to Al-Aksa University. After the settlers departed much Neve Dekalim land had been seized and looted by local clans and militant groups. Explaining the construction of a protective wall around the campus the registrar noted, "After we put up the wall, things became easier." The *Times* had repeatedly condemned Israel's West Bank security wall; Erlanger did not comment on the irony of a Palestinian barrier against Palestinians.[7]

In late June the *Times* reported that Gaza "militants" had emerged from a tunnel dug three hundred yards into Israel, killed two Israeli soldiers and kidnapped nineteen-year-old Cpl. Gilad Shalit. The first soldier to be kidnapped in more than a decade, his capture, which riveted Israelis until his release in a controversial prisoner exchange five years later, was identified by Erlanger as "the latest in a cycle of violence and reprisal." *Times* editors, anticipating the "inevitable" response to Hamas's "provocative behavior," urged Israel to be "as restrained as possible." Ignoring any distinction between aggression and retaliation, they feared "endless rounds of reckless Hamas provocations and inexorable Israeli responses."[8]

From Ramallah, Erlanger explored the replacement of Palestinian Authority "dysfunction and corruption" by Hamas "militants" with a reputation for "discipline, unity and honesty." But its newly acquired power had become "a trap for Hamas, accentuating its divisions and causing new fractures." Israel, he noted, "has long experience in playing off Palestinian divisions and deepening them." But Israel had "its own political third rail – the reputation of its military and the lives of its soldiers." A live soldier in captivity "creates a crisis, pushing both sides in directions they don't necessarily want to go."[9]

Even as rockets from Gaza poured into southern Israel the plight of Gazans, not Shalit in captivity or beleaguered Israeli civilians, dominated *Times* coverage. Erlanger focused on the anguish of Gaza victims of Israeli retaliation for Shalit's kidnapping. He interviewed the Palestinian survivor of an explosion that killed three family members. As one of his fourteen children described the explosion – caused, it turned out, by a Hamas anti-tank rocket – a young woman nearby began to chant: "With our souls, with our blood, we will sacrifice ourselves for our martyr." Gripped by the spectacle, Erlanger described in vivid detail the arrival of dead bodies, wrapped in the flags of Islamic Jihad and Fatah, amid "screaming and ululating" and "cascading sounds of gunfire from militants surging around the courtyard." An Islamic Jihad spokesman promised retribution from "70 suicide bombers."[10]

In the summer of 2006 the simmering Gaza conflict erupted into a two-front war. Responding to a Hezbollah raid from Lebanon that killed eight IDF soldiers and captured two others, Israel sent military forces across the border and fired missiles into the Beirut airport. A "local confrontation," Erlanger and Myre reported, had become a "regional crisis." In Beirut, they noted, "residents gave out sweets in celebration" of the capture of Israeli soldiers.[11]

Times editors recognized that "kidnapping Israeli soldiers to use as bargaining chips … is horrible behavior," as was "lobbing" rockets into Israel. But once again their cautionary admonitions were directed solely to Israel. "Even when acting justifiably in the face of aggression," it "best serves its long-term security interests by acting wisely and proportionally." The editorial urged Israel "to be careful that its far-reaching military responses, however legally and morally justified," did not "advance" the political agenda of its enemies. Israel might be "fully justified" in treating the kidnapping of its soldiers as "unacceptable acts of aggression." But its political and military leaders must not "let themselves be drawn into the provocateurs' game."[12]

It was not a "game" for Israeli civilians. Under a Hezbollah rocket barrage from Lebanon, tens of thousands of Israelis fled from their homes in Safed and other northern towns. As Myre reported, the hospital in Safed was "one of the few places with signs of life." But in the *Times*, Israel invariably was to blame for attacks against it. Ethan Bronner concluded that Israel's recent strategic decisions to "extricate itself from conflict" by building a barrier against West Bank terrorist attacks and evacuating Gaza had been thwarted by its preference for "going it alone, rather than negotiating with its enemies." Nicholas Kristof chastised "impatient Israelis" for escalating the conflict with their vehement response to Hezbollah missiles and kidnappings, to the benefit of "hardliners throughout the Islamic world." He imagined that "real security" depended on "the kind of two-state solution" proposed in 2003 by "Arab and Israeli peaceniks."[13]

Virtually the sole dissenting voice, if rarely and with little evident familiarity with Israel, came from David Brooks, its designated conservative columnist following William Safire's retirement. (Brooks, according to editorial page editor Gail Collins, was "the kind of conservative that wouldn't make our readers shriek and throw the paper out the window.") He described "a return to the elemental conflict between Israel and those who seek to destroy it," with Hamas and Hezbollah encouraged by Iranian support to "set the pace of confrontation." While Israel had tried "to pull back to more sensible borders," its enemies "have gone completely berserk." But the "world's response" (like that of the *Times*) was: "Israel is overreacting."[14]

The Opinion page was flooded with criticism of the Israeli response to Hamas and Hezbollah attacks. Columbia professor Rashid Khalidi, ideologically aligned with the PLO since the 1970s, focused on "the denial of rights to Palestinians and the occupation of Arab lands" by Israel. Columnist Bob Herbert, the *Times* advocate for "progressive journalism," proclaimed that the "spasm of destruction unleashed by Israel in Lebanon" was intolerable. Although "murderous rocket attacks into Israel must be stopped," so must "the wanton killing of innocent civilians including babies and children, who had no connection to Hezbollah."[15]

Israel must understand, according to *Times* editors, that "more civilian deaths in Lebanon won't make Israelis safer." Kristof equated Israel's "Lebanon adventure" with "America's Iraq adventure." Columnist Paul Krugman, an economist not known for Middle East expertise, blamed Israel for relying on "shock and awe rather than either diplomacy or boots on the ground." Thomas Friedman, inserting "primordial, tribal passions" into the moral equivalency mix, bracketed "Palestinian suicide bombings of Israeli cafes and buses" with Israeli retaliation "leveling whole buildings, with the guilty and the innocent inside." Israeli air strikes against Hezbollah targets, an editorial conceded, might be legitimate, but they were doing Israel "more harm than good."[16]

On the "deadliest day" of the three-week conflict more than one hundred Hezbollah rockets landed in northern Israel within less than an hour. Eight Israeli soldiers and four civilians, including a father and his daughter, were killed. After "a slow and fumbling start," Erlanger wrote, Israel was fighting "to win the battle of perceptions," determined to send the message to Palestinians, Hezbollah and their sponsors in Iran and Syria that attacks will be met with "overwhelming force." Previous withdrawals from Lebanon and Gaza, he noted, had not been perceived "as a gesture for peaceful coexistence ... but as a sign of weakness."[17]

The death of an American Israeli soldier, killed by a Hezbollah anti-tank missile in Lebanon, caught *Times* attention. Twenty-two-year-old Michael Levin, raised in a Philadelphia suburb, had dreamed of becoming an Israeli paratrooper. Hailed by his grieving father for his "pioneering spirit," he was "proud to live in a country that 60 years ago was not here." The day his funeral was reported it was overshadowed by a lengthy *Times* story about mourners in the Israeli Arab village of Tarshiha, grieving over three victims of a Hezbollah rocket attack. Their deaths "seemed to swipe the life from this tight-knit Arab neighborhood." Hezbollah rockets had also killed five Israelis in Acre; no *Times* reporter interviewed Jewish mourners.[18]

It took weeks for the *Times,* focused on the damage inflicted by Israeli military retaliation, to acknowledge the toll exacted by attacks against Israeli civilians. With hundreds of Katyusha rockets falling daily in the north, it belatedly noted, the government was temporarily relocating "thousands of residents who are too poor, too sick or unable to leave on their own." Most of the 25,000 residents of the city of Kiryat Shmona had been evacuated; those who remained were living in basements or shelters. With several dozen Israeli civilians (and sixty-five soldiers) killed, and more than five hundred wounded, the evident inability of the vaunted Israeli military to halt the rocket barrage from Lebanon had deepened "psychological damage" to Israelis.[19]

Erlanger identified the Israeli paradox: "The harder the war has been, the more the public wants it to proceed" until Hezbollah no longer posed a threat. Israel was criticized (not least by the *Times*) for overreacting and causing disproportionate damage to the Lebanese civilian population. But Israelis, "nearly universal" in their conviction that the war had become "a matter of survival, not choice," were critical of Prime Minister Olmert for his hesitant leadership. Even a Peace Now leader, insisting "We're not pacifists," noted that the only occupier in Lebanon was Hezbollah. After nearly five weeks of fighting a ceasefire was negotiated by the United Nations. Respected Israeli journalist Nahum Barnea noted in an op-ed column: "We did not win." Israel approached the cease-fire "bruised, conflicted and disturbed."[20]

Times editors conceded that "Given the implacable hatred of its enemies, Israel cannot afford to show weakness." Israelis had "a right to ask" whether Prime Minister Olmert had "rashly raised the ante by demanding the military destruction of Hezbollah," while lacking "any clear and realistic strategy" for achieving it. But for the *Times* the unwelcome alternative to Olmert was Benjamin Netanyahu, "a man with his own long record of costly and impetuous decisions."[21]

Once the Lebanon conflict subsided, *Times* coverage renewed its reflexive focus on Israeli responsibility for dimming peace prospects. Israel, an editorial declared, must impose "a total freeze on settlement building and expansion" and "a prompt easing of the onerous, humiliating and economically strangulating blockades on Palestinian movements within the West Bank." Erlanger explored the plight of a "lost generation of Palestine," comprising "its most radical, most accepting of violence and most despairing" cohort. Israel, the "visible agent of oppression," was responsible for their predicament. With soldiers and settlers the only Israelis with whom they had contact, young Palestinians were "more supportive of armed struggle and terrorism" than their parents. A sixteen-year-old boy from Jenin insisted: "Jews should go back to where they came from. . . . They have no place here."[22]

Erlanger focused on Peace Now allegations (accompanied by "digitized map information" from an unidentified government source) that more than one-third of settlement land occupied "private Palestinian land." The data, Erlanger wrote, "shows a pattern of illegal seizure." But deep into the article he noted that Peace Now had previously erred with an 86% inflation of land seized by the largest settlement of Ma'ale Adumim. Without reliable information for that settlement, Erlanger concluded, the difference between old and new data for "seized land" was "about one percentage point."[23] In translation, there was no substance to the Peace Now report, and little justification for *Times* reliance on it.

Erlanger also reported attending a talk by a twenty-seven-year-old Israeli who recounted four years of military service in the West Bank. The speaker was director of Breaking the Silence, comprising some four hundred former combat soldiers and reservists, "shocked at their own misconduct and that of others," whose stories had been collected and publicly circulated. But he acknowledged that "most behave within decent moral limits." Relying on reports from B'tselem, another left-wing Israeli advocacy group, Nicholas Kristof faulted "hard-line Israeli policies" for "radicalizing young Palestinians, empowering Hamas and Hezbollah," and "nurturing another generation of terrorists in Lebanon."[24]

Thomas Friedman contributed his own quirky proposal for the peace campaign. King Abdullah of Saudi Arabia should lead "an emotional breakthrough" for the revival of Israeli-Palestinian peace talks. Friedman would "humbly suggest" that he pray at the Al-Aksa Mosque on the Temple Mount "to reaffirm the Muslim claim to Arab East Jerusalem." Then the King should visit nearby Ramallah "to offer Israel peace with the whole Arab world in return for full withdrawal." Finally, he would visit Yad Vashem to "sell the deal with Israelis and affirm that the Muslim world rejects the Holocaust denialism of Iran." Friedman had "no doubt" that the majority of Israelis would demand that "their government respond positively" to his fantasy scenario.[25] Nothing was heard but the sound of silence.

Reality intruded once Israel confronted renewed Hamas attacks from Gaza. Sderot, barely one mile east of the border, was its most inviting target. Battered by hundreds of rockets, nearly half its 24,000 residents had fled for safety elsewhere. But the Olmert government, Erlanger wrote, was "feeling constrained by its own weakness and damaged credibility," even as security officials warned that Hamas was "organizing a buildup of weapons, reinforced tunnels and explosive materiel ... that resembles Hezbollah's efforts in southern Lebanon." Sooner or later, they presciently predicted, "Israel will have to confront Hamas in a serious way inside Gaza."[26]

Reporter Isabel Kershner provided a vivid – and, for the *Times,* unusually empathetic – account of Israeli life under siege. After seven years of rocket fire, Sderot, a "bull's eye" for Qassam missiles, had become "a city of fear." She described the "red alert" signaled by the recorded voice of a woman on the city-wide public address system warning of incoming rockets, "inevitably followed by a whistle and a terrifying boom." Residents who had endured nearly three hundred rockets since the 6-month cease-fire ended were "paralyzed by the terror of the last red alert and dread of the next one."[27]

Marking the fortieth anniversary of the Six-Day War, British journalist Adam LeBor contributed a column focused on why *Hatikvah,* the Israeli national anthem, should be "updated." While Israel "strives to be both a Jewish state and a democracy," one-fifth of its population was not Jewish. Therefore "a gesture of inclusion is needed" to encourage "a psychic shift" among Arab and Jewish citizens over "what it means to be an Israeli." His proposed "gesture" would replace the *Hatikvah* reference to "nefesh Yehudi" (Jewish soul) with "nefesh Israeli," thereby promoting "a modern Hebrew (and Arabic) Israeli identity" not predicated on religion. Then Israel would have "an anthem that can be sung by all its citizens."[28]

In the same issue *Times* deputy foreign editor Ethan Bronner contributed a laudatory review of a new book on the Six-Day War by Israeli journalist Tom Segev. He approvingly cited Segev's conclusion that Israel, consumed by Holocaust-driven anxiety, had precipitously launched war against neighboring Arab states poised on its borders to attack "when diplomacy might have sufficed." Its stunning victory "caused such irrational exultation in Israel that it foolishly became an occupier, a role that continues to drag the nation down." Segev, wrote Bronner (soon to become Jerusalem Bureau Chief), was "quite right that Israeli occupation has been cruel and counter-productive, greatly delaying the chances of peaceful coexistence."[29]

Johns Hopkins professor Fouad Ajami provided rare balance and nuance on the *Times* Opinion page. Rejecting the conventional *Times* wisdom of Israeli responsibility for Palestinian violence and disarray, he attributed "Palestinian ruin" to "the masked men of Fatah" who ruled the West Bank and the "masked men of Hamas" who dominated Gaza. No other national movement in the last half-century, Ajami noted, had enjoyed "the indulgence granted to the Palestinians," whose culture had "succumbed to a terrifying cult of violence." Only "a handful of the most romantic Israelis" failed to recognize "the malignancy of the national movement a stone's throw away."[30]

But the *Times* remained captivated by Hamas. Friedman focused on the masks worn by Hamas fighters "to gain power and enhance masculinity." Yaron Ezrahi identified masks as "the uniforms of the new armies of the 21st century," signaling a "new kind of violence" without a face or boundaries. A column by Hamas spokesman Ahmed Yousef infuriated many readers with the favorable publicity bestowed by the *Times* on his terrorist organization. Editorial page editor Andrew Rosenthal (A.M. Rosenthal's son) defended the newspaper, claiming "We look for opinions that are provocative." "The point of the Op-Ed page," wrote public editor Clark Hoyt was "advocacy." Op-ed readers, he asserted, "have seen a wide range of views on the Israeli-Palestinian conflict."[31] But columns by Jewish settlers or their defenders were conspicuously absent.

Between January 2006 and July 2007 the *Times* published twice as many op-eds critical of Israel or espousing an Arab perspective as it did the inverse.

Arab contributors included the prime minister of Lebanon, a prominent PLO official and a senior Hamas adviser in Gaza. No op-ed was published by an Israeli leader, while prominent left-wing Israeli journalists Gershom Gorenberg and Tom Segev explicated the conventional *Times* wisdom that Jewish settlements were the major cause of the conflict. The media monitoring Committee for Accuracy in Media Reporting in America (CAMERA) concluded that the *Times* served as "a vehicle for . . . one-sided advocacy" in the Israeli-Palestinian conflict.[32]

Jewish settlers continued to frame *Times* insistence on Israeli responsibility for the absence of peace. In early August Erlanger reported that hundreds of Israeli riot police, "pelted by rocks and chunks of metal," forcibly evicted two Jewish families from houses they had been "occupying illegally for months" in Hebron. Guided by Rina Castelnuovo, a veteran contract photographer for the *Times*, he described "a small part of Hebron" as "occupied" by Israeli settlers, although Jews had lived in that neighborhood for centuries preceding their evacuation following the Arab pogrom in 1929. The "relatively fierce confrontation" enabled the Israeli government "to show the world" that removing 80,000 settlers beyond the West Bank separation barrier would be difficult.[33]

In a front-page article several days later Erlanger turned his attention to Jerusalem, where a new highway under construction would allow "both Palestinians and Israelis to travel along it – separately." With one lane for each "tribe," Palestinians could drive unimpeded from Ramallah to Bethlehem in a future Palestinian state. But Israelis ("Jewish settlers" were specifically identified) could access ramps leading into Jerusalem that were closed to Palestinians who did not reside in the city. The new road, Erlanger suggested, provided "an ominous map of the future." His primary source was a Jewish lawyer who advised Ir Amim, a left-wing monitoring organization.[34]

The following week the *Times* prominently reported the publication of an instantly controversial book about the "pernicious influence" of "the Israel Lobby" on American foreign policy. Months earlier academic authors John J. Mearsheimer and Stephen Walt, previewing their allegation in the *London Review of Books,* had asserted that while Israel had become "a strategic liability" for the United States "the pro-Israel lobby is so powerful" that "no aspiring politician is going to say so in public." Amid the controversy that swirled around their book, wrote *Times* culture reporter Patricia Cohen, "both authors have stressed that they hold no animus towards Israel or Jews," but claimed that "Israeli policy is fundamentally flawed."[35]

Even after the Israeli withdrawal from Gaza, *Times* coverage remained focused on the Hamas-ruled territory. Columnist Roger Cohen, Anthony Lewis's replacement as a badgering Jewish critic of Israel, recommended more American "hammering" on Israel for its "occupation," although by then the only occupier in Gaza was Hamas. Three months later, noting the desperation of Palestinians "because they are at a dead end," Cohen asserted that Israel's despair might be "quieter" (due to its flourishing economy), but "not the Israeli soul," because four decades of occupation had been "a scourge." His primary source was Palestinian prime minister Salam Fayyad, who was "right" to insist that a return to the 1967 lines "is the only basis for a two-state accord." Cohen's anguish was palpable (because he said so): "Israel is powerful, but Palestinian humiliation is an Israeli and Jewish nightmare. I feel it; many American Jews feel it."[36]

As 2007 ended an editorial recognized that the glow of the peace process had faded. Adhering to their cherished principle of moral equivalence, editors noted that "Israelis and Palestinians have quickly fallen back into predictable destructive patterns." For the *Times,* the Palestinian refusal to act "aggressively" to "disband terrorist and militant groups" was offset by an Israeli tender for three hundred new apartments in Har Homa, a neighborhood in southern Jerusalem. Three weeks later an editorial condemned the "neglect and mistreatment of 1.5 million Palestinians trapped in the Gaza Strip." Hamas had "turned a deaf ear to their plight, refusing to negotiate peace or accept Israel's right to exist." Expressing concern for "innocent Israelis who live along the border with Gaza and must suffer through the constant bombardment," it nonetheless blamed Israel for its "collective punishment" of Gaza residents that would "feed anger and extremism."[37]

Amid the newest wave of cross-border attacks from Gaza, Israeli journalist Daniel Gavron (who several years earlier had declared his preference for "a democratic, multi-ethnic, unitary state" for Israelis and Palestinians) proclaimed in an op-ed column: "Wake up, fellow Israelis, it's over, we've won!" But Israelis had made "a shambles of our Zionist enterprise" by establishing settlements after the Six-Day War. A two-state solution required "a complete withdrawal from the West Bank." Failing that, the only alternative was "some sort of single state, bi-national state or confederation."[38]

Following the launching of two dozen Katyusha rockets from Gaza into Ashkelon, ten miles north of the border, Israel responded forcefully. In "the deadliest day of fighting in more than a year," Steven Erlanger reported, more than fifty Gazans, two-thirds of whom were identified as Hamas "gunmen, " were killed. The likelihood of a two-state solution, lamented a *Times* editorial, "diminishes with every rocket lobbed into Israel from Hamas-controlled Gaza" and, to be sure, "with every Israeli military strike or squeeze on civilian life in Gaza." But the editors realized that even Israelis who favored negotiation with Palestinians could "legitimately ask how Israel can surrender control of the West Bank under current conditions." After a forty-eight-hour Israeli "military incursion" into Gaza several days later, Erlanger filed a six-column report from Jabaliya, where Gazans mourned the death of nearly one hundred Palestinians.[39] There was no report from Ashkelon.

It took a terrorist attack in Jerusalem to refocus *Times* attention inside Israel. Early in March a solitary "gunman" (the preferred *Times* euphemism for "terrorist") killed eight Israelis in the Mercaz HaRav yeshiva. It was, Erlanger reported, "the deadliest attack on Israeli civilians in nearly two years and the first attack inside Jerusalem in four." It drew special attention because the yeshiva was "an ideological base for the settler movement" and "a symbol of the national religious strain of Judaism." Isabel Kershner (who had joined the *Times* following publication of her book about Israel's West Bank separation barrier, with "unbridled Jewish settlement" and "Palestinian tragedy" as its dominant themes) devoted several paragraphs to the Mercaz HaRav murderer. Posters at the mourning tent described him as a martyr who had carried out a "heroic act." The leader of his family clan described him as "well-mannered."[40] Kershner did not report visits to the families of Israeli victims.

Times editors ignored the terrorist attack. Instead, they bracketed Hamas militants, who "will do anything to sabotage Israeli-Palestinian peace efforts," with Israeli retaliation. Just as Arab nations must help Palestinian President Abbas to "pressure Hamas into halting rocket attacks against Israel," so the United States "must persuade Israel" that its "lasting security" requires that Palestinians in the West Bank and Gaza "see more benefits from peace than revenge." Reiterating its familiar remedy, that meant "no further expansion of settlements." Israel's "crushing economic embargo on Gaza," following waves of Hamas rocket attacks, "only feeds furies there and on the West Bank."[41]

In a curious observance of Israel's sixtieth anniversary of independence the *Times* published two sharply critical op-ed columns. Brooklyn-born journalist Jeffrey Goldberg, who had served in the IDF as a military prison guard during the first intifada (and subsequently wrote a book about his dialogue with the Palestinian prisoner he befriended), found Prime Minister Olmert "expansive, and persuasive, on the Zionist need for a Palestinian state." Without it, "in the not-distant future," Goldberg predicted (erroneously), Arabs "under Israeli control will … outnumber the country's Jews." Embracing the demographic doomsday projection popular among settlement critics, he asserted that "the best way to bring about the birth of a Palestinian state is to reverse ... the West Bank settlement project." But American Jewish leaders, he lamented, did not "push" Israel; instead, they "dance so delicately" around it. Goldberg urged "a radical rethinking of what it means to be pro-Israel."[42] Only criticism of the Jewish state, it seemed, sufficed.

In another Independence Day critique Lebanese journalist Elias Khoury complained that "after the Holocaust, it became virtually impossible to condemn any action of the Israeli state" (not, to be sure, in *The New York Times*). Khoury described Jews as "the new invaders" in Palestine who had launched a "comprehensive ethnic cleansing operation" in 1948 (when, as it happened, Jerusalem's Old City was ethnically cleansed of Jews). Israel's "continued occupation of the remaining portions of Palestine in the West Bank and Gaza" (although Gaza, by then, was occupied only by Hamas) "has transformed the nakba from a historic incident to a daily reality." Confronting "invasive settlements" and "the wall of separation," Palestinian lives had become "a hell on earth." Israeli policy (not Arab aggression in 1948, 1967, 1973, and two intifadas) had pushed Palestinians to "the brink of the abyss of fundamentalist tendencies."[43] Such were the sixtieth anniversary wishes to Israel in *The New York Times*.

One month later Nicholas Kristof, attentive to beleaguered and suffering peoples throughout the world, reported his travels through "Israeli colonies" in the West Bank. He focused on Hebron. Without any evident awareness of its place in the biblical narrative, its historical importance as the first capital of ancient Israel, and its home to a vibrant Jewish community until the 1929 Arab pogrom, he launched into a diatribe against its eight hundred Jewish residents – amid 170,000 Arabs. Not only was their presence illegal "in the eyes of much of the world"; they symbolized an Israeli "security regime" that was "suffocating, impoverishing and antagonizing" Palestinians. Jewish settlers, for Kristof, represented "the worst side" of Israel. The "very best side," predictably, were the human-rights groups that "relentlessly stand up for Palestinians" – and Israeli scholars whose work "undermines their own nation's mythologies."[44]

Responding to sharp reader criticism, Kristof insisted that Jewish historical bonds to Hebron did not "confer any right" on Jews to live there. If there was no two-state solution, he warned, there would be a "one-state solution" – and, given the flawed demographic projections that he embraced, "that will mean either the end of Israeli democracy or the end of the Jewish state." Therefore, he concluded, "Zionists should be absolutely clamoring," as Kristof was, "for a Palestinian state."[45]

In July 2008 Prime Minister Olmert, confronting persistent serious allegations of corruption, announced his intention to resign. The primary *Times* concern was whether he retained sufficient "legitimacy or the political traction to make historic concessions to Arab adversaries" before his departure. Brushing aside Olmert's "mismanagement" of the 2006 Lebanon war and his financial scandals, an editorial commended him for understanding that "a two-state solution with the Palestinians is vital for Israel's security." To give Palestinians "a real stake in peace," Israel must impose "a full freeze" on settlement expansion and remove West Bank road blocks that were "strangling" the Palestinian economy. And "a way must be found to help turn Hamas into a legitimate and acceptable negotiating partner."[46]

With new Israeli leadership impending, Jewish settlements continued to dominate *Times* coverage – and frame its criticism. In a six-column analysis of "radical settlers," Isabel Kershner reported the suspicion of Israeli authorities that a pipe bomb explosion outside the home of a Hebrew University professor known for his "impassioned critiques" of settlements was their handiwork. Although there had been "bouts of settler violence for years," this episode might indicate that "elements of Israel's settler movement are resorting to extremist tactics." Tiny groups of "hilltop youth," living in illegal outposts, were exacting a "price" for attempts to dismantle their homes by "taking the law into their own hands." Acting with the potential "to set the tinderbox of the West Bank ablaze," they demonstrated "a deeply religious, almost mystical attachment to the land," while "rejecting any allegiance to the state."[47]

Several days later Ethan Bronner reported the publication by an Israeli newspaper of an "unusually frank and soul-searching" Rosh HaShanah interview with discredited former Prime Minister Olmert. Discarding "long-standing Israeli defense doctrine," Olmert declared that "controlling territories," including all of Jerusalem, was not only outdated but "worthless." His own past endorsement of those policies, he now asserted, was grounded in his unwillingness "to look at reality in all its depth." For Olmert, that meant Israeli withdrawal "from almost all ... if not all the territories."[48]

But events in Gaza soon indicated that even a complete Israeli withdrawal was likelier to bring war than peace. In mid-December persistent Hamas rocket attacks finally provoked "a crushing response." Israeli retaliatory air strikes killed more than 225 Gazans, the highest total in decades. Taghreed El-Khodary, the *Times* Gaza-born reporter, described a "shocking quality" to the Israeli attack, which left Gaza City "a scene of chaotic horror." Many paragraphs further along in his front-page report, he noted that "Hamas is officially committed to Israel's destruction."[49]

Ethan Bronner offered a psychological analysis of the Israeli response. Worried "that its enemies are less afraid of it than they once were, or should be," Israel was attempting "to expunge the ghost of its flawed 2006 war against Hezbollah." Detecting "palpable satisfaction" among Israeli government and military officials with their initial success, he noted "the same satisfaction" at a similar stage of the Lebanon invasion – "before things turned disastrous." *Times* editors conceded that "Israel must defend itself," while Hamas "must bear responsibility" for ending the six-month cease-fire with rocket attacks. But Israel must "make every effort to limit civilian casualties" while the Bush administration "should be pressing Israel to exercise restraint."[50]

Benny Morris, author of an illuminating history of Israel's independence war, explained that many Israelis felt that "the walls – and history – are closing in on their 60-year-old state, much as they felt in early June 1967." The Arab and Islamic worlds would not accept its legitimacy and continued to "oppose its existence," leaving Israelis with "deep foreboding" for the future. Novelist David Grossman, insisting that "restraint, and our duty to protect the lives of Gaza's innocent inhabitants, must remain our commitment," advocated an immediate forty-eight-hour cease-fire. Whether or not Hamas continued to fire rockets, "We will grit our teeth. ... We will not be drawn into using force." Seared by the Lebanon war that had claimed his son's life, he warned that otherwise Israel would once again "get stuck" and be "carried away by a tide of destruction."[51]

As Hamas rockets reached Ashdod, where Isabel Kershner covered the funeral of an Israeli mother of four, and Beersheba, Israel's largest southern city, she reported that "support for a sustained Israeli military campaign remained strong." But Ethan Bronner anticipated "mission creep" as Israeli tanks and troops "poured into Gaza." Destroying Hamas's political infrastructure – an Israeli air attack had killed a senior Hamas leader (along with his four wives and nine children) – would render the prospect of governing Gaza "exceedingly difficult." Bronner conceded that the Israeli strategy might succeed, but "questions still remain: At what human cost?"[52] No such questions were asked of Hamas, whose rockets continued to bombard southern Israel.

Times coverage focused on the plight of civilians in Gaza, not Israel. From a neighborhood in Zeitoun "known to have many supporters of Hamas," where "militants" enjoyed free movement, it ran a six-column front-page story on the Samouni family of nearly one hundred members that suffered thirty deaths while fleeing from house to house to elude Israeli attacks. Their tragic story, publicized by the Red Cross, "horrified many." The following day Erlanger provided a measure of context. Hamas, he wrote, had turned Gaza into "a deadly maze of tunnels, booby traps and sophisticated roadside bombs." Weapons were hidden in "mosques, schoolyards and civilian houses," while "the leadership's war room" was reported by Israeli officials to be located in "a bunker beneath Gaza's largest hospital." Even Israel's critics, Erlanger concluded, agreed that Hamas rocket firings at civilian targets and its use of civilian shields were "violations of the rules of war."[53]

But a fusillade of criticism – of Israel, not Hamas – dominated *Times* opinion pages. Kristof described a "Boomerang Syndrome" in which "extremists on each side sustain each other." When Palestinians were "suffering and humiliated, they find it emotionally satisfying to see Hamas fighting back." Conceding that "when it is shelled by its neighbor, Israel has to do something," it did not have "the right to do *anything*." Columbia professor Rashid Khalidi accused Israel of remaining the "occupying power" in Gaza – even though it had removed all its citizens and soldiers three years earlier. Its "war on the people of Gaza" was designed to "make Palestinians understand ... that they are a defeated people." He mentioned Hamas rockets once, in passing.[54]

Israel was relentlessly criticized, Ethan Bronner wrote, for "bombing an already isolated and impoverished population into the Stone Age." Among Israelis, however, "voices of dissent ... have been rare." Nonetheless, he located them. Israeli Arabs felt "anger and despair." A peace activist complained that Hamas had "killed the peace camp." A "left-leaning" Hebrew University philosophy professor mentioned "several events ... in which he suspected that the wrong decision had been made" by Israelis. But even the Israeli left, Bronner concluded, considered the conflict "almost entirely the responsibility of Hamas, and thus a moral and just struggle."[55]

In another front page article several days later Erlanger focused on "serious accusations and anguished questioning over the legality of [Israel's] military conduct." The "large asymmetry in deaths, especially of civilians, has created an uproar in the Arab world and the West reminiscent of 2006" during the Lebanon war. Western and UN officials, along with Israeli and foreign human rights groups, expressed "shock and disgust," while some called for investigation of "possible war crimes." But "legal experts agree" that Hamas rocket attacks and weapons storage in mosques, schools and ("allegedly") hospitals posed "undue risk" for its own population. Israel, Erlanger concluded, grappled with the "fundamental question": "how does an army fight a terrorist group?"[56]

As a cease-fire took hold after three weeks of fighting, two Gaza-based reporters provided front-page six-column *Times* coverage of the carnage "wrought by the Israeli military" on innocent civilians. Once again they were drawn to Zeitoun, where families "clawed at rubble and concrete" to find the bodies of relatives who died weeks before. They covered a mass funeral, interrupted by "a moment of panic when Hamas militants launched a rocket" nearby.[57] The irony was ignored.

Ethan Bronner wondered whether the "overpowering war by Israel" had weakened Hamas "or simply caused acute human suffering?" Finding "deep rage" among Gazans, he saw little evidence that they "felt such pain from this war that they would seek to rein in Hamas." While Israel had "wildly pressed the attack," Hamas – "the Islamist militia that supposedly embraces death" – had "shied from the fight" by hiding underground. Bronner concluded with a statement from an Israeli security expert at Tel Aviv University: "Both sides understand the value of calculated madness."[58] Once again moral equivalence framed the *Times* narrative.

Bronner candidly confronted the problem of impartial coverage when "no place, date or event in this conflicted land is spoken of in a common language" that "both sides can accept as fair." He feared that he was "only fanning the flames, adding to the misunderstandings and mutual antagonism with every word I write." He described a "narrative disconnect" in which one side stressed the return of Jews to "their rightful home" following "thousands of years of oppression," while the other focuses on "European colonialists" who "stole and pillaged" Palestine and established a country "born in sin." His dilemma was palpable: "Each time I fail to tell the story each side tells itself, I have failed in its eyes to do my job." Bronner saw no alternative to embracing competing narratives, regardless of their veracity, as the definition of objective journalism. So, too, Thomas Friedman conceded that Hamas had provoked "a reckless war that has devastated the people of Gaza," but bracketed it with "fanatical Jewish settlers" who "devour" the West Bank.[59]

The Gaza truce early in 2009 marked an end to the brief war of Hamas aggression that heaped international calumny on Israel. As Israel prepared to inaugurate "a hawkish right-wing government" with Benjamin Netanyahu as prime minister, Bronner cited critics who pointed to "four decades of occupation," settlements, the "economic strangling" of Gaza with the use of "enormous force," and "growing indifference toward the creation of a Palestinian state." With a new Democratic president in Washington who had proclaimed his "desire to press for a two-state solution," a widening gap loomed between Israelis and "many liberal American Jews" – including, as events soon demonstrated, *New York Times* publishers, editors and columnists.[60]

CHAPTER 13

Double Standards:
2009–2014

Between 2009 and 2016 *Times* coverage of Israel was framed within the increasingly strained relationship between a liberal American president and a conservative Israeli prime minister. The diverging views of Barack Obama and Benjamin Netanyahu on the terms of an Israeli-Palestinian accord and the menacing danger of a nuclear Iran cast Israel as the stubborn obstacle to peace in the Middle East. For *Times* editors the prime minister's responses to a proposed settlement freeze were "unconvincing and insufficient"; and his pledge of negotiations without preconditions "rings hollow." Netanyahu, "a smooth talker, will have to do better than vague promises."[1]

Diplomatic correspondent Mark Landler noted a "more unsettled" relationship between the United States and Israel once Barack Obama took office. Israel seemed "rattled" by signs that its "unstinting support" from the Bush administration had faded. Netanyahu's agenda, wrote *Atlantic* journalist Jeffrey Goldberg, "clashes insistently" with Obama's. The Israeli leader's "fixation on Iran," he speculated, might be "a way of avoiding" the peace process with Palestinians amid "escalating pressure from the Obama administration to curb Jewish settlements."[2]

Their first meeting in late March, according to the editors, was "a draw," with Obama insisting that Israel "must stop settlement activity and embrace the two-state solution," while Netanyahu "grudgingly committed to negotiations with the Palestinians" but failed to "utter the words 'two-state solution.'" Obama, they noted, had concluded that the United States "must repair its relations with the Muslim world. Working credibly and even-handedly on a Middle East peace deal is central to that." But Netanyahu "is not likely to make that easy."[3]

Ignoring undiminished Palestinian resistance to any peace agreement with Israel, *Times* reporters identified Jewish settlements as the looming obstacle to

Obama's determination to improve relations with the Muslim world. Impatient with "the slow movement toward Palestinian statehood," wrote Helene Cooper, the president had advised Netanyahu of "the need to stop settlements" and "alleviate some of the pressures that the Palestinian people are under." On the eve of his departure for Cairo to outline his vision of a new Middle East, Obama asserted that Israel "needed to hear the truth, as he saw it." Indicating that he would be "more willing to criticize" the Jewish state than his predecessors, he reiterated his call for a settlement "freeze" entwined with negotiations that would "lead to peace."[4]

As the beneficiary of a pre-departure telephone interview with the president, Thomas Friedman reported Obama's conviction that many Israelis "recognize that their current path is unsustainable," with "tough choices on settlements" required for a two-state solution. And "a lot of Palestinians" realized that "the constant incitement and negative rhetoric" directed at Israel brought no benefits. Obama believed that by "speaking directly to the Arab street" he could make young men "less likely to be tempted by a terrorist recruiter." Friedman could not resist adding: "I think that's right." As an Egyptian friend told him: "when young Arabs and Muslims see an American president who looks like them, has a name like theirs, has Muslims in in his family and comes into their world and speaks the truth, it will be empowering and disturbing. ..."[5]

On the eve of Obama's Cairo speech Ethan Bronner reported "a growing rift" between his administration and the Netanyahu government. It would define American-Israeli relations – and *Times* coverage – for the duration of the Obama presidency. The speech signaled his determination to reach out to the Muslim world, thereby heralding a transformation in American relations with Israel. "I am a Christian," he declared, but he pointedly noted "my father came from a Kenyan family that includes generations of Moslems." America, he insisted, "is not – and never will be – at war with Islam" – although it would "relentlessly confront violent extremists."[6]

The president, reported the *Times*, "reserved some of his bluntest words for Israel," while expressing sympathy for Palestinians, whose plight was "intolerable" under the "daily humiliations, large and small, that come with occupation." Recognizing that "the aspiration for a Jewish homeland is rooted in a tragic history," Obama declared it "also undeniable" that Palestinians had endured "the pain of dislocation for more than 60 years ... in pursuit of a homeland." The only resolution of the conflict, he asserted, was "two states, where Israelis and Palestinians each live in peace and security." Israelis "must acknowledge that just as Israel's right to exist cannot be denied, neither can Palestine's."

Furthermore, the United States "does not accept the legitimacy of continued Israeli settlements."[7] In a conspicuous slight, Obama avoided a stopover in Israel after leaving Egypt.

Times editors proudly "recognized the United States" in Obama's speech after "eight years of arrogance and bullying" (by the Bush administration). Ethan Bronner understood that Obama signaled "one of the biggest shifts in American policy toward the Israeli-Palestinian conflict in three decades." By selecting Jewish settlements as "the opening issue that could begin to untie the Gordian knot of the conflict," the president "wants to send a message to the Arab world that the previous eight years of siding with Israelis are over." Why, Israeli officials wondered, was Obama "focusing so much on the building of homes by Israeli Jews in the West Bank" when Iran is "hurling toward nuclear weapons capacity, Hezbollah was rising to power in Lebanon and Hamas is smuggling long-range rockets into Gaza."[8] There was no better way for the *Times* to assert its patriotic loyalty than by embracing an American president who blamed Israel for Palestinian intransigence.

Ten days later Netanyahu responded at Bar-Ilan University (identified by Isabel Kershner as "an academic bastion of Israel's national religious camp"). In a speech "rich with Zionist rhetoric," he nonetheless "endorsed for the first time the principle of a Palestinian state next to Israel ... on condition that it was demilitarized and the Palestinians recognized Israel as the state of the Jewish people." Reversal of his "longstanding opposition to Palestinian statehood" represented "a concession to American pressure." But Netanyahu "firmly rejected" American demands for a complete settlement freeze. Kershner noted that he frequently referred to the West Bank as Judea and Samaria, "the land of our forefathers," as though Jewish history was irrelevant to Israeli claims.[9]

New York University professor Tony Judt, a passionate teenage Zionist who had turned against Israel after the Six-Day War and subsequently accused it of becoming a "belligerently intolerant, faith-driven ethno-state," berated Netanyahu in an op-ed column. It was "not by chance," he wrote, that Netanyahu spoke at Bar-Ilan, "the heartland of rabbinical intransigence where Yigal Amir learned to hate" Yitzhak Rabin before murdering him. The settlements that Netanyahu was determined to retain for Israel were "nothing but a colonial takeover that the United States has no business subsidizing."[10]

Three months later an editorial expressed concern that Israelis and Palestinians might "squander the best chance for Middle East peace in nearly a decade." Although Netanyahu "hinted" that he would consider a temporary settlement freeze, Israel had approved new construction permits and insisted on completing work in progress on 2,500 housing units. With Palestinian Authority President Mahmoud Abbas refusing to meet with him without a complete settlement freeze, the editors urged Obama to "prod" Netanyahu to "bolder action."[11]

Times allegations of Israeli culpability in Gaza resumed when the UN Human Rights Council, chaired by respected South African judge Richard Goldstone, condemned it for "grave human rights violations" during the recent war. While criticizing Hamas rocket assaults, its "harshest language" accused Israel of "a deliberately disproportionate attack designed to punish, humiliate and terrorize a civilian population." The report, Isabel Kershner wrote, elicited "a furious reaction" among Israelis, with President Shimon Peres labeling it "a mockery of history" that "legitimizes terrorist activity."[12]

The *Times* quickly provided Goldstone with an opportunity to defend his pursuit of "Justice in Gaza." He proclaimed his deep belief in the rule of law and the laws of war, including "the principle that in armed conflict civilians should to the greatest extent possible be protected from harm." In Gaza "all sides flouted that fundamental principle." Israel "could have done much more to spare civilians without sacrificing its stated and legitimate military aims." Neither Goldstone nor *Times* editors confronted the fundamental question identified by former *Haaretz* editor-in-chief David Landau in a *Times* op-ed: "Does the enemy's deployment in the heart of the civilian area shift the line between right and wrong, in morality and in law?"[13]

As the furor over the Goldstone report subsided, Israel once again bore the brunt of *Times* blame for the stymied peace process, which risked making Obama appear "ineffective." His "pivot" to the Middle East, wrote Helene Cooper and Mark Landler, encountered "unmovable resistance" from Israel over a settlement freeze. But the "dark truth," Ethan Bronner concluded, was that "force has produced clearer results in the dispute than talk." Israel had learned to preserve its safety through "deterrence," not diplomacy. Yet Netanyahu, yielding to American pressure, had announced a ten-month settlement freeze, "something no Israeli leader had done before." Although Palestinians "view his steps as either too little or too late or a ruse aimed at buying time," Jewish settlers were "outraged" and Netanyahu confronted a "rebellion" within his own Likud party.[14]

Amid the diplomatic maneuvering the *Times* featured a six-column analysis of a provocative book by Israeli academic Shlomo Sand entitled *The Invention of the Jewish People*. Sand "candidly" stated his intention "to undercut the Jews' claim to the land of Israel" by demonstrating that they did not constitute "a people, with a shared racial or biological past."[15] The prominent review of his quickly discredited book affirmed the enduring discomfort with Jewish nationalism that Adolph Ochs had embedded in his newspaper a century earlier.

With the peace process momentarily invigorated, *Times* reporters refocused their coverage. Isabel Kershner described the struggle of liberal Jewish women against rabbinical Orthodoxy. Demanding the right to wear prayer shawls and pray at the Western Wall, members of an organization known as Women of the Wall had emerged as "the vanguard of a feminist struggle ... to adapt time-honored religious practices for the modern age."[16] As a liberal Jewish woman, Kershner's approval of their struggle was evident.

Ethan Bronner discovered cross-cultural friendship in a Jerusalem hospital. An eight-year-old Israeli (Jewish) boy, "severely wounded by a Hamas rocket," and an eight-year-old Palestinian (Muslim) girl from Gaza, "paralyzed by an Israeli missile," had become friends during their prolonged recovery. "Someone forgot to tell them that they are enemies," Bronner wrote, and "neither understands the prolonged fight over land and identity that divides people here." Even their parents, he observed, "have developed a kinship that defies national struggle."[17] From past wounds, his story wistfully implied, might come future healing between their peoples.

One week later, reiterating the Palestinian victimization narrative that pervaded the *Times*, Bronner reported on the "forsaken" residents of Gaza, where thousands remained homeless and "a pall of listlessness hovers." Guided by B'Tselem, the left-wing organization focused on alleged Israeli human rights violations, he recounted its efforts to convey stories of Palestinian suffering to an Israeli audience. One of its "most interesting videos" revealed the interior of "smuggler tunnels." As the film-maker explained, he "wanted to show the world that the tunnels many think of as dedicated to Hamas arms smuggling are actually the source of basic goods like cooking oil and detergent."[18] There was no mention of Hamas's use of tunnels for cross-border raids into Israel, one of which had resulted in the abduction of IDF soldier Gilad Shalit, still a captive in Gaza four years later.

The following month the Electronic Intifada web site reported that Bronner's son had enlisted in the Israel Defense Forces. Liberal media wondered whether his military service for Israel created "an unacceptable conflict of interest" for Bronner and the *Times*. Executive editor Bill Keller responded: "He's a 20-year-old who makes his own decisions." But Public Editor Clark Hoyt was not persuaded. He recognized Bronner as a "superb" reporter. But the *Times* had "sent a reporter overseas to provide disinterested coverage of one of the world's most intense and potentially explosive conflicts, and now his son has taken up arms for one side." Under these circumstances "even the most sympathetic reader could reasonably wonder how that would affect the father, especially if shooting broke out." Hoyt suggested that he be "assigned elsewhere for the duration of his son's military service."[19] Bronner remained Jerusalem Bureau Chief until 2012.

Palestinian protests against Israeli occupation and mistreatment remained a recurrent theme of *Times* coverage. The eviction of a Palestinian family (from a home they did not own) in "a mostly Palestinian neighborhood" in Jerusalem rekindled "the abiding grievances of Palestinian refugees from the 1948 war." After the Supreme Court upheld a ruling that the property belonged to Jews, "a group of fervent Israeli nationalists" had moved in. Although Jewish land deeds for the property stretched back into the nineteenth century their presence, Isabel Kershner wrote, "complicates the map."

Times editors criticized the Netanyahu government for announcing plans, during a visit by Vice President Biden, to build new housing units in East Jerusalem. The Obama administration was "understandably furious" at Israel for the "slap in the face to Washington," whose demand for the cessation of new settlement building "was – and is – just." Thomas Friedman concurred: Israel's West Bank settlement building and housing development in East Jerusalem was "sheer madness." He worried that Obama will "look like America's most dependent ally can push him around." Biden should have left a farewell note saying "You have lost all contact with reality. Call us when you're serious."[20]

Columnist Maureen Dowd, not known for her Middle East expertise, referred to "the supremely aggravating" Netanyahu and "defiant" Israelis, who "mindlessly let settlement gluttony scuttle any chance for peace." Israeli ambassador Michael Oren responded, reiterating that Netanyahu's assertion of Jerusalem as Israel's "undivided capital," where Jews and Arabs alike "have the right to build anywhere in the city," had been the policy of every Israeli government since 1967.[21]

For nearly a month the Jerusalem housing dispute, and the rift it exposed between the Netanyahu and Obama governments, dominated *Times* coverage. Amid "the gravest diplomatic row" in years, Netanyahu declared in a speech to the American Israel Public Affairs Committee (AIPAC): "The Jewish people were building Jerusalem 3,000 years ago, and the Jewish people are building Jerusalem today." Jerusalem, he asserted, is "not a settlement; it's our capital." *Times* editors were not persuaded. With a peace deal as Obama's priority, the president was "understandably furious at Israel's response." Made to "look weak" by Netanyahu's determination to build homes in East Jerusalem, they found Obama's willingness to challenge Israel "refreshing."[22]

Three months later Israeli naval commandos halted six ships in a flotilla organized by the Free Gaza Movement and a Turkish Human Rights Foundation to break the Israeli blockade of Gaza. Boarding the *Mavi Marmara* from helicopters and speedboats they confronted resistance from activists armed with clubs, iron bars and knives, nine of whom were killed in the ensuing struggle. *Times* editors recognized the intention to provoke a violent Israeli response that would "breathe new life into the Palestinian solidarity movement." But "there can be no excuse for the way that Israel completely mishandled the incident," resulting in "a grievous, self-inflicted wound" that damaged its relations with Turkey, gave "a huge propaganda boost" to Hamas in Gaza, and "complicated" peace talks with the Palestinian Authority. Netanyahu had once again demonstrated that "he prefers bullying and confrontation over diplomacy."[23]

A wave of criticism of Israel flooded the *Times*. Amos Oz complained that the power to "wield force ... has, again and again, intoxicated us." Israel's siege of Gaza and "violent interception" of the flotilla revealed "the mistaken assumption ... that the Palestinian problem can be crushed instead of solved." The only solution was for Israel "to quickly reach an agreement with the Palestinians" for an independent state in the West Bank and Gaza with its capital in East Jerusalem. Obama, wrote Nicholas Kristof, "needs to nudge Israel away from its tendency to shoot itself in the foot, and us along with it."[24]

A four-column op-ed by American Jewish novelist Michael Chabon declared the necessity for Jews "to confront, at long last, the eternal truth of our stupidity as a people," exemplified by the "elite military arm" of Israel. With Jews "every bit as capable of barbarism and stupidity" as other nations, Israel displayed a "rich, inglorious human heritage of block headedness." Tony Judt accused Israel of "pathological habits," especially "its habitual resort to force." Its "botched attack on civilians in international waters" was only the most recent of its "cumulative blunders," leaving Israel as "America's greatest strategic liability in the Middle East." Once again Israel's sole defender in the *Times* editorial pages was Ambassador Oren, who asserted that "Israel has a right and a duty to defend itself from Hamas and its backers."[25]

"What To Do About Israel?" wondered White House correspondent Helene Cooper. As "the list of recent moves by the Netanyahu government that potentially threaten American interests has grown steadily," Israel seemed to be ignoring "the national security concerns of its biggest benefactor." The *Mavi Marmara* episode had "chilled" American relations with Turkey, while

Netanyahu's refusal to halt housing construction in "Arab East Jerusalem" had strained relations with Arab allies.[26]

With the *Mavi Marmara* confrontation under UN investigation, Israeli-Palestinian peace talks were launched in Washington. *Times* editors were "skeptical" that Netanyahu "really wants a deal." Thomas Friedman warned yet again that without a two-state solution "Israel will be stuck with an apartheid-like, democracy-sapping, permanent occupation of the West Bank." When Mahmoud Abbas threatened to terminate negotiations unless the settlement moratorium was extended, Netanyahu (not Abbas) was admonished: "Taking political risks is what leadership is all about." Israel, according to the *Times*, remained the primary obstacle to peace. If Netanyahu was "willing to make the hard choices necessary for peace," the editors complained, "it's not evident these days." He evidently decided that "mugging for his hard-line coalition is more important than working with President Obama to make a peace deal." The burden was on Netanyahu, not Abbas, "to get things moving again."[27]

Amid the diplomatic deadlock the *Times* re-focused on Jerusalem housing. Guided by an "anti-settlement advocate" and a Peace Now "settlement opponent," Ethan Bronner reported "rapidly growing" Israeli housing construction in East Jerusalem. Isabel Kershner described the eviction of a Palestinian family from their home, followed by the arrival of "a group of Jewish settlers" whose "takeover" represented "a new point of Jewish settlement" in the contested city. But six months earlier, she noted, the dispossessed family "lost a legal battle for ownership of the house" when Israeli courts upheld the legality of its sale by a relative. Two weeks later she reported another new Jewish housing project in East Jerusalem on property that had been confiscated from its "absentee" Arab owners after the Six-Day War.[28] Only for Jews in Jerusalem were housing transactions subjected to such rigorous *Times* scrutiny.

Jewish victims of Palestinian terrorist attacks, especially if they were settlers, received considerably less attention. In what Kershner recognized as "the deadliest attack inside a settlement in years," she briefly noted the horrific fatal stabbing of five members of the Fogel family (parents and three children including a three-month old baby) in their Itamar home by "intruders" who were "widely suspected of being Palestinians." Her primary focus was Itamar's location "on a rocky incline" overlooking a nearby Palestinian village and Palestinian claims of justification for killing Israeli civilians, "especially settlers, as a legitimate response to the Israeli occupation."[29]

The Fogel family funeral, which drew 20,000 mourners and dominated Israeli news coverage, was buried within Kershner's emphasis on the announcement of plans to build new housing units in settlement blocs that Israel intended to retain under any accord with Palestinians. She filed a three-column report on Palestinian Authority President Abbas's "abhorrence" of the murders as "abominable, inhuman and immoral," devoting considerably more attention to his response than to the brutally decimated Fogel family.[30]

Two weeks later the *Times* reported that Judge Goldstone had publicly retracted "the central and most explosive assertion" of his damning indictment of Israel for intentionally killing Palestinian civilians during the 2009 Gaza war (which the *Times* had eagerly embraced). Writing in the *Washington Post*, he claimed: "Had I known then what I know now, the Goldstone Report would have been a different document." He withdrew his allegation that Israel had "waged a deliberately disproportionate attack designed to punish, humiliate and terrorize a civilian population." Neither Goldstone nor Ethan Bronner, who wrote the six-column article about his recantation, mentioned that *New York Times* editors had declined to publish it.[31]

But the *Times* welcomed a plea for Palestinian statehood from President Mahmoud Abbas. Recounting his painful experience as a thirteen-year-old Palestinian boy "forced to leave his home" in Safed and "flee with his family to Syria," he described the yearning "to return to their home and homeland." Published one week after Israelis celebrated their sixty-third year of independence, he called for recognition of the State of Palestine within pre-1967 borders while claiming (falsely) that Arabs had accepted the UN Partition Plan twenty years earlier.[32]

The *Times* remained unsparing in its criticism of Netanyahu. In a coordinated Independence Day protest, thousands of Arabs in Syria, Lebanon, Gaza and the West Bank had attempted to breach Israel's borders, resulting in a dozen deaths and many injuries. Israel, an editorial conceded, "must defend its territory" but "credible peace negotiations" might have prevented the casualties. Although "there is blame all around," the editorial focused on Netanyahu's reliance on the regional turmoil of Arab Spring "as one more excuse to hunker down." After the Israeli prime minister urged Congress to oppose the emerging nuclear agreement with Iran, Thomas Friedman concluded that its standing ovation "was bought and paid for by the Israel lobby." Buying and bending Congress to its will, the "powerful pro-Israel lobby" became a recurrent theme for Friedman. To Ambassador Oren, however, it was "the worst anti-Semitic stereotype."[33]

The Op-Ed page remained especially welcoming to Netanyahu's Israeli critics. Ephraim Sneh, retired IDF general and former Deputy Minister of

Defense, conceded that Israel's pre-1967 boundaries were "indefensible." But the necessity for peace with the Palestinians required a return to those boundaries with "a few adjustments." Israeli "nurturing" of West Bank settlements and "maintaining an occupation to protect them" was "a path [that] will lead to disaster." *Haaretz* editor Aluf Benn complained that Netanyahu "should have worked out an agreement on how to reignite the peace process, rather than criticize the American president."[34]

Times columnists joined the chorus of disapproval. Nicholas Kristof complained that Congressional "tomfoolery" in support of Israel only encouraged Netanyahu government "intransigence." Welcoming pressure on Israel from left-wing J-Street, he warned of damage to the relationship between American Jews and Israel as "the face of Israel" shifted from Rabin and Peres to "national religious settlers and the ultra-Orthodox rabbis." With nothing to say about Palestinian obduracy and terrorism he admitted to "double standards" for "democratic allies," demanding "more of Israel partly because my tax dollars support arms and aid" to the Jewish state. Roger Cohen wrestled with allegations that he was "not Jewish enough, or even … a self-hating Jew" because he criticized Israel, "particularly its self-defeating expansion of settlements." But with their history of victimization, Jews "cannot become the systematic oppressors of another people."[35]

Palestinians, *Times* editors conceded, "share the blame" for the blocked peace process. But "the greater onus" fell on Netanyahu, "who has used any excuse to thwart peace efforts." Thomas Friedman confessed that given "the most diplomatically inept and strategically incompetent government" in its history, he had "never been more worried about Israel's future." The primary source for his anguish was *Haaretz* journalist Aluf Benn, who complained that Israel was "increasingly shutting itself off behind fortified walls, under a leadership that refuses any change, movement, or reform." Several days later former Prime Minister Olmert reiterated his own "far-reaching offer" to President Abbas in 2008, including "mutually agreed upon land swaps," a "shared" Jerusalem with Palestinian neighborhoods becoming the capital of Palestine, and Israeli absorption of "a small number of refugees on humanitarian grounds." *Times* editors praised his proposal, bracketing Abbas and Netanyahu for their "inability to make decisions" and refusal "to make any serious compromises for peace."[36]

As peace prospects languished, Jewish settlers remained the focus of *Times* ire. "They are holding land widely considered Palestinian by right," Bronner wrote, thereby "obstructing a two-state solution" (which Palestinians had rejected decades before the first settlement was built). Netanyahu's "hard line on settlements," according to Kristof, "seems like a national suicide policy." Some Israeli friends, Kristof acknowledged, "think I'm unfair and harsh, applying double standards by focusing on Israeli shortcomings." He responded: "Fair enough: I plead guilty," claiming that it was "an act of friendship" to assert that "Israel's leaders sometimes seem to be that country's worst enemies."[37] Double standards were welcome in the *Times,* as long as Israel was their target.

The *Times* rarely missed an opportunity to criticize Netanyahu. In exchange for the release of Sgt. Gilad Shalit in October 2011, Israel freed more than one thousand Palestinian prisoners, nearly three hundred of whom were serving life sentences for terrorist attacks in which more than five hundred Israeli civilians had been murdered. Claiming to "share the joy" of Israelis over Shalit's return after five years of imprisonment, the editors chastised Netanyahu. If he "can negotiate with Hamas," they asked, "why won't he negotiate seriously with the Palestinian Authority?"[38]

Times criticism of Israel was unrelenting. Israeli journalist Gershom Gorenberg, a stanch opponent of Jewish settlements, warned that "the ethnic conflict in the West Bank ... is metastasizing into Israel, threatening its democracy and unraveling its society." With the turmoil of the Arab Spring spreading across the Middle East, Thomas Friedman asserted, Netanyahu should be "strengthening responsible and democratic Palestinian leaders" lest Israel's "democratic character" be undermined. But the prime minister's response was "to do nothing."[39] As always, Israel was to blame.

A detailed CAMERA study of *Times* coverage between August and December 2011 – spanning the peace process, the *Mavi Marmara* episode, the Gaza conflict and Palestinian-Israeli violence – confirmed "a disproportionate, continuous, embedded indictment of Israel that dominates both news and commentary sections." The "overarching message" was "Israeli fault and responsibility for the conflict." Even *Times* public editor Arthur Brisbane acknowledged the "political and cultural progressivism" that "virtually bleeds through the fabric of *The Times.*"[40]

Lengthy articles by Isabel Kershner (at the end of 2011) and Ethan Bronner (at the beginning of 2012) shifted the focus of blame, at least temporarily, from the Netanyahu government to Orthodox "religious violence and fanaticism." Nationwide outrage was sparked by an incident in Beit Shemesh, where the eight-year-old daughter of modern Orthodox American immigrants was targeted for abuse by "ultra-Orthodox zealots" for violating their rigorous dress code. The toxic mix of religion and gender, and the willingness of Israeli governments to trade financial subsidies for ultra-Orthodox votes, provided grist for *Times* criticism.[41]

Iran's looming nuclear threat to Israel, and the possibility of another pre-emptive Israeli air strike, refocused coverage. Framed within moral equivalence, an editorial found "the posturing and saber rattling from both Iran and Israel" to be "frightening." Conceding that "Israel must defend itself," it expressed hope that political leaders would "weigh all of the consequences before they act." The *Times* offered reassurance that despite "strains" in the relationship between Obama and Netanyahu, the president's "commitment to Israel's security" was beyond dispute. Thomas Friedman even claimed that the only question was whether Obama was "the most pro-Israel president in history or just one of the most." Israel had "the right to act on its own," he wrote, but Obama "has built a solid strategic and political case for letting America take the lead."[42] In any disagreement between the United States and Israel the *Times* unfailingly supported America first.

Despite the Iranian threat, Jewish settlements continued to drive *Times* criticism of Israel. An op-ed by Palestinian Parliament member Mustafa Barghouti asserted that "peaceful protest can free Palestine" and "delegitimize the Israeli occupation of the West Bank, which we believe is the last surviving apartheid system in the world." Peter Beinert, a rising star among left-wing journalists, condemned Israel's "pro-settler policies" for transforming the Jewish state into "two Israels: a flawed but genuine democracy within the green line and an ethnically-based non-democracy beyond it." Although boycotting other Jews was "a painful, unnatural act," he nonetheless called for a boycott of settlement products.[43]

In mid-2012 Ethan Bronner was succeeded as Jerusalem Bureau Chief by Jodi Rudoren, previously head of the *Times* Education Bureau, who had grown up in an Orthodox family in a Boston suburb. She quickly displayed her inclination, already deeply embedded in the *Times*, to focus on Palestinian suffering and Israeli transgressions. The "newest heroes of the Palestinian cause," she wrote in one of her early reports, "are gaunt adults, wrists in chains, starving themselves in Israeli prisons." Their hunger strike was "a potential catalyst" for "an Arab-spring-style uprising" in the West Bank.[44]

One week later Rudoren reported from Jenin, where the regional governor, a leader of "the dovish wing of the Palestinian national movement," had died of a heart attack after pursuing street gang members who fired shots at his home. From Ramallah she registered the complaint of Palestinian Authority President Abbas to a J Street delegation that his security forces were "struggling" because

Israel refused to permit a shipment of weapons that would bolster resistance to terrorism. The following week she recounted her visit with the director of the Ministry of Education in Gaza who explained that Hamas-run high schools were preparing to introduce a Hebrew language course so that students would learn "the language of the enemy."[45]

Finally focusing on Israel, Rudoren became critical. Attending the Jerusalem Film Festival, she observed that most films "seemed unable to sensitively portray both sides of the perpetual conflicts" between Arabs and Jews. She criticized a film about secular-religious antagonism for making "little effort to humanize its Arab elements." After visiting the predominantly Arab city of Nazareth, Rudoren wondered about the appropriate role for "a growing Arab minority" in a state "determined to be democratic and Jewish." She interviewed "the left's leading lawyer in Israel," who challenged Israeli "occupation of the Palestinian territories" and represented "hundreds of soldiers refusing to serve" there.[46]

Times editors, long convinced that settlements undermined Israeli democracy, were stunned by a report issued by former Supreme Court Justice Edmund Levy in July 2012 concluding, as settlement defenders had long argued, that they were legal under international law. Constituting a "disastrous blow" to peace prospects, the Levy Report demonstrated the "dispiriting anomaly" that a state founded as a Jewish homeland "is determined to continue ruling 2.5 million Palestinians under an unequal system of laws and rights."[47] The rule of law, so often touted by the *Times* as the standard for criticism of Israel, became irrelevant once it protected settlements.

A subsequent editorial, entitled "Israel's Embattled Democracy," cited (unidentified) "experts" who claimed that the influx of Soviet Jews and high birthrate among ultra-Orthodox Jews strengthened "a cultural mistrust" of democratic values. Furthermore, an expanding Palestinian population was "hastening the day when Jews could be a minority" in their own homeland. Predictably, Prime Minister Netanyahu was to blame for "aggressive settlement building and resistance to serious peace talks with the Palestinians." Consequently, the "basic truths" of Israel's "origins as a democratic state committed to liberal values and human rights" were "in danger of being lost."[48] Once again, the solitary democratic, and Jewish, state in the Middle East was unworthy of editorial approval.

Occasional defense of Jewish settlements on the Op-Ed page was invariably offset by sharp criticism. Settlement leader Dani Dayan asserted that Israel had "legitimately seized the disputed territories of Judea and Samaria in self-defense" in 1967 and its "moral claim to these territories" was "unassailable." He reminded readers: "King David never walked in Tel Aviv, but he did reign in Hebron." But former Knesset Speaker Avraham Burg lamented the demise of "a secular, social democratic country" that had become "a religious, capitalist state" and "just another Middle Eastern theocracy."[49]

In November 2012 Hamas launched a new rocket assault, provoking a pin-point Israeli response that killed its military chief Ahmed al-Jabari. According to *Times* reporters in Gaza, Israel "escalated the risks of a new war in the Middle East" with the (twice-mentioned) "ferocity" of its response. *Times* editors acknowledged that "no country should have to endure the rocket attacks that Israel has endured from militants in Gaza." Recognizing Israel's "right to defend itself," they suggested that "it would be easier to win support for retaliatory action" if it was engaged in "serious negotiations" with the Palestinian Authority "working toward a durable peace agreement."[50]

During the week-long Operation Pillar of Defense nearly 1,500 rockets were fired from Gaza into Israel. Some reached Tel Aviv and the outskirts of Jerusalem, causing "widespread panic and damage." But *Times* headlines told a different story: "Israel Destroys Hamas Prime Minister's Office"; "Israel Takes Tougher Approach." Ethan Bronner reported the suggestions of "many analysts and diplomats" that Israel "needs a different approach to Hamas and the Palestinians based more on acknowledging historic grievances." His primary source, Beirut journalist Rami G. Khouri, claimed that "as long as the crime of dispossession and refugeehood" committed against the Palestinians was not redressed the determination of Palestinian fighters would be enhanced. "Only stupid or ideologically maniacal Zionists," he added, "fail to come to terms with this fact."[51]

As Hamas rockets flew into Israel from Gaza, *Times* op-ed columns overflowed with criticism – of Israel. "I condemn Israel's current leaders for failing to recognize that the best defense is peace," wrote a disillusioned American Israeli in Tel Aviv. A free-lance photographer from Gaza City described Israel, not Gaza, as "the place where bombs come from." A *Jerusalem Post* correspondent accused Israel of "a grave and irresponsible strategic error" for its decision to kill al-Jabari. It was, another Israeli journalist complained, "disproportional punishment," even though he "deserved to die" for his responsibility for the deaths of many Israelis and the abduction of Gilad Shalit. Roger Cohen acknowledged that "no government can accept having its civilians subjected to regular rocket attacks from a neighboring territory." But Israel's actions, he warned, "radicalize the situation, erode middle ground ... and so facilitate continued Israeli occupation of the West Bank, the expansion of settlements there and the steady eclipse of the idea of a two-state peace."[52] What Hamas rockets contributed to peace he declined to mention.

Times reports from Gaza focused on a besieged people suffering from Israeli aggression. Rudoren, embracing its penchant for covering Palestinian deaths, described "the intense, chaotic, lengthy funeral" of a seven-year-old Gaza boy killed along with seven relatives in "the single deadliest attack." Considerably less attention was paid to more than eight hundred rockets fired into Israel, where "normal life," Isabel Kershner wrote, had "come to a halt." Had Netanyahu "pursued serious negotiations on a two-state solution," *Times* editors claimed, "Hamas's nihilistic vision would have far less appeal." Once again Ambassador Oren was the lone dissenter. "Bound by its genocidal theology and crude anti-Semitism," he wrote, "Hamas cannot be induced to make peace." But, he insisted, "it can be deterred from war." Israel had no choice but to "neutralize the rockets and combat the terrorists that target us."[53]

As the Gaza conflict subsided, *Times* coverage pirouetted yet again to the lurking evil of Israeli settlements. The Netanyahu government, responding to the UN General Assembly recognition of Palestine as a non-member state, had announced plans to construct new housing in East Jerusalem and the West Bank while expanding development in the area known as E-1, linking Jerusalem and the Maale Adumim settlement to the east. "Many fear," Rudoren wrote, that by threatening "the meaningful contiguity of a Palestinian state," E-1 construction would "close the chance for a two-state solution." Replete with errors, her article prompted a *Times* correction noting that new settlements "would not divide the West Bank in two," nor would the proposed development in E-1 "make a contiguous Palestinian state impossible." Three weeks later *Times* editors made the identical erroneous claim about E-1.[54] There was no correction.

Editors blamed Netanyahu for "punitive" and "shortsighted" attempts that "threaten to crush" the Palestinian Authority and President Abbas, lauded as "the only credible peace negotiator." Thomas Friedman criticized "far-right settler activists" who were "so arrogant, and so indifferent to U.S. concerns" as to announce plans for new settlements "in the heart of the West Bank." Another editorial criticized Netanyahu's "aggressive new push to expand settlements," warning that "by absorbing the West Bank, Israel would risk its character as a Jewish state because Israeli Jews would become a minority in their own country," a demographic doomsday scenario without credibility.[55]

Israel's sharpest *Times* critics invariably professed their deep friendship with the Jewish State. Its "quieter friends," wrote self-identified "liberal Zionist"

Roger Cohen, "support its pre-1967 borders"; believe that settlement expansion is "self-defeating and wrong"; favor "painful compromises on both sides"; and are "troubled by a rightward nationalist drift in Israel." But the "religious-nationalist Israeli push to keep all the land" contradicted the principles of "freedom, justice and peace" embedded in its Proclamation of Independence.[56]

A cover story in the *Times Magazine*, written by California journalist Ben Ehrenreich, focused on the plight of the West Bank village of Nabi Saleh, where weekly protests against Israeli "occupation" had gained international attention. (Ehrenreich had previously published a Los Angeles *Times* op-ed entitled "Zionism is the Problem" in which he compared the Jewish State to apartheid South Africa.) Presenting Nabi Saleh as the moral counterpoint to the nearby settlement of Halamish, founded by "members of the messianic" Gush Emunim, Ehrenreich described "the tiny village's struggle against the occupation" as a four-year protest against "the entire complex system of control – of permits, checkpoints, walls, prisons – through which Israel maintains its hold on the region." He briefly mentioned, without judgment, the cousin of his host family who had killed a Jewish settler, and another relative who had "escorted" the suicide bomber who killed fifteen Israelis at the Sbarro pizzeria in Jerusalem.[57]

President Obama's first official visit to Israel in March 2013 sparked a week-long flurry of *Times* commentary. Editors, correspondents, columnists, and contributors formed a chorus of praise. An editorial commended the president for "seeking to stir popular enthusiasm for his vision of peace" by addressing an audience of "youthful Israelis," comprising students and "left-wing peace activists" who did "not necessarily share the hardened views of many of their elders." (In translation, Obama had carefully chosen his audience to avoid confronting critics.) Asking them "to empathize with their Israeli-occupied neighbors," Obama inverted Theodor Herzl's famous plea for Jewish statehood: "Just as Israelis built a state in their homeland, Palestinians have a right to be a free people in their own land." In his "all-out effort to connect with the Israeli public," Rudoren noted approvingly, the president even sprinkled his speech with Hebrew phrases.[58]

J-Street president Jeremy Ben-Ami lauded Obama for understanding that "Israel can only uphold the vision of its founders as a democracy and a Jewish homeland if the Palestinian people have a viable and secure state of their own." Obama, Thomas Friedman wrote, "embraced Israelis with both understanding and honesty" by suggesting that their country "collaborate with Palestinians to build a West Bank state that is modern, secular and Westernizing."[59] Nothing pleased the *Times* more than the prospect of Israeli deference to an American president whose liberalism it enthusiastically embraced.

An internal Israeli struggle over religion, gender and identity briefly refocused *Times* coverage. Rudoren described "mounting tension and legal battles" over the mistreatment of women, who confronted gender discrimination in buses and other public spaces, most conspicuously at the Western Wall. (She did not report Muslim gender discrimination inside the nearby al-Aqsa Mosque, where female worshippers were confined to the rear of the shrine.) Rudoren identified an "intensifying culture war" between the growing ultra-Orthodox minority and the secular majority "that poses a threat, if internal, to Israel's social cohesion."[60]

But the "intractable Israeli-Palestinian conflict" inevitably intruded. Roger Cohen, complaining that a "Messianic view" of Israel's destiny dominated its government, called on American Jewish organizations to help deter Israel from "maximalist territorial temptation that inflicts on disenfranchised Palestinians the very exclusion Jews lived" for centuries.[61] Palestinians had become the new Jews, entitled to all the blessings of statehood that the *Times* had opposed for Jews before 1948.

Three days before Secretary of State John Kerry arrived in Israel to attempt to revive the peace process, Rudoren reported Netanyahu's West Bank visit to dedicate an elementary school named for his father. Following the lead of Palestinian negotiator Saeb Erekat, who condemned the visit as "devastating," she labeled its "awkward timing" as reminiscent of the Israeli announcement of new housing units in East Jerusalem during Vice President Biden's visit in 2010. *Times* editors praised Kerry for "doggedly plowing forward" despite the efforts of Israeli "hard-liners" who "tried to undermine his efforts by advocating more West Bank settlements."[62]

Once again Roger Cohen warned that without a two-state peace agreement Israel "cannot remain a Jewish and democratic state." Only peace talks could resolve its "undemocratic system of oppression." But he saw no indication that Israel was prepared to abandon its "maximalist territorial temptation." (Palestinian obduracy was ignored.) Thomas Friedman reminded readers (erroneously): "One should never forget just how crazy some of Israel's Jewish settlers are. They assassinated Prime Minister Yitzhak Rabin when he tried to cede part of the West Bank for peace." (Yigal Amir, Rabin's assassin, was not a settler. He lived in the Israeli city of Herzliya.) *Times* editors reasserted their demographic doomsday scenario that "No good can come if Israel, with its growing Palestinian population, evolves from a Jewish majority state to an Arab majority state . . . and if the long sought dream of a Palestinian state is left to die."[63]

While the *Times* relentlessly blamed Israel for the absence of peace, Rudoren lionized Palestinian stone-throwers. In a front-page story she elevated a seventeen-year-old Palestinian to heroic stature after his fourth arrest for stoning assaults. Like his brothers and father, who had served time in prison simultaneously for their stone-throwing and other illegal activities, Muhammed Abu Hashem symbolized the "Palestinian pushback" against "The Occupation." For Rudoren, rock-throwing was merely a boyhood "rite of passage and an honored act of defiance" among teenagers "with little else to do."[64]

One month later the lead article in the Sunday *Times Review* reiterated its incessant trope: Israeli settlements doomed a two-state solution. Comparing Israel to apartheid South Africa, a (Jewish) University of Pennsylvania political scientist wistfully imagined "the disappearance of Israel as a Zionist project through war, cultural exhaustion or demographic momentum." What "might work" instead, he fantasized, was a post-Zionist Middle East featuring "one mixed state" with an Arab majority population.[65]

In the waning months of 2013 *Times* editors, joined by Roger Cohen, focused their wrath on Prime Minister Netanyahu for his unrelenting opposition to Iranian nuclear development. An editorial chastised his speech at the United Nations for its "sarcasm and aggressive" language, warning that it could be "disastrous" if he exaggerated the Iranian nuclear threat and impeded President Obama's efforts to establish a new relationship with its rulers. For Cohen, "the real challenge to Israel as a Jewish and democratic nation" was not from Iranian nuclear development but from its "failure to achieve a two-state peace with the Palestinians and the prolongation of a West Bank occupation." No democracy, he warned, "can be immune to running an undemocratic system of oppression in territory under its control."[66]

The prevailing *Times* narrative of Palestinian victimization provoked sharp criticism after Isabel Kershner reported the fatal stabbing of an Israeli soldier by a Palestinian teenager who claimed to be avenging prison sentences for relatives convicted of killing two Israelis. Rather than provide a photograph of the Israeli victim, murdered while asleep on a bus, the *Times* (once again) prominently displayed a photo of the assailant's grieving mother. Furious responses from hundreds of readers prompted a reply from Public Editor Margaret Sullivan acknowledging that the photo was "a poor choice, failing to put the focus where it belonged." Senior editors agreed that it was "a regrettable choice."[67] It was, however, a choice that exposed *Times* preoccupation with Palestinian victimization – even when Israelis were the victims.

Then Rudoren, citing Israeli outrage over the prospect of an American nuclear deal with Iran, erroneously claimed that Israel "continues to build West Bank settlements while negotiating with the Palestinians." (Three weeks earlier, in a similar misstatement corrected by the *Times*, she had falsely asserted that Israel was building "3,500 more settlements.")[68] Once again, Rudoren ignored the distinction between building new settlements and new construction within existing settlements.

The final words in 2013 about Israel came from Roger Cohen. His litmus test of its virtue was whether "it gets out of the corrosive business of occupation," thereby rejecting "messianic religious Greater Israel nationalism" for "a democratic state of laws."[69] Yet despite unrelenting criticism from *The New York Times* for subverting democratic values with occupation and settlements, Israel remained the solitary democratic state in the Middle East.

CHAPTER 14

American Loyalty:
2014–2015

During the first week of 2014 the *Times* published an article, an op-ed and an editorial about Israel – all critical. Jodi Rudoren explained why Prime Minister Netanyahu's demand that Israel be recognized as a Jewish state was unacceptable to Palestinian negotiators. In their dispute over "a historical narrative that each side sees as fundamental to its existence," Palestinians claimed that recognition would disenfranchise Arab citizens of Israel and undercut the right of return for Palestinian refugees.[1] For Rudoren, competing "narratives" prevailed over the reality that the voting rights of Israeli Arab citizens had nothing to do with Palestinian recognition.

According to former Shin Bet director Ami Ayalon, Netanyahu failed to understand that time was "running out" for resolving the Israeli-Palestinian conflict. Israel "should be taking independent steps to create the outlines of a two-state reality on the ground," including relinquishing all claims of sovereignty east of its West Bank security fence. Israel must "seize the day," but nothing was expected of Palestinians. An editorial concluded that "neither society will be secure until both can learn to compromise and live as states, side by side."[2] In the new year, moral equivalence still prevailed.

Israel continued to be flayed by op-ed contributors. Avi Shlaim, a leftist critic who had abandoned Israel for England just before the Six-Day War, complained that with American "money, arms and advice" Israel need not pay for "its flagrant violations of international law, and for its systematic abuse of Palestinian human rights." Omar Barghouti, co-founder of the Boycott Divestment and Sanctions movement, challenged Israel's "ethnocratic" identity as "an exclusionary Jewish state" committed to "oppression of the Palestinian people" (although Palestinian citizens comprised one-fifth of its population). Former *Jerusalem Report* editor Hirsh Goodman (Isabel Kershner's husband) lamented that "inexplicably, blindly, Israel is letting itself be branded an apartheid state; even encouraging it with an "apartheid wall," "apartheid roads," and "colonization" of Palestinians.[3]

Then it was Thomas Friedman's turn. In one of his favorite self-appointed roles, as purveyor of Arab peace plans that would return Israel to its precarious pre-1967 borders, he relayed a proposal from Palestinian Authority President Mahmoud Abbas. Following a five-year transitional period, Israeli military forces in the West Bank would be replaced by an "American-led NATO force" and Palestinian police and security units. Like the peace initiative relayed by Friedman from the Saudi King in 2002, proposing a complete Israeli withdrawal to pre-1967 lines, it was a fantasy that bore no relation to any prospect of Israeli acceptance. In a follow-up article he proclaimed that the best way for Israel to contain the boycott campaign was "to freeze all settlement activity" and "give peace its best chance." Otherwise, he warned one week later, Israel "could become some kind of apartheid-like state in permanent control over 2.5 million Palestinians." Roger Cohen chimed in, urging that the Jewish national home be "reinvented" as "a state of laws" by ending the "corrosive occupation."[4]

Times religion columnist Mark Oppenheimer provided a platform for "exceedingly rare" American Orthodox Jews who were driven by their faith to oppose Israel. One favored the "non-statist Zionism" advocated decades earlier by Judah L. Magnes. Another, who supported the Boycott, Divestment and Sanctions movement, refused to rise in his Orthodox synagogue for the prayer for the State of Israel. A Berkeley Talmud professor described Israel as "a moral and political disaster," while a Brooklyn College political scientist explained: "I love being Jewish. I just don't love the state of Israel."[5]

Shifting to the lagging peace process the *Times* published the lament of Birzeit University political scientist (and former Palestinian Authority Cabinet member) Ali Jarbawi. He was especially upset over the Israeli negotiating demand that Palestinians "recognize the Jewishness of the Israeli state." Jarbawi dismissed it as Netanyahu's attempt "to sabotage the peace process . . . while continuing to usurp our land." With Palestinian and Orthodox Jewish critics of Israel embedded in its columns, *Times* editors called on the United States to affirm pre-1967 boundary lines and endorse Jerusalem "as the capital of two states."[6]

Palestinians dominated Jodi Rudoren's coverage from Jerusalem. In the first of two articles a week apart, her front-page report focused on a Palestinian prisoner released from two decades of incarceration for killing a seventy-two-year-old Holocaust survivor. "Demonized as terrorists by Israelis and lionized as freedom fighters by Palestinians," as if murder was nothing more than competing narratives, he was among seventy-eight Palestinians whose negotiated release was intended to facilitate peace negotiations. Noting that "most Israelis – and certainly most victims' relatives" opposed the prisoner releases, Rudoren gave primacy to the daughter of the murdered Israeli, who supported the release "if it advances the peace process."[7]

One week later Rudoren focused on Marwan Barghouti, "the single most popular Palestinian politician," serving five life sentences for complicity in the murder of Israelis. With Palestinian leaders demanding Barghouti's freedom to prevent the collapse of peace talks, she identified him as "the Palestinian parallel" to Jonathan Pollard, the imprisoned American convicted of spying for Israel. For Rudoren, the Palestinian murderer and American spy had "similar symbolic significance" as "a humanitarian cause."[8]

Several days later the *Times* Sunday Review published an opinion column co-written by an Iranian-American historian at Stanford and a University of Haifa political scientist. Entitled "Are Iran and Israel Trading Places?," they suggested that while some Iranian officials had finally realized the dire consequences of "continued intransigence and bellicosity," Israel's "secular democrats are increasingly worried that Israel's future may bear an uncomfortable resemblance to Iran's recent past." Given the rising birthrate among Orthodox Jews and the aspiration of Orthodox parties "to transform Israel into a theocracy," demographic trends "might eclipse any fleeting victories for liberalism in Israel." Secular Israelis might be unable to "halt the country's drift from democracy to theocracy."[9] Israel, in sum, was likely to become the new Iran.

As another round of peace talks verged on collapse a *Times* editorial (predictably) blamed Israel for their failure. Editors reiterated their own guiding principles: a Palestinian state in the West Bank and Gaza based on 1967 lines; land swaps that permitted Israel to retain "some" settlements in exchange for land "comparable in quantity and quality"; Jerusalem as the capital of both Israel and Palestine. Thomas Friedman lauded Secretary of State Kerry for "doing the Lord's work" in negotiations, trying – in vain – "to save Israel from trends that will inevitably undermine it as a Jewish and democratic state."[10]

In mid-June the *Times* reported that three missing Israeli teenagers in the West Bank were "presumed" to have been kidnapped, but "the credulity of the claim was not immediately clear." West Bank violence, Kershner noted, "continues to claim victims on both sides," although no Palestinians had been kidnapped. Israelis were "gripped by the presumed abductions," but Rudoren focused on Arab brothers in Hebron who expressed concern that the Israeli "crackdown" would ruin the forthcoming wedding party of a family member. The mayor of Hebron (whose thriving Palestinian sector had become the commercial hub of the West Bank) described the suffering of the Palestinian people, confined by Israel to "a big jail." Many Palestinians, Rudoren wrote, "questioned whether the abduction even happened."[11]

The *Times* focus quickly shifted from the desperate Israeli search for the missing teenagers (one of whom also held American citizenship) to Israel's "sweeping West Bank arrest campaign." While the initial "crackdown" had "proceeded quietly," Rudoren reported, Israeli soldiers were increasingly confronted by Palestinians throwing rocks, gasoline bombs, grenades and other explosives. During an early morning melee in Dura, near Hebron, a rock-throwing fifteen-year-old Palestinian was fatally shot by an Israeli soldier. Hours later Rudoren visited his mourning mother, wailing in grief as women tried to comfort her with the assurance that "her son had gone to paradise as an Islamic martyr."[12] No visits to families of the missing Israeli teenagers were reported.

In the *Times* narrative Palestinian sorrow overshadowed the fate of kidnapped Israelis. Rudoren focused on competing, and morally equivalent, story lines. "Most" Israelis viewed the yeshiva students as "innocent civilians." But Palestinians viewed "the very act of attending yeshiva in a West Bank settlement as provocation." They complained that the Israeli "security crackdown," with five Palestinians killed during stone-throwing attacks, was "collective punishment against a people under illegal occupation."[13]

Eighteen days after their abduction the bodies of the missing Israeli teenagers were found buried beneath rocks in a field near Hebron. *Times* contributors and columnists blamed Israel, not their Palestinian murderers. The outcry over their disappearance and death, Ali Jarbawi wrote, led to "a portrayal of settlers as victims of terror rather than as illegal occupiers." Roger Cohen, responding to the death of a Palestinian rock-thrower (while remaining silent about the kidnapping and murder of the Israeli teenagers), alleged that Israel's West Bank rule "involves routine coercion, humiliation and abuse to which most Israelis have grown increasingly oblivious." Beyond the Green Line boundary "lies a lawless Israeli enterprise profoundly corrosive, over time, to the noble Zionist dream of a democracy governed by laws." Like Cohen, *Times* editors responded to the murdered Israelis only when there was a Palestinian victim to offset them, describing "an atmosphere in which each side dehumanizes the other."[14]

Early in July Hamas once again launched dozens of long-range rockets from Gaza into Israel, which responded with extensive air attacks and a call-up of 40,000 reservists. Steven Erlanger and Isabel Kershner explained that the

Israeli "crackdown" after the kidnapping and murder of the yeshiva students "appeared to push Hamas to respond from Gaza." Israel, implicitly, was responsible for Hamas aggression. Once again, coverage was accompanied by graphic photos of Gaza family members mourning relatives who were victims of retaliatory Israeli air strikes.[15]

From the East Jerusalem neighborhood of Beit Hanina, Rula Salameh expressed "a Palestinian mother's fear" as (Hamas) rockets exploded nearby. She demanded accountability from the Israeli government for its military campaigns in Gaza and the West Bank and for "the entire occupation, whose violence and cruelty is the dark context" for the renewed conflict. According to Steven Erlanger, "brutality against innocents is not new on either side of the Israeli-Palestinian conflict." Former Jerusalem Bureau Chief Ethan Bronner described the conflict as "an ugly blood-feud" in which the murder of Israeli teenagers had escalated into "devastating Israeli airstrikes that have killed scores and Palestinian rocket attacks that have displaced thousands." For Beirut Bureau Chief Anne Barnard, the plight of Gazans, "trapped between Israel's powerful military machine and the militants of Hamas," was revealed when an Israeli missile (aimed according to Israeli sources at Hamas militants) killed four young cousins playing on a Gaza beach. The children "came quickly to symbolize how the Israeli aerial assaults in Gaza are inevitably killing innocents in this crowded, impoverished sliver of land."[16]

Times coverage was driven by the suffering of Gaza civilians, depicted as the innocent victims of merciless Israeli – not Hamas – aggression. Rudoren frequently shared a by-line with Fares Akram, identified as having "contributed reporting." As Akram revealed in a *Times* interview, "the story of Gaza is my story too." His father, a lawyer and judge employed by the Palestinian Authority in Gaza, had been killed on his farm by an Israeli air strike during the 2009 war. As "a grieving son," Akram found it "hard to distinguish between what the Israelis call terrorists and the Israeli pilots and tank crews who are invading Gaza." Since Rudoren did not speak Arabic, she relied on his selection of sources and translations of their suffering. Responding to allegations of biased coverage, executive editor Dean Baquet evasively asserted: "We're looking for fairness, not balance."[17]

Drawn to Gaza from her posting in Lebanon, Anne Barnard reported on families who were "financially and psychologically depleted" by the endless fighting. She repeated their (false) claim that Israel was to blame for its continuing "occupation" of Gaza, which had ended eight years previously. Palestinian journalist Mohammed Omer succinctly described Gaza, "where nowhere is safe.

Not a mosque. Not a church. Not a school, or even a hospital." Hamas was merely "a convenient villain, someone to blame."[18] He did not mention that Hamas rocket attacks on Israeli civilian targets had provoked and sustained the conflict.

It was "indisputable," Barnard and Rudoren reported, that rockets "can be seen launching from crowded neighborhoods, near apartment buildings, schools and hotels. Hamas fighters have ... stored weapons in mosques and schools." They "operate in civilian areas, draw return fire to civilian structures" and benefit diplomatically from mounting casualties among their own people. Hamas, *Times* editors conceded, deserved "the strongest possible condemnation for storing and launching rockets in heavily populated areas." But "innocents are paying an intolerable cost for being caught in the middle. It is fair to ask whether Israel is doing enough to prevent that."[19]

In *Times* opinion columns, as in its news coverage, Israel was blamed for the turmoil and tragedy in Gaza provoked by Hamas rocket attacks. "I am a Zionist" proclaimed Roger Cohen, before condemning the "perversion" and "betrayal" of Zionism for which "a Messianic Israeli nationalism" was responsible. He remained silent about Hamas rockets. Novelist David Grossman asserted that "in this cruel and despicable bubble, both sides are right. They both obey ... the law of violence and war, revenge and hatred." The solitary dissenter was Amos Yadlin, former head of Israeli Military Intelligence, who cited "Hamas's reckless violence" in locating its tunnels, bunkers and rocket launchers "under or among mosques, hospitals and schools," leaving Gaza civilians as the "shield" for its military aggression.[20]

A bevy of *Times* reporters and columnists reported from Gaza or wrote about it from a safe distance. None were posted in southern Israel, where residents bore the brunt of Hamas aggression. After nearly two weeks of constant rocket attacks, Israeli soldiers spotted armed Hamas fighters exiting from a tunnel inside Israel. The IDF responded with a ground assault into Gaza to destroy the tunnels and halt the rocket fire. The *Times* predictably focused on the toll exacted from Palestinian civilians by Israeli retaliation for the Hamas incursion. The plight of civilians in Gaza, not the thousands of Israelis who fled their homes to escape Hamas mortar and rocket attacks, drove the *Times* narrative.[21]

In Sderot, one mile inside the border, Rudoren discovered Koby Hill, where Israelis could secure "the closest thing to a front-row seat" to observe Hamas rocket fire and Israeli retaliation. She described "prime seats, on a white sofa" reserved for "a dozen middle-aged men" who munched watermelon and cheered the spectacle of the Israeli rocket "show." According to their spokesman, the hill offered a "nice view, good air" where locals could "relax" and enjoy the Israeli military performance. Rudoren noted, in passing, that Sderot had been targeted by 2,322 rockets over the years, while a nearby tunnel had recently provided access for Hamas "militants" to kill four Israeli soldiers.[22]

It took three weeks of rocket attacks from Gaza until the *Times* showed signs of moderating its prevailing narrative that blamed Israel for responding to Hamas aggression. After explosions at a UN school killed sixteen Gaza civilians gathered there for safety, an editorial conceded that Hamas deserved "the strongest possible condemnation" for locating weapons in densely populated areas, while Israel "has reason" to respond "with strong military action" against rocket attacks. But the *Times* ignored a rocket fired from a Gaza hospital parking lot, a war crime reported by a Finnish TV journalist. Nor did it mention a booby-trapped UNRWA clinic whose explosion killed three Israeli soldiers. Only at the end of a lengthy front-page article did reporters refer to five mosques where Hamas weapons were concealed. An opinion column predictably blamed "extremists on both sides" for the war initiated by Hamas.[23]

In early August, with a seventy-two-hour cease-fire in place, an editorial apportioned responsibility for the loss of life and destruction of property. Hamas "knowingly targeted Israeli civilian centers" and "launched weapons from populated areas in what looks like a deliberate effort to draw Israeli fire on innocents." But "in too many cases," Israeli weapons hit schools and shelters and "failed to adequately protect Palestinian citizens."[24] In a war launched and waged by Hamas the *Times* preserved its resolute commitment to moral equivalence.

Immediately after the cease-fire expired Hamas resumed its rocket barrage into Israel. *Times* coverage continued to focus on the plight of Gazans. It identified the first casualty of the renewed Hamas assault as a ten-year-old Palestinian boy killed during a retaliatory Israeli missile attack. Visiting two families in northern Gaza who had made "a tidy home" after their neighborhood was destroyed by Israeli missiles, Rudoren described their "steadfastness" amid sorrow and anger. They were "proud" of Hamas militants who had killed sixty-four Israeli soldiers during a month of fighting. A woman lauded their "genius" because they "shook an entire society with new fear."[25]

The "moral debate" over Israel's "assault" in Gaza was prominently underscored by a front-page *Times* article about a ninety-one-year-old Dutch Holocaust hero who sharply criticized the Jewish state for betraying its professed humanitarian values. Henk Zanoli went to the Israeli Embassy in The Hague to return the medal he had received as a "Righteous Gentile" for his family's efforts to save Jews. Prompted by a recent Israeli airstrike in Gaza that killed six of his relatives by marriage, Zanoli explained in a letter to the Israeli ambassador: "Against this background, it is particularly shocking and tragic that today, four generations on, our family is faced with the murder of our kin in Gaza. Murder carried out by the State of Israel." He had come to realize that "the Zionist project" had "a racist element in it in aspiring to build a state exclusively for Jews." Zanoli's act, according to the *Times* account, "crystallizes the moral debate over Israel's military air and ground assault in the Gaza Strip."[26] The "moral debate" over the burial of the Holocaust in its inside pages had not received as much attention in the *Times*.

One week later the *Times* shifted focus from a disillusioned Holocaust survivor to a disillusioned British Zionist. Headlined "The End of Liberal Zionism," Antony Lerman proclaimed that "what Israel is doing can't be reconciled with their humanism." The "romantic ideal" that had inspired him to make aliya had been shattered by "the land-grabbing settler movement, a growing strain of anti-Arab and anti-immigrant racism, extremist politics, and a powerful, intolerant religious right." Zionism had become "xenophobic and exclusionary, a Jewish ethno-nationalism inspired by religious messianism."[27]

One day after the collapse of a brief cease-fire more than 140 rockets were fired from Gaza into Israel, which responded with massive air strikes against Hamas launching sites and weapon storage facilities. Fares Akram played an increasingly prominent role in *Times* coverage, co-authoring four articles with Rudoren and Kershner (neither of whom spoke Arabic) that focused on civilian damage from Israeli retaliation. Buried in two reports was brief mention of a four-year-old Israeli boy killed in his kibbutz home by a Hamas mortar shell. He was identified (and instantly overshadowed) as "the first Israeli child to be killed in the current conflict," which had claimed the lives of 2,100 Palestinians, "about 500 of them children."[28]

But the death of four-year-old Daniel Tragerman transcended a family tragedy to become a national loss. The Tragerman family lived in Nahal Oz, the border kibbutz where four Israeli soldiers had been killed in the tunnel attack a month earlier. Playing inside a tent in the living room of his home, Daniel froze with fear when he heard the air-raid siren warning, unable to reach the family shelter before mortar shrapnel killed him. The day after his death, which the *Times* mentioned in passing, it devoted an entire article by Akram to a Palestinian teenager who claimed that Israeli soldiers had detained him for five days one month earlier. Although his assertions could not be independently corroborated, and his father "forgot to take photographs" showing his abuse, his detention claim was fit to print, while Daniel Tragerman's death was barely noticed.[29]

Guided by Akram, *Times* reporters had no problem locating displaced and mourning Gazans. Rudoren devoted an article to a long-distance runner and his father at the ruins of their destroyed home. She also reported "a crusader for women's rights" who was reduced from preparing "fresh seafood feasts" to feeding her husband "tuna out of cans." *Times* headlines consistently reflected the plight of Gaza civilian victims while ignoring Hamas responsibility for it. Little notice was given to the departure of thousands of Israeli residents from their border communities, including nearly all residents of Nahal Oz, to escape the unrelenting Hamas rocket assault.[30]

Framed by its fixation on Palestinian victims of Israeli responses to the war launched by Hamas, *Times* distortion was graphically illustrated in a Sunday *Magazine* photo essay after a truce was signed. Entitled "Dust to Dust: On the Ground in Israel and Gaza," it displayed a double-page photograph of massive destruction in the "heavily bombed" Shejaiya neighborhood. Four black and white photos from Gaza were spread across two pages. Two showed the ruins of destroyed mosques; the others revealed women mourning at the funeral of a drone attack victim and men carrying the body of a fourteen-year-old killed in a drone strike. Contrasting color photos showed Israeli children playing in a communal bomb shelter and minor rocket damage to the wall outside an Israeli home near the Gaza border. The concluding double-page photo was a close-up of a ten-year-old Gaza boy killed in an Israeli drone attack, his face cradled in a man's hands. Revealing "the thinking behind the photo essay," the *Magazine* editor explained that the photos were interspersed as a way of emphasizing that "the fates of Israelis and Palestinians are intertwined." But the overriding message was victimized Palestinians (as Rudoren wrote) "amid the conflict's asymmetry."[31]

The *Times* offered an array of retrospective explanations for the causes of the conflict. According to Kershner, Israel had used the Hamas "affiliations" of suspects in the kidnapping and murder of the Israeli teenagers to justify "a major crackdown" with "scores of arrests." That provoked Hamas to fire the rockets that triggered "a full-blown confrontation." For Roger Cohen the Israeli "frenzy" following the kidnappings provided "the context of the drift to war." But, he explained, "oppressed people will rise up."[32] In the *Times*, Hamas was absolved and Israel was blamed for the war that Hamas initiated.

An especially vitriolic contribution came from Israeli-American journalist Mairav Zonszein. Affiliated with an array of left-wing advocacy groups, she referred to the "aggressive silencing of anyone who voices disapproval of

Israeli policies or expresses sympathy with the Palestinians." Israeli society, she lamented (without being silenced), "has been unable and unwilling to overcome an exclusivist ethno-religious nationalism that privileges Jewish citizens." With Israelis "unwilling to listen to criticism, even when it comes from within their own family," she found her perfect forum in *The New York Times,* where criticism of Israel, especially from within the family, was always welcome.[33]

Jewish holy days provided another opportunity for Roger Cohen to interweave his Jewish identity with criticism of Israel. Acknowledging "the excruciating difficulty of waging war against an enemy deployed among civilians," he nonetheless concluded that "the death of a single child to an Israeli bullet seems to betoken some failure in the longed-for Jewish state." (Cohen had remained silent about the death of Daniel Tragerman from a Hamas rocket attack.) The "terrible thing" about Israel was its denial of "humanity to the stranger."[34]

Times coverage had become indistinguishable from criticism of the Jewish state. Rudoren was intrigued by Israelis who had relocated to Berlin, drawn by its "cosmopolitan flair, vibrant arts scene and advanced public transportation." Searching for a better life than Israel afforded, the son of a Holocaust refugee had returned to his father's Germany for want of opportunities in Tel Aviv. Although emigration from Israel was lower than ever, a *Times* headline reading "Exodus from Israel to Germany" was irresistible.[35]

Another headline called attention to "A House-by-House Struggle for Control of a Jerusalem Neighborhood." Silwan, home to a community of Yemenite Jews during the pre-state years, had subsequently become a Palestinian enclave. But "in the dark of night," Kershner reported, Jewish settlers, beneficiaries of "a multimillion-dollar series of complex and shadowy transactions," had moved into twenty-five housing units in the neighborhood. "The national and religious contest for control of the area," she wrote, "is taking place house by house."[36] Presumably ethnic segregation that excluded Jews was preferable.

Israel, wrote Israeli-born Palestinian journalist Rula Jebreal, "is increasingly becoming a project of ethno-religious purity and exclusion" (repeating Mairav Zonszein's allegation a month earlier of Israel's "ethno-religious nationalism"). Ranking the Law of Return among the most "discriminatory Israel laws," she condemned the integration of ultra-Orthodox Jews into Israeli society as "a new, religiously inspired racism" that further disadvantaged Palestinian Israeli citizens. When asked by an Israeli journalist whether the *Times* might subject Palestinian racism to the same scrutiny, Opinion editor Matt Seaton responded that it would cover Palestinian racism as "soon as they have [a] sovereign state to discriminate with."[37]

Times reporters were drawn to celebrations of Palestinian terrorist attacks no less than to funerals of Palestinian victims of Israeli retaliation. Kershner and Rudoren visited a refugee camp outside Ramallah to interview relatives of a Palestinian teenager who had become an overnight "heroic figure" for his fatal stabbing of an Israeli soldier in Tel Aviv. His young admirers displayed signs proclaiming "We are people who love death while our enemies love life." A song called "Run Over the Settler" had become popular. The reporters noted in passing that six Israelis had been killed in terrorist attacks within the past month.[38] Their funerals were unreported.

One week later, in the deadliest attack on Israeli civilians in more than three years, two Palestinians armed with a gun, knives and axes murdered three rabbis, a worshipper and a police guard in a Jerusalem synagogue. Noting that eleven Israelis, including an infant, had been killed within the past month, Rudoren and Kershner cited a "cycle of violence and mutual dehumanization" by "extremists on both sides." (No Israeli "extremists" were identified.) A *Times* editorial transformed the synagogue murders into "a tragedy for all Israelis and Palestinians," whose communities seemed "increasingly locked in a cycle of hatred and hopelessness."[39] Jews were murdered by Palestinians but both peoples suffered.

In the waning days of 2014 *Times* columnists and editors weighed in with dire forecasts about Israel's future. Thomas Friedman, echoing a trope long favored by Anthony Lewis, feared that "scary religious nationalist zealots" might lead Israel into the "dark corner" of a "South African future," even as soon as the forthcoming national elections in March. "Uneasiness inhabits Israel," Roger Cohen lamented, as "Israelis are questioning their nation and its future." He relied on Amos Oz, "the conscience of a liberal and anti-Messianic Israel," who anticipated that without a two-state solution (which Palestinians had repeatedly rejected) there would either be an Arab state or "an Israeli dictatorship, probably a religious nationalist dictatorship." An editorial accused Israel of "narrowing the space for a peace deal by expanding settlements." Palestinians, to be sure, had rejected peace decades before the first settlement was built.[40] As usual, Israel was to blame for Palestinian intransigence.

The steady drumbeat of *Times* criticism continued. An American Israeli explained his avoidance of military service: "I don't want to be part of a system whose main task is the violent occupation of millions of people." After a Palestinian stabbed twelve Israelis in Tel Aviv, Kershner wrote about the (pious but not extremist) terrorist, his mother and family, and their sparsely furnished apartment. Nothing was written about the victims, their families or their homes. Rudoren expansively reviewed a documentary showing "previously unaired admissions of brutal behavior" by Israeli soldiers during the Six-Day War. The director admitted to "trying to revamp the prevailing Israeli narrative of triumph in 1967."[41] Rudoren eagerly publicized his effort.

Israeli national elections in March 2015 refocused *Times* coverage. Although they "should constitute a triumph, a celebration of democracy," Nicholas Kristof wrote (from the West Bank), settlements "mar the elections, and the future of the country." Accompanied, as *Times* journalists often were, by a member of the anti-settlers group B'Tselem, he cited violence by settlers against Arab property, including poisoned olive trees and slashed automobile tires. (He noted, in passing, that some settlers "have been murdered by Palestinians.") Conceding that there were "far worse human rights abuses in the Middle East," the Israeli occupation was "particularly offensive" to Kristof because it was "underwritten with our tax dollars."[42]

Two weeks before the Israeli election Prime Minister Netanyahu, addressing Congress at the invitation of Republican members, warned of the impending Iranian nuclear threat. *Times* editors were infuriated by the "rapturous welcome" he received from "fawning lawmakers." A dismaying example of "exploitative political theater," it was "made worse because it was so obviously intended to challenge President Obama's foreign policy," which the *Times* effusively embraced. Netanyahu's "obsessive Iran demonization" also perturbed Roger Cohen. To be sure, "the Islamic Republic is repressive" and "hostile to Israel." But Netanyahu's focus on Iran was "a cleverly manipulated distraction" from "the real long-term threat to Israel as a Jewish and democratic state": Palestine.[43]

A "cloud" hung over Netanyahu's election victory, Kershner reported. His "increasingly shrill" campaign "reaffirmed his reputation as a cynical, calculating politician." Friedman questioned whether "a Jewish democratic Israel survives his tenure." *Times* editors were unusually vitriolic, labeling him "desperate, and craven," guilty of "duplicity," "demagogy," and "fear-mongering." Netanyahu, they complained, "has gone into overdrive" to oppose an impending American nuclear agreement with Iran. Although "Iran's threats toward Israel and its involvement in terrorist activities are heinous and unacceptable," the agreement should not be conditioned on their cessation.[44] The patriotic loyalty of the *Times* was affirmed.

Israelis in Jerusalem had become increasingly vulnerable to attacks by lone Palestinians who targeted them with knives, guns, and motor vehicles. They were often reported by Diaa Hadid, hired in response to Public Editor Margaret Sullivan's suggestion that the *Times* could improve its coverage by employing an Arabic-speaking reporter. Hadid not only spoke Arabic; she had previously written for Electronic Intifada, a pro-Palestinian news site, and served as a public relations officer for *Ittijah*, a pro-Palestinian NGO. After the 9/11 attacks, she wrote: "I can't look at Israelis any more. . . . I don't want to be friends with them. I don't want to talk to them."[45]

In one of her early *Times* articles Hadid cited the detention of two Palestinian boys, ages seven and twelve, for throwing stones at an Israeli bus as "the latest example of Israel's crackdown on children, even the very young." She explained that "many Palestinians" saw rock-throwing as "a central weapon in their resistance to Israel's occupation." (She noted, in passing, that a four-year-old Israeli girl had recently died from injuries "caused by Palestinian rock throwers.") Reporting from a hamlet in the Negev desert, where seventy Bedouin families faced eviction from state-owned land, Hadid described it as "a rallying cry for Arab citizens who see it as a demonstration of . . . their second-class status in Israel" and their victimization by its "racist policy."[46]

Opinion articles reinforced the prevailing *Times* narrative of Israeli malfeasance. Tel Aviv University philosophy professor Anat Biletzky contrasted the "universal democratic values which are often loudly touted in official Israel" with Netanyahu's "bold, unadorned Zionist norms of exclusive Jewish rights and exclusion of Arab citizens." The story of Israel, she concluded, "is a sad story." Writing about "Israel's Charade of Democracy," B'Tselem executive director Hagai El-Ad described "the democratic façade that obscures an undemocratic and oppressive reality" of Israeli occupation.[47]

Times reporters pursuing human interest stories invariably emphasized the plight of Palestinians. Visiting Hebron, "the most tense and fraught patch of the occupied West Bank," Rudoren focused on Mohammad Abu Halaweh, whose butcher shop in a once volatile neighborhood had been shuttered closed by the Israeli military for twenty years. No residents of the tiny Jewish enclave appeared in her report, except for a reference to settlers "who began squatting in the neighborhood – where Jewish history is centuries old," after the Six-Day War. Her primary cited sources were B'Tselem and Youth Against Settlements.[48]

A *Times* headline, reporting "Man Dies After West Bank Attack," did not identify either the Israeli victim or his Palestinian assailant. In a two-sentence paragraph Isabel Kershner mentioned Malachi Rosenfeld, a twenty-six-year-old Hebrew University student who was shot while driving with three other Israelis near a settlement. Several days later, at considerably greater length, the *Times* reported the killing of a teenage Palestinian stone-thrower by the driver of an Israeli military vehicle whose windshield had been smashed. Kershner's lengthy description of his mourning family was accompanied by a photograph of weeping Palestinian women. Diaa Hadid reported B'Tselem's challenge to the military account of his death, questioning Israel's ability to conduct an impartial investigation.[49]

With the mid-July signing of the American nuclear agreement with Iran over Prime Minister Netanyahu's unrelenting opposition, there was a concluding flurry of criticism of the Israeli leader. *Times* editors found it "deeply unsettling" that he had dismissed it as a "historic mistake." Netanyahu, according to Rudoren, "battered Israel's critical alliance with the United States by alienating President Obama with his aggressive approach." Thomas Friedman (implicitly identifying Israel with Syria) presumed that since Israel plays by "'Hama rules' – war without mercy" – it already possessed "significant deterrence against an Iranian bomb." He cited an equally "existential" threat: Israel's failure to vacate the West Bank, which would leave it "governing so many Palestinians it could no longer be a Jewish democracy."[50]

With the Iran nuclear agreement signed, Palestinian victimization once again dominated *Times* coverage. A Palestinian researcher for B'Tselem, telling a story of "dispossession and oppression," recounted how two generations of his family had been expelled from their homes. One week later the West Bank village of Duma received international attention following the night-time fire-bombing of the home of a Palestinian family. An eighteen-month-old child was killed, and his brother and parents were hospitalized with severe burns. (The father and mother subsequently died of their injuries.) Israel, wrote Hadid and Rudoren, "has long been criticized for not vigilantly investigating price-tag attacks or punishing their offenders." But even Israeli leaders, Hadid noted, denounced the attack as "an act of terrorism, a term usually reserved for Palestinian attacks against Israelis."[51]

Kershner reported the "rare outpouring of self-reproach and soul-searching" among Israelis across the political spectrum. Israel faced a "quandary": how to "maintain democratic values while effectively fighting anti-democratic forces and terrorism within its own population." Amid the "outpouring of outrage," Rudoren described "a time of deep questioning across Israel" that "underscored both the endless conflict with the Palestinians and its own internal struggle to balance a rising religiosity with civil rights." In an op-ed column writer Etgar Keret wondered whether Israelis "still care about justice."[52]

The perceived threat to Israeli democracy posed by Jewish extremists dominated *Times* coverage. A "crackdown on Jewish terrorism suspects" framed a lengthy report on "a shadowy network" of "young Jewish zealots" who advocated "fomenting unrest to bring about the collapse of the State of Israel … and establishing a Jewish kingdom based on the laws of the Torah." Kershner provided a detailed account of "this latest generation of Jewish militants," living in West Bank outposts, "answering to no parental or rabbinical authority." With Rudoren she reported the arrest of Meir Ettinger, a prominent member of the "radical group of Israeli settlers" known as "hilltop youth" (and the grandson of Rabbi Meir Kahane). They identified him as "the name and face of what critics call a scourge on Israeli society."[53]

The "settler terrorism" of American Jews was scrutinized by Oxford Lecturer (and Massachusetts native) Sara Yael Hirschhorn, who explored the "long list of settler extremists with American roots." While "speaking fluent liberalese," American settlers remained "deafeningly silent on recent acts of Jewish terrorism." American Jews "can no longer condone these blind spots and damning silences when it comes to Jewish extremism in Israel."[54]

During a violent September in Jerusalem, Hadid reported the death of a sixty-four-year-old Jewish man after (unidentified) "attackers" pelted his car with rocks, causing him to lose control and crash into a pole. Palestinians, she explained in exculpation, "frequently argue that rocks and crude incendiary devices are among their only weapons to press for independence, and to defend themselves against Israeli forces during confrontations." Indeed, for some young Palestinians rock-throwing had become "a rite of passage." Kershner noted that Israel had "harshly criticized" Palestinian Authority President Mahmoud Abbas for his videotaped statement that "Al Aqsa is ours, the Church of the Holy Sepulcher is ours, it is all ours. They [Jews] have no right to defile them with their filthy feet."[55] The *Times* had not previously reported his slanderous comments.

While America has "a responsibility to help assure the security of Israel," the editors wrote, "Israel undermines stability by failing to negotiate peace with the Palestinians." In an adjacent column Roger Cohen (who confessed to writing it "in a break from shul, on an empty stomach" on Yom Kippur) cited the Jewish "covenant of ethics" to criticize Israeli "acquiescence to the injustice of dominion over another displaced people, the Palestinians." Seizing the holy day opportunity to criticize settlers while touting his own religious observance, he reiterated his preference for love of the stranger over "the all-or-nothing conviction of the Messianic Jewish settler."[56]

Under the headline "Historical Continuity Proves Elusive at Jerusalem's Holiest Place," *Times* reporter Rick Gladstone questioned whether the ancient

Jewish Temples had been located on the Temple Mount, the site of frequent recent clashes. Although they were "integral to Jewish religious history and to Israel's disputed assertions of sovereignty over all of Jerusalem," his suggestion of the absence of a definitive answer regarding their location was contradicted by centuries of Jewish history, texts and archeological evidence. Several days later an Editors' Note rejected his erroneous allegation, noting: "archeological and historical uncertainties about the site ... do not directly challenge Jewish claims to the Temple Mount."[57]

During the first week of October (which marked the beginning of what became known as the "stabbing" intifada) the *Times* reported a cluster of fatal Palestinian knifing attacks against Israelis. Failing to distinguish assailant from victim, Kershner noted that "intensifying violence has claimed lives on both sides in recent days." Rudoren noted that "bodies have piled up over the past week – four Israelis killed in two Palestinian attacks, four Palestinians slain by Israeli troops." She, too, did not distinguish between victims and assailants. Israel, Kershner reported, was "struggling to contain a spasm of violence." But its "resort to live fire, often with lethal consequences, is increasingly opening Israel up to criticism," especially in the *Times*. With evasive vagueness she cited the claim by "some critics" who argued that "some videos" of Israeli police responses have turned Israelis, "in the eyes of some people," from "victims" into "aggressors."[58]

In Jerusalem, where five Israelis were murdered in two dozen knifing attacks within two weeks, Kershner and Rudoren noted that at least twelve "suspects," whose identity was not revealed, had been fatally shot by Israeli security forces and citizens. The Israeli response, but not the Palestinian attacks, "exposed the deep and complex fissures" in the city. The "uptick in aggression," Rudoren wrote, had not begun with "the two dozen attacks that have killed seven Israeli Jews." East Jerusalem, she noted, had been "a hotbed" for more than a year since a "Jewish extremist" kidnapped and killed a sixteen-year-old Palestinian boy. There was no mention of the kidnapping and killing of three Israeli teenagers that triggered that murder.[59]

After Palestinian President Abbas falsely claimed on television that a thirteen-year-old Arab boy "had been executed on a Jerusalem street," a hospital photo showed him recovering, spoon-fed by an Israeli nurse. Kershner evaded the blatant Abbas lie, merely noting that "conflicting versions of reality have always been part of the seemingly intractable Israeli-Palestinian conflict." For many Arab residents of East Jerusalem, Rudoren wrote in exculpation, violence was "a consequence" of their feeling like "neglected stepchildren" who were not "wanted" in the city by Jews.

One week later Rudoren wrote about Palestinian musicians who produced "scores of militaristic, often violent tunes," forming "an intifada soundtrack" that circulated on YouTube and Facebook. Among the titles were "Stab the Zionist and Say God is Great" and "Let the knives stab your enemy," while "Continue the Intifada" urged listeners to "Say hello to being a martyr." Citing criticism that the songs were "weak musically," she and her colleague Rami Nazzal refrained from probing whether they might constitute incitement. The Israeli-Palestinian conflict, Rudoren wrote several days later, "is one of dueling narratives ... fueled by incendiary material swirling around social networks and harsh rhetoric from leaders on both sides." While Israeli Jews see "a spate of random attacks against innocents," Palestinians saw "excessive force not only against attackers but anyone who looks like them."[60] For Rudoren there were no facts to report, only competing narratives.

Following "a spate of stabbings" by Palestinians in the Hebron region, *Times* coverage focused on the grievances of local Arab residents. Noting that twenty Palestinians had been killed during October in demonstrations and "alleged attacks," Hadid and Nazzal relied on the claim of a local Hamas official that "Israeli occupation was driving the uprising." Their only mention of a Jewish resident was a "settler" who killed a "youth" who tried to stab him. Stating that Hebron was "holy to both Muslims and Jews," they misidentified it as the birthplace of the biblical patriarch Abraham; nor did they mention its prominent place in Jewish history millennia before the emergence of Islam.[61]

Reporting from Jerusalem, Kershner and Nazzal described "a looplike dynamic of Israeli-Palestinian violence." Stabbings of Israelis, followed by "swift, often deadly" Israeli responses accompanied by "graphic video footage," inspired "replica Palestinian attacks." Young Palestinian attackers, they implied, were merely passive actors in an impersonal "loop," victims of Israeli aggression rather than assailants who triggered the violence. One week later Kershner barely noted the death of Ezra Schwartz, an eighteen-year-old American yeshiva student murdered while delivering food packages to Israeli soldiers at the Gush Etzion highway junction south of Jerusalem. Her primary focus was an agreement between Israel and the Palestinian Authority to provide high-speed service to cellphone carriers in the West Bank.[62]

With liberal female reporters – Rudoren, Kershner, and Hadid – providing *Times* coverage from Israel, women (especially Arab women) received unprecedented attention. Kershner devoted an article to Israeli police superintendent Luba Samri, who described herself as "a proud Arab with Palestinian roots" who was dedicated to "peace and coexistence." Noting "a changing gender dynamic in Palestinian society," Hadid (sharing a byline with Rami Nazzal) estimated that "women and girls" had accounted for one-fifth of Palestinian attackers since October. And, "for perhaps the first time in a patriarchal society they are acting on their own, without consulting any male authorities." Young women "need only grab a knife from the kitchen to join the fight."[63]

In mid-December Hadid and Nazzal reported that violence had "mostly faded" in Jerusalem, the result of strict Israeli security measures including "sweeping arrests," close monitoring of social media and the destruction of attackers' homes. But Palestinians complained that Israelis were "going too far, taking vindictive steps to remind them who is in charge." Since mid-October, the reporters noted, Palestinians had killed eighteen Israelis and an American citizen while more than 115 Palestinians were killed. To be sure, sixty were "shot dead while attacking Israelis" while the others were "protesters" throwing firebombs and rocks at Israeli soldiers.[64]

By the waning days of 2015 *Times* coverage of Israel was indistinguishable from criticism of Israel, especially from its Jewish columnists and reporters. Roger Cohen lamented that with Yitzhak Rabin's assassination two decades earlier, "Reason ebbed. Rage flowed. The center eroded. Messianic Zionism ... supplanted secular Zionism," making it "impossible for Israel to be a democratic and Jewish state." Isabel Kershner focused on Breaking the Silence, "a leftist organization of combat veterans" determined to expose "the grim reality" of Israel occupation that (according to the headline) "Incites Furor." Its revelations, an Israeli professor suggested, indicated that Israel was "moving away from a liberal democratic model."[65]

Jodi Rudoren completed her term as Jerusalem Bureau Chief with a blistering critique of Israel. Unwilling to assert sovereignty over the West Bank or grant democratic rights to its inhabitants, Israel chose "the undermining of its own democracy," leaving "colonized Palestinians" to suffer from "oppression and humiliation." Messianic Zionism, she concluded, was responsible for making it "impossible for Israel to be a democratic and Jewish state."[66]

Asserting the "myopia" of her critics (while ignoring her own), Rudoren subsequently claimed that her reporting was "more complicated and nuanced" than they acknowledged. Targeting "well financed professional advocates" who focused on "undermining *New York Times'* credibility" (a thinly veiled reference to CAMERA), she dismissed "pro-Israel types" who accused her of "self-hatred, of selling out 'my people.'" Rejecting assertions of a double standard, she defended her focus on understanding Palestinian perpetrators of violence, rather than their Israeli victims, as "more useful." The victims, after all, were "random"; it seemed inconsequential to Rudoren that they were targeted because they were Jews.[67]

Rudoren echoed her *Times* Jewish predecessors in Jerusalem: Joseph Levy, who sought to undermine the Zionist pursuit of Jewish statehood; and Thomas Friedman, who lacerated its Israeli reality. Friedman, Anthony Lewis, and Roger Cohen comprised a trio of liberal Jewish columnists who relentlessly reprimanded Israel for its perceived mistreatment of Palestinians and resistance to Palestinian statehood. A bevy of liberal op-ed contributors, disproportionately Israeli and American Jews, comprised a chorus of disapproval of the Jewish state. Editorials repeatedly criticized one of the world's liveliest democracies. Confronting the disquieting presence of a Jewish state that disregarded assimilationist norms, the Ochs-Sulzberger publishing dynasty still felt compelled to affirm its patriotic American loyalty.

Epilogue: 2016

In January 2016 Peter Baker, who covered the White House during the Obama presidency, replaced Jodi Rudoren as Jerusalem Bureau Chief. But his prolonged absence on book leave left the *Times* with intermittent coverage of Israel. With Diaa Hadid unabashedly enamored of Palestinians, and James Glanz (*Times* science reporter before his appointment as Baghdad bureau chief in 2007) a novice in Israel, only Isabel Kershner provided a semblance of informed coverage – filtered, to be sure, through liberal lenses. Consequently, what the *Times* ignored would become as revealing as what it reported.

Three days into the new year Hadid's admiring exploration of liberal Palestinian culture in Haifa, not the West Bank or Gaza, described a social scene comprising "cool kids": "coifed, pierced and tattooed women and men" who had "unfurled a self-consciously Arab milieu that is secular, feminist and gay friendly." She was charmed by the "liberal Arab renaissance" that she imagined (without a shred of supporting evidence) to be "reminiscent of the city during British rule" – before Jewish statehood quashed "a lively Arab cultural life."[1] She ignored the absence of a similar Arab oasis of tolerance and freedom anywhere in the Middle East but Israel.

Reader complaints "from all sides" prompted a quick response from Public Editor Margaret Sullivan, whose recommendation that *Times* coverage in Israel expand to include "a native Arab speaker on staff who can penetrate Palestinian society with understanding and solid news judgment" had led to Hadid's hiring. (Sullivan did not indicate whether she had also recommended a fluent Hebrew speaker to provide similar penetrating coverage of Israeli society.) She praised Hadid's article, "written vividly" about "a subject worth exploring," while suggesting (too mildly for critics) that it needed "more political and historical information to put it in perspective." Hadid dismissed readers' objections based on "their own political beliefs about Palestinians and Israel."[2] She remained silent about her own political beliefs.

Hadid's defining attribute as a journalist, as it had been before she joined the *Times*, was Palestinian advocacy. One week later she stirred another hornet's nest of criticism when she reported that a cluster of Palestinian families faced eviction from their "tiny, crammed apartments" in the Old City of Jerusalem, where they had lived "for decades." They claimed that the evictions, based on "seemingly arcane violations of their rental agreements, are part of a broader agenda to create Jewish enclaves inside the historic Muslim Quarter." With "Palestinian advocacy groups" as Hadid's primary sources, the predictable culprits were "Jewish organizations reclaiming properties they owned before Israel was established in 1948."[3]

An "Editors' Note" rebuked Hadid, citing her "incomplete description of the legal disputes in several cases" based solely on tenants' accounts. Her article "should have included additional information from court documents or from the landlords." CAMERA, which claimed credit for prompting the Editor's Note, pointedly wondered: "Was Hadid's lack of objectivity unknown to the *Times* when they hired her? Or was it why they hired her?"[4]

Within a two-week period Isabel Kershner contributed a flurry of articles that provided revealing glimpses of her own priorities. Noting that Bedouins comprised "one of the poorest and most neglected sectors of Israeli society," largely "left out" of its technological initiatives, she focused on "an all-Bedouin company that offers expertise on Internet and mobile technologies." Mixing "technology with tradition," it hired Bedouin women and permitted mid-day Muslim prayer. It was, she noted in passing, financed by an Israeli technology investor.[5] Kershner, like Hadid, had little to say about a tolerant Israeli society where gay Palestinians and Bedouin women enjoyed social and economic opportunities unrivaled in the Arab world.

Terrorism by, not against, Jews dominated Kershner's reporting. She visited a West Bank settler outpost where "young extremists" belonging to a "Jewish terrorist network" were responsible for launching "the Revolt" that had recently claimed the lives of a Palestinian child and his parents. One week later, reporting the stabbing of a pregnant Israeli woman shopping in a West Bank store, she noted that it occurred while "a funeral convoy was making its way to Jerusalem." The funeral was for Dafna Meir, mother of four, fatally stabbed in the presence of three of her children at the entrance to their home in the settlement of Otniel. Kershner had not previously reported her hideous murder, which dominated Israeli news. "Much of the world," she could not resist noting (in a repetitive *Times* refrain), "considers the settlements illegal and an obstacle to the establishment of an independent Palestinian state."[6]

Kershner paid close attention four days later to the fatal shooting of a thirteen-year-old Palestinian girl, armed with a knife, who ran at an Israeli security guard at the entrance to a settlement near her home. The shooting, Kershner noted, "came amid a wave of Palestinian stabbings and attempted stabbings, car rammings and gun attacks," mostly by teenagers, that within four months had killed two dozen Israelis and an American student, attacks largely overlooked in her reporting. Two days later a *Times* headline reported "Palestinian Assailants Are Killed" – before mentioning their "Knife Attack on 2 Israeli Women."[7]

Then it was the editors' turn. "Considering the relentless attacks on Israel's very existence," they conceded, "Israelis are understandably on high alert to defend themselves." But moral equivalence intruded: "Palestinians have been victims of assaults and acts of vandalism by Jewish extremists." And "Israel is moving quickly to establish facts on the ground that preclude a Palestinian state, leaving Palestinians increasingly marginalized and despairing." Roger Cohen reiterated his familiar lament: "Nothing can excuse Israel's relentless pursuit of the very occupation that undermines it." UN Secretary General Ban Ki Moon, condemning terrorism "categorically," quickly shifted his op-ed focus to "Palestinian frustration and grievances" over "a harsh, humiliating and endless occupation."[8]

Steven Erlanger contributed a flurry of articles about beleaguered Palestinians and aggressive Israelis. He reported the anguish of a "heartbroken father" who lamented the "lost hope and dignity" that drove his son to stab an Israeli soldier. Zionism, Erlanger asserted, "was never the gentlest of ideologies." The return of Jews to their biblical homeland and renewed Jewish sovereignty, he claimed, "always carried within them the displacement of those already living on the land."[9] Zionism, in his iteration, was little more than cruel conquest.

Times scrutiny of Israel invariably shaded into criticism of Israelis. Thomas Friedman complained that Prime Minister Netanyahu's "lust to hold onto his seat of power is only surpassed by his lack of imagination to find a secure way to separate from Palestinians." Focusing on an imprisoned Palestinian hunger striker (described by the Shin Bet as "a known extremist who praised and incited attacks"), Hadid condemned Israel's practice of administrative detention as "a contentious tactic." Kershner described the plight of an eighty-one-year-old Israeli woman (who had escaped the Nazis as a child) on an El-Al flight, where an ultra-Orthodox man expressed his wish not to be seated next to her. "Many feminists and advocates of religious pluralism in Israel and abroad," Kershner wrote, ask "Why?"[10] Palpable gender discrimination in Palestinian society was not scrutinized in the *Times*.

History, Roger Cohen wrote, demonstrated that "the Jewish state was needed." That, he preened, is "why I am a Zionist." But he quickly segued: "Today, it is Palestinians ... who are dehumanized through Israeli domination, settlement expansion and violence," leaving the West Bank as "the tomb of Israel as a Jewish and democratic state."[11] Palestinians, for Cohen, were the new Jews.

Between October 2015 and April 2016 there were nearly two hundred Palestinian attacks (or attempted attacks) against Israelis. But in the *Times* one Israeli soldier's deadly response to the stabbing of his partner received the most prominent coverage. Kershner noted that "Israeli and Palestinian human rights groups have long accused the military of whitewashing criminal behavior and being incapable of investigating itself."[12] To the contrary: the soldier was charged with manslaughter, tried and found guilty by an Israeli court.

Reporting from the West Bank as the *Times* de facto Palestinian advocate, Diaa Hadid devoted two articles to twelve-year-old Dima, the youngest Palestinian inmate incarcerated by Israel. Impelled by the desire "to kill Jews because 'I wanted to be a martyr,'" Dima explained, she had "stuffed a knife from the family kitchen under her long school shirt" and skipped school hoping to stab a security guard at a nearby settlement. Hadid described her arrest in effusive detail, even mentioning her first menstruation during her interrogation. She was enthralled by accounts of Palestinian girls, sharing an Israeli prison cell, who kept busy tossing baskets, playing shuffle ball, attending classes, and having their hair braided by an Israeli Arab prisoner. Hadid viewed them not as perpetrators of violence but as targets of "a broad Israeli crackdown on young Palestinians." Released from her four-month prison sentence six weeks early to "a hero's welcome" in her hometown of Halhoul, Dima disclosed that she had "intended to kill" the guard and "boasted of not having cried."[13]

In mid-May James Glanz and Rami Nazzal (who supplemented his *Times* reporting with tours for those "looking into the reality of Palestine") provided expansive coverage of the imminent opening of the Palestinian Museum in Birzeit, north of Ramallah. In nearly one thousand words they described the Palestinian struggle "to build political and civic institutions while resisting Israel's occupation"; the plan to feature "artistic interpretations of things like keys and photographs that Palestinians around the world have kept from the homes they fled or were forced from in what is now Israel"; and the imminent "high-profile opening ceremony a few days after the 68th anniversary of what Palestinians call the Nakba, or catastrophe" of Israel's founding. Gazing at the sparkling new building, "rising above a terraced garden with carefully selected trees," a museum sponsor exulted: "It's as if the building is coming out of the womb, the Palestinian Mother Nature."

The museum, Glanz and Nazzal enthused, would "have almost everything: a stunning, contemporary new building; space to celebrate and redefine Palestinian art, history and culture; an outdoor amphitheater; a terraced garden." There was, however, a conspicuous omission: "one thing the museum will not have," they wrote, "is exhibitions." Nonetheless, the museum's chairman explained, Palestinians were "so in need of positive energy" that it seemed "worthwhile to open even an empty building."[14] Glanz and Nazzal, enraptured by the prospect, did not contemplate what an empty museum might reveal about Palestinian history and culture.

The better to criticize Israel, *Times* reporters were drawn to extremist Jewish settlers. Guided by award winning Israeli-American filmmaker Shimon Dotan, whose critical film "The Settlers" had just opened in Israel, Glanz visited Yishuv Hadat, home to "the reclusive and politically explosive" settlers known as "hilltop youth." Comprising "a tiny fraction" of 400,000 Israeli settlers, they nonetheless guided Glanz's narrative of "raw but canny" and "street smart" youths whose "virulent racism, glorification of violence and a desire to replace the modern state of Israel with a full-scale biblical kingdom that would extend as far as Iraq" inspired "acts of defiance and violence to achieve their aims." Focusing on a miniscule number of settler "hippies," Glanz publicized their fantasies.[15] As Jewish "terrorism" had driven *Times* coverage of pre-state Zionism, so settler "terrorism" was embedded in its post-1967 narrative.

The lead editorial that day lacerated Prime Minister Netanyahu's invitation to Avigdor Lieberman to become minister of defense. While serving as foreign minister, Lieberman's "ultranationalist positions on Palestinians, settlements and the Israeli-Palestinian conflict" were "a disaster." His appointment "would make a mockery of any possible Israeli overtures to the Palestinians" that *Times* editors craved. Claiming to know what Netanyahu "seems to think" and "may also believe" about peace prospects, editors accused him of "a risky and cynical gamble" that "bringing peace to his shaky coalition" was, at least for now, sufficient.[16]

The next day Thomas Friedman chimed in, citing "Israel's desire to destroy itself." He attributed it to Netanyahu's "steady elimination of any possibility that Israel will separate itself from the Palestinians in the West Bank." As a result of the prime minister's "dog paddling," Israel "sinks ever deeper into a de facto binational state controlled by Jewish extremists." For "those of us who care about Israel's future," concluded the caring Friedman, "this is a dark hour."[17] In the *Times*, Palestinians had no responsibility for their stateless plight.

One month later Diaa Hadid and Myra Noveck (previously identified by the *Times* Executive Editor as "not a reporter" but a "long-time news assistant") reported the brutal fatal stabbing by a Palestinian "teenager" of a thirteen-year-old Israeli girl asleep in bed in her Kiryat Arba home, adjacent to Hebron. Hallel Yaffa Ariel was stabbed eighteen times. Her room, shared with two younger sisters, was "soaked in blood." Reporting the gruesome murder that reverberated throughout Israel, Hadid and Noveck focused on the murderer, not his victim. They conjectured that he "may have been trying to emulate a young woman from his hometown" who had rammed her car into a bus stop at the Kiryat Arba entrance several days earlier. He had posted poems on his Facebook page praising her bravery, asking "Grave, where are you? Why don't you ask of me?" *Times* reporters (unlike a *Times of Israel* journalist) did not track his previous Facebook posts supporting attacks against Israelis and promising "We will die as martyrs." About Hallel Yaffa Ariel they noted only that she was related to Uri Ariel, "Israel's right-wing housing minister."[18]

Two days later Hadid focused on Israeli restrictions imposed on Palestinians following recent deadly attacks – "the harshest measures" since the kidnapping and murder of three Israeli teenagers in 2014. Many paragraphs along, in passing, she noted that the day after Ariel's grisly murder unidentified "gunmen" fired on an Israeli car near Hebron, killing the father, seriously wounding the mother, and injuring their two children when the car overturned. Updating recent violence, she cited "more than thirty Israelis dead," immediately adding: "More than 210 Palestinians have also been killed, most while carrying out attacks or when thought to be about to do so." Hadid concluded that Palestinian attacks reflected "growing despair by young Palestinians in particular over lives constrained by Israel's decades-long military occupation."[19] The loop of blame was closed: (Israeli) occupation fed (Palestinian) despair that understandably resulted in murder (of Israelis).

With little evident interest in Israeli society, Glanz and Nazzal teamed up to report an incongruous Palestinian hobby. In "the violent East Jerusalem slum of Issawiya," where burning trash filled the air with "an acrid stench," Palestinian families "who struggle to share tiny, cramped homes" were nonetheless raising "exquisitely groomed Arabian horses." The *Times* reporters cited "many Palestinians" who claimed that their affection for horses "helps them to endure life under Israeli occupation."[20] Nazzal's selection of appropriate subjects for *Times* coverage was evident. Even horses fed criticism of Israel.

Two weeks later Hadid reported at length State Department displeasure with Israel "for taking steps to build hundreds of housing units in Jewish neighborhoods in East Jerusalem" that were "corrosive to the cause of peace." The new housing tenders had been publicized by Ir Amim, a left-wing activist group that collaborated with Palestinian organizations in monitoring "settlement activity" in East Jerusalem. Many paragraphs further along was the statement by a senior adviser to the Mayor of Jerusalem that the new tenders were part of a master building plan that had been in place for years.[21] The *Times* did not mention that the planned construction would be in areas that Israel intended to retain under any peace agreement.

Lacking Israeli subjects of interest other than the cruelties of occupation, Hadid (whose blatant Palestinian advocacy infused her reporting) returned to transgendered Palestinians. She focused on "Ms. Abu Hanna," who had grown up as a boy in Nazareth stealing "his mother's makeup and his sister's dresses." After the "scandal" of his new identity riled his family, he fled to Haifa and then to Tel Aviv. Inspired by meeting "a woman who told her that she used to be a man," (s)he grew up to become "Israel's first transgender beauty queen." Eagerly anticipating a forthcoming "global transgender pageant," she planned to represent Israel "because it is a democracy that has given me peace between my soul and my body." But gay and transgender "activists," Hadid noted, described her decision to represent Israel as "pinkwashing": "how Israel markets its gay-friendly reputation to shift focus from military occupation."[22]

With little else of interest to report, and without an on-site Jerusalem Bureau Chief, the *Times* focused mid-summer attention on its favorite Israeli target of opprobrium (except for settlers): Prime Minister Netanyahu. Ruth Margalit, an Israeli writer living in New York, explored "How Benjamin Netanyahu is Crushing Israel's Free Press" as part of "a broader attack ... on Israel's democratic institutions." Proclaiming that "an atmosphere of intimidation has begun to take hold in many, if not most, of the country's newsrooms," she virtually ignored *Haaretz,* long the reliable (and not intimidated) journalistic bastion of the Israeli left.[23]

August 18, 2016 marked 120 years of Ochs-Sulzberger ownership of *The New York Times.* It still lacked a functioning Jerusalem Bureau Chief. (Peter Baker, on book leave until September, was reassigned to Washington four months later to cover the Trump White House.) Its reporting from Israel came from journalists whose evident liberal bias constricted and distorted their coverage (although Palestinian advocate Diaa Hadid had faded away). Persistent editorial criticism of Israel was complemented by an array of columnists and op-ed contributors who (with few exceptions) reiterated deeply embedded *Times* uneasiness with a Jewish state that challenged its liberal credo and assimilationist priorities.

The *Times* continued to embrace the patriotic and liberal values implanted by Adolph Ochs and inherited by his Sulzberger successors. Judaism is a religion, not a national identity. Zionism threatened the allegiance of American Jews to the United States; Israel posed the ominous menace of dual loyalty. Criticism of Zionism and Israel confirmed American patriotism. All the news "fit to print" became news that revealed *New York Times* unease with the idea and eventual reality of a thriving Jewish and democratic state in the biblical homeland of the Jewish people.

Afterword

My first encounter with *The New York Times* came in October 1945. My father showed me the photo of an exultant baseball player greeted by jubilant teammates as he crossed home plate after hitting the grand-slam home run that clinched the pennant for the Detroit Tigers. Hank Greenberg, he proudly revealed, was our cousin. That moment transformed me into a faithful *Times* reader although, to be sure, the sports pages long remained my primary focus.

A resolute creature of habit, I continued to begin each day with *The New York Times* as my breakfast companion. Along the way I realized that the *Times* had a Jewish problem. This book is the result of my quest to understand when and why its proud signature motto, *"All the News That's Fit to Print,"* was distorted by abiding discomfort with Zionism and the restoration of Jewish national sovereignty in the Land of Israel after nearly two thousand years of exile, dispersion, and the horrific tragedy of the Holocaust.

Acknowledgments

It has been a pleasure to work with Academic Studies Press. Its willingness to publish a critical analysis of *The New York Times* is an admirable example of publishing integrity. Senior Editor Alessandra Anzani was attentive to my inquiries and concerns, invariably responding with understanding and reassurance. Editorial Coordinator Eileen Wolfberg paid meticulous attention to my manuscript. I appreciate the careful scrutiny of Copy Editor Ariana Kosareva. Production Editor Kira Nemirovsky, joined by Daria Pokholkova, patiently guided me through the concluding stages of editing and was helpfully responsive to an array of questions and suggestions. Sales & Marketing Coordinator Matthew Charlton was helpful and reassuring.

I am the beneficiary of decades of rewarding friendship with Bill Novak, Daniel Horowitz, Stanley Fisher, Michael Rosenthal, Edward Alexander, Irle Goldman, Martin Abramowitz, and Joel and Sara Leeman, all of whom gave encouragement when it was most needed. Seth Lipsky offered the wisdom of his experience as journalist and editor. I am grateful to Leslie H. Fishel, Jr., Saul Benison and William E. Leuchtenburg who, decades ago, guided my journey to becoming a historian.

Permission to reprint material that originally appeared elsewhere was granted by *The Jewish Advocate, The Jewish Press, American Thinker, New York Observer* and *The Jerusalem Report. The Times of Israel* generously provided a blog site. I am grateful to Ruth Wisse and Neal Kozodoy for guiding portions of Chapter 2 into *Mosaic*. I am especially grateful to *The Algemeiner* and editor Dovid Efune, who welcomed my submissions and enabled me to fulfill my boy-hood ambition to become a journalist.

The staff of The Brooke Astor Reading Room in The New York Public Library facilitated my research in the *New York Times* Archive and granted per-mission to quote from material in its collection. The Israel State Archives gave permission to quote from the Joseph Levy Papers. Wellesley College Professor

Lisa Rodensky and Jessica D. Gaudreau guided my application for a publication stipend, which the College generously provided.

My first visit to Israel, forty-five years ago, was transformative, compelling me to reexamine my life as an assimilated Jew. The following year I lived in Jerusalem, where I was connected in deeply rewarding ways to Jewish history and life and to the Jewish calendar. At Tel Aviv University, where I was Fulbright Professor, Haggai Hurvitz and Rafi Amir were my inspirational teachers. Frequent visits to Israel followed, as did another sabbatical year in Jerusalem a decade later. By then Israel had become an inseparable part of my life. Its historically unprecedented national rebirth remains an embedded source of inspiration.

In my family Jeff, Pamela, Shira and Rebecca, and a rising generation of wonderful grandchildren – Cole, Dalia, Jonah, Sophia and Isabelle - inspire pride, joy and love. Jeff has long been a pillar of support. I am proud that we have followed an identical path as historians and authors, with his *Imperial Boredom* moving toward publication as this book followed a parallel trajectory. Susan stood by me in good times and bad, endured my breakfast commentaries on *The New York Times* and untangled computer mysteries and my mistakes. Pasha reminded me that purring demands attention, even in the middle of a sentence.

JSA
December 2018

Bibliography

The New York Times on-line archive, my primary source, provides access to every published article about Zionism and Israel since 1896. It was supplemented by an array of books about the *Times* written by its own journalists, admirers and – rarely – critics.

The Horatio Alger story of Adolph S. Ochs is recounted in Gerald W. Johnson, *An Honorable Titan* (New York: Greenwood Press, 1946) and Doris Faber, *Printer's Devil to Publisher* (New York: Messner, 1963). Biographies and memoirs by *Times* reporters and editors include: Arthur Krock, *Memoirs: Sixty Years on the Firing Line* (New York: Funk & Wagnalls, 1968); Harrison E. Salisbury, *Without Fear or Favor: The New York Times and its Times* (New York: Times Books, 1980); David K. Shipler, *Arab and Jew: Wounded Spirits in a Promised Land* (New York: Broadway Books, 1986); Thomas L. Friedman, *From Beirut to Jerusalem* (New York: Anchor Books, 1989); Max Frankel, *The Times of My Life and My Life with The Times* (New York: Dell, 1999); Isabel Kershner, *Barrier: The Seam of the Israeli-Palestinian Conflict* (London: Palgrave Macmillan, 2005); Greg Myre and Jennifer Griffin, *This Burning Land: Lessons from the Front Lines of the Transformed Israeli-Palestinian Conflict* (New Jersey: Wiley, 2010).

Other informative books about the *Times* include: Meyer Berger, *The Story of The New York Times, 1851–1951* (New York: Simon and Schuster, 1951); Gay Talese, *The Kingdom and the Power* (New York: World Pub. Co., 1969); Joseph C. Goulden, *Fit to Print: A.M. Rosenthal and His Times* (New Jersey: Stuart, 1988); Edwin Diamond, *Behind the Times: Inside The New York Times* (New York: Villard Books, 1994); Richard F. Shepard, *The Paper's Papers: A Reporter's Journey through the Archives of The New York Times* (New York: Random House,1996); Susan E. Tifft and Alex S. Jones, *The Trust: The Private and Powerful Family Behind The New York Times* (Boston: Little, Brown and Co., 2000). Stephen Karetzky and Peter E. Goldman, *The Media's War against Israel* (New York: Steimatzky, 1986) analyzes, among other subjects, the *Times* "Propaganda War against Israel." Deborah E. Lipstadt, *Beyond Belief: The American Press and the Coming of the Holocaust 1933–1945* (New York: Free Press, 1986) locates the *Times* within the broader journalistic response to, and evasion of, the Holocaust. Laurel Leff's *Buried by The Times: The Holocaust and America's Most Important Newspaper* (New York: Cambridge University Press, 2005) is a meticulous analysis – and withering critique – of *The New York Times* dismissal of the Nazi slaughter of six million Jews as "a relatively unimportant story."

Notes

CHAPTER 1

1. For Adolph S. Ochs's early years, see Doris Faber, *Printer's Devil to Publisher* (New York: Messner, 1963).

2. Oscar S. Straus, *The Origin of Republican Form of Government in the United States of America* (New York: G.P. Putnam's Sons, 1885); Naomi W. Cohen, *Encounter with Emancipation: The German Jews in the United States 1830–1914* (Philadelphia: Jewish Publication Society, 1984), 161–70; Michael A. Meyer, "America: The Reform Movement's Land of Promise," in Jonathan Sarna (ed.), *The American Jewish Experience* (New York: Holmes & Meier, 1997); Hasia R. Diner, *A Time for Gathering: The Second Migration 1820–1880* (Baltimore: Johns Hopkins University Press, 1992).

3. Gerald W. Johnson, *An Honorable Titan: A Biographical Study of Adolph S. Ochs* (New York: Greenwood Press, 1946), 126–27; Meyer Berger, *The Story of The New York Times 1851–1951* (New York: Simon and Schuster, 1951); Doris Faber, *Printer's Devil to Publisher: Adolph S. Ochs of The New York Times* (New York: Messner, 1996); Susan E. Tifft and Alex S. Jones, *The Trust: The Private and Powerful Family Behind the New York Times* (New York: Little Brown, 1999).

4. Theodor Herzl, *The Jewish State* (New York: New York Federation of American Zionists, 1917); reprint ed. New Orleans: Quid Pro Books, 2014.

5. "Topics of the Times," *New York Times*, August 11, 1897.

6. "The Jewish State Idea," *New York Times*, August 15, 1897; "Zionist Congress in Basel," *New York Times*, August 31, 1897.

7. "A Jewish State in Palestine an Impossibility," *New York Times*, September 5, 1897.

8. "The President of the Zionist Congress," *New York Times*, November 14, 1897; "Opposed to Zionism," *New York Times*, May 14, 1899.

9. "The Evil of Zionism," *New York Times*, January 19, 1902.

10. "Zionism Attacked by Rabbi Silverman," *New York Times*, November 24, 1902; "The Solution of the Jewish Problem," *New York Times*, December 8, 1902.

11. Theodor Herzl Obituary, *New York Times*, July 4, 1904.

12. "Opposed to Jewish Colonies," *New York Times*, December 8, 1905.

13. Count Leo Tolstoy, "Zionism," *New York Times*, December 9, 1906.

14. "Zionism's Hope Here," *New York Times*, July 29, 1907.

15. "Mr. Schiff Finds a Flaw in Zionism," *New York Times*, August 23, 1907.

16. "Judaism Defined as a Gift of Birth," *New York Times*, November 11, 1909; "What America Means to Jews," *New York Times*, January 18, 1911.

17. "Roosevelt Speaks to Jewish Delegates," *New York Times*, January 19, 1911.

18. "Schiff Opposes Zionist Movement," *New York Times*, January 8, 1914; "Rabbis Hear Schiff Put America First," *New York Times*, November 10, 1915.

19. Gerald Sorin, *A Time for Building: The Third Migration 1880–1920* (Baltimore: Johns Hopkins University Press, 1992), 206–71.

20. Allon Gal, *Brandeis of Boston* (Cambridge: Harvard University Press, 1980), 124–36; Melvin Urofsky, *Louis D. Brandeis: A Life* (New York: Pantheon Books, 2009).

21. "Duties of American Jews," *New York Times*, January 4, 1915.

22. "A New Palestine if the Allies Win," *New York Times*, March 22, 1915.

23. Tifft and Jones, *The Trust*, 92–93, 95–97.

24. "Brandeis Named for Highest Court," *New York Times*, January 29, 1916.

25. "Mr. Brandeis for the Supreme Court," *New York Times*, January 29, 1916; "Found Turks Eager to Sell Palestine," *New York Times*, May 22, 1916.

26. "Jacob Schiff Quits Jewish Movements," *New York Times*, June 5, 1916; "Mr. Schiff and His Critics," *New York Times*, June 6, 1916.

27. "Sees Zionism's End in Russian Revolt," *New York Times*, April 5, 1917; "Mr. Schiff Not for Zionism," *New York Times*, May 21, 1917.

28. Henry Moskowitz, "Palestine Not a Solution of Jewish Problem," *New York Times*, June 10, 1917.

29. "Britain Favors Zionism," *New York Times*, November 9, 1917.

30. "The Zionists," *New York Times*, November 24, 1917.

31. "Jewish Nation Not Wanted in Palestine," *New York Times*, November 25, 1917; Henry Morgenthau, "The Future of Palestine," *New York Times*, December 12, 1917.

32. Ralph P. Boas, "Program of Zionism Menaces Jewish Unity," *New York Times*, December 16, 1917.

33. "Zionism Already Begun in Palestine," *New York Times*, June 9, 1918.

34. "Americanism vs. Zionism," *New York Times*, December 22, 1918.

35. Julius Kahn, "Why Most American Jews Do Not Favor Zionism," *New York Times Magazine*, February 16, 1919; "31 Prominent Jews Send Letter to President Wilson," *New York Times*, March 5, 1919.

36. "These Piping Times," *New York Times*, April 7, 1920; "10 Killed in Jerusalem," *New York Times*, April 9, 1920; "Not a Jewish State," *New York Times*, February 6, 1921.

37. Edwin L. James, "Scores Are Killed in Palestine Riots," *New York Times*, May 4, 1921. For an account of the riots see Gudrun Kramer, *A History of Palestine* (Princeton: Princeton University Press, 2008), 208–11.

38. "Jews in Palestine Tillers of the Soil," *New York Times*, February 17, 1921; "Business in Palestine," *New York Times*, March 20, 1921; "Palestine Called California of East," *New York Times*, December 25, 1921.

39. John Finley, *A Pilgrim in Palestine* (New York: C. Scribner's Sons, 1919), 47, 233–35, 239–40.

40. "Pope Criticizes Jews," *New York Times*, June 14, 1921; "Zionism a Fallacy, Says Morgenthau," *New York Times*, June 27, 1921; T. Walter Williams, "Palestine is Still a Land of Problems," *New York Times*, July 10, 1921.

41. "Finds Unrest in Palestine," *New York Times*, February 10, 1922; "Palestine and the Zionists," *New York Times*, April 16, 1922; Dr. Joseph Collins, "Paving Way for a New Crusade," *New York Times*, April 30, 1922.

42. "Palestine's Health Needs," *New York Times*, May 7, 1922.

43. Adolph S. Ochs, "The Truth About Palestine," *The American Israelite* (April 27, 1922), 3–8. New York Times Company records. Adolph S. Ochs papers. The New York Public Library. Astor, Lenox, and Tilden Foundations. Reprinted with permission of the New York Public Library.

44. "Quo Vadis?," *New York Times*, May 14, 1922; "A Dangerous Movement," *New York Times*, May 28, 1922.

45. "Palestine's Health Needs," *New York Times*, May 7, 1922; "Relics of Arabs, Byzantines and Romans Found by Americans," *New York Times*, September 3, 1922; Dr. Arthur Ruppin, "Palestine Industries Thriving," *New York Times*, November 26, 1922; "Blindness Waning in Palestine," *New York Times*, December 7, 1922.

46. "Ask Jews to Drop Yiddish and Wine," *New York Times*, January 25, 1923.

47. "Palestine Gaining," *New York Times*, May 1, 1924; "Hebrew University Gets $100,000 Gift," *New York Times*, May 25, 1924; Johnson, *Honorable Titan*, 260–61.

48. "City of David Located," *New York Times*, February 3, 1924; "Tombs of Bible Heroes Are Unearthed," *New York Times*, November 16. 1924.

49. "Balfour Dedicates Hebrew University," *New York Times*, April 2, 1925.

50. "Rabbi Criticizes Hebrew University," *New York Times*, April 13, 1925.

51. T. Walter Williams, "Refuge, Not Nation, Sought by Zionists," *New York Times*, May 2, 1925.

52. "Rabbis Discuss Jews in America," *New York Times*, October 11, 1925.

53. "The Zionist Enterprise," *New York Times*, November 20, 1926; Letter, "Dr. Pritchett's Report," *New York Times*, December 1, 1926; "Pritchett Defends Report," *New York Times*, December 5, 1926.

54. "Fosdick Sees Ruin Ahead for Zionism," *New York Times*, May 25, 1927.

CHAPTER 2

1. Laurel Leff, *Buried by The Times* (New York: Cambridge University Press, 2005), 207; Naomi W. Cohen, *The Year after the Riots* (Detroit: Wayne State University Press, 1988), 75, 99, 192 n. 30.

2. Joseph M. Levy, "Continue Research at Kiriath-Sepher," *New York Times*, June 24, 1928.

3. Levy, "Palestine Outlook Growing Brighter," *New York Times*, June 10, 1928.

4. "Jerusalem Easter a Colorful Affair," *New York Times*, April 29, 1928; Levy, "Palestine Assists Cultural Activity," *New York Times*, May 13, 1928; Levy, "Palestine Schools Cover

All Grades," *New York Times*, August 5, 1928; Levy, "Jews in Palestine Need Farm Credits," *New York Times*, October 7, 1928.

5. "Palestine Awaits New Commissioner," *New York Times*, August 26, 1928.
6. "Wailing Wall Fast Day Proclaimed," *New York Times*, October 19, 1928.
7. Levy, "Jews Seek Redress for Brutal Action," *New York Times*, October 28, 1928.
8. "Palestine Season Brings Prosperity," *New York Times*, January 20, 1929; Levy, "Jerusalem Moves to Abolish Begging," *New York Times*, March 24, 1929.
9. "Arab Mob Invades Wailing Wall Lane," *New York Times*, August 17, 1929; "Funeral Causes Jerusalem Clash," *New York Times*, August 22, 1929.
10. See Jerold S. Auerbach, *Hebron Jews: Memory and Conflict in the Land of Israel* (Lanham, MD: Roman & Littlefield, 2009), 67–72.
11. Levy, "12 Americans Killed by Arabs," *New York Times*, August 26, 1929; "8 Americans Listed in 70 Hebron Dead," *New York Times*, August 27, 1929.
12. Levy, "British Troops Fight Moslems," *New York Times*, August 28, 1929; Levy, "Moslems in Open Revolt," *New York Times*, August 29, 1929.
13. Adolph S. Ochs to Lilian Wald, September 5, 1929, Adolph Ochs MSS. New York Times Company records. Adolph S. Ochs papers. The New York Public Library. Astor, Lenox, and Tilden Foundations. Reprinted with permission of the New York Public Library.
14. "Palestine Snipings Keep Fears Alive," *New York Times*, October 6, 1929; "Sheikh Instigated Hebron Massacre," *New York Times*, October 13, 1929.
15. "Troops Seize Arab Chiefs," *New York Times*, August 30, 1929; "Zionists Divide on Palestine Riots," *New York Times*, September 8, 1929; "Zionism Called Unsound," *New York Times*, September 8, 1929.
16. Levy, "Arabs Call Strike on Rules for Jews," *New York Times*, October 15, 1929.
17. Levy, "Arabs Close Ranks against Zionists," *New York Times*, November 4, 1929.
18. See Arthur A. Goren (ed.), *Dissenter in Zion* (Cambridge, MA: Harvard University Press, 1982), 398–400, 440; Norman Bentwich, *For Zion's Sake: A Biography of Judah L. Magnes* (Philadelphia: Jewish Publication Society of America, 1954); Anthony Cave Brown, *Treason in the Blood* (Boston: Houghton Mifflin, 1994), 56.
19. Brown, *Treason in the Blood*, 56–76, 86–96; H. St. J. B. Philby, *Arabian Days* (London: R. Hale, 1948), 207–9, 235–36.
20. H. St. John Philby to Lord Passfield (November 1, 1929) and Levy to the Grand Mufti (November 3, 1929), Joseph M. Levy Papers 695/4, Israel State Archives, Jerusalem. Reprinted with permission. See also Susan Hattis Rolef, "The Zionists and St. John Philby," 34 *Jewish Social* Studies (April 1972), 110–15.
21. Levy, "Students Hiss Head of Hebrew College," *New York Times*, November 19, 1929; "Dr. Magnes Scored in Jewish Press," *New York Times*, November 22, 1929; Goren, *Dissenter in Zion*, 38–40; Bentwich, *For Zion's Sake*, 178–81.
22. See Cohen, *The Year after the Riots*, 72–75, 100; Rolef, "Zionists and Philby," 111; Goren, *Dissenter in Zion*, 40.

23. "Urges Palestine as World Holyland," *New York Times*, November 21, 1929; Levy, "Suggests Solution for Palestine Ills," *New York Times*, November 24, 1929.

24. Ibid.

25. Ibid.

26. Cohen, *The Year after the Riots*, 100.

27. Levy, "Dr. Magnes Replies to Zionist Critics," *New York Times*, January 7, 1930; "Magnes Defends Arab Conciliation," *New York Times*, January 12, 1930.

28. "Morgenthau Says Zionism Must Fail," *New York Times*, February 10, 1930; "Thomas Mann on Zionism," *New York Times*, April 13, 1930; "Finds Racial Issue in Palestine Acute," *New York Times*, April 15, 1930.

29. "Schulman Assails Zionist Ideal," *New York Times*, August 24, 1930; "The Palestine Report," *New York Times*, October 22, 1930.

30. Levy, "Wall Only Symbol in Palestine Fight," *New York Times*, July 5, 1931.

31. Levy, "Palestine Problem Far From Solution," *New York Times*, July 19, 1931 .

32. Nahum Sokolow, "Palestine Faces the Future," *New York Times*, August 14, 1932.

33. "To the Holy Land Comes Prosperity," *New York Times*, June 4, 1933.

34. Ochs to Levy, June 28, 1933; Ochs MSS, New York Times Company records. Adolph S. Ochs papers. The New York Public Library. Astor, Lenox, and Tilden Foundations. Reprinted with permission.

35. Levy, "German Jews Find Jobs in Palestine," *New York Times*, September 17, 1933; Levy, "Jewish Refugees Loyal to Germany," *New York Times*, October 8, 1933.

36. Levy, "22 Die in Palestine in Riots by Arabs," *New York Times*, October 28, 1933; Levy, "Arabs Riot Again," *New York Times*, October 29, 1933.

37. Levy, "Palestine Tension Laid to Both Sides," *New York Times*, November 12, 1933.

38. "Zionists World Aim Voiced," *New York Times*, January 6, 1933; Walter Duranty, "Odessa Made Over," *New York Times*, April 20, 1933.

39. P.W. Wilson, "Bible Stories Borne Out by Archeology," *New York Times*, January 7, 1934.

40. Levy, "Racial Separation in Palestine Urged," *New York Times*, January 21, 1934.

41. Levy, "11 Killed, 50 Hurt in Palestine Riots," *New York Times*, April 20, 1936; "Deaths Rise to 20 in Palestine Riots," *New York Times*, April 21, 1936; "Tension is Still High," *New York Times*, April 23, 1936.

42. Levy, "Arabs and Jews Fight in Palestine," *New York Times*, May 22, 1936; Levy, "Arab Revolt," *New York Times*, May 27, 1936; Levy, "Palestine Unrest," *New York Times*, May 28, 1936; Levy, "5 Die in Palestine," *New York Times*, May 29, 1936; Levy, "Arabs Get Threat of Mass Penalties," *New York Times*, May 31, 1936.

43. Levy, "Family Feud Seen behind Arab Riots," *New York Times*, June 14, 1936.

44. Levy, "Arab Youths Plan to Widen Killings," *New York Times*, June 5, 1936; Levy, "Family Feud Seen behind Arab Riots," *New York Times*, June 14, 1936; Levy, "Palestine Gripped by a Reign of Fear," *New York Times*, June 28, 1938; Levy, "Palestine Terror Makes All Unsafe," *New York Times*, August 16, 1936.

45. Levy, "Peace Remote in Palestine," *New York Times*, September 8, 1936.

46. "Palestine Inquiry Proves Difficult," *New York Times*, November 15, 1936.
47. "Arab Case is Held Hurt in Palestine," *New York Times*, January 24, 1937.
48. "Partition of Palestine," *New York Times*, July 8, 1937.
49. "Palestine Peace Seen," *New York Times*, July 18, 1937.
50. "Vignettes of Peace in Troubled Palestine," *New York Times*, August 15, 1937.
51. Levy, "Palestine Outlook Continues Gloomy," *New York Times*, July 24, 1938; Levy, "Revenge of Arabs Alarms Palestine," *New York Times*, July 27, 1938.
52. "Palestine Arabs Repeat Demands," *New York Times*, September 12, 1937.
53. Levy, "Palestine Outlook Continues Gloomy," *New York Times*, July 24, 1938; Levy, "Dissension Injures Jews," *New York Times*, August 11, 1938; Levy, "Arabs in Palestine Talk of Holy War," *New York Times*, August 22, 1938.
54. Levy, "Ibn Saud Appeals to U.S.," *New York Times*, January 5, 1939; Levy, "Pessimism Grips Palestine," *New York Times*, March 12, 1939; Levy, "Jews in Palestine Hope Despite Plan," *New York Times*, March 19, 1939.
55. Levy, "Britain is Warned by Zionist Leader," *New York Times*, May 14, 1939.
56. Levy, "Pessimism Grips Palestine," *New York Times*, March 12, 1939; Leff, *Buried by the Times*, 207.

CHAPTER 3

1. "Inner Strife Rends Arabs in Palestine," *New York Times*, September 29, 1930; "The Week in Europe; the Palestine Policy," *New York Times*, October 26, 1930.
2. "Nazis to Hold 5,000 in Camp at Dachau," *New York Times*, April 5, 1933; "Odessa Made Over on Soviet Model," *New York Times*, April 30, 1933; "Palestine Council Fought," *New York Times*, December 29, 1935.
3. Shepard, *The Paper's Papers*, 301.
4. Ibid., 75.
5. Leff, *Buried by The Times*, 27.
6. Deborah Lipstadt, *Beyond Belief: The American Press and the Coming of the Holocaust 1933–1945* (New York: Free Press, 1986), 170, 171n.
7. Leff, *Buried by The Times*, 24, 31, 42.
8. Ibid., 31.
9. "Palestine Fights Fatal," *New York Times*, June 8, 1939.
10. Leff, *Buried by The Times*, 195–96; "The Struma Disaster," *New York Times*, March 13, 1942.
11. Leff, *Buried by The Times*, 65, 201.
12. Ibid., 292–93.
13. "Arab-Jewish Deal in Palestine Urged," *New York Times*, June 14, 1942; Leff, *Buried by The Times*, 2–3, 12–16.
14. "Allies Are Urged to Execute Nazis," *New York Times*, July 2, 1942; David Wyman, *The Abandonment of the Jews: America and the Holocaust* (New York, Pantheon Books: 1984),

95; Richard Breitman and Allan J. Lichtman, *FDR and the Jews* (Cambridge, MA: Harvard University Press, 2013), 244.

15. "Battle is Reported in Warsaw's Ghetto," *New York Times*, May 7, 1943; "All Warsaw Jews Held 'Liquidated'," *New York Times*, May 15, 1943; "Pole's Suicide Note," *New York Times*, June 4, 1943; "Nazis Speed Massacre of Jews," *New York Times*, June 5, 1943; Leff, *Buried by The Times*, 172–74, 220–21.

16. "The White Paper," *New York Times*, February 12, 1944.

17. Sulzberger to Jacob Billikopf, January 8, 1944; Sulzberger to Mrs. Ben Marks, January 31, 1944, New York Times Company records. Arthur Hays Sulzberger papers. The New York Public Library. Astor, Lenox, and Tilden Foundations. Reprinted with permission.

18. "Nazi Death Factory Shocks Germans," *New York Times*, April 18, 1945.

19. Max Frankel, "150th Anniversary: 1851–2001: Turning Away From the Holocaust," *International New York Times*, November 14, 2001.

20. Leff, *Buried by The Times*, 196–99; for a condensed account, see Leff, "A Tragic 'Fight in the Family': The New York Times, Reform Judaism and the Holocaust," *American Jewish History*, 88 (March 2000), 3–51.

21. "Arab-Jewish Deal in Palestine Urged," *New York Times*, June 14, 1942; Judah Magnes, "Palestine Moves," *New York Times*, November 1, 1942; "Asks Evaluation of British Effort," *New York Times*, November 6, 1942; Leff, *Buried by The Times*, 198.

22. Leff, *Buried by The Times*, 201.

23. "Battle is Reported in Warsaw's Ghetto," *New York Times*, May 7, 1943; "Pole's Suicide Note Pleads for Jew," *New York Times*, June 4, 1943.

24. Lipstadt, *Beyond Belief*, 219–20; "British May Sift Palestine Turmoil," *New York Times*, November 8, 1944; "Old Rivalry Fans Palestine Strife," *New York Times*, November 26, 1944.

25. Anne O'Hare McCormick, "American Boys Find Tel-Aviv Like a Home Town," *New York Times*, January 6, 1945; McCormick, "Palestine Learns That Big Powers Rule World," *New York Times*, January 8, 1945; McCormick, "Three Conflicting Elements in Palestine," *New York Times*, January 10, 1945; McCormick, "Events Increase Pressure for Jewish State in Palestine," *New York Times*, January 13, 1945; McCormick, "Palestine Refugees Upset Appeal of Reason," *New York Times*, January 15, 1945; McCormick, "Palestine Settlement Must Come From Outside," *New York Times*, January 22, 1945; McCormick, "New Currents Stir the World of Genesis," *New York Times*, January 29, 1945.

26. Judah Magnes letter, "Compromise for Palestine," *New York Times*, February 17, 1945.

27. Sulzberger to Horace Kallen, January 16, 1945, New York Times Company records. Arthur Hays Sulzberger papers. The New York Public Library. Astor, Lenox, and Tilden Foundations. Reprinted with permission. Leff, *Buried by The Times*, 322, 324.

28. "Palestine's and Europe's Jews," *New York Times*, November 14, 1945.

29. Clifton Daniel, "Jewish Majority in Palestine Asked," *New York Times*, March 9, 1946; Daniel, "Zionist Says Jews Can Handle Arabs," *New York Times*, March 12, 1946; "Palestine Group Approves Magnes," *New York Times*, March 15, 1946; Daniel, "Inquiry Hopes Fade on Palestine Issue," *New York Times*, March 17, 1946.

30. Julian Meltzer, "Life Goes On in Palestine," *New York Times*, June 23, 1946; Daniel, "Britain Launches Army Drive," *New York Times*, June 30, 1946; "Largest Mass Arrest," *New York Times*, July 1, 1946.

31. Meltzer, "Jerusalem Bomb Kills 41," *New York Times*, July 23, 1946; Daniel, "Zionist Terrorists Say They Set Bomb," *New York Times*, July 24, 1946.

32. McCormick, "The Crisis of Palestinian Leadership," *New York Times*, July 24, 1946.

33. Sulzberger Address, 80th anniversary of Congregation Mizpah, Chattanooga, October 26, 1946. New York Times Company records. Arthur Hays Sulzberger papers. The New York Public Library. Astor, Lenox, and Tilden Foundations. Reprinted with permission.

34. Gene Currivan, "Palestine Swept by Terror Revival," *New York Times*, January 3, 1947; S. J. Gordon, "Twofold Danger Confronts the British," *New York Times*, January 5, 1947; Meltzer, "Palestine Now Sees a Climactic Struggle," *New York Times*, February 2, 1947; Meltzer, "Formula for Troubled Palestine," *New York Times*, February 16, 1947.

35. "The People Who Live between Two Closed Doors," *New York Times*, February 1, 1947.

36. Gertrude Samuels, "Children Who Have Known No Childhood," *New York Times*, March 9, 1947; "Palestine Powderkeg," *New York Times*, March 9, 1947.

37. Daniel, "Agency Represents Most of the Jews in Palestine," *New York Times*, May 11, 1947.

38. Daniel, "Zionists Show U.N. A Desert in Bloom," *New York Times*, June 27, 1947.

39. "U.N. Is Asked to Bar Jewish State," *New York Times*, June 9, 1947.

40. Currivan, "3 Slain on Zionist Vessel," *New York Times*, July 18, 1947.

41. "Exodus 1947," *New York Times*, July 20, 1947; Currivan, "Jews Shipped Back to Port in France," *New York Times*, July 21, 1947; "Exodus Refugees Firm," *New York Times*, August 18, 1947; Editorial, "Odyssey of the Exodus," *New York Times*, September 11, 1947.

42. "The Alternatives to a U.N. Solution," *New York Times*, October 13, 1947.

43. Currivan, "Irgun Threatens War on Haganah," *New York Times*, October 27, 1947; Currivan, "Palestine Groups Fight 'Civil War,'" *New York Times*, November 2, 1947.

44. "Ben-Gurion Urges One Zionist Force," *New York Times*, October 17, 1947; "Irgun Threatens War on Haganah," *New York Times*, October 24, 1947.

45. Editorial, "The Partition of Palestine," *New York Times*, November 30, 1947; "British Soldiers Join Jews for Celebration," *New York Times*, December 1, 1947.

46. "Palestine," *New York Times*, November 30, 1947.

47. Samuel Pope Brewer, "Arabs and Jews Arming for a Palestine Test," *New York Times*, December 14, 1947.

48. "World Challenge Stressed to Jews," *New York Times*, January 18, 1948; William M. Blair, "Warns Jews Here on One Citizenship," *New York Times*, January 19, 1948;

49. Joseph M. Proskauer letter, *New York Times*, January 21, 1948; Lessing Rosenwald letter, *New York Times*, January 29, 1948.

50. "Red 'Fifth Column' for Palestine Feared," *New York Times*, January 1, 1948.

51. Brewer, "Palestine Fighting Grows," *New York Times*, January 4, 1948; Brewer, "Huge Job of Building a Small State," *New York Times*, January 11, 1948; Brewer, "Jerusalem Diary," *New York Times*, February 1, 1948.

52. "Truce Call Hailed by Magnes Group," *New York Times*, March 29, 1948; "Rosenwald Urges Trusteeship Plan," *New York Times*, April 8, 1948.
53. McCormick, "As the Days Tick Off in Palestine," *New York Times*, May 1, 1948.
54. McCormick, "Recognizing the Realities in the New Palestine," *New York Times*, May 15, 1948.
55. "War in Palestine," *New York Times*, May 2, 1948; "Palestine and Destiny," *New York Times*, May 10, 1948.
56. Dana Adams Schmidt, "All New State's Energy is Dedicated to Defense," *New York Times*, May 16, 1948.
57. "U.N. Palestine Vote Held 'Sordid Story,'" *New York Times*, May 15, 1948; Schmidt, "The Two Worlds of Palestine," *New York Times*, May 24, 1948; Tifft and Jones, *The Trust*, 23.
58. Currivan, "City with a Mission," *New York Times*, May 23, 1948.
59. Currivan, "'B.G.', Key Man of Israel," *New York Times*, June 6, 1948.
60. Currivan, "Besieged 5 Months," *New York Times*, May 29, 1948; Currivan, "Life Goes On in Israel," *New York Times*, May 30, 1948.
61. See Ari Shavit, *My Promised Land: The Triumph and Tragedy of Israel* (New York: Spiegel & Grau, 2013), Ch. 5; Leon Wieseltier, "The State of Israel," *New York Times*, November 21, 2013. For a sharp critique see Rick Richman, "Lydda 1948: The Dog That Didn't Bark," *Commentary* (December 31, 2014).
62. Currivan, "City with a Mission," *New York Times*, May 23, 1948.
63. "ll-Day Fight Over," *New York Times*, May 29, 1948.
64. "Dr. Judah Magnes Dead at Age of 71," *New York Times*, October 28, 1948.
65. Sidney Gruson, "50,000 Arabs Live in Peace in Israel," *New York Times*, October 26, 1948; Gruson, "State of Israel," *New York Times*, November 7, 1948.

CHAPTER 4

1. Anne O'Hare McCormick, "There is No Present Tense in Israel," *New York Times*, February 13, 1949.
2. Editorial, "Spring in Palestine," *New York Times*, February 14, 1949.
3. "4,000 Yemen Jews Flown to Israel," *New York Times*, March 5, 1949.
4. Emanuel R. Freedman to Currivan, May 16, 1949. New York Times Company records. Foreign Desk records. The New York Public Library. Astor, Lenox, and Tilden Foundations. Reprinted with permission.
5. Gene Currivan, "Bitter Immigrants in Israel," *New York Times*, July 18, 1949.
6. Editorial, "Birthday in Israel," *New York Times*, May 4, 1949.
7. Editorial, "Peace in Palestine," *New York Times*, July 22, 1949.
8. Gertrude Samuels, "From Munich to Haifa," *New York Times Magazine*, August 21, 1949.
9. Gertrude Samuels, "The Three Great Challenges to Israel," *New York Times Magazine*, October 16, 1949.

10. Gertrude Samuels, "Report from Dafne in Galilee," *New York Times Magazine*, December 18, 1949.

11. "Israel Upbraided for 'Unity' Claims," *New York Times*, March 2, 1950.

12. Currivan, "Joyous Passover Planned in Israel," *New York Times*, April 1, 1950; Editorial, "Israel's Second Birthday," April 23, 1950.

13. Currivan, "Iraqi Jews Flown by Lift to Israel," *New York Times*, May 22, 1950; Gruson, "Israel to Maintain Immigration Rate," *New York Times*, December 20, 1950.

14. Irving Spiegel, "Leader Stresses Israeli Identity," *New York Times*, September 10, 1950; "M" to Maurice Spector, March 27, 1951. New York Times Company records. Foreign Desk records. The New York Public Library. Astor, Lenox, and Tilden Foundations. Reprinted with permission.

15. Spiegel, "Israeli 'Influence' in U.S. Is Opposed," *New York Times*, April 14, 1951; Spiegel, "Judaism Council Rebukes Zionists," *New York Times*, April 16, 1951.

16. Flora Lewis, "Ben-Gurion: Man on a Mountain Top," *New York Times Magazine*, May 6, 1951.

17. Lessing Rosenwald Letter, *New York Times*, June 6, 1951; Lessing Rosenwald Letter, *New York Times*, December 21, 1951.

18. Editorial, "Treaty with Israel," *New York Times*, August 25, 1951; "Israel Needs Help," *New York Times*, September 20, 1951; Editorial, "The Arab Refugees," *New York Times*, December 20, 1951.

19. Dana Adams Schmidt, "Israel Deeply Stirred by German Talks Issue," *New York Times*, January 13, 1952.

20. Editorial, "The Arab Refugees," *New York Times*, January 22, 1952.

21. Thomas Sugrue, "Individual – and Universal," *New York Times*, January 27, 1952; Spiegel, "Foe Scores Zionism as Totalitarianism," *New York Times*, April 4, 1952.

22. Spiegel, "Zionists Accused of Swaying Youth," *New York Times*, April 5, 1952; Spiegel, "Council Attacks 'Jewish Vote' Idea," *New York Times*, April 7, 1952.

23. "Joyous Israelis Ignore Troubles to Mark 4th Independence Day," *New York Times*, April 30, 1952; Editorial, "Israel's Fourth," *New York Times*, April 30, 1952.

24. Dana Adams Schmidt, "Israel's Stress and Strain Show Up," *New York Times*, May 4, 1952.

25. Schmidt, "Israel Uses the Bible as a 'Divining Rod,'" *New York Times Magazine*, September 21, 1952.

26. Editorial, "The Arab Refugees," *New York Times*, November 9, 1952; Schmidt, "Israel Marks Progress but Has Big Problems," *New York Times*, November 16, 1952.

27. Spiegel, "For a Thirsty Land," *New York Times*, January 1, 1953; Schmidt, "Pioneers in Negev Imitate Ancients," *New York Times*, April 25, 1953.

28. Schmidt, "Break with Russians Adds to Israel's Woes," *New York Times*, February 15, 1953.

29. Editorial, "An Appeal for Human Rights," *New York Times*, February 17, 1953.

30. Editorial, "Israel's Fifth," *New York Times*, April 21, 1953.

31. Spiegel, "Judaism Council Assails Zionists," *New York Times*, May 8, 1953; Spiegel, "'Luring' of Youths to Israel Opposed," *New York Times*, May 9, 1953; Spiegel, "Zionists' Concepts Called Dangerous," *New York Times*, May 11, 1953.

32. Kenneth Love, "Arabs' Case vs. Israel," *New York Times*, October 25, 1953.

33. Editorial, "Israel vs. Jordan," *New York Times*, November 20, 1953.

34. McCormick, "A Dispute That Grows Worse with Time," *New York Times*, November 21, 1953; Editorial, "Censure is Not Enough," *New York Times*, November 26, 1953.

35. Gertrude Samuels, "Refugees to Israel, Five Years Later," *New York Times Magazine*, October 3, 1954; Samuels, "Israel: Five Years of Change," *New York Times*, November 7, 1954.

36. Brilliant, "Israel Cuts Pace of Westernizing," *New York Times*, March 2, 1955.

37. Editorial, "Arms to Egypt," *New York Times*, September 1, 1954; Harry Gilroy, "Israel is Adjusting Policies," *New York Times*, September 5, 1954; "Israel is Worried by Suez Agreement," *New York Times*, October 20, 1954; "U.S. Offers Arabs Refugee Solution," *New York Times*, November 25, 1954; C.L. Sulzberger, "Human Misery and Political Ferment in the Levant," *New York Times*, January 31, 1955.

38. Spiegel, "Judaism Council Assails Zionists," *New York Times*, March 18, 1955; Spiegel, "Special Interest for Jews Decried," *New York Times*, March 20, 1955.

39. Love, "Israeli Settlers Grow with Town," *New York Times*, August 28, 1955.

40. Sulzberger, "Refugees and Peace in Divided Palestine," *New York Times*, October 10, 1955.

41. Sulzberger, "Problems of Creating an Israeli Nation," *New York Times*, October 12, 1955; Sulzberger, "The Advance of Disaster in the Middle East," *New York Times*, October 26, 1955.

42. Editorial, "Refugees But No Refuge," *New York Times*, December 2, 1955.

43. "Zionist Appeals in U.S. Deplored," *New York Times*, December 4, 1955.

44. Editorial, "Reproof to Israel," *New York Times*, January 20, 1956.

45. Harry Gilroy, "Dam Brings Lake to Judea's Hills," *New York Times*, February 5, 1956; Osgood Caruthers, "Chance for Israel-Arab Peace," *New York Times*, February 12, 1956; James G. McDonald letter, "Toward Middle East Peace," *New York Times*, March 4, 1956.

46. "Scholar with a Mission," *New York Times*, March 7, 1956.

47. Homer Bigart, "War in the Middle East," *New York Times*, April 1, 1956; Bigart, "In Israel: Tension on Gaza Strip," *New York Times*, April 15, 1956.

48. Editorial, "The Truth About Palestine," *New York Times*, June 2, 1956.

49. Lawrence E. Davies, "Ex-Officer Quits Judaism's Council," *New York Times*, July 22, 1956; Editorial, "'National' But Irrational," *New York Times*, August 7, 1956.

50. Editorial, "The Israeli Raids," *New York Times*, September 27, 1956.

51. Joseph D. Heff, "Israel Sticks to Reprisal Raids," *New York Times*, September 30, 1956; Moshe Brilliant, "Ben-Gurion at 70 – Audacious as Ever," *New York Times Magazine*, October 14, 1956.

52. Editorial, "Israel and Egypt," *New York Times*, October 20, 1956.

53. Schmidt, "U.S.-Israeli Ties Badly Strained," *New York Times*, October 31, 1956.

54. Editorial, "Crisis in the Middle East," *New York Times*, October 31, 1956; Editorial, "War in the Middle East," *New York Times*, November 1, 1956.

55. Editorial, "Suez Balance Sheet," *New York Times*, November 9, 1956.

56. C.L. Sulzberger, "Fate – As Seen by Premier Ben-Gurion," *New York Times*, November 14, 1956.

57. Arthur Krock, "Leadership of a World We Never Made," *New York Times*, November 15, 1956.

58. Brilliant, "Israelis Feel Stronger Despite Loss of Friends," *New York Times*, November 25, 1956.

59. Editorial, "The Palestine Refugees," *New York Times*, January 4, 1957. The most reliable estimate of Palestinian refugee numbers, provided in the careful scholarship of Efraim Karsh, *Palestine Betrayed* (New Haven: Yale University Press, 2010), is 583,000–609,000.

60. "Zionists' Foe Pays A Visit to Israel," *New York Times*, January 21, 1957.

61. Editorial, "Israel's Position," *New York Times*, February 9, 1957; Editorial, "Warning on Sanctions," *New York Times*, February 12, 1957.

62. Editorial, "Aqaba and Gaza," *New York Times*, February 19, 1957.

63. James Reston, "Some Chickens Coming Home to Roost," *New York Times*, February 21, 1957; Editorial, "The Crux of the Matter," *New York Times*, February 26, 1957; "Mideast Contradictions," *New York Times*, April 19, 1957; Editorial, "Mideastern Munich," *New York Times*, April 27, 1957.

64. Spiegel, "Israel is Victory of Zionists' Hopes," *New York Times*, April 2, 1957.

65. Ibid.

66. "Judaism Leader Here Charges Zionism Prevents an Objective View of Mideast," *New York Times*, April 28, 1957; Richard F. Shepard, *The Paper's Papers* (New York: Random House, 1996), 305–6.

67. Max Frankel, *The Times of My Life and My Life with the Times* (New York: Dell, 1999), 44, 401; Edwin Diamond, *Behind the Times: Inside The New York Times* (Chicago: University of Chicago Press, 1995), 44.

CHAPTER 5

1. Lawrence Fellows, "Israel Seizes Nazi Chief," *New York Times*, May 24, 1960; "Eichmann's Trial Worries Israelis," *New York Times*, May 29, 1960; Editorial, "The Eichmann Trial," *New York Times*, June 8, 1960.

2. Editorial, "The Eichmann Trial," *New York Times*, June 8, 1960.

3. Fellows, "Israel Determined to Try Gestapo Man," *New York Times*, June 12, 1960.

4. David Ben-Gurion, "The Eichmann Case as Seen by Ben-Gurion," *New York Times Magazine*, December 18, 1960.

5. Sulzberger to Turner Catledge, April 3, 1961, New York Times Company records. Arthur Hays Sulzberger papers. The New York Public Library. Astor, Lenox, and Tilden Foundations. Reprinted with permission. William G. Weart, "Zionism Attacked on Eichmann Case," *New York Times*, May 8, 1961.

6. Homer Bigart, "Warsaw Saga Stirs Trial of Eichmann," *New York Times*, May 4, 1961; Bigart, "Eichmann Takes Stand at Trial," *New York Times*, June 21, 1961; Fellows, "Eichmann Trial Seen by Israelis," *New York Times*, June 25, 1961; Bigart, "Israelis Stress Eichmann Image," *New York Times*, July 9, 1961; Fellows, "Eichmann Trial Assessed," *New York Times*, July 23, 1961.

7. Arthur Hays Sulzberger, November 8, 1961, New York Times Company records. Arthur Hays Sulzberger papers. The New York Public Library. Astor, Lenox, and Tilden Foundations. Reprinted with permission.

8. Editorial, "Holding the Peace Line," *New York Times*, May 19, 1967; "Arabs and Israel," *New York Times*, May 21, 1967.

9. "Rumbling in Mideast," *New York Times*, May 24, 1967; "Foreign Affairs: The Edge of Infinity," *New York Times*, May 24, 1967.

10. Terence Smith, "Reserve Call-Up Costly to Israel," *New York Times*, May 29, 1967; Smith, "On One Side, Syria, Sea on the Other," *New York Times*, May 30, 1967; Smith, "Israelis in Jerusalem," *New York Times*, June 5, 1967.

11. Tom Wicker, "Lethal Legalisms in the Middle East," *New York Times*, May 30, 1967; C.L. Sulzberger, "The Deadliest Game," *New York Times*, May 31, 1967.

12. James Reston, "A War's First Hours," *New York Times*, June 6, 1967.

13. Reston, "Israelis Think the War Has Been Won," *New York Times*, June 7, 1967.

14. Smith, "Israelis Weep and Pray beside the Wailing Wall," *New York Times*, June 8, 1967.

15. Anthony Lewis, "British Bid Israel Check Her Sweep," *New York Times*, June 8, 1967.

16. Seth S. King "Along with Terrain, Israel Gets Burden of 900,000 Refugees," *New York Times*, June 8, 1967.

17. Reston, "Tel Aviv: The Israeli Strategy," *New York Times*, June 9, 1967; Sidney Gruson, "For the Israelis There Are Some Border Problems," *New York Times*, June 9, 1967.

18. Editorial, "Bind Up the Wounds," *New York Times*, June 10, 1967.

19. "Mideast Upheaval," *New York Times*, June 11, 1967.

20. Editorial, "The Holy City," *New York Times*, June 13, 1967.

21. Sulzberger, "The Bible as Policy," *New York Times*, June 16, 1967; "Israel's Opportunity," *New York Times*, June 19, 1967.

22. Editorial, "Positive Notes at Khartoum," *New York Times*, September 2, 1967; Palestine National Charter, Article 20.

23. James Feron, "Occupation Frictions," *New York Times*, August 10, 1967.

24. Feron, "Hebron Settlers May Stay in Town," *New York Times*, May 16, 1968.

25. Amnon Rubenstein, "'Damn Everybody' Sums Up the Angry Mood of Israel," *New York Times Magazine*, February 9, 1969.

26. David Binder, "9 Israelis on Olympic Team Killed," *New York Times*, September 6, 1972; "Murder in Munich," *New York Times*, September 6, 1972.

27. Editorial, "Aftermath of Munich," *New York Times*, September 8, 1972.

28. "Jerusalem's Report," *New York Times*, October 7, 1973; Editorial, "Mideast Explodes," *New York Times*, October 7, 1973; Editorial, "Peace Shattered," *New York Times*, October 8, 1973.

29. Charles Mohr, "Israel Confident But Also Somber," *New York Times*, October 9, 1973; "Suicidal Course," *New York Times*, October 9, 1973.

30. Editorial, "From Bad to Worse . . ." *New York Times*, October 10, 1973.

31. Edward W. Said, "Arab and Jew: 'Each is the Other,'" *New York Times*, October 14, 1973.

32. Terence Smith, "Little Israeli Hope of Peace Pact," *New York Times*, October 15, 1973; Sol Stern, "Mideast War as Seen through Eyes of 2 Israeli Reservists," *New York Times*, October 18, 1973; Reston, "The Hidden Compromise," *New York Times*, October 19, 1973; Ayman el-Amir, "In Consideration of the Arab View," *New York Times*, October 19, 1973.

33. Amnon Rubenstein, "The Israelis: No More Doves," *New York Times Magazine*, October 21, 1973.

34. Charles Mohr, "Israelis Tighten Grip," *New York Times*, October 24, 1973.

35. Smith, "Many Israelis Feel It's Far from Over," *New York Times*, October 29, 1973; Editorial, "Start Talking," *New York Times*, October 30, 1973.

36. Paul Hofmann, "The U.N. Vote," *New York Times*, November 11, 1973; Lewis, "The U.N. and Zionism," *New York Times*, November 13, 1973.

37. A.M. El-Messiri, "Zionism and Racism," *New York Times*, November 13, 1975.

38. I.F. Stone, "Zionism and Peace," *New York Times*, November 23, 1975; Nathan Glazer, "Zionism Examined," *New York Times*, December 13, 1975.

39. Editorial, "Israel's Dilemma," *New York Times*, May 11, 1976.

40. "Hostages Freed as Israelis Raid Uganda Airport," *New York Times*, July 4, 1976; "Key to Raid's Success," *New York Times*, July 5, 1976; "A Legend is Born," *New York Times*, July 6, 1976.

41. Smith, "Israel's Dilemma," *New York Times*, May 11, 1976; Smith, "Hijacking Rescue Lifts Israeli Spirit," *New York Times*, July 7, 1976.

42. William Farrell, "A Day in the Life of Menachem Begin," *New York Times*, June 14, 1977.

43. Farrell, "The New Face of Israel," *New York Times*, July 17, 1977.

44. Marvin Kalb, "A Journey through a Land of Doubts," *New York Times Magazine*, July 17, 1977.

45. William Safire, "The Authentics," *New York Times*, August 4, 1977.

46. Beverly Bar-Illan, "Appointment in Samaria," *New York Times*, September 3, 1977.

47. Max Frankel, *The Times of My Life*, 404–7.

48. Bernard Gwertzman, "Carter Voices Worry to Israel," *New York Times*, January 30, 1978; Smith, "Israel is Said to Have Altered Dayan Pledge," *New York Times*, January 31, 1978; Farrell, "3 Israeli Outposts," *New York Times*, February 1, 1978; Farrell, "How Much More 'Give' Can Begin Afford?," *New York Times*, February 5, 1978.

49. Charles Mohr, "Behind Israeli Settlements Rift," *New York Times*, February 17, 1978; "Israelis Are Debating the Meaning of Security," *New York Times*, February 26, 1978.

50. Editorial, "Israel's Unsettling Settlements," *New York Times*, July 28, 1977; Editorial, "The West Bank by Any Other Name," *New York Times*, September 14, 1977; Editorial, "Unsettling the West Bank," *New York Times*, October 15, 1977; "Israeli Rights and Wrongs," *New York Times*, November 1, 1977.

51. Farrell, "Allon Says Begin ... Perils Peace Effort," *New York Times*, March 9, 1978.

52. "Thousands in Israel Rally to Back Begin," *New York Times*, April 16, 1978.

53. Editorial, "How Big is Israel?" *New York Times*, March 7, 1978; Leon Wieseltier, "Auschwitz and Peace," *New York Times*, March 10, 1978.

54. Brilliant, "Fatah Admits Raid," *New York Times*, March 12, 1978.

55. Tom Wicker, "A Message for Mr. Begin," *New York Times*, March 12, 1978; Editorial, "To Break the Cycle of Hate," *New York Times*, March 14, 1978; Editorial, "Israel Poses A Test," March 16, 1978; Rosenthal to Robert B. Semple, March 17, 1978, A.M. Rosenthal papers. Manuscripts and Archives. The New York Public Library. Astor, Lenox, and Tilden Foundations. Reprinted with permission.

56. Cynthia Ozick, "Letter to a Palestinian Military Spokesman," *New York Times*, March 16, 1978.

57. Sabah Kabbani, "Mr. Carter, the Palestinians and Israel," *New York Times*, March 17, 1978; Anwar el-Sadat, "Egypt's Efforts to Promote Peace," *New York Times*, March 21, 1978.

58. Lewis, "Americans and Israel," *New York Times*, March 27, 1978.

59. Lewis, "The Hour of Grace," *New York Times*, April 3, 1978.

60. Editorial, "Mr. Begin's Jewish Critics," *New York Times*, April 23, 1978.

61. James Farrell, "The Furor Surrounding Begin," *New York Times*, July 25, 1978; Flora Lewis, "Territory and Temperament Thwart a Middle East Peace," *New York Times*, August 6, 1978.

62. Russell Baker, "Withdrawal Pains," *New York Times*, December 30, 1978.

63. Editorial, "A Tortured View of Israel's Conduct," *New York Times*, February 9, 1979; Safire, "Back in Balance," *New York Times*, March 5, 1979; Anthony Lewis, "The Risks of Peace," *New York Times*, March 8, 1979.

64. Editorial, "Vows for a Treaty Signing," *New York Times*, March 26, 1979.

65. Flora Lewis, "Sadat and Begin," *New York Times*, March 27, 1979; Roger Kandell, "Israeli Peace Movement, Outflanked by Begin," *New York Times*, March 28, 1979; Anthony Lewis, "This Year in Jerusalem," April 12, 1979; Anthony Lewis, "Do I Not Have Fears," *New York Times*, April 23, 1979.

66. Gwertzman, "2 New Settlements Approved," *New York Times*, April 24, 1979.

67. Editorial, "Israel Digs into West Bank," *New York Times*, April 25, 1979.

68. Paul Hofmann, "Arabs on West Bank Reject Gesture," *New York Times*, May 14, 1979.

69. Anthony Lewis, "The Crisis of Zionism," *New York Times*, June 7, 1979.

CHAPTER 6

1. A.M. Rosenthal to David Shipler, May 14, 1979, A.M. Rosenthal papers. Manuscripts and Archives. The New York Public Library. Astor, Lenox, and Tilden Foundations. Reprinted with permission.

2. David Shipler, *Arab and Jew* (New York: Penguin Books, 1986), xiii, 8–9.

3. Shipler, "World Criticism is Remote, and Irrelevant to the West Bank Settlers," *New York Times*, July 29, 1979.

4. "Moshe Dayan Interview," *New York Times*, October 28, 1979; Shipler, "Among Israel's Cabinet," *New York Times*, November 4, 1979.

5. Shipler, "In Hebron," *New York Times*, February 5, 1980.

6. Shipler, "Palestinians in Gaza," *New York Times*, February 19, 1980.

7. Anthony Lewis, "From Bondage to Freedom," *New York Times*, March 31, 1980.

8. Shipler, "Those Crucial Settlements," *New York Times Magazine*, April 6, 1980.

9. Shipler, "For Israelis, Borders Are Not Just Lines On the Map," *New York Times*, April 13, 1980; Editorial, "Bombs of Dishonor," *New York Times*, June 3, 1980.

10. Shipler, "At Hebron Shrine," *New York Times*, April 20, 1980.

11. Dov Ronen, "Palestinians and Israelis," *New York Times*, May 2, 1980.

12. Shipler, "5 Are Killed in Palestinian Attack," *New York Times*, May 3, 1980; Shipler, "3 West Bank Arabs Deported," *New York Times*, May 4, 1980.

13. Shipler, "The Hebron Raid," *New York Times*, May 5, 1980; Shipler, "Armed Jews Hold Funeral Procession," *New York Times*, May 6, 1980.

14. Anthony Lewis, "The Bad and the Impossible," *New York Times*, May 5, 1980; Editorial, "A West Bank Eulogy," *New York Times*, May 13, 1980; Walter Reich, *Stranger In My House* (New York: Holt, Rinehart and Winston, 1984), 84.

15. Shipler, "Martyr for Israel's Hard-Liners," *New York Times*, May 12, 1980; Shipler, "Israel Acts to Curb Terrorism by Jews," *New York Times*, May 15, 1980.

16. Editorial, "A West Bank Eulogy," *New York Times*, May 13, 1980.

17. Letter, Rabbi Ralph Pelcovitz, *New York Times*, May 22, 1980.

18. Shipler, "Jewish Settlers' Power Grows," *New York Times*, June 5, 1980; Shipler, "Burst of Fury," *New York Times*, June 8, 1980.

19. Frankel, *The Times of My Life*, 398.

20. Ibid., 399–404.

21. Editorial, "Israel's Illusion," *New York Times*, June 9, 1981.

22. Editorial, "The Fallout from Baghdad," *New York Times*, June 14, 1981.

23. Jacobo Timmerman, "The World Demands Too Much of the Jews," *New York Times*, June 14, 1981; Sidney Zion, "Genesis Rewritten," *New York Times*, July 31, 1981; Safire, "The Jewish De Gaulle," *New York Times*, August 30, 1981.

24. *New York Times*, June 14, 1981; June 25, 1981; July 31, 1981.

25. Safire, "The Jewish De Gaulle," *New York Times*, August 30, 1981.

26. Shipler, "Begin's Visit," *New York Times*, September 6, 1981.

27. Editorial, "True Grit with Mr. Begin," *New York Times*, September 6, 1981; Editorial, "Merchants at the Summit," *New York Times*, September 14, 1981.

28. Flora Lewis, "Thinking of Israel's Future," *New York Times*, September 14, 1981.

29. Eqbal Ahmad, "Replacing Camp David," *New York Times*, November 4, 1981.

30. Shipler, "In Sinai, Jews Dig In," *New York Times*, September 12, 1981.

31. Shipler, "Golan Heights Annexed," *New York Times*, December 15, 1981; Nadav Safran, "Begin's Heights of Risk," *New York Times*, December 16, 1981.

32. Shipler, "Begin: The Guerilla as Master Politician," *New York Times*, December 20, 1981; Shipler, "Begin Contends U.S. Policies Treat Israel Like a 'Vassal,'" *New York Times*, December 21, 1981.

33. Safire, "Reagan 'Suspends' Israel," *New York Times*, December 24, 1981; Flora Lewis, "Symbols Are Important," *New York Times*, December 25, 1981; James Reston, "Where Are We Going?," *New York Times*, December 27, 1981.

34. Michael Elkins, "Self-Searching in Israel," *New York Times*, March 7, 1982.

35. Anthony Lewis, "Destroying the Dream," *New York Times*, April 1, 1981; Anthony Lewis, "Other Israeli Voices," *New York Times*, April 29, 1982.

36. Flora Lewis, "How to Grow Horns," *New York Times*, April 29, 1982.

37. Shipler, "Israel's Double Gamble," *New York Times*, April 14, 1982.

38. Shipler, "Dreams of Peace Seem Hollow," *New York Times*, April 25, 1982.

39. Shipler, "West Bank Occupation Leaves Scars," *New York Times*, May 2, 1982; Amnon Rubenstein, "Annexing Arab Anger," *New York Times*, May 12, 1982.

40. Shipler, "Why Israelis Invaded Now," *New York Times*, June 7, 1982.

41. Shipler, "For Israel, Victory is Only the First Step," *New York Times*, June 13, 1982.

42. Edward Said, "Begin's Zionism Grinds On," *New York Times*, June 11, 1982; "A Place for the Palestinians," *New York Times*, June 16, 1982.

43. "Tragic Mideast Puzzle," *New York Times*, June 17, 1982; "Out of This Nettle," *New York Times*, June 17, 1982.

44. Editorial, "A Place for the Palestinians," *New York Times*, June 16, 1982; Editorial, "Judging Israel," *New York Times*, July 1, 1982; Editorial, "It's the P.L.O. That Has to Move," *New York Times*, July 21, 1982.

45. Editorial, "A Crisis of Conscience Over Lebanon," *New York Times*, June 16, 1982.

46. Fouad Ajami, "The Oasis Goes Dry," *New York Times*, June 21, 1982.

47. Flora Lewis, "The Higher Courage," *New York Times*, June 24, 1982.

48. Shipler, "Some Israelis Fear Their Vietnam is Lebanon," *New York Times*, June 27, 1982; Joseph C. Goulden, *Fit to Print: A.M. Rosenthal and His Times* (Secaucus, NJ: Stuart, 1988), 322–23.

49. Shipler, "Killings A Shock," *New York Times*, September 20, 1982; Editorial, "The Horror, and the Shame," *New York Times*, September 21, 1982.

50. Shipler, "In Israel, Anguish Over the Moral Questions," *New York Times*, September 24, 1982; Editorial, "Israel's Soul, and Security," *New York Times*, September 26, 1982.

51. Reston, "The Tragedy of Begin," *New York Times*, September 22, 1982; Anthony Lewis, "Averting Their Eyes," *New York Times*, September 23, 1982; Anthony Lewis, "In the Name of God, Go," *New York Times*, September 27, 1982; "No From the P.L.O.," *New York Times*, November 28, 1982.

52. Thomas Friedman, "The Beirut Massacre," *New York Times*, September 26, 1982; Editorial, "Israel Finds Its Voice," *New York Times*, September 29, 1982.

53. Shipler, "Sharon Comes to Symbolize A Country's Moral Crisis," *New York Times*, February 13, 1983.

54. Editorial, "A Cry of Conscience," *New York Times*, February 9, 1983; "The Verdict," *New York Times*, February 13, 1983.

55. Shipler, "Israel: Voices of Moral Anguish," *New York Times Magazine*, February 27, 1983.

56. Shipler, "Jews From Asia and Europe," *New York Times*, April 6, 1983; Shipler, "Sephardim Are Transforming Israel's Political Map," *New York Times*, April 8, 1983.

57. "Israelis Will Pull Back," *New York Times*, August 21, 1983.

58. Shipler, "More Schoolgirls in West Bank Fall Sick," *New York Times*, April 4, 1983; Shipler, "In West Bank, Humiliation as an Israeli Weapon," *New York Times*, May 31, 1983.

59. Shipler, "Begin Announces He Plans to Quit," *New York Times*, August 29, 1983; Editorial, "A Flame Burns Out," *New York Times*, August 31, 1983.

60. Anthony Lewis, "Mr. Begin's Legacy," *New York Times*, September 1, 1983; Safire, "Israel after Begin," *New York Times*, September 15, 1983.

61. Shipler, "Begin's Era in Israeli Politics," *New York Times*, September 16, 1983.

62. Shipler, "Jews and Arabs of Israel," *New York Times*, December 27, 1983.

63. Shipler, "Arabs and Jews of Israel," *New York Times*, December 28, 1983; Shipler, "Israeli Arabs: Scorned, Ashamed," *New York Times*, December 29, 1983.

64. Morton Dolinsky, Letter to Editor, *New York Times*, January 10, 1984.

65. Shipler to Rosenthal, January 3, 1984, A.M. Rosenthal papers. Manuscripts and Archives. The New York Public Library. Astor, Lenox, and Tilden Foundations. Reprinted with permission.

66. Shipler, "Terrorists Seize a Bus in Israel," *New York Times*, April 13, 1984; Shipler, "News of Hijacking Denied to Israelis," *New York Times*, April 14, 1984; Shipler, "Hijacker's Death: Question in Israel," *New York Times*, April 19, 1984.

67. Shipler, "Israelis Publish Hijacking Photo," *New York Times*, April 26, 1984; Shipler, "Arabs were Slain by Israeli Guards," *New York Times*, May 29, 1984; Anthony Lewis, "To Thine Own Self Be True," *New York Times*, May 31, 1984; Shipler, *Arab and Jew*, 86–91.

68. Shipler, "A Divided Israel," *New York Times*, July 7, 1984.

69. Shipler, *Arab and Jew*, xiii–xiv, 9, 62, 72, 148–49.

CHAPTER 7

1. Thomas L. Friedman, *From Beirut to Jerusalem* (New York: Farrar, Straus, Giroux, 1989), 10.

2. Ibid., 4–5.

3. Middle East Peace Group Letter, Brandeis *Justice* (November 12, 1974); Jerold S. Auerbach, "Thomas Friedman's Israel: The Myth of Unrequited Love," in Edward Alexander (ed.), *With Friends Like These: The Jewish Critics of Israel* (New York: SPI Books, 1993), 59–74.

4. Friedman, *From Beirut to Jerusalem*, 6–8, 54–57, 144.

5. Ibid., 165.

6. Ibid., 166.

7. Friedman to A.M. Rosenthal, July 3, 1984; July 8, 1984, A.M. Rosenthal papers. Manuscripts and Archives. The New York Public Library. Astor, Lenox, and Tilden Foundations. Reprinted with permission.

8. Friedman, "The Power of Fanatics," *New York Times*, October 7, 1984.

9. Friedman, "Israel's Dilemma: Living with a Dirty War," *New York Times Magazine*, January 20, 1985.

10. Friedman, "Legacy of War," *New York Times*, May 26, 1985.

11. Friedman, *From Beirut to Jerusalem*, 313–21, 511.

12. Friedman, "West Bank Arabs," *New York Times*, August 11, 1985.

13. Friedman, "Kahane Appeal," *New York Times*, August 5, 1985; Friedman, *From Beirut to Jerusalem*, 144.

14. Friedman, "The Palestinian-Israeli Fight," *New York Times*, October 3, 1985.

15. Friedman, "Port in Israel Described as Target," *New York Times*, October 11, 1985; Editorial, "The Duty of Nations," *New York Times*, October 11, 1985.

16. Friedman, "Hijackers in Custody," *New York Times*, October 12, 1985.

17. Friedman, "Double Blow to Arafat," *New York Times*, October 16, 1985; Friedman, "Settlers Threaten Disobedience," *New York Times*, November 6, 1985.

18. Friedman, "'Shocked' Israel Investigates Charges by U.S. of Espionage," *New York Times*, November 25, 1985; Friedman "The Secret Spy Inquiry," *New York Times*, November 26, 1985; Editorial, "Israel's Stutter," *New York Times*, November 30, 1985; Friedman, "The Pain Israel is Feeling for Spying," *New York Times*, December 8, 1985.

19. Friedman, "Abu Nidal," *New York Times*, January 1, 1986; Friedman, "In West Bank," January 5, 1986.

20. Friedman, "America in the Mind of Israel," *New York Times Magazine*, May 25, 1986.

21. Friedman, "Israeli Army Films Its Troubles in Lebanon," *New York Times*, June 11, 1986.

22. Friedman, "Israel's Bus-Stop War," *New York Times*, June 12, 1986; Friedman, "Swastikas Deface Israeli Synagogues," *New York Times*, June 16, 1986; Friedman, "Israel's Uneasy Mix of Religion and State," *New York Times*, June 22, 1986.

23. Friedman, "Israel Raid: New Tactic," *New York Times*, September 26, 1986; Friedman, "Israeli Funeral," *New York Times*, October 9, 1986.

24. Friedman, "Confluence of State, Temple and Gender Issues," *New York Times*, October 12, 1986; Friedman, "Israel's Leadership Problem," *New York Times Magazine*, October 12, 1986.

25. Friedman, "The Peres Record," *New York Times*, October 13, 1986; Friedman, "Israel's Other Half," *New York Times*, October 21, 1986.

26. Friedman, "Weight of Politics, Prejudice Bends the Law," *New York Times*, December 21, 1986.

27. Friedman, "Palestinians under Attack," *New York Times*, January 12, 1987.

28. Friedman, "Jerusalem Journal," *New York Times*, January 21, 1987.

29. Friedman, "Israel: Israel," *New York Times Magazine*, February 1, 1987.

30. Friedman, "Pioneers Return on Film," *New York Times*, February 15, 1987.

31. Friedman, "Treblinka Trial," *New York Times*, March 13, 1987.

32. Friedman, "An Islamic Revival," *New York Times*, April 30, 1987.

33. Friedman, "Using Songs, Israelis Touch Arab Feelings," *New York Times*, May 3, 1987.

34. Friedman, "Shape of Religious Future in Israel," *New York Times*, June 29, 1987; Friedman, "American Jews Are Voicing Their Disquiet," *New York Times*, July 5, 1987.

35. Friedman, "My Neighbor, My Enemy," *New York Times Magazine*, July 5, 1987.

36. Friedman, "Freewheeling Tel Aviv," *New York Times*, July 21, 1987.

37. Friedman, "Road to Power," *New York Times*, August 4, 1987.

38. Friedman, "Artists vs. An Endless War," *New York Times*, August 9, 1987.

39. Friedman, "Will Israel Finally Get a Constitution?," *New York Times*, August 16, 1987.

40. Friedman, "Rage in Jerusalem on Sabbath Films," *New York Times*, August 25, 1987.

41. Friedman, "Report Sees 'Big Brother' in Israeli Data," *New York Times*, September 12, 1987; Friedman, "A Long Fuse Burns Slowly," *New York Times*, October 18, 1987.

42. Friedman, "A Forecast for Israel: More Arabs Than Jews," *New York Times*, October 19, 1987.

43. Friedman, "Israelis Seem Ambivalent on Violence," *New York Times*, November 8, 1987.

44. Friedman, "Israel Pays the Price," *New York Times*, November 29, 1987.

45. Friedman, "Israel Rebuts U.S. Charges," *New York Times*, December 24, 1987; Friedman, "Palestinians and Unrest," *New York Times*, December 25, 1987.

46. Friedman, "How Long Can Israel Deny Its Civil War," *New York Times*, December 27, 1987; Friedman, "Palestinian Cause Turns to Fury," *New York Times*, December 28, 1987; Friedman, "In Jerusalem, Sharon Apartment Causes A Stir," *New York Times*, December 31, 1987.

47. Friedman, "Israel Puts Army on Street Control," *New York Times*, January 2, 1988; Friedman, "For Israeli Soldiers," *New York Times*, January 5, 1988.

48. Friedman, "Riots Unify the Unity Government," *New York Times*, January 10, 1988.

49. Friedman, "For Arabs and Israelis, Maybe It Never Ends," *New York Times*, January 31, 1988.

50. Friedman, "Reality Time in Mideast," *New York Times*, December 19, 1988.

51. Friedman, *From Beirut to Jerusalem*, 252–67.

52. Ibid., 269–71.

53. Ibid., 273–81, 314–15.

54. Ibid., 382–88.

55. Ibid., 391–92, 421–22, 433–37, 444–45, 469–79.

56. Ibid., 437, 450.

57. Ibid., 166.

CHAPTER 8

1. Anthony Lewis, "West Bank Choice," *New York Times*, November 29, 1987; Anthony Lewis, "The Worst Option," *New York Times*, December 17, 1987.

2. Editorial, "Israel Can Do Better," *New York Times*, December 25, 1987; Editorial, "Who Will Plead for Gaza," *New York Times*, December 27, 1987; Editorial, "Blame for All in Gaza," *New York Times*, January 8, 1988.

3. A.M. Rosenthal, "The Making of Gaza," *New York Times*, December 22, 1987.

4. Alexander M. Schindler, "Israel's Time Bomb," *New York Times*, December 24, 1987.

5. Flora Lewis, "Israel's Survival Issue," *New York Times*, January 8, 1988; Edward Said, "Some Satisfaction for the Palestinians," *New York Times*, January 8, 1988; "Editorial Blame for All in Gaza," *New York Times*, January 8, 1988.

6. Anthony Lewis, "End of an Illusion," *New York Times*, January 17, 1988; Anthony Lewis, "Mr. Rabin's Policy," *New York Times*, January 21, 1988.

7. Editorial, "What Israel is Losing," *New York Times*, January 24, 1988.

8. "Some Israeli Views on the Consequences of Occupation," *New York Times*, January 24, 1988.

9. Shipler, "U.S. Jews Torn Over Arab Beatings," *New York Times*, January 26, 1988.

10. Steven Erlanger, "For Jews Israel is Anguish and Hope," *New York Times*, January 27, 1988; Anthony Lewis, "No Way Out?," *New York Times*, January 28, 1988; Woody Allen, "Am I Reading the Papers Correctly?," *New York Times*, January 28, 1988.

11. Roni C. Rabin, "Israeli Doves Call for End of Occupation," *New York Times*, February 11, 1988.

12. Editorial, "A Mideast Vehicle," *New York Times*, February 3, 1988; Editorial, "Harshness and Hope in Israel," *New York Times*, February 19, 1988.

13. Anthony Lewis, "Going to Jerusalem," *New York Times*, February 21, 1988.

14. Sari Nusseibeh, "A Palestinian View," *New York Times*, February 21, 1988; Yaron Ezrahi, "An Israeli View," *New York Times*, February 21, 1988.

15. Letter from Amos Oz, et al., *New York Times*, February 21, 1988.

16. Letter from Eugene V. Rostow, *New York Times*, February 21, 1988.

17. Editorial, "The P.L.O., No and Yes," *New York Times*, March 2, 1988; Anthony Lewis, "Friends of Israel," *New York Times*, March 6, 1988; A.M. Rosenthal, "No Suicide for Israel," *New York Times*, March 8, 1988; Flora Lewis, "Time to Speak to Israel," *New York Times*, March 9, 1988.

18. Anthony Lewis, "Home Truths, Hard Truths," *New York Times*, March 10, 1988.

19. William Safire, "Blinking Green Light," *New York Times*, March 17, 1988; Anthony Lewis, "Passing in the Night," *New York Times*, March 27, 1988; Anthony Lewis, "The Future of Israel," *New York Times*, April 3, 1988; Anthony Lewis, "A Fateful Choice," *New York Times*, April 17, 1988.

20. Anthony Lewis, "Toward the Extreme," *New York Times*, April 24, 1988; "The Price of Occupation," *New York Times*, May 15, 1988.

21. A.M. Rosenthal, "The Unholy War," *New York Times*, May 3, 1988.

22. Joel Brinkley, "Jerusalem Day," *New York Times*, May 15, 1988; Brinkley, "Dip in Terrorism," *New York Times*, May 16, 1988; Brinkley, "Israel Chides State Department Aide," *New York Times*, May 21, 1988; "Swing to the Left," *New York Times*, May 28, 1988; Brinkley, "On the West Bank," *New York Times*, May 29, 1988.

23. Anthony Lewis, "Garbage In, Garbage Out," *New York Times*, June 16, 1988.

24. Anthony Lewis, "A Chance to Talk," *New York Times*, June 23, 1988; Anthony Lewis, "Through A Glass Darkly," *New York Times*, June 26, 1988.

25. "The Untelevised Struggle," *New York Times*, June 20, 1988.

26. Brinkley, "Israel Stunned by Bribery Plot," *New York Times*, September 7, 1988.

27. Anthony Lewis, "Before It is Too Late," *New York Times*, September 18, 1988.

28. "Zionism's Arab Stepchild," *New York Times*, September 21, 1988.

29. Meron Benvenisti, "Two Generations," *New York Times Magazine*, October 16, 1988.

30. Thomas Friedman, "Peace," *New York Times Magazine*, October 30, 1988; "Israeli Civilians Killed," *New York Times*, October 31, 1988.

31. Editorial, "In Israel: Hard Lines Grow Harder," *New York Times*, November 3, 1988.

32. Anthony Lewis, "A Vote for Deadlock," *New York Times*, November 3, 1988; Flora Lewis, "U.S. Owes Israel a Warning," *New York Times*, November 6, 1988.

33. Brinkley, "Two Israels Clash," *New York Times*, November 6, 1988; Brinkley, "Issues of Faith, More Than Land," *New York Times*, November 8, 1988.

34. Brinkley, "Angry American Jews Press Shamir," *New York Times*, November 19, 1988; John Kifner, "American Jews Protest Israeli Threat to Identity," *New York Times*, November 21, 1988; Flora Lewis, "What is a Jew For?," *New York Times*, December 11, 1988.

35. Anthony Lewis, "'Let's Start Talking,'" *New York Times*, December 11, 1988; Anthony Lewis, "End of the Beginning," *New York Times*, December 18, 1988.

36. A.M. Rosenthal, "The Anointing of Arafat," *New York Times*, December 20, 1988; William Safire, "Welcome, Mr. Arens," *New York Times*, December 22, 1988.

37. Friedman, "Reality Time in Mideast," *New York Times*, December 19, 1988.

38. Safire, "Welcome Mr. Arens," *New York Times*, December 22, 1988; John Kifner, "In Alleys of Nablus," *New York Times*, January 1, 1989; Anthony Lewis, "Not a Zero-Sum Game," *New York Times*, January 1, 1989.

39. Editorial, "Israel Stands Still," *New York Times*, December 21, 1988.

40. Kifner, "Israelis Pull Together and Rightward," *New York Times*, December 25, 1988; Editorial, "In U.S., Glum Expectations," *New York Times*, January 18, 1989; Editorial, "It's Israel's Move," *New York Times*, January 19, 1989.

41. Brinkley, "Israel Reviews Military Tactics," *New York Times*, January 29, 1989; Brinkley, "The Palestinian Cost," *New York Times*, February 21, 1989; Brinkley, "Israel and P.L.O.," *New York Times*, February 24, 1989.

42. Youssef M. Ibrahim, "A Legacy of the Uprising," *New York Times*, March 15, 1989.

43. A.M. Rosenthal, "The Middle East Lie," *New York Times*, March 21, 1989.

44. Anthony Lewis, "Time for Straight Talk," *New York Times*, October 8, 1989.

45. Hal Wyner, "Israeli Brutality, Press Timidity," *New York Times*, October 8, 1989.

46. Norman Podhoretz, "Israel Isn't Suicidal," *New York Times*, October 22, 1989.

47. Anthony Lewis, "It Can Happen There," *New York Times*, October 29, 1989.

48. Brinkley, "Inside the Intifada," *New York Times Magazine*, October 29, 1989.

49. Jack Rosenthal, "Costs of the Intifada," *New York Times*, November 5, 1989; Anthony Lewis, "Self-Inflicted Wound," November 19, 1989.

50. Brinkley, "The Arab Uprising after Two Years," *New York Times*, December 10, 1989.

51. Brinkley, "Soviet Jews Leave at a Record Pace," *New York Times*, December 14, 1989.

52. Flora Lewis, "Israel and Relevance," *New York Times*, December 27, 1989.

CHAPTER 9

1. Brinkley, "A Stream of Soviet Emigrès," *New York Times*, January 28, 1990.

2. Brinkley, "Native Israelis Slip Quietly Away," *New York Times*, February 11, 1990; Editorial, "Soviet Jews, Arab Fears and Israel," *New York Times*, February 23, 1990.

3. Brinkley, "Shamir at Home Caused Storm Abroad," *New York Times*, February 5, 1990; Brinkley, "West Bank's Garden Views," *New York Times*, March 4, 1990.

4. A.M. Rosenthal, "The Middle East Kangaroo," *New York Times*, January 28, 1990; Rosenthal, "The President's Bomb," *New York Times*, March 8, 1990; Brinkley, "Angry at U.S. Rebuff," *New York Times*, March 11, 1990; Editorial, "The Right Bush Push on Israel," *New York Times*, March 15, 1990.

5. Editorial, "Slouching in Jerusalem," *New York Times*, April 24, 1990; Brinkley, "Israel Defends Aid to Settlers," *New York Times*, April 25, 1990.

6. Anthony Lewis, "Israel Against Itself," *New York Times*, April 27, 1990; Anthony Lewis, "Realizing a Dream," *New York Times*, May 8, 1990.

7. Editorial, "Whose Terror Teams, Mr. Arafat?" *New York Times*, June 1, 1990; Flora Lewis, "March of Folly, Again," *New York Times*, June 12, 1990; Editorial, "There's No Tolerating Terror," *New York Times*, June 13, 1990.

8. Brinkley, "Death in Jerusalem," *New York Times*, October 15, 1990.

9. Editorial, "Israel's Second Blunder," *New York Times*, October 11, 1990; Editorial, "Israel's Friends, and Enemy," *New York Times*, October 18, 1990.

10. Anthony Lewis, "The Israeli Tragedy," *New York Times*, October 12, 1990; Anthony Lewis, "Self-Inflicted Wounds," *New York Times*, October 19, 1990.

11. William Safire, "Of Stones and Walls," *New York Times*, October 11, 1990; Meir Rosenne, "If Only the Jews," *New York Times*, October 18, 1990.

12. Sabra Chartrand, "Palestinians Are Buoyed," *New York Times*, January 21, 1991; Brinkley, "Israeli Tension Eases," *New York Times*, January 21, 1991.

13. A.M. Rosenthal, "Bill of Reckoning," *New York Times*, January 22, 1991.

14. Char Arand, "Made Homeless by Missiles," *New York Times*, January 25, 1991; Brinkley, "Missiles Provoke Debate in Tel Aviv," *New York Times*, January 29, 1991; Brinkley, "Israelis Patience is Thin," *New York Times*, January 30, 1991.

15. Norman Podhoretz, "Unleash the Israelis," *New York Times*, February 1, 1991.

16. Editorial, "Dubious Justice in Israel," *New York Times*, February 1, 1991; Anthony Lewis, "The Old Order," *New York Times*, February 4, 1991; Anthony Lewis, "When News is a Crime," *New York Times*, March 4, 1991.

17. Eugene V. Rostow, "Don't Strong-Arm Israel," *New York Times*, March 19, 1991; A.M. Rosenthal, "Talk in Jerusalem," *New York Times*, March 26, 1991.

18. Brinkley, "Ethiopian and Israeli Jews Exult," *New York Times*, May 26, 1991; Brinkley, "Israelis Rush to Help Ethiopian Arrivals," *New York Times*, May 27, 1991; Editorial, "Exodus Above the Red Sea," *New York Times*, May 29, 1991.

19. Clyde Haberman, "Setback for Likud," *New York Times*, June 24, 1992; Editorial, "New Promise for Peace in Israel," *New York Times*, June 25, 1992; Anthony Lewis, "A New Life," *New York Times*, June 28, 1992; A.M. Rosenthal, "The Israeli Gamble," *New York Times*, June 20, 1992.

20. Edwin Diamond, *Behind the Times* (Chicago: University of Chicago Press, 1993), 373.

21. Haberman, "Israeli People Divided," *New York Times*, September 1, 1993; Editorial, "An Open Door to Mideast Peace," *New York Times*, September 5, 1993; Friedman, "The Brave New Middle East," *New York Times*, September 10, 1993.

22. Benjamin Netanyahu, "Peace in Our Time?," *New York Times*, September 5, 1993; Haberman, "Violence Rejected," *New York Times*, September 10, 1993.

23. A.M. Rosenthal, "The Road to Palestine," *New York Times*, September 3, 1993.

24. Friedman, "Old Warriors Now Face Task of Building," *New York Times*, September 14, 1993.

25. Editorial, "Beyond the Shock of Recognition," *New York Times*, September 10, 1993.

26. Editorial, "Enough!," *New York Times*, September 14, 1993; Editorial, "Mideast: Now a People's Peace," *New York Times*, September 15, 1993; Friedman, "An American's Respite," *New York Times*, September 19, 1993; Shipler "Victims and Enemies," *New York Times*, September 19, 1993.

27. Joel Greenberg, "Palestinians Slay 2 Israeli Hikers," *New York Times*, October 10, 1993; "Increase in Attacks Feared," *New York Times*, October 11, 1993; Greenberg, "2 Jews Attacked in West Bank," *New York Times*, November 8, 1993.

28. Auerbach, *Hebron Jews*, 123–27.

29. Haberman, "New Clashes Likely," *New York Times*, February 26, 1994; Greenberg, "Sounds of Chanting and Gunfire Echo," *New York Times*, February 26, 1994.

30. Alison Mitchell, "A Killer's Path of Militancy," *New York Times*, February 26, 1994; Editorial, "The Horror in Hebron," *New York Times*, February 26, 1994.

31. Haberman, "Palestinians Battle Israelis," *New York Times*, February 27, 1994; David Firestone, "Seed Planted in Brooklyn," *New York Times*, February 27, 1994; Shipler, "Never Again," *New York Times*, February 27, 1994.

32. Rosenthal, "The Worth of Israel," *New York Times*, March 1, 1994.

33. Editorial, "Hatred Stalks the Settlements," *New York Times*, March 1, 1994; Chris Hedges and Joel Greenberg, "Before Killing, Final Prayer," September 28, 1994. For an illuminating, if sharply critical, analysis of American Jewish settlers see Sara Yael Hirschhorn, *City on a Hilltop: American Jews and the Israeli Settler Movement* (Cambridge, MA: Harvard University Press, 2017).

34. Editorial, "Hamas Tries to Blow Up the Peace," *New York Times*, October 21, 1994.

35. Rosenthal, "Terror and the West," *New York Times*, October 21, 1994.

36. Editorial, "'Holy War,' Fragile Peace," *New York Times*, January 24, 1995.

37. Haberman, "Israelis Mourn," *New York Times*, January 24, 1995.

38. Greenberg, "Suspect Says He Tried to Kill Rabin Before," *New York Times*, November 5, 1995.

39. Serge Schmemann, "Peres Takes Over," *New York Times*, November 5, 1995.

40. Editorial, "The Rabin Assassination," *New York Times*, November 5, 1995; Friedman, "The Death of Israel's Everyman," *New York Times*, November 5, 1995.

41. John Kifner, "Israelis Investigate Far Right," *New York Times*, November 8, 1995.

42. Netanyahu, "McCarthyism in Tel Aviv," *New York Times*, November 10, 1995.

43. Anthony Lewis, "On God's Orders," *New York Times*, November 6, 1995.

44. Amos Oz, "An Unsentimental Dove," *New York Times*, November 6, 1995.

45. Ze'ev Chafets, "Israel's Quiet Anger," *New York Times*, November 7, 1995.

46. Alan Cowell, "Among Hard-Liners in Hebron," *New York Times*, November 7, 1995.

47. Schmemann, "West Bank Settlers Feel Betrayed," *New York Times*, November 17, 1995.

48. Friedman, "How About You?," *New York Times*, November 8, 1995.

49. Editorial, "Burying a Man of Israel," *New York Times*, November 7, 1995.

50. Frank Rich, "Jew against Jew," *New York Times*, November 8, 1995; Greenberg, "Grief and Guilt," *New York Times*, November 8, 1995.

51. A.M. Rosenthal, "For Peace in Israel," *New York Times*, November 7, 1995.

52. Yossi Klein Halevi, "Soldiers of Zion," *New York Times*, November 15, 1995.

53. Kifner, "Belief to Blood," *New York Times*, November 19, 1995.

54. Schmemann, "Revenge is Claimed," *New York Times*, February 26, 1996; Schmemann, "Peres Promises a War on Hamas," *New York Times*, February 27, 1996; Editorial, "Terror in Israel," *New York Times*, February 28, 1996.

55. Editorial, "Terror in Israel," *New York Times*, February 28, 1996; Schmemann, "Terror Isn't Alone as a Threat," *New York Times*, March 3, 1996.

56. Schmemann, "Israeli Rage Rises as Bomb Kills 19," *New York Times*, March 4, 1996.

57. Schmemann, "Peres Government Vows," *New York Times*, March 5, 1996.

58. Anthony Lewis, "It's Up to Arafat," *New York Times*, March 4, 1996.

59. A.M. Rosenthal, "Now It's Israel's Job," *New York Times*, March 5, 1996.

60. Editorial, "Israel Votes," *New York Times*, May 26, 1996.

61. Schmemann, "Peres and His Foe," *New York Times*, May 27, 1996; Friedman, "Bibi and Gennadi," *New York Times*, May 29, 1996; Schmemann, "A Man of Promise," *New York Times*, May 31, 1996.

62. Schmemann, "Final Tally Today," *New York Times*, May 31, 1996.

63. Editorial, "Leading a Divided Israel," *New York Times*, May 31, 1996; Schmemann, "The 'American' Premier," *New York Times*, June 1, 1996; Schmemann, "Telling Israeli Vote," *New York Times*, June 2, 1996.

64. Rosenthal, "Israelis Vote for Peace," *New York Times*, May 31, 1996.

CHAPTER 10

1. Editorial, "Netanyahu's Reassuring Start," *New York Times*, June 20, 1996.

2. Schmemann, "Arab-Israeli Clash," *New York Times*, September 26, 1996; Joel Greenberg, "Among Arabs, Dashed Hope," *New York Times*, September 27, 1996.

3. Adam Goodheart, "Archeology is Destiny," *New York Times*, October 1, 1996; Friedman, "Bibi and Bill," *New York Times*, October 2, 1996; Rashid Khalidi, "What 'Final Status'?," *New York Times*, October 3, 1996; Anthony Lewis, "'Another Such Victory,'" *New York Times*, October 4, 1996; Chris Hedges, "A Shadow Over the Middle East," *New York Times*, October 4, 1996.

4. Schmemann, "Hebron Deal is All But Done," *New York Times*, January 1, 1997.

5. Anthony Lewis, "Israel in Danger," *New York Times*, January 3, 1997; Editorial, "A Clearer Road to Mideast Peace," *New York Times*, January 16, 1997.

6. Editorial, "The Disappearing Hebron Deal," *New York Times*, January 4, 1997; Rosenthal, "The Hype on Hebron," *New York Times*, January 7, 1997; Friedman, "Half-Pregnant in Hebron," *New York Times*, January 5, 1997; Schmemann, "A Softening of the Hawk," *New York Times*, January 15, 1997; Friedman, "What Hebron Tells Us," *New York Times*, January 15, 1997; Friedman, "The Unsilent Majority," *New York Times*, January 19, 1997; Editorial, "A Convergence of Views in Israel," *New York Times*, January 29, 1997.

7. Schmemann, "Hamas Takes Responsibility," *New York Times*, July 31, 1997; Schmemann, "Israelis Threaten Major Crackdown," *New York Times*, August 1, 1997.

8. Schmemann, "The Cold Comfort of Hot-Headed Enemies," *New York Times*, August 3, 1997.

9. Editorial, "Terror and Peace in Israel," *New York Times*, July 31, 1997; Friedman, "The Terrorist Question," *New York Times*, August 4, 1997.

10. Schmemann, "The Horror Has Become Near Routine," *New York Times*, September 5, 1997.

11. Editorial, "Israel, Beyond the Bombings," *New York Times*, September 5, 1997; Anthony Lewis, "No Peace, No Security," *New York Times*, September 5, 1997.

12. Schmemann, "Netanyahu's Hard Line," *New York Times*, September 9, 1997.

13. Rosenthal, "The Half-Century War," *New York Times*, September 9, 1997.

14. Deborah Sontag, "Five Years after Accord," *New York Times*, September 14, 1997; A.M. Rosenthal, "Listen to the Man," *New York Times*, September 25, 1998.

15. Editorial, "The Rustle of Mideast Diplomacy," *New York Times*, September 29, 1998; Sontag, "Israeli Hawk Gets Foreign Ministry," *New York Times*, October 10, 1998.

16. Sontag, "24 Wounded as Arab Hurls Grenades," *New York Times*, October 1, 1998; Sontag, "In Hebron," *New York Times*, October 15, 1998.

17. Friedman, "The Morning After," *New York Times*, October 25, 1998; Editorial, "New Political Equations," *New York Times*, October 27, 1998.

18. Anthony Lewis, "People of the Law?," *New York Times*, May 1, 1999; Editorial, "Oslo and the Israeli Election," *New York Times*, May 4, 1999; Rosenthal, "100 Brave Arabs," *New York Times*, May 7, 1999.

19. Sontag, "Leftist Dove is Netanyahu's Favorite Campaign Target," *New York Times*, May 9, 1999.

20. Greenberg, "A Land of Tribes, Again," *New York Times*, May 9, 1999; Editorial, "Divisive Politics in Israel," *New York Times*, May 11, 1999.

21. Sontag, "Israel's Battle Fatigue," *New York Times*, May 18, 1999; Editorial, "Reviving Hope for Mideast Peace," *New York Times*, May 24, 1999; Rosenthal, "Girl with a Skullcap," *New York Times*, May 28, 1999.

22. Friedman, "Just Do It," *New York Times*, July 4, 2000; Editorial, "Rendezvous at Camp David," *New York Times*, July 6, 2000.

23. Karen Armstrong, "No One People Owns Jerusalem," *New York Times*, July 16, 2000.

24. Leah Rabin, "To Fight for Peace," *New York Times*, July 18, 2000.

25. Friedman, "Good Fences," *New York Times*, July 21, 2000; John Kifner, "Summits: The Holy City," *New York Times*, July 23, 2000.

26. John F. Burns, "Jerusalem's Mood," *New York Times*, July 26, 2000; Editorial, "Failure at Camp David," *New York Times*, July 26, 2000; Friedman, "It Ain't Over Till It's Over," *New York Times*, July 26, 2000.

27. Safire, "Why is Arafat Smiling?," *New York Times*, July 27, 2000.

28. AP Report, "Palestinians and Israelis in a Clash at Holy Site," *New York Times*, September 28, 2000; William A. Orme, Jr., "Israelis Criticized for Using Deadly Force," *New York Times*, October 4, 2000; Orme, Jr., "Flash Points in West Bank and Gaza," *New York Times*, October 5, 2000.

29. Orme, Jr., "A Young Symbol of Mideast Violence," *New York Times*, October 2, 2000.

30. Editorial, "Conflagration in the Middle East," *New York Times*, October 3, 2000; Greenberg, "Old Anger of Israeli Arabs Finds Vent," *New York Times*, October 3, 2000.

31. Allegra Pacheco, "Israel's Doomed Peace," *New York Times*, October 5, 2000; Friedman, "Time to Choose, Yasir," *New York Times*, October 6, 2000.

32. Greenberg, "Unapologetic Sharon," *New York Times*, October 5, 2000.

33. Sontag, "Once Again, Us vs. Them," *New York Times*, October 9, 2000; Editorial, "Dousing the Mideast Fire," *New York Times*, October 10, 2000.

34. Greenberg, "As Dreams of Peace Take Flight," *New York Times*, October 13, 2000; Sontag, "Israel in Shock," *New York Times*, October 14, 2000.

35. Anthony Lewis, "But There is No Peace," *New York Times*, October 14, 2000; Shipler, "Forsaking Trust, the Middle East Hurtles Backward," *New York Times*, October 15, 2000.

36. Friedman, "Ritual Sacrifice," *New York Times*, October 31, 2000; Friedman, "Diplomacy by Other Means," *New York Times*, November 3, 2000.

37. Editorial, "An Elusive Mideast Truce," *New York Times*, November 3, 2000.

38. Sontag, "Sharon Easily Ousts Barak," *New York Times*, February 7, 2001.

39. Sontag, "Dreams of Peace Seem to be Fading," *New York Times*, February 6, 2001; Orme, Jr., "Warrior Who Confounds," *New York Times*, February 7, 2001.

40. Dennis Ross, "Peace, One Very Small Step," *New York Times*, February 9, 2001.

41. Sontag, "16 Killed by Suicide Bomber," *New York Times*, June 2, 2001; Greenberg, "Victims' Accounts of a Night of Horror," *New York Times*, June 3, 2001.

42. Anthony Lewis, "The Price of Occupation," *New York Times*, June 2, 2001; Friedman, "Cease-Fire Umpteen," June 19, 2001.

43. Sontag, "Quest for Mideast Peace," *New York Times*, July 26, 2001. For a sharp critique of the Sontag article see Robert Satloff, "The *Times* Tries to Rewrite History: Times Bomb," *The New Republic* (August 13, 2001).

44. Editorial, "Looking Back at Camp David," *New York Times*, July 28, 2001.

45. Haberman, "Melee at Jerusalem's Most Sacred Site," *New York Times*, July 30, 2001.

46. Yossi Beilin and Yaser Abed Rabbo, "A Mideast Partnership Can Still Work," *New York Times*, August 1, 2001; Anthony Lewis, "Is There No Choice?," *New York Times*, August 4, 2001.

47. Friedman, "Civil Peace Requires Civil War," *New York Times*, August 7, 2001; Editorial, "Mr. Arafat's Role," *New York Times*, August 8, 2001.

48. Haberman, "At Least 14 Dead as Suicide Bomber Strikes Jerusalem," *New York Times*, August 10, 2001.

49. Haberman, "Israelis Grieve and Strike Back," *New York Times*, August 11, 2001.

50. Haberman, "Making Targets of Each Other's Symbols," *New York Times*, August 12, 2001.

51. Editorial, "The Mideast Maelstrom," *New York Times*, August 11, 2001; Schmemann, "Terror Calls the Tune," *New York Times*, August 12, 2001.

52. Tom Segev, "A Retreat to the Familiar Ground of Zionism," *New York Times*, August 12, 2001.

53. David Grossman, "Trapped in a Body at War with Itself," *New York Times*, August 25, 2001.

CHAPTER 11

1. Greenberg, "Protesting Tactics in West Bank," *New York Times*, February 2, 2002.

2. Uri Dan, "The 'Resister' – Full Disclosure," *Jerusalem Post* (February 2, 2002).

3. Yasir Arafat, "The Palestinian Vision of Peace," *New York Times*, February 3, 2002.

4. Editorial, "Averting Disaster in the Mideast," *New York Times*, February 4, 2002.

5. Friedman, "Dear Arab League," *New York Times*, February 6, 2002; Friedman, "An Intriguing Signal from the Saudi Crown Prince," *New York Times*, February 17, 2002.

6. Editorial, "A Peace Impulse Worth Pursuing," *New York Times*, February 21, 2002.

7. Henry Siegman, "Will Israel Take a Chance?," *New York Times*, February 21, 2002.

8. Safire, "Masterly Inactivity," *New York Times*, February 25, 2002; Dore Gold, "Only Buffer Zones Can Protect Israel," *New York Times*, February 27, 2002.

9. Editorial, "Arafat and the Beirut Summit," *New York Times*, March 26, 2002; Joel Brinkley, "Bomb Kills At Least 19 in Israel," *New York Times* March 28, 2002.

10. Schmemann, "Dire Day," *New York Times*, March 28, 2002.

11. Editorial, "Mideast Peace, Mideast Carnage," *New York Times*, March 29, 2002; Editorial, "The Limits of Force," *New York Times*, March 30, 2002.

12. Brinkley, "Frantically Figuring the Results," *New York Times*, April 2, 2002; Ben-Dror Yemini, "The Avraham Burg Syndrome," YNet news.com, January 6, 2015.

13. Nicholas D. Kristof, "The Boomerang Syndrome," *New York Times*, April 4, 2002; Friedman, "The Hard Truth," *New York Times*, April 3, 2002.

14. Schmemann, "Mideast Turmoil," *New York Times*, April 1, 2002; Editorial, "Time for American Leadership," *New York Times*, April 2, 2002; James Bennet, "Arabs' Grief in Bethlehem," *New York Times*, April 4, 2002.

15. Brinkley, "Hamas Spirits Soar," *New York Times*, April 4, 2002; Editorial, "The President Steps In," *New York Times*, April 5, 2002.

16. Editorial, "The Cancer of Suicide Bombing," *New York Times*, April 3, 2002; Kristof, "Kids with Bombs," *New York Times*, April 5, 2002.

17. Safire, "Sharon on Survival," *New York Times*, April 4, 2002; Editorial, "The President Steps In," *New York Times*, April 5, 2002; Editorial, "Moving Past War in the Mideast," *New York Times*, April 7, 2002.

18. Schmemann, "The Method of This Madness," *New York Times*, April 7, 2002; Friedman, "Lifelines to the Future," *New York Times*, April 7, 2002.

19. James Bennet, "In Nablus's Casbah," *New York Times*, April 8, 2002; Schmemann, "Fighting is Fierce," *New York Times*, April 8, 2002; Editorial, "Ariel Sharon's Costly Defiance," *New York Times*, April 9, 2002.

20. Schmemann and Brinkley, "At Least 8 Killed in Suicide Bombing," *New York Times*, April 10, 2002. For a careful analysis see "What Really Happened in Jenin?," Jerusalem Center for Public Affairs (May 2, 2002).

21. Kristof, "Fatal Delusions," *New York Times*, April 9, 2002; Greenberg, "Detainees," *New York Times*, April 10, 2002.

22. Allegra Pacheco, "Life Under Siege," *New York Times*, April 10, 2002.

23. Bennet, "The Aftermath," *New York Times*, April 12, 2002; Bennet, "Jenin Refugee Camp's Dead," *New York Times*, April 13, 2002.

24. Safire, "On Being an Ally," *New York Times*, April 11, 2002; Editorial, "Bulldozing Hope in the Mideast," *New York Times*, April 12, 2002.

25. Nitsan Alon, "Why Israel's Mission Must Continue," *New York Times*, April 12, 2002.

26. Schmemann, "After Secretary Meets Sharon," *New York Times*, April 13, 2002; Bennet, "Refugee Camp is a Scene of Vast Devastation," *New York Times*, April 14, 2002.

27. Paolo Pellegrin and Scott Anderson, "The Cleanup," *New York Times*, April 15, 2002; Kristof, "Behind the Rage," *New York Times*, April 16, 2002.

28. Editorial, "The Powell Mission," *New York Times*, April 15, 2002; Editorial, "Mission Impossible," *New York Times*, April 18, 2002.

29. Brinkley, "Israelis Mourn Their Dead," *New York Times*, April 19, 2002; Schmemann, "Not Quite an Arab-Israeli War," *New York Times*, April 22, 2002; Friedman, "What Day Is It?," *New York Times*, April 24, 2002.

30. Kifner and Greenberg, "A Morning Commute," *New York Times*, June 19, 2002.

31. Greenberg, "He Was Arab and Israeli," *New York Times*, June 20, 2002.

32. Editorial, "Palestinian Death Knell," *New York Times*, June 20, 2002.

33. Dexter Filkins, "Pair of Bombers Kill 23 in Israel," *New York Times*, January 6, 2003.

34. Editorial, "Israel's Misaimed Anger," *New York Times*, January 8, 2003.

35. Editorial, "Sharon's Paradoxical Victory," *New York Times*, January 29, 2003.

36. Amos Oz, "The Two Cowards," *New York Times*, August 19, 2003.

37. Martin Indyk, "Let the Fight for Peace Begin," *New York Times*, August 21, 2003; Bennet, "The Illusions of Progress," *New York Times*, August 23, 2003.

38. Editorial, "The Crumbling Mideast Cease-Fire," *New York Times*, August 22, 2003.

39. Friedman, "The Wailing Wall," *New York Times*, September 7, 2003.

40. Friedman, "Passions and Interests," *New York Times*, October 2, 2003.

41. John F. Burns, "Bomber Left Her Family With a Smile and a Lie," *New York Times*, October 7, 2003.

42. Burns, "A War-Weary People Reach Out," *New York Times*, October 12, 2003.

43. Editorial, "A Turn for the Worse in the Mideast," *New York Times*, October 7, 2003.

44. Greg Myre, "Immigrant's Life in the Shadow Ends," *New York Times*, February 2, 2004; Greg Myre and Jennifer Griffen, *This Burning Land* (New York: John Wiley & Sons, 2011), 130–32, 166–69, 184, 185–89, 285, 292.

45. Editorial, "Gaza First," *New York Times*, February 4, 2004.

46. Bennet, "Bombers Kill 10 in Israel," *New York Times*, March 14, 2004; "Death in Gaza," *New York Times*, March 23, 2004.

47. Myre and Elissa Gootman, "Sharon Suffers a Party Setback," *New York Times*, May 3, 2004; Schmemann, "Disrupting the Zero-Sum Game," *New York Times*, May 4, 2004; Editorial, "The Gaza Quagmire," *New York Times*, May 20, 2004; Kristof, "The Bush and Kerry Tilt," *New York Times*, May 26, 2004.

48. Steven Erlanger, "Hope, Skepticism and Fear," *New York Times*, February 8, 2005; Editorial, "Reason for Cheer in the Middle East," *New York Times*, February 9, 2005.

49. Erlanger, "It's the Middle East," *New York Times*, February 13, 2005.

50. Editorial, "Midsummer Mideast Madness," *New York Times*, July 23, 2005; Erlanger and Dina Kraft, "Israeli Soldiers Pour In," *New York Times*, August 17, 2008.

51. Erlanger, "Tearfully but Forcefully, Israel Removes Gaza Settlers," *New York Times*, August 18, 2005; Erlanger, "Gaza Pullout," *New York Times*, August 22, 2005.

52. Editorial, "Gaza Reality Check," *New York Times*, August 18, 2005; Editorial, "Ariel Sharon's Statesmanship," *New York Times*, August 24, 2005; Editorial, "The Battle for Israel's Future," *New York Times*, August 31, 2005.

53. Erlanger, "Gazans Revel," *New York Times*, September 13, 2005; Friedman, "Rooting for Bibi," *New York Times*, September 23, 2005.

54. Erlanger, "Israel Steps Up Reprisals," *New York Times*, October 28, 2005.

55. Editorial, "Life after Ariel Sharon," *New York Times*, January 6, 2006.

CHAPTER 12

1. Bennet, "History Interrupted," *New York Times*, January 8, 2006; Editorial, "Dismay Among the Palestinians," *New York Times*, January 17, 2006.

2. Friedman, "The Weapon of Democracy," *New York Times*, February 15, 2006; Friedman, "Let Hamas Sink or Swim on Its Own," *New York Times*, February 17, 2006.

3. Erlanger, "A New Landscape," *New York Times*, March 20, 2006.

4. Editorial, "The Face of Hamas," *New York Times*, April 19, 2006.

5. Greg Myre, "Coalition in Place," *New York Times*, May 5, 2006; Jonathan D. Tepperman, "Colonial Drift," *New York Times*, May 7, 2006.

6. Editorial, "Palestinian Peace Politics," *New York Times*, June 10, 2006.

7. Erlanger, "A Campus for 'Scholars, Not Fighters,'" *New York Times*, June 21, 2006.

8. Erlanger, "Militants' Raid on Israel," *New York Times*, June 26, 2006; Editorial, "Hamas Provokes a Fight," *New York Times*, June 29, 2006.

9. Erlanger, "Hamas," *New York Times*, July 2, 2006.

10. Erlanger, "Israel Vows to Fight," *New York Times*, July 10, 2006; Erlanger, "Once Again, Gazans Displaced," *New York Times*, July 12, 2006.

11. Erlanger, "Attack in Gaza," *New York Times*, July 13, 2006.

12. Editorial, "Israel's Two-Front Battle," *New York Times*, July 13, 2006; Editorial, "Playing Hamas's Game," *New York Times*, July 15, 2006.

13. Ethan Bronner, "Drawn Back into the Fire," *New York Times*, July 16, 2006; Kristof, "Feeding the Enemy," *New York Times*, July 18, 2006.

14. David Brooks, "As Israel Goes for Withdrawal," *New York Times*, July 16, 2006.

15. Rashid Khalidi, "The Terrorism Trap," *New York Times*, July 23, 2006; Bob Herbert, "Find a Better Way," *New York Times*, July 24, 2006.

16. Editorial, "No More Foot-Dragging," *New York Times*, July 25, 2006; Friedman, "On the Eve of Madness," *New York Times*, July 28, 2006; Editorial, "A Right Way to Help Israel," *New York Times*, July 29, 2006; Kifner, "Israel is Powerful," *New York Times*, July 30, 2006.

17. Editorial, "Cease-Fire Diplomacy," *New York Times*, August 2, 2006; Kifner, "200 Missiles Hit Israel," *New York Times*, August 3, 2006.

18. Dina Kraft, "A Soldier's Funeral," *New York Times*, August 4, 2006.

19. Friedman, "Buffett and Hezbollah," *New York Times*, August 9, 2006.

20. Erlanger, "Left or Right, Israelis Are Pro-War," *New York Times*, August 9, 2006; Erlanger, "Lebanon Cease-Fire Begins," *New York Times*, August 14, 2006.

21. Myre, "With Guns Silent," *New York Times*, August 18, 2006; Editorial, "Testing Time for Israel's Leaders," *New York Times*, August 19, 2006.

22. Editorial, "Palestinians at War," *New York Times*, January 15, 2007; Erlanger, "Years of Strife and Lost Hope," *New York Times*, March 12, 2007.

23. Erlanger, "West Bank Sites on Private Land," *New York Times*, March 14, 2007.

24. Kristof, "Talking About Israel," *New York Times*, March 18, 2007; Erlanger, "Israeli Soldiers Stand Firm," *New York Times*, March 23, 2007.

25. Friedman, "Abdullah's Chance," *New York Times*, March 23, 2007.

26. Isabel Kershner, "Olmert Visits Israeli Town," *New York Times*, May 18, 2007; Taghreed El-Khodary and Erlanger, "Israel and Palestinian Militants," *New York Times*, May 22, 2007; Erlanger, "Israelis Don't Want Gaza to be Their Next Lebanon," *New York Times*, May 23, 2007; Erlanger, "Israelis Bomb Hamas Targets," *New York Times*, May 27, 2007.

27. Kershner, "Rockets Fray Nerves," *New York Times*, June 1, 2007.

28. Adam LeBor, "New Lyrics for Israel," *New York Times*, June 18, 2007.

29. Bronner, "Holding a Mirror Up to Israeli Destiny," *New York Times*, June 18, 2007.

30. Fouad Ajami, "Brothers to the Bitter End," *New York Times*, June 19, 2007.

31. Friedman, "Behind the Masks," *New York Times*, June 20, 2007; Clark Hoyt, "The Danger of the One-Sided Debate," *New York Times*, June 24, 2007.

32. http://www.camera.org/index.asp?x_context=2&x_outlet=118&x_article=1441.

33. Erlanger, "Police Fight to Remove West Bank Settlers," *New York Times*, August 8, 2007.

34. Kershner, "Olmert and Abbas Meet," *New York Times*, August 7, 2007.

35. Kershner, "The Kibbutz Sheds Socialism," *New York Times*, August 27, 2007.

36. Roger Cohen, "A Return to the Mother of Conflicts," *New York Times*, August 30, 2007; Cohen, "Bush's Best Hope," *New York Times*, November 26, 2007.

37. Erlanger, "Israeli Army, a National Melting Pot," *New York Times*, December 31, 2007; Editorial, "Trapped in Gaza," *New York Times*, January 24, 2008.

38. Daniel Gavron, "Israel's Secret Success," *New York Times*, February 11, 2008.

39. Erlanger and El-Khodary, "Israel Takes Gaza Fight to Next Level," *New York Times*, March 2, 2008; Editorial, "Slipping Away," *New York Times*, March 3, 2008; Erlanger, "Picking Up Pieces," *New York Times*, March 6, 2008.

40. Erlanger and Kershner, "Gunman Kills 8," *New York Times*, March 7, 2008; Kershner, "Israel Approves Home Building in West Bank Settlement," *New York Times*, March 10, 2008.

41. Editorial, "Talk, But No Peace," *New York Times*, March 8, 2008.

42. Jeffrey Goldberg, "Israel's American Problem," *New York Times*, May 18, 2008.

43. Elias Khoury, "For Israelis, an Anniversary," *New York Times*, May 18, 2008.

44. Kristof, "The Two Israels," *New York Times*, June 22, 2008.

45. Kristof, "Tough Love for Israel," *New York Times*, July 24, 2008.

46. Kershner, "Olmert to Resign," *New York Times*, July 31, 2008; Helene Cooper, "Israel's Political Situation," *New York Times*, August 1, 2008; Editorial, "Perils of an Israeli Transition," August 18, 2008.

47. Kershner, "Radical Settlers Take on Israel," *New York Times*, September 26, 2008.

48. Bronner, "Olmert Says Israel Must Leave West Bank," *New York Times*, September 30, 2008.

49. El-Khodary and Bronner, "More Than 225 Die in Gaza," *New York Times*, December 28, 2008.

50. Bronner, "Israel Reminds Foes," *New York Times*, December 29, 2008; Editorial, "War Over Gaza," *New York Times*, December 30, 2008.

51. Benny Morris, "Why Israel Feels Threatened," *New York Times*, December 30, 2008; David Grossman, "Fight Fire with a Cease-Fire," *New York Times*, December 31, 2008.

52. Kershner, "In a Broadening Offensive," *New York Times*, January 2, 2009; Bronner, "Is Real Target Hamas Rule?," *New York Times*, January 4, 2009.

53. El-Khodary and Kershner, "For Arab Clan, Days of Agony," *New York Times*, January 10, 2009; Erlanger, "Gaza War Full of Traps," *New York Times*, January 11, 2009.

54. Kristof, "The Gaza Boomerang," *New York Times*, January 8, 2009.

55. Bronner, "Israelis United on Gaza War," *New York Times*, January 13, 2009.

56. Erlanger, "Weighing Crimes and Ethics," *New York Times*, January 17, 2009.

57. Sabrina Tavernise and El-Khodary, "Shocked and Grieving Gazans," *New York Times*, January 19, 2009.

58. Bronner, "Parsing Gains of Gaza War," *New York Times*, January 19, 2009.

59. Bronner, "The Bullets in My In-Box," *New York Times*, January 25, 2009.

60. Bronner, "Israel Confronts Deeper Isolation," *New York Times*, March 19, 2009.

CHAPTER 13

1. Editorial, "An Agenda for Mr. Netanyahu," *New York Times*, May 12, 2009.

2. Jeffrey Goldberg, "Israel's Fears, Amalek's Arsenal," *New York Times*, May 17, 2009.

3. Mark Landler and Helene Cooper, "Keeping Score on Obama vs. Netanyahu," *New York Times*, May 21, 2009; Editorial, "Mr. Obama and Mr. Netanyahu," *New York Times*, May 23, 2009.

4. Cooper, "Weighing Tactics on Israeli Settlements," *New York Times*, June 1, 2009.

5. Kershner, "Israel and U.S. Can't Close Split," *New York Times*, June 2, 2009; Friedman, "Obama on Obama," *New York Times*, June 3, 2009.

6. Bronner, "Israelis Say Obama is Ignoring Past Understandings," *New York Times*, June 4, 2009.

7. Jeff Zekeny and Cooper, "A Blunt Obama," *New York Times*, June 5, 2009.

8. Editorial, "The Cairo Speech," *New York Times*, June 5, 2009; Bronner, "New Focus on Settlements," *New York Times*, June 6, 2009.

9. Kershner, "In Reversal, Netanyahu Backs Palestinian State," *New York Times*, June 15, 2009.

10. Tony Judt, "Fictions on the Ground," *New York Times*, June 22, 2009.

11. Editorial, "Squandering the Moment," *New York Times*, September 5, 2009.

12. Neil MacFarquhar, "U.N. Inquiry Sees Gaza War Crimes," *New York Times*, September 16, 2009.

13. Richard Goldstone, "Justice in Gaza," *New York Times*, September 17, 2009; David Landau, "The Gaza Report's Wasted Opportunity," *New York Times*, September 20, 2009.

14. Cooper and Landau, "Obama Pivots," *New York Times*, September 13, 2009; Bronner, "The Painful Truth in Mideast Talks," *New York Times*, October 20, 2009; Editorial, "Diplomacy 101," *New York Times*, November 28, 2009; Bronner, "Surprising Role for Netanyahu," *New York Times*, December 16, 2009.

15. Patricia Cohen, "Book Calls Jewish People an 'Invention,'" *New York Times*, November 24, 2009.

16. Kershner, "Challenging Traditions at the Heart of Judaism," *New York Times*, December 22, 2009.

17. Bronner, "A Mideast Bond," *New York Times*, December 31, 2009.

18. Bronner, "Gaza Journal," *New York Times*, January 6, 2010.

19. Clark Hoyt, "Too Close to Home," *New York Times*, February 6, 2010.

20. Editorial, "Diplomacy 102," *New York Times*, March 11, 2010; Friedman, "Driving Drunk in Jerusalem," *New York Times*, March 14, 2010; Landler and Bronner, "Israel Feeling Rising Anger," *New York Times*, March 16, 2010.

21. Bronner, "Israelis Resist Demands from U.S.," *New York Times*, March 17, 2010; Maureen Dowd, "Bibi's Tense Time Out," *New York Times*, March 17, 2010; Michael B. Oren, "A Disagreement, Not a Crisis," *New York Times*, March 18, 2010.

22. Bronner, "Clash Over Building," *New York Times*, March 21, 2010; Landler, "As U.S. and Israel Meet," *New York Times*, March 23, 2010; Editorial, "Mr. Obama and Israel," *New York Times*, March 27, 2010.

23. Editorial, "Israel and the Blockade," *New York Times*, June 2, 2010.

24. Amos Oz, "Israeli Force, Adrift on the Sea," *New York Times*, June 2, 2010; Kristof, "Saving Israel From Itself," *New York Times*, June 3, 2010; Editorial, "A Credible Investigation," *New York Times*, June 4, 2010.

25. Michael Chabon, "Chosen, But Not Special," *New York Times*, June 6, 2010; Judt, "Israel without Clichés," *New York Times*, June 10, 2010.

26. Cooper, "What to Do About Israel," *New York Times*, June 10, 2010.

27. Kershner and Landler, "Killing of 4 Israeli Settlers," *New York Times*, September 1, 2010; Landler and Cooper, "Settlements … are Clouding Peace Talks," *New York Times*, September 3, 2010; Editorial, "Another Start for Peace Talks," *New York Times*, September 4, 2010; Editorial, "The Sunday Deadline," *New York Times*, September 24, 2010; Editorial, "They Need to Talk," *New York Times*, October 7, 2010; Bronner, "Netanyahu's New Offer," *New York Times*, October 12, 2010.

28. Bronner, "West Bank Settlement Boom," *New York Times*, December 23, 2010; Kershner, "Eviction of a Palestinian Family," *New York Times*, November 24, 2010; Kershner, "Bulldozers Move In," *New York Times*, January 10, 2011.

29. Kershner, "Suspecting Palestinians," *New York Times*, March 13, 2011.

30. Kershner, "Israel to Step Up Pace of New Construction," *New York Times*, March 14, 2011; Kershner, "Abbas Condemns Killing of Jewish Family," *New York Times*, March 15, 2011; Kershner, "Neighbor's Blood Binds Settlers," *New York Times*, March 16, 2011.

31. Bronner and Kershner, "Head of U.N. Panel Regrets," *New York Times*, April 3, 2011; Bronner and Jennifer Medina, "Investigator on Gaza," April 20, 2011; Richard Goldstone, "Reconsidering the Goldstone Report," *The Washington Post*, April 1, 2011; Michael B. Oren, *Ally* (New York: Random House, 2016), 99–103.

32. Mahmoud Abbas, "The Long Overdue Palestinian State," *New York Times*, May 17, 2011. See Oren, *Ally* (248), for his complaint to editorial page editor Andy Rosenthal about Abbas's false claim and Rosenthal's evasion, which Oren labeled "chicanery."

33. Editorial, "President Obama and the Arab Spring," *New York Times*, May 18, 2011; Kershner, "Elusive Line Defines Lives," *New York Times*, September 7, 2011; Editorial, "Israel's Embattled Democracy," *New York Times*, July 21, 2012; Margaret Sullivan, "Photo of a Palestinian Mother," *New York Times*, November 19, 2013; Oren, *Ally*, 227.

34. Ephraim Sneh, "Bad Borders, Good Neighbors," *New York Times*, July 11, 2011; Aluf Benn, "Israel's Lost Chance," *New York Times*, July 30, 2011.

35. Kristof, "Seeking Balance on Mideast," *New York Times*, August 4, 2011; Cohen, "Jews in a Whisper," *New York Times*, August 21, 2011.

36. Friedman, "Israel: Adrift at Sea Alone," *New York Times*, September 18, 2011; Ehud Olmert, "Peace Now, or Never," *New York Times*, September 22, 2011; Editorial, "The Palestinians' Bid," *New York Times*, September 23, 2011.

37. Bronner, "Tensions Simmer in West Bank," *New York Times*, September 24, 2011; Bronner, "Israelis Happy at Home," *New York Times*, September 29, 2011; Kristof, "Is Israel Its Own Worst Enemy?," *New York Times*, October 10, 2011.

38. Editorial, "Gilad Shalit's Release," *New York Times*, October 19, 2011.

39. Gershom Gorenberg, "Israel's Other Occupation," *New York Times*, November 27, 2011; Friedman, "The Arab Awakening and Israel," *New York Times*, November 20, 2011.

40. Ricki Hollander and Gilead Ini, *Indicting Israel*, CAMERA Monograph Series (2012), 5–8 *ff*. For a contrary view, see Neil Lewis, "The *Times* and the Jews," *Columbia Journalism Review* (January 13, 2012). Lewis was a *Times* news correspondent between 1985 and 2009.

41. Kershner, "Israeli Girl ... at the Center of Attention," *New York Times*, December 28, 2011; Bronner and Kershner, "Israeli Women Core of Debate," *New York Times*, January 15, 2012.

42. Amos Yadlin, "Israel's Last Chance to Strike Iran," *New York Times*, March 1, 2012; Editorial, "Iran, Israel and the United States," *New York Times*, March 6, 2012; Friedman, "Israel's Best Friend," *New York Times*, March 7, 2012.

43. Mustafa Barghouti, "Peaceful Protest Can Free Palestine," *New York Times*, February 22, 2012; Peter Beinert, "To Save Israel, Boycott the Settlements," *New York Times*, March 19, 2012.

44. Jodi Rudoren, "Palestinians Go Hungry," *New York Times*, May 4, 2012.

45. Rudoren, "A Model City," *New York Times*, May 10, 2012; Rudoren, "West Bank Leader," *New York Times*, May 13, 2012; Rudoren, "The Fight Over Who Fights in Israel," *New York Times*, May 20, 2012.

46. Rudoren, "Service to Israel Tugs at Identity," *New York Times*, July 12, 2012; Rudoren, "When the Lights Go Down," *New York Times*, July 21, 2012; Rudoren, "A Champion for the Displaced," *New York Times*, July 27, 2012.

47. Editorial, "Wrong Time for New Settlements," *New York Times*, July 10, 2012.

48. Editorial, "Israel's Embattled Democracy," *New York Times*, July 21, 2012.

49. Dani Dayan, "Israel's Settlers Are Here to Stay," *New York Times*, July 25, 2012; Avraham Burg, "Israel's Fading Democracy," *New York Times*, August 5, 2012; Daniel Byman and Natan Sachs, "Stopping Extremist Settlers," *New York Times*, August 16, 2012.

50. Fares Akram and Kershner, "Violence Surges on Israeli-Gaza Border," *New York Times*, November 10, 2012; Kershner and Akram, "Ferocious Israeli Assault," *New York Times*, November 14, 2012.

51. Bronner, "Israel Takes Tougher Approach," *New York Times*, November 16, 2012; Laura Aburamadan, "Trapped in Gaza," *New York Times*, November 16, 2012.

52. Gershon Baskin, "Israel's Short-Sighted Assassination," *New York Times*, November 16, 2012; Rudoren and Akram, "Mistaken Lull," *New York Times*, November 17, 2012; Cohen, "Gaza without End," *New York Times*, November 19, 2012.

53. Editorial, "Hamas's Illegitimacy," *New York Times*, November 19, 2012; Oren, "Hamas Left Israel No Choice," *New York Times*, November 20, 2012; Editorial, "A New Israel-Hamas Cease-Fire," *New York Times*, November 21, 2012.

54. Rudoren and Mark Landler, "Housing Move," *New York Times*, November 30, 2012; Rudoren, "Dividing the West Bank," *New York Times*, December 1, 2012.

55. Erlanger, "West Bank Land, Empty," *New York Times*, December 17, 2012; Editorial, "The Fading Mideast Peace Dream," *New York Times*, December 20, 2012.

56. Cohen, "Israel's True Friends," *New York Times*, January 7, 2013; Cohen, "Zero Dark Zero," *New York Times*, February 28, 2013.

57. Rashid Khalidi, "Is Any Hope Left for Mideast Peace?," *New York Times*, March 12, 2013; Ari Shavit, "The Old Peace is Dead," *New York Times*, March 12, 2013; Friedman, "Obama Goes to Israel," *New York Times*, March 12, 2013.

58. Landler and Rudoren, "In Israel, Obama Seeks to Offer Reassurance," *New York Times*, March 20, 2013; Landler, "Obama Urges Young Israelis," *New York Times*, March 21, 2013.

59. Jeremy Ben-Ami, "A Friend Spoke Truth to Friends," *New York Times*, March 22, 2013; Friedman, "Israel: Bits, Bites and Bombs," *New York Times*, March 23, 2013.

60. Rudoren, "Israel Moves to End Gender Segregation," *New York Times*, May 8, 2013; Rudoren, "Standoff at Western Wall," *New York Times*, May 10, 2013; Rudoren, "Israel Prods Ultra-Orthodox," *New York Times*, June 6, 2013; Rudoren, "Trying to Revive Peace Talks," *New York Times*, June 18, 2013.

61. Cohen, "Why American Jews Matter," *New York Times*, June 20, 2013.

62. Rudoren, "Before Kerry Visit," *New York Times*, June 24, 2013; Editorial, "Kerry's Quest," *New York Times*, June 30, 2013.

63. Cohen, "The Two-State Imperative," *New York Times*, July 22, 2013.

64. Editorial, "Inching Forward in the Mideast," *New York Times*, July 25, 2013.

65. Editorial, "In a West Bank Culture of Conflict," *New York Times*, August 4, 2013; Rudoren, "In a West Bank Culture of Conflict," *New York Times*, August 4, 2013; Ian S. Lustick, "Two-State Illusion," *New York Times*, September 4, 2013.

66. Cohen, "Bibi's Tired Iranian Lines," *New York Times*, October 3, 2013; Cohen, "If Not Now, When?," *New York Times*, October 17, 2013.

67. Kershner, "Attack on Israeli Worsens Tensions," *New York Times*, November 13, 2013; Silwa Gawadreh, "Photo of Palestinian Mother Was the Wrong Choice," *New York Times*, November 19, 2013.

68. Cohen, "Israel's Iran Dilemma," *New York Times*, November 25, 2013.

69. Cohen," My Jewish State," *New York Times*, December 31, 2013.

CHAPTER 14

1. Rudoren, "Sticking Point in Peace Talks," *New York Times*, January 1, 2014.

2. Ami Ayalon, "Israel Must Seize the Day," *New York Times*, January 1, 2014; Editorial, "The Ticking Mideast Clock," *New York Times*, January 3, 2014.

3. Avi Shlaim, "Israel Needs to Learn Some Manners," *New York Times*, January 30, 2014; Omar Barghouti, "Why Israel Fears the Boycott," *New York Times*, January 31, 2014.

4. Friedman, "Abbas's NATO Proposal," *New York Times*, February 2, 2014; Friedman, "The Third Intifada," *New York Times*, February 4, 2014; Cohen, "The B.D.S. Threat," *New York Times*, February 10, 2014; Friedman, "Israel's Big Question," *New York Times*, February 11, 2014.

5. Mark Oppenheimer, "A Conflict of Faith," *New York Times*, February 14, 2014.

6. Ali Jarbawi, "Defining the Jewish State," *New York Times*, March 6, 2014; Editorial, "Peace Process on Life Support?," *New York Times*, March 28, 2014.

7. Rudoren, "Remaking a Life," *New York Times*, March 29, 2014.

8. Abbas Milani and Israel Waismel-Manor, "Are Iran and Israel Changing Places?," *New York Times*, April 8, 2014.

9. Editorial, "Time to Move On," *New York Times*, April 14, 2014.

10. Friedman, "Not the Same Old, Same Old," *New York Times*, April 15, 2014.

11. Kershner, "Israeli Teenagers Said to Be Kidnapped," *New York Times*, June 13, 2014; Kershner, "Rift Bared as Palestinians Aid Israel," *New York Times*, June 14, 2014; Rudoren, "Tensions Mount as Troops Scour Hebron," *New York Times*, June 16, 2014.

12. Kirshner, "Abduction of Young Israeli Hitchhikers," *New York Times*, June 16, 2014.

13. Rudoren, "2 Mothers Embody a Divide," *New York Times*, June 29, 2014.

14. Ali Jarbawi, "The Deadly Politics of Revenge," *New York Times*, July 2, 2014; Cohen, "Lawless Holy Land," *New York Times*, July 3, 2014; Editorial, "Four Horrific Killings," *New York Times*, July 7, 2014.

15. Erlanger and Kershner, "Israel and Hamas Trade Attacks," *New York Times*, July 8, 2014; Rula Salameh, "A Palestinian Mother's Fear," *New York Times*, July 9, 2014.

16. Kershner, "Air Sirens Puncture Life," *New York Times*, July 9, 2014; Erlanger, "Killing of Palestinian Youths," *New York Times*, July 10, 2014; Bronner, "A Damaging Distance," *New York Times*, July 11, 2014; Anne Barnard, "Boys Drawn to Gaza Beach," *New York Times*, July 16, 2014.

17. Kristof, "Leading through Great Loss," *New York Times*, July 16, 2014; "Trouble Underfoot on Israeli Kibbutz," *New York Times*, July 18, 2014; Kristof, "Who's Right and Wrong in the Middle East," *New York Times*, July 19, 2014; Margaret Sullivan, "Not the Time for Antiseptic Coverage," *New York Times*, July 22, 2014; "Gaza: When Home is a War Zone," *New York Times*, August 6, 2014. For Fares Akram see "New York Times' Gaza Correspondent Exposed as Arafat Fan," http://honestreporting.com/new-york-times-gaza correspondent (August 24, 2014).

18. Kristof, "Leading through Great Loss," *New York Times*, July 16, 2014; Nathan Thrall, "How the West Chose War in Gaza," *New York Times*, July 22, 2014.

19. Rudoren, "For Israelis on Edge of Battle," *New York Times*, July 23, 2014; "Gaza's Mounting Death Toll," *New York Times*, July 25, 2014.

20. Amos Yadlin, "To Save Gaza, Destroy Hamas," *New York Times*, July 25, 2014; David Grossman, "An Israel Without Illusions," *New York Times*, July 27, 2014; Ali Jarbawi, "Israel's Colonialism Must End," *New York Times*, August 4, 2014.

21. Editorial, "Israel's War in Gaza," *New York Times*, July 18, 2014.

22. Margaret Sullivan, "Not the Times for Antiseptic Coverage," *New York Times*, July 22, 2014; Cohen, "Zionism and Its Discontents," *New York Times*, July 29, 2014.

23. "Gaza's Mounting Death Toll," *New York Times*, July 24, 2014; Cohen, "Gaza and Its Discontents," *New York Times*, July 29, 2014; Ali Jarbawi, "Israel's Colonialism Must End," *New York Times*, August 4, 2014.

24. Editorial, "Making the Gaza Cease-Fire Last," *New York Times*, August 6, 2014; Akram, "Gaza: When Home is a War Zone," *New York Times*, August 6, 2014.

25. Rudoren and Akram, "A Boy at Play in Gaza," *New York Times*, August 8, 2014; Rudoren, "In Gaza, Grief, Anger – and ... Pride," *New York Times*, August 10, 2014.

26. Christopher F. Schuetze and Anne Barnard, "Resisting Nazis, He Saw Need for Israel," *New York Times*, August 16, 2014.

27. Antony Lerman, "The End of Liberal Zionism," *New York Times*, August 22, 2014.

28. Akram and Rudoren, "Executions in Gaza," *New York Times*, August 22, 2014; Kershner and Akram, "Israeli Strike Destroys Apartment Tower," *New York Times*, August 23, 2014; Akram and Kershner, "Israel Says Missile Strike Killed Hamas Official," *New York Times*, August 24, 2014.

29. Akram and Rudoren, "Teenager Cites Ordeal as Captive," *New York Times*, August 24, 2014.

30. Rudoren, "For a Gaza Athlete," *New York Times*, August 25, 2014; Rudoren and Akram, "As Truce Holds," *New York Times*, August 27, 2014. For one reader's response see Richard A. Block, "Why I'm Unsubscribing from the New York Times," *Tablet* (August 28, 2014).

31. "Dust to Dust," *New York Times Magazine*, August 31, 2014; Jake Silverstein, "Editor's Note," *New York Times*, August 28, 2014.

32. Ali Jarbawi, "Israel's Lessons from the Gaza War," *New York Times*, September 4, 2014; Cohen, "A War of Choice in Gaza," *New York Times*, September 8, 2014.

33. Mairav Zonszein, "How Israel Silences Dissent," *New York Times*, September 26, 2014.

34. Cohen, "The Community of Expulsion," *New York Times*, October 6, 2014; Akram, "In Gaza's Rubble," *New York Times*, October 6, 2014.

35. Kershner, "A House-by-House Struggle," *New York Times*, October 15, 2014; Rudoren, "In Exodus From Israel," *New York Times*, October 16, 2014.

36. Kershner, "More Jewish Settlers Move In," *New York Times*, October 20, 2014.

37. Rula Jebreal, "Minority Life in Israel," *New York Times*, October 27, 2014; Tamar Sternthal, "New York Times editor admits holding Palestinians to a lower standard," *The Times of Israel* (October 29, 2014).

38. Kershner and Rudoren, "A Leaderless Palestinian Revolt," *New York Times*, November 11, 2014.

39. Rudoren and Kershner, "Israel Shaken by 5 Deaths in Synagogue Assault," *New York Times*, November 18, 2014. For Public Editor Margaret Sullivan's favorable assessment of *Times* coverage of the Israeli-Palestinian conflict, see "The Conflict and the Coverage," *New York Times*, November 22, 2014. For Jodi Rudoren's critique of the "very noisy group of advocates" who criticized her coverage, see *The Algemeiner* (November 25, 2014). For critical

CAMERA analysis of *Times* coverage see Gilead Ini, "New York Times Opinion Bias by the Numbers," camera.org, November 10, 2014.

40. Friedman, "This Israeli Election Matters," *New York Times*, December 16, 2014; Editorial, "The Embattled Dream of Palestine," *New York Times*, December 19, 2014; Cohen, "What Will Israel Become?," *New York Times*, December 20, 2014.

41. Moriel Rothman-Zecher, "Why I Won't Serve Israel," *New York Times*, January 11, 2015; Rudoren, "Disillusioned by War," *New York Times*, January 25, 2015.

42. Kristof, "The Human Stain," *New York Times*, February 26, 2015; Kristof, "The Two Israels," *New York Times*, February 28, 2015.

43. Editorial, "Mr. Netanyahu's Unconvincing Speech," *New York Times*, March 3, 2015; Cohen, "Netanyahu's Iran Thing," *New York Times*, March 6, 2015; Paul Krugman, "Israel's Inequality Election," *New York Times*, March 13, 2015.

44. Editorial, "An Israeli Election Turns Ugly," *New York Times*, March 17, 2015; Friedman, "Go Ahead, Ruin My Day," *New York Times*, March 18, 2015; Rudoren and Michael D. Sheer, "Netanyahu Reopens Door," *New York Times*, March 19, 2015; Rudoren and Julie Hirschfield Davis, "Netanyahu Apologizes," *New York Times*, March 23, 2015; Editorial, "Keeping Palestinian Hopes Alive," *New York Times*, March 24, 2015; Editorial, "Israel's Unworkable Demands," *New York Times*, April 7, 2015.

45. CAMERA, "Diaa Hadid, Former NGO Worker, Keeps Up Advocacy Work at *New York Times*" (December 17, 2015).

46. Hadid, "Palestinian Women Join Effort," *New York Times*, April 16, 2015; Hadid, "Israel Detains Palestinian Boys," *New York Times*, April 30, 2015; Hadid, "Village of Bedouins Faces Eviction," *New York Times*, May 16, 2015.

47. Anat Biletzki, "Making It Explicit in Israel," *New York Times*, May 11, 2015; Hagai El-Ad, "Israel's Charade of Democracy," *New York Times*, May 31, 2015.

48. Rudoren, "Businesses' Doors Creak Open," *New York Times*, June 24, 2015.

49. Kershner, "Israeli Man Dies in Attack," *New York Times*, June 30, 2015; Kershner, "Israeli Forces Kill Palestinian Teenager," *New York Times*, July 3, 2015; Hadid, "Video in Death of Palestinian," *New York Times*, July 13, 2015; Chuck Freilich, "A Good Deal for Israel," *New York Times*, July 19, 2015; "What *The New York Times* Won't Show Readers," CAMERA, July 6, 2015.

50. Editorial, "An Iran Nuclear Deal," *New York Times*, July 14, 2015; Rudoren, "Netanyahu May Turn Iran Deal to his Favor," *New York Times*, July 16, 2015.

51. Nasser Nawaja, "Israel, Don't Level My Village," *New York Times*, July 23, 2015; Hadid and Rudoren, "Jewish Arsonists Suspected," *New York Times*, July 31, 2015; Hadid, "Censure and Clashes," *New York Times*, August 1, 2015.

52. Kershner, "Israeli Justice," *New York Times*, August 3, 2015; Rudoren, "Soul-Searching in Israel," *New York Times*, August 6, 2015.

53. Rudoren and Kershner, "Israel Detains Kahane's Grandson," *New York Times*, August 4, 2015; Rami Nazzal and Kershner, "Father of Palestinian Toddler," *New York Times*, August 8, 2015.

54. Sara Yael Hirschhorn, "Israeli Terrorists, Born in the U.S.A.," *New York Times*, September 4, 2015.

55. Hadid, "Jewish Man Dies as Rocks Pelt His Car," *New York Times*, September 14, 2015; Kershner, "Amid Jerusalem Clashes," *New York Times*, September 18, 2015.

56. Cohen, "Jews as Far as Possible," *New York Times*, September 24, 2015.

57. Rick Gladstone, "Historical Certainty Proves Elusive," *New York Times*, October 8, 2015; Kershner and Rudoren, "Attack by Palestinians Kill 3 Israelis," *New York Times*, October 13, 2015.

58. Rudoren and Hadid, "Israel Says 5 From Hamas Confess," *New York Times*, October 5, 2015; Kershner, "Survivor of Jerusalem Stabbing Recounts Attack," *New York Times*, October 6, 2015; Kershner, "Stabbings, and Deadly Responses," *New York Times*, October 12, 2015; Editorial, "The Cycle of Violence," *New York Times*, October 15, 2015.

59. Kershner and Rudoren, "Jerusalem Grows More Grim," *New York Times*, October 14, 2015; Kershner and Robert Mackey, "Conflicting Accounts of Jerusalem Strife," *New York Times*, October 15, 2015; Rudoren, "East Jerusalem, Bubbling Over with Despair," *New York Times*, October 17, 2015.

60. Kershner, "Anger Spreads with 5 Attacks," *New York Times*, October 17, 2015; Rudoren and Nazzal, "Palestinian Anger … Gets a Violent Soundtrack," *New York Times*, October 22, 2015; Rudoren, "The Dueling Narratives," *New York Times*, October 27, 2015.

61. Rudoren, "American-Israeli Teacher," *New York Times*, October 29, 2015; Hadid, "Israel Restricts Palestinian Entry," *New York Times*, October 30, 2015.

62. Kershner and Nazzal, "Violent Loop Engulfs Youths," *New York Times*, November 10, 2015; Kershner, "5 Killed in Tel Aviv and West Bank," *New York Times*, November 19, 2015.

63. Kershner, "An Arab, Muslim, and Israeli Officer," *New York Times*, October 30, 2015.

64. Hadid and Nazzal, "Young Palestinian Woman Joins West Bank Turmoil," *New York Times*, December 17, 2015.

65. Hadid and Nazzal, "Jerusalem Attacks Subside," *New York Times*, December 17, 2015; Kershner, "Israeli Veterans' Criticism," *New York Times*, December 24, 2015.

66. Cohen, "The Assassination in Israel That Worked," *New York Times*, December 17, 2015.

67. Alexandra Lapkin, "The New York Times Jerusalem Bureau Chief," *The Jewish Advocate* (November 27, 2015), 7; Laura Kelly, "Maintaining Empathy," *International Jerusalem Post* (January 1–7, 2016), 11–12.

EPILOGUE

1. Hadid, "In Haifa, a Liberal Arab Culture Blossoms," *New York Times*, January 3, 2016.

2. Sullivan, "More Context Needed in Article on Haifa Culture," *New York Times*, January 8, 2016.

3. Hadid, "Evictions in Walled Old City," *New York Times*, January 15, 2016.

4. CAMERA, "Diaa Hadid, Recycling Old Stories about the Old City" (January 15, 2016).

5. Kershner, "All-Bedouin Tech Company," *New York Times*, January 9, 2016.

6. Kershner, "Israel Faces New Brand of Terrorism," *New York Times,* January 11, 2016; Kershner, "Stabbing of an Israeli Woman," *New York Times,* January 18, 2016.

7. Kershner, "Palestinian Girl with Knife Killed," *New York Times,* January 23, 2016; Kershner, "Palestinian Assailants are Killed," *New York Times,* January 25, 2016.

8. Editorial, "The Fading Two-State Solution," *New York Times,* January 22, 2016; Cohen, "Israel's Image Issue," *New York Times,* January 28, 2016; Ban Ki Moon, "Don't Shoot the Messenger, Israel," *New York Times,* January 31, 2016.

9. Erlanger, "Anger in a Palestinian Town," *New York Times,* January 19, 2016; Erlanger, "Israel Mired in Ideological Battles," *New York Times,* January 29, 2016; Erlanger, "Who Are the True Heirs of Zionism?," *New York Times,* February 4, 2016.

10. Friedman, "The Many Mideast Solutions," *New York Times,* February 10, 2016; Kershner, "She Was Asked to Switch Seats," *New York Times,* February 26, 2016.

11. Cohen, "An Anti-Semitism of the Left," *New York Times,* March 7, 2016.

12. Kershner, "Israel Soldier Detained," *New York Times,* March 24, 2016; Hadid, "In West Bank," *New York Times,* April 13, 2016.

13. Hadid, "Israel Frees Palestinian Girl," *New York Times,* April 24, 2016; Hadid, "Surge in Palestinian Youths in Prison," *New York Times,* April 29, 2016.

14. James Glanz and Nazzal, "Palestinian Museum Prepares to Open," *New York Times,* May 16, 2016.

15. Glanz, "A Window into the West Bank's 'Wildest, Most Violent' Areas," *New York Times,* May 24, 2016.

16. Editorial, "A Baffling, Hard-Line Choice," *New York Times,* May 24, 2016.

17. Friedman, "Netanyahu, Prime Minister of the State of Israel-Palestine," *New York Times,* May 25, 2016.

18. Hadid and Myra Noveck, "Palestinian, 19, Stabs 13-Year-Old to Death," *New York Times,* June 30, 2016; Dov Lieber, "Kiryat Arba Killer had a Death Wish," *The Times of Israel,* June 30, 2016.

19. Hadid and Somini Sengupta, "Israel Imposes Restrictions," *New York Times,* July 2, 2016.

20. Glanz and Nazzal, "For Palestinians, Raising Arabian Horses is 'the Hobby of the Poor,'" *New York Times,* July 13, 2016.

21. Hadid, "Building Plan by Israel 'Corrosive,'" *New York Times,* July 29, 2016.

22. Hadid, "A 'Seed of Hope' for Transgender People," *New York Times,* July 30, 2016.

23. Ruth Margalit, "How Benjamin Netanyahu is Crushing Israel's Free Press," *New York Times,* July 31, 2016. See the critique by Liel Leibovitz, "Sorry, 'New York Times,' But Israel's Press is doing Just Fine," www://tabletmag.com/jewish-news-and-politics/209643/Israel (August 1, 2016).

Author's Note

Jerold S. Auerbach is the author of eleven previous books: *Labor and Liberty* (1966); *Unequal Justice: Lawyers and Social Change in Modern America* (a *New York Times* Noteworthy Book, 1976); *Justice without Law?* (1983); *Rabbis and Lawyers: The Journey from Torah to Constitution* (1990); *Jacob's Voices: Reflections of a Wandering American Jew* (1996); *Are We One? Jewish Identity in the United States and Israel* (2001); *Explorers in Eden: Pueblo Indians and the Promised Land* (2006); *Hebron Jews: Memory and Conflict in the Land of Israel* (2009); *Brothers at War: Israel and the Tragedy of the Altalena* (2011); *Against the Grain: A Historian's Journey* (2012); and *Jewish State Pariah Nation: Israel and the Dilemmas of Legitimacy* (2014).

His articles have appeared in *Harper's, The Wall Street Journal, The New York Times, The Jerusalem Post, The New Republic, Commentary, The Forward, The New York Sun, The Jerusalem Report, The Jewish Press, Mosaic* and on-line in *The Algemeiner, American Thinker* and *The Times of Israel*. His articles about *The New York Times* and Israel can be found at https://www.tumblr.com/blog/jacobsvoice.

A Guggenheim Fellow, Fulbright Lecturer at Tel Aviv University, Visiting Scholar at the Harvard Law School, and recipient of two College Teachers Fellowships from the National Endowment for the Humanities, Jerold S. Auerbach is Professor Emeritus of History at Wellesley College, where he taught for forty years.

Index

CPSIA information can be obtained
at www.ICGtesting.com
Printed in the USA
JSHW031351080621
15688JS00003B/166

9 781618 118981